Afghan Communism
and
Soviet Intervention

Afghan Communism
and
Soviet Intervention

Henry S. Bradsher

OXFORD
UNIVERSITY PRESS

OXFORD
UNIVERSITY PRESS

Great Clarendon Street, Oxford ox2 6dp

Oxford University Press is a department of the University of Oxford.
It furthers the University's objective of excellence in research, scholarship,
and education by publishing worldwide in

Oxford New York

Athens Auckland Bangkok Bogotá Buenos Aires Calcutta
Cape Town Chennai Dar es Salaam Delhi Florence Hong Kong Istanbul
Karachi Kuala Lumpur Madrid Melbourne Mexico City Mumbai
Nairobi Paris São Paulo Singapore Taipei Tokyo Toronto Warsaw
with associated companies in Berlin Ibadan

Oxford is a registered trade mark of Oxford University Press
in the UK and in certain other countries

ISBN 0 19 579506 7

This edition in Oxford Pakistan Paperbacks, 2000

Printed in Pakistan at
Mehran Printers, Karachi.
Published by
Ameena Saiyid, Oxford University Press
5-Bangalore Town, Sharae Faisal
PO Box 13033, Karachi-75350, Pakistan.

CONTENTS

1221

PREFACE

This book supersedes the author's *Afghanistan and the Soviet Union*, which was published in 1983 and updated in 1985. As the Communist period in Afghanistan ended, simply adding post-1985 developments to that book would not have been adequate. So much new information had become available on the period that it covered—about Afghan political developments that led to the Communist period, the Soviet process of making decisions on Afghanistan, and many other things—that a fresh assessment was needed.

Therefore, this is a completely rewritten version of events covered in the earlier book, beginning with the emergence of modern political trends in Afghanistan, as well as a description of the final period through Soviet disengagement and the collapse of Communist control in 1992. The narrative ends with the collapse; the chaos that followed is only briefly introduced. Some material that was in the earlier book has been condensed while much new information has been added. Some points that had been analytical conclusions are now presented as documented facts. At the same time, this book seeks to make clearer the underlying causes and trends of the whole tragic interaction between Afghanistan and the Soviet Union. And it naturally drops an assumption made earlier. Like many others, I failed to foresee in 1983 or in the first few months after Mikhail S. Gorbachev became the Soviet leader in 1985 that the USSR would change its foreign and military policies, weaken, and ultimately collapse. I had assumed that an enduring Soviet superpower would hold onto Afghanistan indefinitely, trying to mould it into an acquiescent part of Moscow's empire. Fortunately, I was wrong.

While writing the first book and continuing the study of Afghan and Soviet affairs that led to this second book, I have added to my knowledge of Afghanistan from journalistic visits there in the 1960s and '70s, and of Soviet affairs from residence in Moscow as a journalist in the 1960s. Many people—Americans, Soviets, Pakistanis, Indians, British, and others—have helped me understand the two subjects and their linkage in the Afghan war. In particular, Afghan friends from the 1960s who survived the murderous years after 1978 as well as many new Afghan acquaintances have shared facts and perceptions about their complex country. Interviews and conversations in recent years in the United States, Britain, Germany, the Soviet Union, Russia, Peshawar, Islamabad, Rawalpindi, and New Delhi have broadened the picture.

While these personal contacts and my own analysis have shaped this book, it makes extensive use of texts of speeches and declarations, academic writings, and the work of the many journalists who recorded the period in both official media and independent publications. Those few reporters—mostly Western, but some Soviet ones also—who accepted the dangers of seeing for themselves what was happening during the war in Afghanistan deserve particular thanks for their contribution.

So far as possible, I have tried to tell this story in the words of the participants or of their official chronicles. Sources have been identified in detail, with a translated version cited when used instead of the original. If the narrative is sometimes complicated by alternative versions of an event or a range of statistics, it is because there is no clear truth. Any writer who purports to give simple, clear facts about Afghanistan or the Soviet involvement there should be read with skepticism. Supposed facts coming out of Afghanistan are often only partial truths, and many flat statements made in official Soviet and Afghan media in the early 1980s were flatly contradicted by those same media at the end of the '80s. Some things will never be known with any exactitude, such as the numbers of casualties, *mujahideen* fighters, or refugees. Varied spellings follow the varied sources.

INTRODUCTION

Behind the history of modern day Afghanistan are two intertwined stories. One is of the modernization throes of Afghanistan. The other is the story of the last imperialistic thrust of the Soviet Union.

The two came together because the search for ways to improve an isolated, backward Asian kingdom led a small number of Afghans to embrace the Soviet model of Communism. Once they had achieved power almost accidentally, most other Afghans rejected their naive attempt to remake society in order to impose that model. The USSR went to their support. This turned a remote civil war into a world issue.

The Soviet Union did not become involved in its longest war because of any intrinsic importance of Afghanistan to Moscow. Ensuring Afghan adherence to Marxism-Leninism was not a goal that in itself could justify such an involvement. Instead, the involvement showed Soviet determination, at the height of Leonid I. Brezhnev's power, to assert Moscow's authority wherever the USSR perceived danger or opportunity. After the determination of the Afghan people to maintain their independence had bloodied the Soviets while devastating their own country, the imperialistic thrust ended. But, again, Afghanistan was not the cause. Moscow's abandonment of the Kabul regime was a result of long-festering Soviet internal weaknesses, some of which had been exacerbated by the Afghan war. Belated recognition of those weaknesses, rather than any battlefield defeat or the war's immediate costs, produced the changed Kremlin thinking that led to the Soviet Army's withdrawal from Afghanistan. Those weaknesses later brought the collapse of Soviet

Communist power and of the USSR itself. Aid to Kabul ended.

Without Soviet aid, Afghan Communists lost power. Afghanistan turned inward to resume its struggle over modernization. The Soviet model had been discredited. Another model, of greater reliance on Islam for answers, had been strengthened. Traditional factors of national unity had been weakened, leaving uncertainty about Afghanistan's political structure and coherence. And a land that stumbled into war while seeking economic development had been blasted backward into an even more desperately primitive economic condition.

A fundamental reason for this conflict was that Afghanistan had turned to the Soviet Union for armaments in the mid-1950s. **Chapter 1** examines Prime Minister Mohammad Daoud's desire for a better army partly to confront neighbouring Pakistan over an ethnic-based territorial dispute, partly to overcome traditionalist opposition to the changes brought about by economic aid from the Soviet Union, the United States, and other countries. Soviet aid enhanced the appeal of the Communist model to break Afghanistan out of its backwardness. Marxist study groups developed in 1965 into a tiny Communist party, the People's Democratic Party of Afghanistan (PDPA). In reaction to the Marxists, groups that became known as Islamist were created to search in religion for an answer to the growing pressures of a changing world. Some Afghan military officers who imbibed Communism during training in the USSR shunned emerging political groups, as did some bureaucrats who became secret Communists. The Soviet-influenced officers enabled Daoud to abolish the monarchy in a 1973 *coup d'état*. He soon excluded the officers and known PDPA members from his traditionalist strongman leadership, while suppressing Islamist opposition to aspects of modernization. The unexplained murder of a key PDPA member caused Daoud to arrest party leaders.

Fearing exposure, leftist military officers overthrew Daoud's government on 27 April 1978, as described in **Chapter 2**. The soldiers turned power over to the PDPA. The Soviet political police, the KGB, helped organize the new regime. It soon split. The PDPA's Parcham faction led by Babrak Karmal was ousted by the new president, Nur Mohammed Taraki's Khalq faction. After purging the old governing establishment and suppressing public hostility, the regime decreed a series of supposed reforms that challenged Afghanistan's social, economic, and religious customs. This provoked rebellion in the name of religion by warriors for Islam, the *mujahideen*. During an uprising in Herat in March 1979, the USSR refused the regime's pleas for help from Soviet troops, though it supplied better weapons and more military advisers. The Soviet embassy in Kabul began trying to ameliorate regime policies. Excesses were blamed primarily on Taraki's Khalqi deputy, Hafizullah Amin. Moscow thought Taraki should get rid of Amin, but instead, Amin seized power on 14 September 1979 and had Taraki suffocated. Amin knew the Soviets opposed him, but he needed their aid. The Soviets knew Amin distrusted them, but they were committed to his regime while lacking the ability to control him. The civil war against the regime worsened, bloodshed increased, the Afghan army faded. Amin appealed for help from Soviet troops.

Chapter 3 discusses Moscow's decision to commit the Soviet Army to Afghanistan. The decision was based on an exaggerated impression of guerrilla strength and regime weakness. A small clique around Brezhnev made the decision without much consideration of the implications or possible consequences. The basic reasons were the determination to support a client regime, to prevent a rollback of Communism, to protect the sensitive Soviet Central Asian border from the example of an anti-Communist Islamic victory, and to uphold Soviet military and diplomatic prestige. The invasion was not seen as a step toward projecting military power beyond Afghanistan, nor was it expected to worsen already poor relations with the West. Soviet troops that arrived unopposed in Afghanistan seized key installations on 27 December 1979, killed Amin, and installed Karmal in power. President Jimmy Carter of the United States called it 'a grave threat to peace' and imposed sanctions on the USSR. Some Western countries did not observe all the sanctions.

The Afghan people demonstrated against the Soviet Army and its local puppets. Desertions decimated the Afghan army. **Chapter 4** relates the difficulties of Karmal's Parcham-led regime. Soviet advisers controlled the government, the armed forces, and the political police, KhAD, headed by Mohammed Najibullah. Efforts to build popular support for the regime were unsuccessful. Sheltered by Moscow's protection and need for local front men, the always incompetent PDPA grew increasingly corrupt and irresponsible. Force was used to ensure control. The regime and the Soviet Army committed human rights violations extensively. In a savage situation, the *mujahideen* sometimes replied with atrocities against regime supporters.

Faced with an intractable problem, bogged down militarily, the Soviet Union decided to drop the unsuccessful Karmal. On 4 May 1986 it replaced him with Najibullah as PDPA general secretary, and later as president, **Chapter 5** reports. Najibullah launched a Soviet-directed effort to broaden the regime's popular support with new shadow political parties and illusory elections. While the resistance spurned this 'national reconciliation', the numerous Khalqis in key jobs opposed it as a betrayal of PDPA principles. Wastefully used Soviet aid kept the regime alive in a wrecked economy.

How many Afghans died in the war will never be known. **Chapter 6** cites estimates from 1.3 million to two million. Others, uncounted and probably in hundreds of thousands, were wounded, maimed, crippled. Well over half of Afghanistan's pre-war population was killed or was displaced as refugees internally and abroad. Refugee camps in Pakistan became centres for recruiting and training *mujahideen*. The Pakistani armed forces' Interservices Intelligence Directorate (ISI) channelled refugees into seven Afghan resistance groups that it selected. It favoured Islamists for reasons of both Pakistani domestic politics and intended future influence in Afghanistan. The seven groups represented Afghanistan's majority of Sunni Muslims. Iran supported resistance groups from the excluded minority Shi'ite Muslims.

Chapter 7 considers the war in the Soviet period. The USSR's 40th Army reached a peak strength of about 120 000 men in Afghanistan. Few were trained or equipped for mountain warfare against guerrillas. The Soviets tried to rebuild the desertion-riddled Afghan army but never gave it the latitude to develop independent capabilities. Troops of the interior ministry and KhAD, plus regional militias, brought Kabul's claimed military force to 300 000. The number of *mujahideen* varied by definition; some were full-time fighters, more were occasional warriors. As Soviet and regime forces grew stronger and more experienced, so too did the resistance. The guerrillas' cause was popular in the United States. Its Congress forced more and better armaments into a covert military aid programme by the Central Intelligence Agency than CIA managers sought. ISI distributed the resulting $3 billion worth of American arms aid plus about the same value of CIA-organized aid that was financed by Saudi Arabia. *Mujahideen* use of American-supplied Stinger anti-aircraft missiles beginning in September 1986 reduced the Soviet advantage of airpower over foot-slogging guerrillas.

The war had a slowly increasing effect on the USSR. Initially, Kremlin leaders censured the fact that Soviet soldiers were fighting and dying in Afghanistan. But, as **Chapter 8** relates, politically motivated glimpses of the grim reality began to appear in a situation in which, a government newspaper conceded, the Soviet 'people did not accept this war'. After Mikhail S. Gorbachev became the Soviet leader in March 1985, the full horror of the war began to be publicly reported. Also finally discussed were the corruption and inequities in selecting conscripts for Afghanistan duty, and the indifference toward wounded and crippled veterans. In May 1988 the USSR began issuing casualty figures that ultimately totalled 14 750 dead and 50 000 wounded.

The Soviet Army did not leave Afghanistan because of the costs in blood, roubles, or damaged international relations. Gorbachev recognized the Afghan involvement as a barrier to the improved East-West relations that were needed to refocus Soviet energies on worsening domestic problems and obtain Western aid. **Chapter 9** analyses the long, meandering negotiating effort that covered the army's withdrawal. United Nations' peace efforts beginning in 1981 had gone nowhere. But after declaring in February 1986 that Afghanistan was 'a bleeding wound' for the USSR, Gorbachev began pressing the reluctant Soviet military, KGB, and Kabul regime to end Soviet Army involvement. Accords were signed under United Nations' auspices on 14 April 1988 by Afghanistan, Pakistan, the USSR, and the United States, providing for Soviet troops to withdraw by 15 February 1989. The United States insisted, over Soviet objections, that it would continue to provide supplies to the *mujahideen.*

Afghan, Soviet, and American officials expected Najibullah's regime to collapse quickly once Soviet troops were gone, **Chapter 10** reports. The final troops left on schedule after Gorbachev had personally authorized the last major Soviet war atrocity, destruction of villages along the mountain road north from Kabul. The Afghan army pulled back from many garrisons that had been held only with Soviet help. In some areas, wanton killing and looting by victorious *mujahideen* undercut their cause and steeled regime soldiers to fight harder because there seemed to be no option of amnesty. During the Soviet withdrawal, Najibullah failed to broaden his popular base. Infighting intensified in Kabul between Khalqis and Parchamis and in Peshawar among *mujahideen* leaders. Efforts to work out a political agreement among Kabul, Peshawar, and their supporters were unsuccessful.

Unexpectedly, tenaciously, the regime held on for another three years without the Soviet Army but with massive Soviet aid. **Chapter 11** discusses this period. With Pakistan's ISI and Saudi agents pulling strings, the seven Peshawar groups put together an interim government in the hope of quickly taking charge in Kabul. Corrupt, nepotistic, and incompetent, it sat in Pakistan without influence while guerrilla commanders inside Afghanistan tried without success to create an alternative leadership. The PDPA failed to attract new support while changing its name to the Watan (Homeland) Party. Directed by ISI officers, some *mujahideen* tried in early 1989 to capture Jalalabad in order to make it the interim government's capital. But not all *mujahideen* supported Pakistan's effort to put in power its favourite Islamist, Gulbuddin Hekmatyar. The four-month seige failed. The *mujahideen* proved generally unable to turn guerrilla talents into conventional warfare victories.

The crumbling of the USSR combined with ethnic and regional factionalism among Afghan regime supporters finally gave the *mujahideen* victory. KGB, military, and other Soviet officials who had insisted on continuing to provision Kabul's fight lost power after trying to overthrow Gorbachev in August 1991. This opened the way for Moscow to halt aid that it could no longer afford, as **Chapter 12** describes. In January 1992 Pakistan abandoned ISI's determination to install Islamist favourites in Kabul by military force. It opted for a settlement involving all political elements. United Nations' efforts to put together a temporary leadership representing regime, *mujahideen*, royalist, and other Afghan elements, were overtaken by events. With Soviet money no longer available to pay his mercenaries, northern militia leader Abdul Rashid Dostam switched sides from Kabul to *mujahideen* commander Ahmad Shah Massoud. A cabal of regime officials helped Dostam's troops seize downtown Kabul as Najibullah tried to flee. Hekmatyar threatened to capture the capital. In this chaotic situation, other *mujahideen* leaders from Peshawar arrived in Kabul on 28 April 1992 to assume nominal power. The Communist period was over, but there was no peace.

Chapter 13 briefly examines the legacies of the Afghan Communist period in the former Soviet Union and in Afghanistan, but it does not attempt to trace the civil war that raged after 1992. Many of the Soviets who fought in Afghanistan became prominent in politics, in the USSR successor republics' shrunken armed forces, in crime. Many others were neglected, forgotten, broken, crippled. For Afghanistan the legacies were more profound, the human and property damage greater. The unsettled results of the Communist period led to a struggle for control of Kabul that devastated the capital. It was partly a struggle for personal power. More basically, it was a struggle over the authority of a central government, over the role of Islam in government, over adjusting to the modern world. Afghanistan's pre-war polity was gone. Much time and pain were needed to find a new form for the nation—if it remained unified. New cultural and social conventions were needed in a formerly consensual society that had become confrontational. A devastated country had to be rebuilt. One phase of political experimentation and civil war were over for Afghanistan. But peace was tragically elusive.

CHAPTER 1

PROBLEMS OF MODERNIZATION

The experiment with Communism that ended by wrecking Afghanistan began with an effort to modernize an isolated, backward central Asian kingdom. Economic and military aid from the country's big northern neighbour, the Soviet Union, caused a small group of Afghans to look to Moscow for a model of political organization and economic development. When they came to power almost accidentally in 1978, they unleashed forces that killed and displaced half of Afghanistan's people and left the country torn by post-Communist conflict.

After World War II, the Afghan royal family turned to the United States for help in building the first all-weather roads and other development projects. American economic aid by 1979 totalled $378.17 million in gifts and $154.7 million in loans. The royal family was initially wary of its Soviet neighbour. It began using Soviet trade routes northward in 1950, however, as a result of a dispute with its southeastern neighbour, Pakistan. The royal family came from the Durrani branch of Afghanistan's dominant Pushtun ethnic group. The dispute arose from Afghan efforts to gain control of the area inhabited by Pushtuns—Kabul called it Pushtunistan—and the Baloch ethnic group that lay across the Durand Line, the *de facto* border with Pakistan that had been drawn for British India in 1893.

After the United States decided to arm Pakistan as an anti-Communist ally, over Kabul's objections, Afghan Prime Minister Mohammad Daoud Khan turned to the USSR for economic aid in 1954. From 1954 until the Soviet invasion in 1979, Afghanistan received $1.265 billion worth of Soviet economic aid. Only $173.1 million of this was in gifts; the rest was to be repaid primarily by natural gas piped from fields that Soviet technicians developed in northwestern Afghanistan.[1] 'Our economic aid to Afghanistan did not promote social and economic progress in the country to the degree which we had anticipated,' Soviet economists eventually conceded. Much of the aid was wrongly used or looted, and the Soviet industrialization model did not provide for essential efforts to increase production of food and consumer goods.[2]

Feuding with a rearming Pakistan, Daoud started talking to Moscow in late 1954 about military aid. A July 1956 agreement began the orientation of the Afghan army and air force to Soviet ways. Their technical language became Russian, and they became dependent upon Soviet expertise and spare parts. Through 1979, Soviet military aid was valued at $1.25 billion, and some 3725 Afghan military personnel had received training in the USSR—where they were exposed to ideological indoctrination.

Turning to the USSR for military aid had a catalytic effect in the hothouse of Kabul University and intellectual circles in the capital. Soviet economic aid had already aroused curiosity about the applicability to Afghanistan of a Marxist— or, more accurately, Stalinist—development model. The Soviet military connection focused the intellectual searching of the growing educated class. Soon after the conclusion of the military aid agreement, discussion groups began to be formed to consider Communism in the semi-secrecy required by Daoud's police state. From the groups would emerge the People's Democratic Party of Afghanistan (PDPA). There was also the opposite effect of galvanizing those who rejected Marxism for Islamic religious reasons compounded by knowledge of colonial practices in Soviet Central Asia. They turned to Islam. From them emerged leaders of the major *mujahideen* organizations that fought the PDPA.

In addition to these two elements that came to dominate Afghan politics from 1978 onward were two other elements, dominant up to 1978 but eclipsed after that. One was the royal establishment of religious leaders, large landowners, big merchants, senior government officials and military officers, and other key supporters of Daoud and his first cousin and brother-in-law, King Mohammad Zahir Shah. They saw the turn to Moscow as furthering their interests in building the economic and military strength of the central government, and, as a result, its national authority and their personal power. Although some of them served the PDPA regime or became minor *mujahideen* leaders, after 1978 most were killed by the PDPA or fled abroad. The second element was those technocrats who ran the government, economy, education, and armed forces for Daoud and the king without rising into the royal establishment or secretly choosing Marxism—most of the new leftists earned their living as technocrats. The apolitical technocrats were modernizers who accepted a Western perspective for Afghanistan. They believed that Soviet aid could be absorbed into a mixture of free enterprise and some state capitalism under their elite guidance. Once in power, the Communists killed some of the best technocrats out of vindictiveness or a fear of allowing alternative leadership to remain available for possible Soviet efforts to install a more competent and popular government. Some technocrats stayed at their jobs and struggled against great odds to keep basic services running. But by a 1985 estimate, 90 per cent of Afghans with higher education from non-Communist universities had been killed, imprisoned, or scattered into exile.[3]

AFGHAN LEFTISTS

The first of five identifiable leftist study groups was convened in 1956 by Nur Mohammed Taraki. A self-made man, born in 1917, Taraki had the kind of plebeian background that a true Communist was supposed to have but that others often fabricated to hide a bourgeois upbringing. A concern for social justice came out in the novels and short stories that he wrote, possibly with a Soviet subsidy by the early 1960s. Taraki the literary man was a dreamer, a teahouse talker rather than a schemer or organizer, a man with lofty goals but little realistic sense of how to achieve them, a vain man easily deluded by flatterers. These characteristics became his undoing. Amid the unrest of social change caused by modernization, Taraki's Marxism attracted village lads who had come to Kabul on educational scholarships.

The second leftist study group was organized in 1960. It was oriented more toward upper middle-class urban sons of the Kabul establishment. Many of them were from the Tajik ethnic group in northeastern Afghanistan, or were so urbanized as speakers of the Tajiki language Dari that was predominant in Kabul, as to appear Tajik. This group was founded by Babrak Karmal and Mir Akbar Khyber.[4] Karmal, born in 1929, was a gregarious politician noted for fiery oratory. The privileged son of an establishment family, but chastised by three years in prison for challenging the royal regime, then tempered by working in government, Karmal had a more realistic sense of what was possible in Afghan society than the introverted Taraki did. Perhaps Karmal's motivating drive was more to achieve power than Taraki's, less to benefit the poor masses of whom he lacked Taraki's personal knowledge. Both understood Communism more in terms of promising progress and social justice than in the ideological terms then defined by Moscow as Marxism-Leninism or in the reality of Soviet dictatorship. Karmal was converted to Communism while in prison by Khyber, a military high school graduate four years his senior. Khyber was 'a rather mysterious figure...[who played] an important part in [the] radicalization of the intelligentsia.... He seems to have been the only one to have had a real Marxist orientation'.[5] Where Khyber got it is uncertain.

The other three known study groups were not so important. One was headed by Ghulam Dastagir Panjshiri, a literature teacher at Kabul Teachers College and later a ministry of information and culture employee. It included Shahrollah Shahpar. Another was led by Mohammed Taher Badakhshi and was composed mostly of students from Badakhstan province. The fifth group was headed by the otherwise unknown Mohammed Zahir Ofaq.[6]

A number of others who became pro-Soviet leftists in the late 1950s and early '60s were not involved in groups that merged into the PDPA. There was an advantage for Moscow in having supporters who were not identified with leftist politics and therefore detectable by Afghan police, and who could be more influential in advocating policies dictated from Moscow if their connections were hidden. Several civilians can be singled out on the basis of their actions and reputations. One is Mohammad Hassan Sharq, a physician who ran Daoud's secretariat when he was prime minister, became a deputy prime minister when Daoud was president, and later was prime minister under President Najibullah. Another was Nematullah Pazhwak, the recipient of a doctorate in literature from Columbia University under the American aid programme who, as the king's interior minister, helped bring Daoud back to power in 1973 before later serving PDPA regimes. Yet another was Mohammed Khan Jallalar, who from 1972 through 1989 was the minister of finance or trade in every government except Taraki's and Amin's.[7]

It is easier to identify soldiers who became secret leftists, probably as a result of indoctrination or even recruitment by Soviet intelligence services during their training in the USSR. Although all eventually became associated with PDPA factions, they never were so much factional players as a separate force whose role became a key to understanding PDPA infighting. They included men who staged both the 1973 *coup d'état* that made Daoud president and the 1978 coup that killed him and opened the way for PDPA rule.

The best known are air force pilot Abdul Qadir and tank commander Mohammed Aslam Watanjar. Others include helicopter pilot Assadullah Sarwari, radar specialist Sayed Mohammed Gulabzoy, and tank officers Sher Jan Mazdooryar and Mohammed Rafi.[8]

THE ISLAMISTS

The fourth political element to emerge was composed of those who turned to Islam for answers to questions raised by modernization, particularly the Soviet role in it. The oft-used term 'fundamentalist' Muslims is inadequate for them, not least because of its connotations outside Afghanistan. It obscures a distinction between different attitudes toward religion as a factor in politics. Those who wanted to preserve Afghanistan's distinctive mixture of Islamic and pre-Islamic traditions were, in general, part of the royal establishment or technocrats. Others wanted to seek in Islamic writings a different social and governmental structure. The fourth element sought to combine modern—even revolutionary—thinking with religion, although over the years it moved increasingly toward using its definition of religious rules to set social standards. This element will be identified here as Islamist.[9]

Most of the Islamists were rural lads who had earned by merit admission to the theology faculty or the scientific and technical faculties of Kabul University. Exposed to Marxist proselytizing and other uncertainties of intellectual life in the capital, they sought in religion both a barrier and an answer to alien thoughts. The Islamist movement began to develop at Kabul University in 1957, gathering in semi-secrecy around members of the theology faculty who included Sibghatullah Mojaddedi. Student members of the group included Burhanuddin Rabbani and Abdul Rasul Sayyaf.

FORMATION OF A COMMUNIST PARTY

Daoud's pursuit of the Pushtunistan issue led to a break in relations with Pakistan in 1961 that hurt Afghanistan economically. In order to back the country out of this dead end, he relinquished the prime minister's job on 3 March 1963, and King Zahir Shah began a decade of presiding indecisively over government by commoners. The prospect of open politics in this constitutional decade caused the leftist study groups to begin cooperating later in 1963. When parliamentary elections were scheduled for August and September 1965, they united to formalize their cooperation as the PDPA.[10]

Twenty-seven men met 'in semi-secrecy in the middle of the night' of 1 January 1965 in Taraki's living-room. This 'first PDPA congress' approved the party's 'constitutional and organizational principles' and elected a central committee of seven full members and four candidate members. Taraki was named the committee's secretary general.[11] As the leader of the second most important study group, Karmal was named a party secretary, the second-ranked position. The leaders of two other study groups, Panjshiri and Badakhshi, became full committee members. The other three full members were medical Dr Saleh Mohammed Ziray from Taraki's group, economist Soltan Ali Keshtmand from Karmal's, and Shahpar from Panjshiri's. The leader of the fifth study group, Ofaq, reportedly attended the meeting but did not become a full committee member. Three of the candidate committee member positions went to Taraki's group, one to Karmal's.[12] A Soviet specialist on Afghan affairs later identified this group sharing as the appearance of 'the deep-rooted factionalism' that plagued the party.[13]

The other two men besides Taraki and Karmal who became leaders of Communist Afghanistan emerged in the PDPA's first few years. One was Hafizullah Amin, the other Sayyed Mohammed Najibullah Ahmadzai—who later used just the name Najibullah or Najib. Their background has a contrast similar to those of their original patrons: Amin, like Taraki, from a poorer provincial family than Najibullah, who, like Karmal, had prosperous urban origins. But they shared a pragmatic toughness that led them both into responsibility for secret police atrocities—and both died violently.

Amin, born in 1929, graduated from Kabul University as a scholarship student and became first a teacher and then high school principal in Kabul. Under the American aid programme, Amin earned a Master's degree in educational administration in 1958 from Columbia University in New York City. Amin said in 1979 that he had gained his political awareness while taking summer courses at the University of Wisconsin in 1958 and on his return home contacted Taraki. But after deposing Taraki and becoming president, Amin claimed with greater political correctness that 'my stay in the United States is not the reason for my political beliefs. My beliefs and thoughts emanate from the reality of the ideology of the working class'.[14]

Najibullah was, by some accounts, one of the students who attended the PDPA founding congress. Born in 1947, he was the son of a 1960s Afghan trade representative in Peshawar, the capital of Pakistan's Pushtun ethnic area, whose job included passing out money to encourage Pushtunistan agitation. In one of Kabul's elite high schools he met Karmal's younger half-brother, Mahmud Barialay, and was introduced to Karmal's study group. His political agitation earned two periods in jail.[15]

PDPA Goals

Taraki's supporters described him in 1976 as a 'long-standing Communist' and said the founding congress set the party goal of 'building a socialist society in Afghanistan based on adapting the morals of general truths and the Marxist-Leninist revolutionary principles to conditions in

Afghanistan'. They said the congress 'established our Marxist-Leninist party...the Communist Party of Afghanistan'.[16] That name was too inflamatory in an Islamic society, however, so the relatively neutral name of People's Democratic Party was adopted for public use.

A PDPA constitution, which apparently was written later, said the party,

> whose ideology is the practical experience of Marxism-Leninism, is founded on the voluntary union of the progressive and informed people of Afghanistan: the workers, peasants, artisans, and intellectuals of the country.... The main principle and guideline of the structure of the PDPA is democratic centralism...[defined as] adherence of lower officials to the decisions of higher officials....

In this and in organizational details, the party followed dictatorial patterns of the Communist Party of the Soviet Union (CPSU). The constitution held members responsible for 'expanding and strengthening Afghan-Soviet friendly relations...'.[17]

In its early days, Karmal said in 1985, the PDPA's 'social structure...was mostly restricted to intellectuals'— administrators and doctors, teachers and students, writers and other bourgeois types. He complained of 'the low level of political class awareness of the workers' strata' and said '[t]he semiclandestine nature of the party made it difficult to create a broad structural organization and to broaden its links with the masses'.[18] Out of Afghanistan's estimated population of 15 million, industrial workers numbered only about 20 000 in the 1960s and had risen to about 38 000 in 1978 plus another 50 000 or so in construction, and most farmers were illiterate and uninformed.[19] But, following Lenin's example of arrogating to his middle-class clique the authority to know what was best for the proletariat, a PDPA spokesman explained in 1979, 'It is not necessary that the workers should be leading. A working-class party does not mean that the majority is constituted by workers, but rather that the members are equipped with the ideology of the working class'[20]—as they chose to define it.

The PDPA turned to Kabul University and the capital's residential high schools as the easiest recruiting grounds, emphasizing the inequities of the royal system. Before it began trying to recruit in the armed forces, however, Abdul Qadir had established his own organization of pro-Soviet military officers on 17 September 1964. Qadir's underground group, variously identified by Soviet sources as the Afghan Armies' Revolutionary Organization or the United Communist Front of Afghanistan, reportedly numbered 600 to 800 officers by the time of the April 1978 coup. It was in close touch with—if not controlled and directed by—the Soviet Defence Ministry's Main Intelligence Directorate, or GRU. The GRU operated separately from the Soviet Committee for State Security, or KGB, which influenced the civilian Marxist study groups that became the PDPA.[21]

THE SPLINTERED LEFT

With Karmal sparking a period of radical politics as a member of the first parliament of the constitutional decade, a new press law made it possible for six newspapers to open in 1966. The PDPA began publication 11 April 1966 of 'its propaganda organ', named *Khalq* (People, or Masses). Taraki was the publisher. The first two issues contained a PDPA policy statement. Making no mention of Islam, it began with an analysis of Afghanistan as 'a country with a feudal economic and social system'. It blamed 'the pathetic condition' of the Afghan people on 'feudal lords', some big businessmen, foreign traders, 'corrupted bureaucrats', and others. The statement called for a new, noncapitalist economic system and proposed a number of social and economic changes. The PDPA's economic naïveté was apparent in an idealistic pronouncement on minimum-wage laws, guaranteed vacations with pay, no work for children under the age of 15—the ones who tended flocks and wove rugs, both jobs basic to the economy—and other ideas befitting a mature industrial nation. And the statement said 'progressive and democratic elements...support the struggles of the people of Pushtunistan'. The Soviet Union was praised without being named.[22] The CPSU newspaper *Pravda* commented in 1990 that the statement had shown a striking 'desire to skip natural stages of socioeconomic development, and the underestimation of public opinion and of Afghan nationalism...'.[23]

The government closed *Khalq* after six issues as part of official pressure that was one factor in causing the recently united leftist movement to splinter. Other factors were personal ambitions, social and class differences that stimulated diverse ideas of ideology and tactics, ethnic tensions, and contrasting models offered by the USSR and by China, which was then plunging into the Great Proletarian Cultural Revolution. Ziray said in 1987 a 'lack of mutual confidence and understanding, and doubt and suspicions, were destroying the [PDPA's] internal relations.... Splits became more serious as a result of different leaders' struggles to achieve power'.[24]

The PDPA, with only 515 members in 1966,[25] split into two major factions composed of Taraki's and Karmal's original groups, while the soldier Communists whose loyalty ran directly to Moscow remained outside it as a third force. Karmal had never been happy with taking second place in the PDPA to the older man. Taraki's supporters scoffed at Karmal's faction as 'the royal Communist party' because of it sought to flatter 'such a progressive king' and work within the system. But Karmal was more realistic about the Left's weakness in the absence of a sizeable, politically aware proletariat, and its need therefore to build its strength slowly by co-opting other elements. After several incidents, Karmal broke completely with Taraki's organization in May 1967.

He took with him a majority of the full members of the founding central committee—Panjshiri, Shahpar, and Keshtmand—and others. Only Ziray and Badakhshi from the original full committee membership stuck with Taraki.[26]

Each faction claimed to be the true PDPA, calling the other a splinter group. Taraki's faction became known as Khalq, from the newspaper. While Taraki was denied official permission to start any other paper, Karmal received permission to start one—proof in Taraki's eyes that Karmal was being used by the government to divide and weaken the leftist movement. Karmal's paper, which lasted about two years and 100 issues, was named *Parcham* (Banner, or Flag), which became the name for his faction.[27]

The Parcham faction was oriented toward urbanized, westernized members of the upper middle class from a number of ethnic groups, especially Tajiks and detribalized Pushtuns. Khalq was predominately Pushtun and embraced a wider economic and social cross-section of the population with a more diverse background. Parcham was comfortable with a pragmatic willingness to seek alliances on the long road to Communism; Khalq lacked social access to upper class alliances and so emphasized class struggle and a hard line. Moscow maintained contacts with both factions, although Karmal was closer to the Soviet embassy in Kabul.[28]

In late 1984, when Parcham dominated the PDPA regime in Kabul, the party said the 1967 split had weakened party effectiveness. It went on:

> [T]he appearance of deviationist, tribal, clan, national sectarian, nationalist and group tendencies, rightist and leftist opportunistic inclinations, adventurism, egoism, deviation from constitutional, organizational and political principles, and other qualities...[had been caused by] the general backwardness of socioeconomic relations in the countryside; the lack of growth of political and class awareness; the low level of the knowledge of revolutionary theory of the majority of members of the party, along with the shortage of awareness of the experiences of the national, progressive, workers and democratic parties and

movements and their creative approach in the specific conditions of our society; weakness in fully and correctly understanding the Afghan society, the characteristics and the level of development of the class composition of the country; and the lack of correct understanding of the tactic and strategy of the working class during the phases of growth and development of the revolution and proletarian internationalism....[29]

Adding to this woolly rhetoric, Karmal said the intellectuals who composed most of the early PDPA membership had a very low level of 'class political awareness', were confused about 'the revolutionary facts', and were too selfish and personally ambitious to work for the common good.[30]

Other Leftists

After the split, Badakhshi took his study group entirely out of the PDPA and founded a new party, *Setem-i-Melli* (Against National Oppression), that focused on Tajik resentment of Pushtun dominance.[31] An obscure fourth splinter was later identified as led by Dr Abdul Karim Zarghun, whom Najibullah claimed to have brought back into the party in 1978.[32]

For a time in the late 1960s and early '70s the PDPA factions were eclipsed in size and popular appeal by a separate leftist party. This was *Shu'la-yi-Jawed* (Eternal Flame), named for its short-lived newspaper and commonly known as *Shola*. Tracing its roots back to 1946, the party emerged in 1964 from a Maoist-oriented study group that preached an anti-Soviet message. It controlled the Kabul University students' organization for several years, and it particularly recruited Hazaras. These people, a minority from central Afghanistan of Shi'ite Muslims in a predominately Sunni Muslim country, were the poorest labourers in Kabul.[33]

Despite the king's failure to approve a legal basis for political parties, some members of the royal establishment and the technocracy coalesced into organizations. Prime Minister Mohammed Hashim Maiwandwal created the Progressive Democratic Party in 1966 to try to marshal support for his programmes, but it faded after he resigned in 1967.[34] Another group was the Afghan Social Democratic Party. But such groups lacked the intensity or dedication of the leftists or the Islamists, and they failed to offer alternatives for a restive younger generation.

ISLAMIST ORGANIZATION

The growing organizational strength on the left encouraged Islamists to become organized. Under the influence of theology professors, a student movement called *Sazman-i Jawanan-i Musulman* (Organization of Muslim Youth) developed as a militant force that fought the PDPA factions and Maoists. Opposed to both Communist and Western influences, the Muslim Youth and the professors behind it denounced the traditional elite and the king personally. With a strong Tajik element in their ethnic mix, they also opposed Pushtun nationalism and the Pushtunistan cause. In 1972 Rabbani became the head of a council that in theory directed the Muslim Youth.[35]

Two of the students recruited by the professors were Gulbuddin Hekmatyar and Ahmad Shah Massoud, future leaders of the war against the PDPA regime and the post-Communist struggle for control of Afghanistan. Hekmatyar became an opportunist responsible for torture and murder of his supposed allies in his drive for personal power in the name of Islam. The equally devout but more pragmatic Massoud was a superb guerrilla fighter and clever political manoeuverer who exercised strong leadership without projecting Hekmatyar's messianic aura.

Hekmatyar was born in 1949 among Ghilzai Pushtuns—the other Pushtun branch, rivals of the royal Durranis—who had been transplanted to Konduz in the northern Tajik area.

He joined the Muslim Youth while an engineering student at Kabul University and became the organization's fourth leader—and only leader to survive official repression—as well as secretary of the council. The secretary's job included supervision of the Islamists' militant wing of student demonstrators and agitators. Opposing Western styles, Hekmatyar's militants 'sprayed acid in their faces' when women did not wear veils, and 'when women wore stockings, they shot at their legs', a classmate of his said later.[36] Massoud, born in 1953, was the son of a brigadier in Zahir Shah's army from the Panjshir valley, a lush alpine area inhabited by Tajiks. After attending Kabul's elite French-language high school, he was an engineering student in the Soviet-run Polytechnic Institute when political developments disrupted his education. As a junior member of the Muslim Youth, he helped recruit military members in the early 1970s.[37]

RETURN OF DAOUD

By the early 1970s, amid demonstrations and clashes between leftists and Islamists in Kabul, regional drought and famine, governmental corruption and inefficiency, Zahir Shah's experiment with constitutional democracy was widely considered a failure. During the constitutional decade, Daoud had been a disruptive presence off stage, smouldering with resentment over having been barred from politics. His discussion group of old colleagues was joined—the year is uncertain—by Karmal, who was the son of one of Daoud's trusted generals and was widely suspected of being Daoud's agent in the leftist movement. On 17 July 1973, several hundred troops seized control of Kabul against little resistance, and Kabul Radio announced that Afghanistan had become a republic. An announcement the next day said a 'central committee' had named Daoud founder, president, and prime minister of the republic, with personal control of the defence and foreign ministries.

The central committee is not known to have met again after endorsing Daoud, and the names of its members were never made public. Some of them were Karmal's Parchamis whose 'participation in the Daoud administration...had been sanctioned by Soviet intelligence', a KGB official wrote later, and they 'shared information with Soviet secret agencies'.[38] There is, however, little reason to believe that either the Soviets or Parcham controlled events, although Soviet military advisers would have known what tank and air force units were doing. Watanjar headed the coup's tank force and Abdul Qadir led the air force—both men were members of the pro-Soviet Afghan Armies' Revolutionary Organization. An independent Communist, Pazhwak, as interior minister directed police during the coup.[39] It is unclear what authority Daoud had over them, but after becoming president he moved behind a cloak of secrecy to reduce the influence of leftist soldiers and civilians. Qadir was assigned to head a military meat packing plant, and other coup officers were dismissed or sent abroad as ambassadors.[40]

As Daoud defiantly rejected any 'imported ideology', both Parcham and Khalq went into slumps of rejection.[41] But Moscow nurtured the two factions in a way that it apparently had been doing since the PDPA was founded, or even before in supporting the predecessor study groups. The CPSU had for decades been secretly funding such Communist groups abroad.[42] A KGB officer acting on behalf of the CPSU central committee's international department regularly held separate, clandestine meetings with Taraki and Karmal at the Kabul residence of another KGB man, the correspondent for the Soviet news agency, Tass. Beginning in early 1977, on Taraki's instructions Amin began separate clandestine meetings with a KGB officer to report on the state of the Afghan army and Khalqi recruiting efforts in it.[43] There is no indication that the KGB coordinated Khalqi recruiting with the GRU, which already had strong influence in the armed forces through Qadir and Watanjar.

As he eliminated leftists from power, Daoud increasingly turned to old supporters, including the apparently pro-Soviet Jalallar and Sharq, and crushed several real or suspected plots against his regime. A coup plot by the Islamists was thwarted in December 1973. Islamist leaders tried to come to terms with Daoud but failed because he considered the religious right to be the main threat to his modernization ideas.[44] The Islamists had been trying to establish cells in the army since 1972. Massoud said that two days after Daoud's *coup* he and other Muslim Youths began contacting military officers to try to organize their own *coup*. When their efforts were discovered, five persons were killed in the first publicly acknowledged political executions in Afghanistan in more than 40 years. Estimates of the number of Islamists killed during the Daoud regime run up to 600.[45] Rabbani, Massoud, Hekmatyar, and 20 or more other plotters fled to Pakistan.[46]

FAILED UPRISINGS

The Islamists received a friendly reception in Pakistan. Afghanistan's constitutional governments had relegated the Pushtunistan issue to the background, but Daoud revived it. Shortly after Daoud took power, Pakistani Prime Minister Zulfikar Ali Bhutto had his foreign ministry create an 'Afghan cell', or committee, to oversee policy. Bhutto seized on the Islamists as a tool for countering any new Pushtunistan pressure. He assigned this tool to the Pakistani armed forces' Interservices Intelligence Directorate (ISI), which combined intelligence with paramilitary responsibilities, in cooperation with the Frontier Constabulary. ISI began a programme that taught guerrilla warfare skills to at least 5 000 Islamists. Hekmatyar and Massoud were in the first three-month course for commanders. About 150 commanders were trained, some 90 of whom survived to become important *mujahideen* leaders in the 1980s.[47] A Pakistani general said later that the United States played a role, presumably in secret cooperation with Pakistan, by financing potential future Afghan leaders after 1973.[48]

In July 1975 newly trained Islamists under Pakistani direction tried to incite uprisings against Daoud's government. They failed, and Daoud had hundreds of youths and dozens of religious leaders executed.[49] The survivors made their way back to Peshawar, where ISI continued to support them for a time, as did Pakistan's elitist, right-wing *Jamaat-i Islami* (Islamic Society) and others. The Islamists soon split. In general, those trained in Afghan religious schools and Dari speakers from the north, including Massoud, followed the Tajik professor Rabbani. He sought a broad coalition that adapted to ethnic and political realities while accommodating liberal Muslim intellectuals. Most radical students from Kabul's secular schools, especially speakers of the Pushtun language, Pashto, followed the Pushtun Hekmatyar. He defied traditional lines of authority and most political conventions, scorning liberal views, to create a disciplined, militant personal following.[50] By 1977 the two main groups based in Peshawar were Rabbani's *Jamiat-i Islami Afghanistan* (Afghanistan Islamic Society) and Hekmatyar's *Hezb-i Islami Afghanistan* (Afghanistan Islamic Party). Both groups slumped into impotence amid bitterness and infighting as Pakistani interest in helping them waned.[51]

DAOUD'S FOREIGN RELATIONS

With the Soviets unhappy with his squeezing leftists out of his regime, Daoud began to play down the counter productive Pushtunistan issue and improve relations with neighbouring Pakistan as well as Iran and the Western countries. He sought to reduce the Soviet role in

Afghanistan's economy by getting more foreign aid from Iran and other nations. In early 1974 he began arranging for Afghans to receive military training in India and Egypt, where they could practise on Soviet-made weapons like the ones at home, but without being subjected to Marxist indoctrination. He also removed Soviet military advisers from lower echelons of the Afghan armed forces, cutting their total numbers sharply. Just before he fell, he began arranging military training in Pakistan—a striking indication of how much relations had changed between the two countries.[52]

By December 1975, when Soviet President Nikolai S. Podgorny visited Kabul, Soviet-Afghan relations had noticably cooled. In addition to foreign policy changes, Daoud had created his own National Revolutionary Party and banned all other parties—a final blow to Parcham's hopes.[53] The communique on the visit dropped the references to 'cordiality, friendship' of earlier occasions and spoke instead of 'frankness'[54]—a Soviet code word for unresolved differences. Daoud convened a *loya jirgah*, the traditional meeting of Pushtun tribal leaders and elders of other Afghan ethnic groups to ratify national policy decisions. It adopted on 13 February 1977 a new constitution with a single-party system and then elected him president. A month later Daoud, who was increasingly annoyed with covert Soviet activities in Afghanistan, named a new cabinet that omitted leftists except Jalallar, and included some known anti-Communists.

Daoud had become concerned over evidence of Soviet subversive activity. After he had decided to ask CPSU General Secretary Leonid I. Brezhnev if this activity were officially sanctioned, Moscow invited Daoud to make another visit. The public record of his 12 to 15 April 1977 visit is normal. But, according to Abdul Samad Ghaus, the Afghan foreign ministry's director general who participated in the talks, the second round of talks by full delegations erupted into an angry confrontation. After promising more aid, a 'visibly very ill' Brezhnev complained that an increased number of Western aid personnel were in Afghanistan, including close to the Soviet border. They were spies, and the USSR wanted the Afghan government to get rid of them. Daoud, his face 'hard and dark', replied that Brezhnev's statement was unacceptable and a flagrant interference in Afghan internal affairs. 'We will never allow you to dictate to us how to run our country and whom to employ in Afghanistan,' Daoud declared. Daoud then got up abruptly to leave, pausing to shake Brezhnev's hand only on repeated urging from the Afghan minister in charge of foreign affairs, while bluntly rejecting Brezhnev's offer of a private meeting.[55]

PDPA UNITY—IN NAME

What Taraki later characterized as Daoud's 'capitulat[ion] to the reactionaries within and without' provoked Afghan Communists into action. Parcham and Khalq saw the need to paper over their rift in preparation for an uncertain future.[56] Unification efforts were accelerated, a CPSU official said, because Daoud had begun 'preparations for the complete elimination of the PDPA'.[57] The efforts were troubled. Taraki had scorned Parcham's early efforts to recruit soldiers as not in accord with the Marxist definition of a worker revolution. After seeing the ease with which leftist military officers had accomplished the 1973 coup and given Parcham an initial foothold in Daoud's new regime, however, Khalqi leaders decided that they needed military supporters, that perhaps the revolution did not need to await the development of a strong, politically conscious proletariat. Amin was assigned responsibility for recruiting military men for Khalq.[58] Some Parchami soldiers switched to Khalq when Karmal went into a slump in 1975, but mostly Amin found new recruits with a message emphasizing nationalism and such problems as Daoud's favouritism and poor military pay and conditions. Estimates differ of military adherents—none more than hundreds—but Khalq might have come to have more than Parcham, while Abdul Qadir's separate pro-Soviet officer group was larger than either.[59]

Khalq said in late July 1975 that it was ready to discuss in secrecy 'unity and the union of forces' with Parcham. Talks began the following month but quickly broke down, leading to further bitter polemics both in clandestine pamphlets in Kabul and in foreign Communist publications. But by 1976 Moscow apparently felt the time had come for unity to oppose Daoud as well as prepare for some eventual succession to the 64-year-old president, who had not allowed any acknowledged political heir to emerge. With no other organized political force in Kabul, the Islamists having been broken and driven out, the PDPA seemed to have a good chance of picking up the pieces after Daoud—if the party was unified and ready. The Soviet-influenced Communist Party of India and other foreign Communists reportedly became involved in trying to broker unity. Karmal wrote later that unity was achieved 'with the help of [unspecified] international friends and brothers'.[60]

A secret PDPA unification conference was held in Kabul in July 1977. The two factions' sizes at the time is uncertain, but a reasonable estimate is a maximum of 2500 Khalqis and 1000 to 1500 Parchamis.[61] The conference named a new 30-member central committee, equally divided between Khalqis and Parchamis. Taraki became general secretary, Karmal a secretary—the jobs they had taken at the founding congress in 1965. All factional civilian activities were supposed to be unified immediately. Later however, there were charges of secretly keeping separate cells, and Taraki said that unity was strictly a formality, since Parcham was not trusted.[62]

In the sharing of assignments, Najibullah, who became a central committee member, was appointed to a group for liaison with the USSR,[63] a role in which he apparently developed close ties with the KGB. Factional activities in the armed forces were treated differently. Khalq was unwilling to merge its military cells, which it claimed were larger than Parcham's, with people whom it suspected of continued willingness to work with Daoud, thereby creating a danger of betrayal. Each faction continued to try to recruit its own military supporters, causing confusion and hostility.

Khalq later claimed that Amin prepared Khalqi military officers to be ready 'in case someone else toppled Daoud or in case Daoud attacked the party or arrested Comrade Taraki', and the officers held ten practices for a *coup*.[64] When the KGB reported this, Moscow apparently thought any coup attempt would be crushed. It sent word to Taraki that an uprising against Daoud would be irresponsible and 'fraught with dire consequences for the PDPA and all other left-wing forces in the country...'. Nonetheless, PDPA officials later said they were planning to overthrow Daoud in the Afghan month spanning July and August 1978. However events forced a *coup* three months earlier.[65]

Whatever the plans, there was no unity. Karmal later accused Amin of 'divisive factional activities' that caused the PDPA central committee to decide to oust Amin, but the decision was not carried out because Amin was protected by 'some invisible hand...'.[66] The hand presumably was Taraki's. The history of the pre-*coup*, period published while Taraki was president, said he defended Amin 'against all sorts of intrigues and propagandas...[and] treacherous or erroneous blows dealt him by some [party] elements...'.[67]

REPRESSION AND MURDER

In 1977 the government took increasingly harsh, repressive steps. Daoud, whose doctor reportedly said he was growing senile, had become paranoid about his problems. His younger brother, Naim, and six cabinet ministers broke with him temporarily in November 1977 over the inflexibility of his increasingly unrealistic policies. In winning back their cooperation, Daoud began to realize that his policies were creating apathy and stagnation. On 17 April 1978, he reportedly told close associates that he would broaden his regime by bringing in technocrats and liberals, announce reforms, and eventually hold elections.[68]

Later the same day, two unidentified men knocked on the door of Mir Akbar Khyber, called him outside, and murdered him. That set in train events that led 10 days later to the murder of Daoud. Parcham's ideologue, Khyber was also its key organizer, filling the role for Karmal that Amin filled for Taraki. The PDPA circulated *shabnahmas* (night letters)—surreptiously distributed pamphlets or handbills—accusing the government of the murder. Shortly after becoming president, Taraki repeated this charge, but then Khyber was forgotten by the Khalqi regimes of Taraki and Amin. After Karmal was put in power by Soviet troops, his mistress Anahita Ratebzad said there was evidence that Khalq's Amin was responsible for the murder.[69] The presumed reason was conflict between the two factions over recruiting military officers. Karmal's regime did not follow up this charge nor pay any tribute to Khyber's major contributions. Instead, by 1983 the regime returned to blaming Daoud for the murder. A 1988 Soviet propaganda tract said the mystery remained unsolved.[70]

Khyber became in death a convenient martyr for the Communists. The PDPA turned out for his funeral on 19 April an unusually large crowd for Kabul, perhaps 15,000 persons. Taraki and Karmal made strong orations, blaming both 'imperialism' and Daoud's government, and reportedly calling for the overthrow of the government by force. After his officials had studied police tapes of the speeches for a week, Daoud ordered the arrest of PDPA leaders for subversion.[71]

NOTES

1. For a detailed account of the beginning of foreign aid, see Henry S. Bradsher, *Afghanistan and the Soviet Union* (Durham, 1983, 2nd edn., 1985).
2. *World Economics and International Relations*, No. 10, 1988: 107-12.
3. Sayd B. Majrooh, 'Past and Present Education in Afghanistan—A Problem for the Future', in Bo Huldt and Erland Jansson, eds., *The Tragedy of Afghanistan: The Social, Cultural and Political Impact of the Soviet Invasion* (London, 1988), p. 87; Barnett R. Rubin, 'The Old Regime in Afghanistan: Recruitment and Training of a State Elite', *Central Asian Survey*, Vol. 10, No. 3.
4. Raja Anwar, *The Tragedy of Afghanistan: A First-hand Account* (London, 1988), p. 40.
5. Olivier Roy, 'The Origins of the Afghan Communist Party', *Central Asian Survey*, Vol. 7, Nos. 2/3: 45.
6. A. M. Baryalai, ed., *Democratic Republic of Afghanistan Annual, 1979*, [hereafter *DRA Annual, 1979*] (Kabul, 1979), pp. 1115-16; Anwar, *Tragedy*, pp. 28-9, 40; Anthony Arnold, *Afghanistan's Two-Party Communism: Parcham and Khalq* (Stanford, 1983), p. 182. Ofaq's name sometimes appears as Ofagh.
7. Conversations with Afghan exiles; Ludwig W. Adamec, *A Biographical Dictionary of Contemporary Afghanistan* (Graz, 1987), pp. 76, 149, 175; Roy, 'Origins', pp. 50-51; Arnold, *Afghanistan's Two-Party*, pp. 179-80; M. Mobin Shorish, book review, *Slavic Review*, Vol. 44, No. 1: 134.
8. Adamec, *Biographical Dictionary*, pp. 8, 63, 106, 168-9, 198; Arnold, *Afghanistan's Two-Party*, pp. 179-86; Aleksandr Morozov, 'Our Man in Kabul, Part 1', *New Times*, No. 38, 1991: 38; Anwar, *Tragedy*, p. 112.
9. Eden Naby, 'Islam within the Afghan Resistance', *Third World Quarterly*, April 1988: 794; Robert L. Canfield, 'Islamic Sources of Resistance', *Orbis* 29, 1: 65; Olivier Roy, *Islam and Resistance in Afghanistan* (Cambridge, 1986, 2nd edn. 1990), pp. 3-4. Roy first defined this element as Islamist.
10. Kabul Radio, 30 [*sic*] November 1984, in Foreign Broadcast Information Service, *Daily Report, South Asia* [hereafter *FBIS/SA*], 9 November 1984, pp. C1-7.
11. Ibid.; Kabul Radio, 10 January 1985, in *FBIS/SA*, 14 January 1985, p. C2; anonymous, 'The Establishment of the Marxist-Leninist Party in Afghanistan', obtained privately by the author in 1980, published in 1983 in Arnold, *Afghanistan's Two-Party*, pp. 160-77.

12. Kabul Radio, 10 January 1985, in *FBIS/SA*, 14 January 1985, p. C2; US Embassy Kabul cable 3511, 3 May 1978, in Muslim Students Followers Imam, *Spynest Revelations: Vol. 29, Afghanistan* (Tehran, 1981) [hereafter *Spynest*], p. 57; Arnold, *Afghanistan's Two-Party*, pp. 180-81, 186-7, 197; 'Establishment of the Marxist-Leninist Party', p. 2; Anwar, *Tragedy*, p. 42.

13. Valdimir Plastun in *Pravda*, 8 May 1990, p. 4, in FBIS, *Daily Report, Soviet Union* [hereafter *FBIS/SU*], 11 May 1990, p. 13.

14. *DRA Annual, 1979*, pp. 629-30; Adamec, *Biographical Dictionary*, p. 20; US Embassy Kabul, cable 6788, 11 September 1979, in *Spynest* Vol. 29, p. 59; Kabul Radio, 13 November 1979, in FBIS, *Daily Report, Middle East* [hereafter *FBIS/ME*], 19 November 1979, pp. S1-3.

15. Afghan exiles; *New Times*, No. 22, 1986: 24-5; *Voyenno-Istoricheskiy Zhurnal*, No. 7, 1989: 35; *New York Times*, 16 January 1987, p. A6. M. Hassan Kakar, *Afghanistan: The Soviet Invasion and the Afghan Response, 1979-1982* (Berkeley, 1995), quotes Karmal as saying in 1986 that he and Barialay were full brothers; p. 65.

16. 'Establishment of the Marxist-Leninist Party', p. 2.

17. US Embassy Kabul, airgram A-60, 3 July 1978.

18. Kabul Radio, 10 January 1985, in *FBIS/SA*, 14 January1985, p. C4.

19. *Pakistani Progressive*, March-April 1980, in *MERIP Reports*, July-August 1980, p. 21; Basil G. Kavalsky, 'Afghanistan, the Journey to Economic Development' (unpublished World Bank study, 1977), p. 17; *Voprosy Filosofii*, No. 8, 1980: 60-71, in *FBIS/SU* Annex, 6 October 1980, pp. 1-12.

20. *New York Times*, 9 September 1979, p. 3; Halliday, 'Revolution in Afghanistan', p. 24.

21. Yuri V. Gankovskiy, interview, Washington, 6 April 1988; A. A. Lyakhovskiy and V. M. Zabrodin, 'Secrets of the Afghan War, Part 1', *Armiya*, Nos. 3-4, 1992: 72-7; V. G. Korgun, 'Afghanistan in Contemporary Times', in Yuri V. Gankovskiy, *A History of Afghanistan* (Moscow, 1982), p. 293.

22. 'Establishment of the Marxist-Leninist Party', p. 2; *Khalq*, 11 April 1966, in English by Taraki's translation service, obtained privately by the author, 1980; published in 1983 in Arnold, *Afghanistan's Two-Party*, pp. 137-48.

23. *Pravda*, 28 June 1990, p. 6, in *FBIS/SU*, 3 July 1990, p. 20.

24. Kabul Radio, 19 October 1987, in FBIS, *Daily Report, Near East and South Asia* [hereafter *FBIS/NE*], 29 October 1987, p. 38.

25. Kabul Radio, 18 October 1987, in *FBIS/NE*, 23 October 1987, p. 33.

26. 'Establishment of the Marxist-Leninist Party', pp. 6, 8.

27. Ibid., pp. 3-4, 8; Kabul Radio, 30 [*sic*] November 1984, in *FBIS/SA*, 9 November 1984, p. C2.

28. Morozov, 'Our Man, 1', pp. 36-7; Eliza Van Hollen, 'Soviet Dilemmas in Afghanistan', State Department (Washington, 1980).

29. Kabul Radio, 30 [*sic*] November 1984, in *FBIS/SA*, 9 November 1984, p. C2.

30. Kabul Radio, 10 January 1985, in *FBIS/SA*, 14 January 1985, p. C4.

31. Louis Dupree, 'Red Flag Over Hindu Kush, Part 1: Leftist Movements in Afghanistan', *American Universities Field Staff Reports, Asia* [hereafter *AUFS/A*], No. 44, 1979: 8; Korgun, 'Afghanistan in Contemporary Times', p. 285; Anwar, *Tragedy*, p. 56.

32. 'Establishment of the Marxist-Leninist Party,' p. 10; Kabul Radio, 11 March 1990, in *FBIS/NE*, 13 March 1990, pp. 41-2.

33. Arnold, *Afghanistan's Two-Party*, p. 39; Anwar, *Tragedy*, pp. 58-9; Eden Naby, 'The Changing Role of Islam as a Unifying Force in Afghanistan', in Ali Banuazizi and Myron Weiner, eds., *The State, Religion, and Ethnic Politics: Afghanistan, Iran, and Pakistan* (Syracuse, 1986), p. 139; Grant M. Farr, 'The New Afghan Middle Class as Refugees and Insurgents', in Farr and Merriam, *Afghan Resistance*, p. 136; Korgun, 'Afghanistan in Contemporary Times', pp. 277-8, 289.

34. Ibid., p. 271; Farr, 'New Afghan Middle Class', p. 135.

35. Roy, *Islam and Resistance*, pp. 71-4; 'The Islamic Movement in Afghanistan: Memoirs of Dr Tawana', *AFGHANews*, 1 May 1989, p. 6.

36. Adamec, *Biographical Dictionary*, p. 71; Roy, *Islam and Resistance*, pp. 71-3; State Department, 'Afghanistan: Eight Years of Soviet Occupation', (Washington, December 1987), p. 8; *Defis Afghans*, February-June 1988, pp. 16-21, in Joint Publications Research Service, *Near East-South Asia Report* [hereafter *JPRS-NEA*], No. 88-076 (Washington), 26 October 88, p. 37; *The Resistance*, 1 February 1988; *Guardian*, 5 January 1988, p. 17.

37. Adamec, *Biographical Dictionary*, p. 104; Roy, *Islam and Resistance*, pp. 71-4; Edward R. Girardet, *Afghanistan: The Soviet War* (New York, 1985), p. 78.

38. Morozov, 'Our Man, 1', p. 39. Morozov said the KGB met secretly with Karmal for some years before 1978, but Karmal denied ever being a 'KGB agent'—probably a matter of definition; *Trud*, 24 October 1991, pp. 1, 4, in JPRS, *Soviet Union, International Affairs* [hereafter *JPRS-UIA*], No. 91-027, 27 November 1991, p. 56.

39. Dupree, 'Red Flag, Part 1', p. 12.

40. Anwar, *Tragedy*, p. 76; Korgun, 'Afghanistan in Contemporary Times', p. 299; M. F. Slinkin, *A History of the Armed Forces of Afghanistan, 1747-1977* (Moscow, 1985), pp. 170-91. Kakar,

Afghanistan, attributes to the leftist soldiers strong influence on Daoud's regime, pp. 13, 60, 88.

41. US Embassy Kabul, airgram A-24, 30 April 1975; Ghaus, *Fall*, p. 190; conversations with Afghan exiles, 1980-81, 1986; Halliday, 'Revolution in Afghanistan', p. 29; Kabul Radio, 12 May 1978, in *FBIS/ME*, 15 May 1978, pp. S1-4.

42. *Izvestiya*, 11 and 17 February 1992, pp. 3 and 2, in FBIS, *Daily Report, Central Eurasia* [hereafter *FBIS/CE*], 5 March 1992, pp. 92-6, and *FBIS/SU*, 25 February 1992, p. 7.

43. Aleksandr Morozov, 'Our Man in Kabul, Part 2', *New Times*, No. 39, 1991: 33; Aleksandr Morozov, 'The KGB and the Afghan leaders', *New Times*, No. 24, 1992: 36.

44. Roy, *Islam and Resistance*, p. 75; Ghaus, *Fall*, p. 189.

45. Tahir Amin, 'Afghan Resistance: Past, Present, and Future', *Asian Survey*, April 1984, p. 377.

46. Richard Mackenzie, 'Afghan Rebels Never Say Die', *Insight*, 25 January 1988, p. 13; Slinkin, *History of the Armed Forces*, p. 177; Korgun, 'Afghanistan in Contemporary Times', p. 300; conversations with Afghan exiles, 1985.

47. Abdul Rasheed (Rashid), 'Final Report: The War in Afghanistan, Past and Present', manuscript dated November 1986, pp. 60-61; *Far Eastern Economic Review*, 30 January 1981, pp. 32-3; Gen. Khalid Mahmud Arif, *Working with Zia: Pakistan's Power Politics 1977-1988* (Karachi, 1995), p. 306.

48. Maj.-Gen. Nasirullah Babar Khan, quoted in *New York Times*, 23 April 1989, p. 16.

49. *Far Eastern Economic Review*, 30 January 1981: 32-3; Roy, *Islam and Resistance*, p. 75; Robert G. Wirsing, 'Pakistan and the War in Afghanistan', *Asian Affairs*, Summer 1987: 74; Korgun, 'Afghanistan in Contemporary Times', p. 300.

50. *Far Eastern Economic Review*, 29 February 1980: 21-2; talks with Afghan exiles, 1980-81, 1985; Roy, *Islam and Resistance*, pp. 77-8.

51. Ibid.; Foreign and Commonwealth Office [hereafter, FCO], 'Afghanistan: Opposition Groups' (London, 1980); Richard Mackenzie, 'Essential Justice After a Massacre', *Insight*, 22 January 1990: 28-9; Arif, *Working with Zia*, p. 306.

52. US Embassy Kabul, airgram A-28, 17 April 1974, and cable 778, 5 February 1975.

53. Halliday, 'Revolution in Afghanistan', p. 30; Dupree, 'The Democratic Republic of Afghanistan, 1979', *AUFS/A*, No. 3 (1979); Ghaus, *Fall*, 168-9.

54. *Izvestiya*, 11 December 1975, pp. 1-3, in *FBIS/SU*, 17 December 1975, p. J1-3.

55. Ghaus, *Fall*, pp. 174, 178-9.

56. *Die Zeit*, 9 June 1978, in *FBIS/ME*, 9 June 1978, pp. S1-5; Korgun, 'Afghanistan in Contemporary Times', p. 303.

57. Rostislav A. Ulyanovskiy, 'The Afghan Revolution at the Current Stage', *Problems of History of the Soviet Communist Party*, No. 4, 1982: 84-95.

58. *DRA Annual, 1979*, p. 22.

59. Anwar, *Tragedy*, p. 89; *Economist*, 2 August 1980. Gankovskiy said (interview, Washington, 6 April 1988) that in April 1978 Amin's Khalqi military group had 'more than 500' members, while the Parchami group organized by Nur Ahmad Nur had 600 officers, and both were outnumbered by Qadir's 800-man independent leftist officer group. Morozov, 'Our Man, 1', pp. 37-8, says Amin listed about 300 Khalqis in the army just before the 1978 *coup*.

60. Bradsher, *Afghanistan*, pp. 69-71; *World Marxist Review*, April 1980: 53; Anwar, *Tragedy*, p. 86; Halliday, 'Revolution in Afghanistan', p. 31; Arnold, *Afghanistan's Two-Party*, p. 54.

61. Dupree, 'Red Flag Over the Hindu Kush, Part V: Repressions, or Security Through Terror Purges, I-IV', *AUFS/A*, Vol. 28, No. 3 (1980): 3.

62. Korgun, 'Afghanistan in Contemporary Times', p. 303; Anwar, *Tragedy*, p. 86; *DRA Annual, 1979*, pp. 24-5; report from CPSU to East German leader Erich Honecker, 13 October 1978, quoting Taraki, in *Cold War International History Project Bulletin* [hereafter *CWIHPB*], Washington, Nos. 8-9, Winter 1996/1997: 135.

63. State Department, 'Afghanistan: Seven Years of Soviet Occupation', (Washington, December 1986), p. 12.

64. *DRA Annual, 1979*, 26, 40.

65. Morozov, 'Our Man, 1', p. 37; Anwar, *Tragedy*, p. 90, citing *Kabul Times*, 3 May 1978, and *Kabul New Times*, 8 January 1980.

66. *World Marxist Review*, April 1980: 53.

67. *DRA Annual, 1979*, p. 26.

68. Louis Dupree, 'The Marxist Regimes and the Soviet Presence in Afghanistan: An Ages-Old Culture Responds to Late Twentieth-Century Aggression', in M. Nazif Shahrani and Robert L. Canfield, eds., *Revolutions & Rebellions in Afghanistan: Anthropological Perspectives* (Berkeley, 1984), pp. 60-61.

69. Kabul Radio, 12 May 1978 and 1 January 1980, in *FBIS/ME*, 15 May 1978 and 2 January 1980, pp. S1-4 and S2.

70. Anwar, *Tragedy*, p. 93; Kakar, *Afghanistan*, pp. 200-201; Rustem Galiullin, *The CIA in Asia: Covert Operations against India and Afghanistan* (Moscow, 1988), p. 110.

71. State Department, cable 108913, 28 April 1978; Dupree, 'Afghanistan Under the Khalq', *Problems of Communism*, July-August 1979: 34; Anwar, *Tragedy*, p. 92; Ghaus, *Fall*, pp. 196-7.

CHAPTER 2

THE GREAT SAUR *COUP d'ÉTAT*

Daoud's order for the arrest of PDPA leaders ended an era in Afghanistan, and began a tumultuous, destructive period culminating in a Soviet invasion. The order led to what the Communists called 'the Great Saur Revolution', for the month in the Afghan calendar, but was actually a *coup d'état*. The country came under the control of a narrowly based, sharply divided Communist movement that was utterly unprepared and generally incompetent for responsibility attained unexpectedly, even accidentally.

Police arrested Taraki and four other PDPA leaders shortly after midnight on the morning of 26 April 1978. All were taken to prison except Amin, who was placed under house arrest, according to the PDPA's official history.[1] This history—or mythology—asserts that while under house arrest Amin issued instructions for the *coup*. Soviet experts flatly rejected the account, however. A leading Soviet academic specialist on Afghanistan, Yuri V. Gankovskiy, characterized versions of it as 'fairy tales for children'.[2]

According to the official history, when police came to Amin's house the unprepared conspirator had his wife hastily hide a list of military officers 'involved in the revolution'. At 6:30 a.m. Amin sent his teenage son with instructions for Sayed Mohammed Gulabzoy—an air force officer whose allegiance apparently was more to Qadir's group than to a PDPA faction—to tell others at air force headquarters to attack the government at 9 a.m. the next day. Amin used relatives to summon other party members and wrote out for them two copies of a detailed plan for the *coup*. Watanjar was to command ground forces, Qadir to direct air force units, and 20 others were given assignments. Amin finished writing at 10:30 a.m., and at 10:45 more police arrived to take him to prison.[3]

If true, this amazing development might have been a result of simple incompetence by the Afghan police. There were also reports that Amin had secret connections through PDPA penetrations of the police, through a childhood friendship with a senior policeman, or as an informer himself.[4] But the preponderance of evidence is that the Amin did not organize the *coup* while under house arrest. His claimed master plan was written after the fact. The explanation for the *coup* that best fits all the evidence is that military officers acted on their own in fear of exposure of their leftist connections by the arrested PDPA leaders and resulting execution by an enraged Daoud.[5] Despite efforts to blacken Amin's name after his death, Karmal's regime never sought to correct the official history. Admitting a non-PDPA *coup* might have been as politically awkward as investigating Khyber's murder.

A CONFUSED *COUP*

According to Gankovskiy, four military officers met to discuss the 26 April arrests. They were Qadir, head of the Marxist officers group; Watanjar and Gulabzoy, who worked with Amin; and Mohammed Rafi, who worked with Parchami organizer Nur Ahmad Nur Panjwa'i. The officers decided to revolt rather than risk exposure and death. A Soviet military history journal said 'a military *coup* was carried out...under the command of the chief of staff of the country's air force and air-defence forces, Abdul Qadir'.[6]

On Thursday, 27 April 1978, Watanjar, the deputy commander of the Fourth Armoured Brigade stationed at the Pul-i-Charki military base a few miles east of Kabul, led 50 or 60 tanks to the Arg, the walled palace complex in downtown Kabul where Daoud had his office and residence. When some 600 rebels began attacking the Arg about noon, as Daoud was inside meeting his cabinet to consider the fate of the PDPA prisoners, the 1800 presidential guards barracked there resisted. About 4 p.m. Qadir had some 20 jet fighter-bombers from Bagram air base, north of Kabul, begin strafing and rocketing the palace. Daoud's efforts to call in reinforcements were unsuccessful. Soviet sources said 43 soldiers died, Taraki said 72 soldiers and others died, Amin said the overall death toll was 101, and opponents' estimates of deaths went into the thousands.[7]

Rebel soldiers captured Kabul Radio around 5:30 p.m. About the same time, other rebels freed Taraki, Amin, Karmal, and other leaders from the city prison. Official accounts diverge on whether Taraki or Amin took charge and issued orders from the radio station.[8] The only independent evidence, from Kabul Radio's broadcasts, is that neither was in command. Qadir announced at 7 p.m. that Daoud had been overthrown—which was premature, because the palace was not completely captured and Daoud and his family killed until about 4 the next morning. 'The power of the state fully rests with the revolutionary council of the armed forces,' Qadir declared without reference to the PDPA or any civilian leadership. The broadcasts identified Qadir as head of the council, and Watanjar's name was also mentioned, but no reference was made to the political leaders.[9] At 10 p.m.

the revolutionary council of the national armed forces' broadcast a brief policy statement, still without mention of the PDPA or a civilian leadership. It promised 'preservation of the principles of the sacred teachings of Islam, establishment of democracy, freedom and security of the individual, and...[a foreign] policy of positive active neutrality....[10]

Within a day or two, Kabul had returned to normal; the rest of the country remained calm.

Moscow reacted publicly as if this were just another
military *coup* in some Third World country of only moderate
interest. For three days, Tass called it a *coup d'état* and said
the armed forces' council had seized power, without
indicating any involvement by political parties or the general
public.

PDPA IN CHARGE

Najibullah later described the *coup* as an 'uprising of the
military officers...as a result of which political power was
transferred to the PDPA'.[11] The transfer was never explained.
Late on 30 April Kabul Radio was still broadcasting an
account by the official Bakhtar News Agency that 'the
national armed forces are in complete control of the
situation'.[12] Then the station began broadcasting 'Decree
No. 1 of the Revolutionary Council of the Democratic
Republic of Afghanistan', which was said to have been issued
at 3 p.m. on 30 April. Ignoring the military council, and
therefore leaving the public unclear what had become of it,
the decree said the revolutionary council was 'the supreme
governmental power in the country'. No details about the
revolutionary council were given except to identify Taraki as
both its president and the country's prime minister, with
other officials to be appointed shortly.[13]

The record of the period issued by the new regime claimed
that Taraki or Amin had been in charge all along. It ignored
the existence of the military council except for one
statement—unheard in broadcasts at the time—that the
council was said to have issued at 9 p.m. on 29 April:

> In order that this revolution...performs its grave democratic
> and national duties in creative all-round and effective manner,
> the Revolutionary Council of the Armed Forces transferred all
> high state power to the Revolutionary Council of the
> Democratic Republic of Afghanistan and merged itself in the
> latter council.

A Soviet book said the military council 'headed by Colonel Abdul Kadir,...which directed the revolutionary *coup*, adopted' this decision.[14]

What happened behind the scenes during those first three days, why the soldiers agreed to hand over power to the politicians, was left unclear. One view, held by some Khalqis, was that the soldiers never really had power, and the PDPA central committee spent the three days deciding whether to hide its hand behind the soldiers.[15] A Soviet account indicated Moscow got the pro-Soviet officers to stand aside. It said the head of KGB foreign intelligence, Vladimir A. Kryuchkov, and a deputy, Oleg D. Kalugin, flew to Kabul 'almost immediately after the April *coup*'. Kryuchkov was 'primarily responsible for the formulation of the new Afghan leadership' so that it met 'certain conditions: complete loyalty to the USSR, an equal proportion of representatives from the 'Khalq' and 'Parcham' factions, and absence of...ties with Western special [intelligence] services', this account said. But Kalugin said he and Kryuchkov did not visit Afghanistan until August 1978, and he doubted that Kryuchkov had gone earlier.[16] Taraki told Soviet Ambassador Aleksandr M. Puzanov on 29 April that Afghanistan would 'belong to the socialist camp' led by the USSR.[17]

RESURGENT FACTIONALISM

Decree No. 2 at 9 a.m. on 1 May said the council's second meeting had 'unanimously elected Babrak Karmal as vice-president'. Three deputy prime ministers were named to represent the three power elements: Karmal for Parcham, Amin for Khalq while also becoming foreign minister, and Watanjar represented the armed forces while also becoming minister of communications. Qadir became minister of national defence, and 16 other cabinet posts were announced. Whether by Kryuchkov's arrangement or just negotiated compromise, government jobs under Taraki were divided almost equally between Khalqis and Parchamis plus a few soldiers, although Karmal objected to making room for the soldiers.[18]

This arrangement quickly proved unstable. Confrontations between Khalqis and Parchamis had begun by 19 May. On 22 May Amin had the armed forces' political department publish a pamphlet that made him the organizer and hero of a Khalqi coup.[19] This, and the question of the party role of independent soldiers who had been in the *coup*, escalated arguments at a PDPA politburo meeting on 24 May. Beginning on 11 June, Parchamis appealed to Puzanov to intercede with Taraki. In a showdown on 12 June, personal differences exacerbated a dispute over seeking 'immediate radical transformations', as Taraki wanted, or following Karmal's 'more flexible and cautious approach'. Karmal reportedly sought support from Qadir, who was reluctant to become too closely identified with either faction.[20]

Advisers from the CPSU's International Department, who had arrived in Kabul after the *coup*, tried to reconcile the feuding factions. These outsiders 'were simply ignorant of the specific features of Afghan society', and they 'often did not understand the complicated social and tribal structure of the state and the basic alignment of political forces', a Soviet journal later conceded. It added that the suspiciousness and outright hostility within the PDPA were too much for them to overcome.[21]

Purge of Parchamis

Karmal complained to Puzanov on 18 June, 'I do not know what is going on in the country—they have isolated me...'.[22] By 10 July most senior Parchamis had been banished abroad. Karmal went reluctantly as ambassador to Czechoslovakia, Najibullah as ambassador to Iran. A reorganization of the PDPA, after 'lengthy discussion', was announced on 8 July.[23] Amin took Karmal's position as a party secretary. In the government, Watanjar was demoted to replace Nur as interior minister, leaving Amin as Taraki's only deputy prime minister as well as being foreign minister. Amin also controlled the new political police, *Da Afghanistan da Gato da Satalo Adara* (Organization for the Protection of the Security of Afghanistan), known as AGSA, with Assadullah Sarwari as its acting boss. Known Parchamis were fired from official jobs, many being arrested and tortured in efforts to discover the names of secret Parchamis.[24]

After decapitating Parcham, the Khalqis went after the other element in the revolutionary council—the independent leftist soldiers. Kabul Radio announced on 17 August, the discovery of an 'anti-revolutionary network' led by Defence Minister Qadir, the army chief of staff, Maj.-Gen. Shapur Ahmedzai, and others. They were arrested.[25] Qadir seems to have been trying to maintain his own separate group, if not as an organized bloc then at least as a loose association of officers not directly beholden to Khalq. For thus resisting total control they were branded Parchamis,[26] even though Qadir had worked with both factions while joining neither. The PDPA politburo named Taraki as defence minister, saying Amin 'shall also help in the [ministry's] affairs'. Within a few days, another leftist soldier in the cabinet, Rafi, and a civilian Parchami, Planning Minister Keshtmand, were arrested along with virtually every other known or suspected Parchami and many non-aligned leftists. Many were tortured, some to death. Anyone involved in Marxist politics who was not with Khalq was considered to be against it.[27] But, other than handwritten confessions tortured out of key figures, no evidence was presented of a full-blown plot. Keshtmand's confession said, 'Karmal argued that the present Khalqi state was isolated from the people, and the latter were dissatisfied'.[28] This was a dangerous truth.

On 6 September the government ordered home the banished Parchami ambassadors—but they all disappeared into Eastern Europe—while Qadir and three others were secretly sentenced to death.[29] According to a KGB official, in mid-1979 Amin dispatched a team to assassinate Karmal in Prague, where he had stayed on in exile after losing the ambassador's post, but Czechoslovak counterintelligence 'spotted and neutralized' the group.[30] At a 27 November meeting Taraki said that Amin had earlier become both a politburo member and party secretary, the key job combination in any Leninist party. Now, Taraki said, Amin and his deputy Shah Wali 'are administering the party and Khalqi organizations' affairs through related commissions'. Resentment grew over Amin's high-handed behaviour.[31]

NEW POLICIES

Taraki announced his regime's policies on 9 May. Following the statement published in 1966 in *Khalq*, he promised 'democratic land reforms', 'ensuring the equality of rights of women', and increasing 'the state sector of the national economy...'. A foreign policy of non-alignment and good relations with all neighbours singled out 'cooperation with the USSR', and he called for 'understanding and peaceful political talks' with Pakistan to solve the Pushtunistan problem. But the PDPA tried to hide its ideology, denying that it was a Communist party. Puzanov reported that Taraki told him the PDPA will inform the people 'later' about its true goals.[32]

Justifying the policy decisions, Amin tried to explain away the lack of a properly Marxist proletariat movement. 'It is not necessary,' he said, that the working class 'should be in the majority so that the working class revolution takes place', since 'the working class revolutionary ideology is the torch of our revolution and' the PDPA. Since 'the working class has not yet developed as a political force', the army should take power and then 'working-class ideology should be spread through the army...'.[33] In support, a Soviet commentator rejected the idea that the PDPA 'political vanguard' should 'sit impassively on the shore of a vast sea of human privation and suffering...wait[ing] until the political conscience of millions would awaken completely.... No, [it] chose [instead to lean] on the army to take political power, and, in the process of social transformation, to involve the millions in the revolution'.[34] But the millions never got involved.

A SOVIET ROLE?

It became an article of faith for many anti-Communist Afghans and numerous foreign observers that the USSR had somehow played a critical role in destroying Daoud and bringing the PDPA to power. An indirect role was clear. Afghan soldiers trained by Moscow had been encouraged to be dissatisfied with the status quo. The CPSU had urged unification of Khalq and Parcham. But the Soviets professed to be amazed by an unexpected *coup*.[35] Brezhnev told US President Jimmy Carter that the Soviets first heard of the *coup* on the radio and had not instigated it.[36] Gankovskiy said that when Qadir, Watanjar, Rafi, and Gulabzoy decided to move against Daoud, they sent a messenger to inform the Soviet embassy, but he was turned away by the duty officer there, who accused him of trying to stage a provocation.[37] The American secretary of state at the time, Cyrus Vance, who had access to all United States intelligence on the subject, wrote later that 'we had no evidence of Soviet complicity in the *coup*...[although t]here was room for doubt...'.[38] Pakistan's foreign secretary, Agha Shahi, wrote that 'Pakistan viewed the upheaval, in the absence of reliable evidence of a foreign hand, as an internal Afghan affair...'.[39]

However, a curious point arose later. On 30 June 1989, the Soviet council of ministers adopted a decree extending the benefits granted to veterans of the 1979-89 Soviet military involvement in Afghanistan. The same benefits were given to Soviet 'soldier-internationalists' who had seen combat in countries that Moscow had aided while not being formally involved in their wars. On the list, with Soviet combat in Korea from 1950 to 1953, in Vietnam from 1 July 1965 to 31 December 1974, and other countries, were listed Soviet 'servicemen who took part in combat operations...in Afghanistan from 22 April 1978 to 30 November 1979'.[40] There is no public record of a Soviet combat role in the *coup*, much less beginning 22 April—five days before the *coup*. But this dating seems to confirm reports that some of the 350 Soviets advising the Afghan armed forces were with the rebels who seized control of Kabul airport and helped launch the warplane attacks from Bagram.[41] It is unlikely—indeed, virtually impossible—that the tightly controlled advisers got involved in a *coup* without high-level authorization, yet the dating for benefits indicates some were involved. Involvement does not, however, mean instigation.

Soviet Ambassador Puzanov, an alcoholic 72-year-old dropout from Kremlin politics, was asked to meet Taraki on the evening of 27 April. After some delay in getting Moscow's permission, Puzanov met him 28 or 29 April at the Tass correspondent's house where KGB officers used to meet Taraki.[42] This led to Puzanov's extending Soviet diplomatic recognition to the regime just half an hour after Decree No. 1 was broadcast on April 30. Moscow did not publicize this, however. Not until three days later, after India and other countries had publicly accepted the new regime, did Soviet President Leonid I. Brezhnev, Premier Alexei N. Kosygin, and Foreign Minister Andrei A. Gromyko send their government's congratulations according to normal protocol.[43]

MOSCOW, THE THIRD WORLD, AND AFGHANISTAN

Moscow's attitude toward the new Afghan regime reflected the Brezhnev leadership's belief that the USSR was capable of expanding its influence anywhere in the world. In 1978 Soviet leaders did not recognize the structural weaknesses then building up that would undermine the country a decade later, nor did they appreciate the USSR's limited economic ability to play an adventurous role in the Third World. Not only was the cost of foreign aid kept an official secret but also distorted pricing and confused accounting made it impossible for even the leaders to determine aid's true economic burden in meaningful terms of choices or alternatives.

Looking back from the perspective of President Mikhail S. Gorbachev's 'new thinking' in 1989, a Soviet foreign ministry journal condemned 'simplistic ideas' about the Third World. These had arisen, it said, partly from inadequate information and partly from 'distortions in systematic studies.... The dogmatic mode of thought and action, the authoritarian, command style which prevailed in the [Soviet] internal life was spread to the sphere of foreign policy and the academic studies on which it relied'.[44] Dogmatic thinking was reinforced by the superficial successes achieved through the Brezhnev regime's fixation on building up armed strength at the expense of the civilian economy. Soviet military textbooks had by 1977 come to define the armed forces' role as giving 'support and aid to liberated countries in suppressing the imperialist export of armed counter-revolution'.[45]

The implied promise that Soviet bloc armies would go to the aid of Moscow-recognized Marxists in the Third World was partially based on a perception of a 'Vietnam syndrome'—that the United States had lost the political will to use its military power in Third World situations after the fall of Saigon in 1975.[46] A military book that said in 1972 that mobile Soviet forces may be required to help countries fighting 'internal reaction' added a telling comment that would prove hauntingly applicable to the Soviet involvement in Afghanistan: 'The experience of American aggression in Vietnam has indicated that, however strong a military presence may be from a military-technical standpoint, it will not of itself guarantee the achieving of political success.[47] The apparent lessons of Vietnam seemed to promise Moscow more latitude for opportunistic Third World activities without encountering meaningful opposition from Washington.

The first secret Soviet reaction to the coup beyond Puzanov's cautious diplomacy was the KGB visit. Kryuchkov not only structured the new Kabul leadership out of people whom the KGB had long supported and encouraged, but also won agreement on opening a KGB office in Kabul to work with the new regime—while keeping a clandestine residency there to spy on it. Kryuchkov later made frequent secret visits to Kabul to supervise developments.[48] Taraki and Amin were receptive to advice. They were later paraphrased as telling Moscow, 'We have power, but we don't know what to do with it. Please dispatch here as many advisers as possible for our armed forces, the PDPA, and each of our ministries. Teach us to manage the state, and we will do everything as we are taught'.[49] Moscow responded with a flood of advisers who virtually took over the regime, as is discussed in Chapter 4.

Western observers were mystified about the nature of the new Afghan regime. Some declared the 19th-century 'Great Game' of British-Russian imperial competition in Central Asia to be over, with the Russians as winners. But United States officials carefully avoided pronouncements that might complicate keeping open lines for trying to influence the new regime. The US embassy in Kabul said on 10 May that it had 'not yet been able to determine [if] the new Afghan government indeed qualifies as a "Communist" regime' according to the terms of the American Foreign Assistance Act of 1961, which prohibited aid to 'any Communist country'.[50] None the less, countries other than the USSR that bordered Afghanistan—Pakistan, Iran, and China—were disturbed by the prospect of a pro-Soviet leftist neighbour.[51]

THE PURGE

As the KGB 'sent people capable of organizing and *directing* the actions of the Afghan state security organs' to Kabul, according to a Soviet report,[52] a wide-ranging purge began. Taraki described it as 'weeding out from the state machinery anti-revolutionary, anti-democratic elements, and elements opposed to the interests of the people', as well as those considered guilty of 'sabotage,...corruption, bad reputation, bribery, cruelty, oppression, and administrative inefficiency...'. A 'revolutionary military court' was set up to dispense summary justice for offenses against the revolution or 'against the interests of the people and against national interests'[53]—whatever the PDPA decided those to be.

Members of the extended royal family were arrested. Since the family represented the Durrani branch of southern Pushtuns, while Khalqis were predominately from the Ghilzai confederation of eastern Pushtuns, many Afghans perceived the coup as little more than a traditional clash in which the Ghilzais had finally defeated their old Durrani rivals. Also arrested were non-political technocrats—former cabinet ministers and Western-educated officials were particularly targeted—most non-Communist military officers above the rank of major, and some businessmen and Islamic religious leaders. Hundreds, perhaps thousands, of former officials were killed. At the new Pul-i-Charki prison just east of Kabul, where torture was routine, an estimated average of 50 persons were shot or buried alive nightly.[54] Summarizing the situation in October 1978, the CPSU said mass

repressions...are being carried out without regard to law, and are directed not only at class enemies of the new regime ('Muslim Brothers,' supporters of the monarchy, etc.), but also at persons who could be used for revolutionary interests; that brings out discontent among the populace, undermines the authority of the revolutionary government, and leads to the weakening of the new regime.[55]

Karmal later complained that 'there was not the necessary number of [Afghan] managers and specialists at all levels who could combine devotion to the revolution with sufficient vocational and theoretical training'. Najibullah said 'experienced and professional cadres [were replaced] by individuals lacking professional skills under the pretext of political loyalty...'.[56] Soviets filled the gap, taking over running much of the new regime. Soviet military advisers and technicians in the Afghan armed forces, who had numbered 350 at the time of the coup, were up to 650 by early June and at least 1000 a year later. General Vasiliy P. Zaplatin was rushed to Kabul in May to direct the creation of a Soviet-model 'political administration' in the armed forces to insure loyalty and reliability. Within a year, between 2000 and 2500 Soviet economic advisers were in the country.[57]

BEGINNING OF RESISTANCE

By late May, exiles in Peshawar led by Rabbani had established a National Rescue Front of nine factions that became the forerunner of *mujahideen* party politics. Afghanistan's estimated 320 000 traditional Islamic teachers, the mullahs (*mullahian*), were treated as opponents by Taraki, who charged that religion was being used as an obstacle to 'the progressive movement of our homeland'. After religious leaders had been alienated, Karmal's regime recognized too late that 'the thinking of the predominately illiterate population is still being formed mainly by the mullahs'.[58]

Actions that the Afghan people saw as violating both traditions and Quranic propriety stirred resistance. Years later Najibullah summarized 'a series of serious practical blunders' that 'aggravated the situation in the country and even launched armed confrontation'.[59] As Khalqis from Kabul took over local administrations and turned schools and medical clinics into propaganda centres, they were set upon by outraged villagers. Among numerous, varied reports of what different observers believed to be the first armed rebellion was an early battle in Paktia province. Within a week of the coup, road workers from the Jadran tribe forced their military escort to flee and then captured the fort at Wazi from an infantry company. Other small revolts soon drove regime officials from the Nuristani provinces northwest of the Khyber Pass and from Badakhshan province, and in some places such as Asmar army units surrendered peacefully to rebellious local tribesmen.[60]

Most early rebellions were sparked by hostility to PDPA imposition of rigid state control over loosely governed rural areas, then fuelled by rejection of decreed social changes. But eventually predominant as the core and sustenance of the resistance was the feeling that Islam was in danger. Taraki said he wanted to 'clean Islam...of the ballast and dirt of bad traditions, superstition, and erroneous belief. Thereafter, we will have progressive, modern, and pure Islam' that would support him.[61] Many religious leaders who resisted efforts to bend religion to his support were tortured and killed. The concept of national unity despite ethnic and geographic diversity had been based on a common religion, and an Islamic world view pervaded social customs and attitudes. Religion thus became the critical element in the long, costly fight against the PDPA and its Soviet backers. It made the Afghan resistance into a *jihad*, a war declared by religious authorities to defend Islam against enemies of the faith, and made its participants *mujahideen*, those engaged in a *jihad*.

PDPA REFORMS

The PDPA instituted reforms partly to prove its Marxist credentials, partly to ensure that its promises were not seen as empty and thus risk weakening leftist support, and partly to carry out naively idealistic hopes of rapid modernization that lacked an appreciation of conditions and attitudes in the demonstrably change-resistant society outside Kabul. The 'basic lines of the revolutionary duties of the government', announced by Taraki on 9 May, began with land reform, went through 'abolition of old feudal and pre-feudal relations' and 'ensuring the equality of rights of women and men in all social, economic, political, cultural, and civil aspects', included universal and compulsory education, and concluded with such ideals as free health services and elimination of unemployment and illiteracy.[62] Karmal later claimed to have 'written and compiled' the 'basic lines' of revolutionary duties for Taraki and helped write the decrees to put them into effect before being exiled. The claim was unwise, since the unrealistic decrees fuelled rebellion, and dubious, since his limited influence reportedly was on the side of caution.[63]

Despite initial promises to go slow, the new regime had within half a year issued sweeping decrees. Amin explained later, 'We preferred to take up the revolutionary reforms at the time when...[opponents] were not yet...well-organized...'.[64] The first reform decree[65] promised the use of Afghanistan's many mother tongues for education and publication. Education had been only in Pashto or Dari, with English as the compulsory foreign language in upper school. Now English was replaced by Russian. The decree enhanced regional separatism and could have made Russian the national link language, as Moscow had made Russian a tool of control in Soviet Central Asia by limiting regional intercommunication through the emphasis of localized language differences.

The second decree was to free 'peasants from the yoke of oppressing exploiters' by eliminating land mortgages and rural indebtedness. Without the credit that moneylenders and big landowners had provided, however, many farmers lacked the means to buy seeds and other essentials. Agriculture suffered. Some debtors who cited the decree in refusing to pay, were murdered by angry lenders, but many ignored the decree and continued to pay their debts because debts had Islamic religious sanction. The third decree was 'for insuring of equal rights of women with men...and for removing the unjust patriarchial feudalistic relations between husband and wife'. It sought to ameliorate the system of a groom's family paying money and goods to a bride's family that sometimes amounted to two or three years' income of the groom, to regulate the age of marriage, to enhance the status of women, and to make related social changes. In what villagers regarded as an insult to their honour, the government tried to have girls join boys in new schools instead of keeping them separate. Although these changes conformed with Islamic injunctions—a point the regime arrogantly neglected to make—they challenged pre-Islamic customs and economic relations at the heart of Afghan society while dealing with symptoms rather than social causes. By stirring resentment of rural males, the decree actually set back the slow development of women's rights.

The last major reform decree, issued 28 November on land reform, said landless farm workers and other 'deserving persons' would receive free land from those with holdings over fixed limits. But the facts of land ownership were only vaguely known. This was the most extreme case of what Karmal later called the 'insufficient maturity by the PDPA', which 'lacked the necessary experience...to guide economic and cultural development'.[66] Little was done to set up the farm cooperatives and new credit facilities mentioned in the decree because skills, experience, and capital were lacking. Many poor farmers, dependent upon their landlords for credit, resisted change that went against the Quran's ban on usurping another's possessions. The disruptions caused an estimated one-third of arable land to go untilled. More than any other decree, but compounding the effects of earlier ones, land reform aroused and disrupted the countryside as resisting landlords and mullahs were shot in front of other villagers.[67] Taraki announced on 15 July 1979 that land reform had been triumphantly completed ahead of schedule, but it later was admitted to have been a disaster that, at Soviet urging, was abandoned prematurely in an effort to contain rural opposition. Najibullah called it one of the 'main mistakes' of PDPA leaders, who lacked an 'accurate understanding of the country's conditions and situation...'.[68]

Soviet media initially 'made unfounded and exaggerated claims for the [Afghan] regime's successes' with the reform decrees, but realized later that, 'We were the victims of our own illusions'.[69] Moscow media eventually conceded that '[o]rdinary people lost faith in the revolutionary regime.... [The] main mistake...[of trying] to go too fast without taking account of the complex mosaic of Afghan society and its Islamic and ethnic traditions...[was] partly at the prompting of advisers from the USSR...'.[70]

THE AFGHAN-SOVIET PACT

The flood of Soviet advisers into Afghanistan and the role they came to play was not made public, and Moscow avoided acknowledging the extent of Kabul's dependence. The first demonstration of Afghanistan's new status came when Taraki visited Moscow. He and Brezhnev signed, on 5 December 1978, a treaty of friendship and cooperation that became the Kremlin's justification for sending troops into Afghanistan a year later. More specific than the generally noncommittal but similar treaties that Moscow had already made with ten other Third World countries, it said the USSR and Afghanistan 'shall consult each other and take by agreement appropriate measures to ensure the security, independence, and territorial integrity of the two countries...[and] shall continue to develop cooperation in the military field...'.[71] While in Moscow, Taraki agreed to expand the PDPA's relations with the CPSU, which had already 'helped us organize party work'. He also signed an agreement to establish a permanent inter-government commission on economic cooperation[72] that eventually supervised large Soviet subsidies to sustain the Afghan urban economy.

DEATH OF THE AMERICAN AMBASSADOR

As Soviet aid increased, the United States and other Western countries tried to maintain small aid programmes rather than drive Afghanistan into total dependence on Moscow.[73] This policy broke down with the killing on 14 February 1979 of the American ambassador, Adolph 'Spike' Dubs. He was seized by four members of *Setem-i-Melli*, the predominately Tajik party founded in 1968 by PDPA defector Badakhshi to oppose Pushtun domination. The kidnappers told Afghan authorities they wanted to exchange Dubs for three imprisoned party members. In a confused situation, Afghans headed by Amin refused to negotiate. Despite objections of United States diplomats on the scene, who wanted time to try to work out a solution, Afghan police supported by Soviet advisers rushed the kidnappers. Dubs and two kidnappers were killed; police apparently killed the other two soon after.[74]

Outraged, the United States accused the Soviet Union of involvement in the bungling that caused Dubs' death. Moscow denied it. President Carter slashed economic aid programmes for Afghanistan—that were becoming impossible to carry out because of spreading guerrilla resistance—and stopped plans to resume a military training programme, which had already been rejected by the PDPA regime.[75] Most American official personnel left the country, and on 14 August Carter signed a law prohibiting further aid. Aid programmes of other non-Communist countries were halted at about the same time because of the turmoil and insecurity.

GROWING CONFLICT—AND SOVIET INVOLVEMENT

Armed resistance to the Communist regime grew in the winter of 1978-9. Many army deserters joined the resistance, which broadened and diversified into groups that were Islamist, traditionalist, and Maoist.[76] A network of guerrilla training camps and supply routes expanded in Pakistan and, to a lesser extent, in Iran.[77] But as the first anniversary of the Saur *coup* approached, resistance was sporadic, and towns were under control. Then the confidence of regime and Soviet officials was shattered by an uprising in Herat, the economic and administrative centre of western Afghanistan.

Communist activists in Herat had dealt brutally with real and potential opponents. Hundreds were buried alive. On 15 March 1979 a rebellion erupted, starting with or quickly joined by the Afghan army's 17th division that was stationed there. Mobs hunted down and butchered Khalqis and their Soviet advisers with age-old barbarism. Some were skinned alive. Among the 3000 or more killed before loyal troops from Qandahar restored order five days later were dozens of Soviet advisers and their families.[78]

Amin showed no alarm in a 17 March telephone conversation with Gromyko, but Taraki panicked. In phone calls on 17 and 18 March to Kosygin, Taraki pleaded that Soviet troops in Afghan disguise be sent 'to save the revolution'. Kosygin replied that it would 'not be possible to conceal this' from the world, and within two hours '[e]veryone will begin to shout that the Soviet Union's intervention in Afghanistan has begun'. He promised instead 'to quickly deliver military equipment and property to you and to repair helicopters and aircraft...for free'.[79]

The Herat uprising qualified the Afghan problem as one of those 'crisis situations...when [the USSR's] interests and those of our allies were at stake' that caused the ruling CPSU politburo to set up a special commission 'of personnel from various departments...to formulate proposals and coordinate actions'. The commission on Afghanistan was established shortly after Taraki's appeals. Politburo members were Foreign Minister Gromyko, KGB chief Yuriy V. Andropov, and Defence Minister Dmitry F. Ustinov. Also participating was the CPSU secretary for relations with such countries as Afghanistan, Boris N. Ponomarev.[80]

Taraki flew to Moscow to press his request for help on 20 March. First he met with the politburo commission. Kosygin told him that, 'if our troops were introduced, the situation in your country would not only not improve, but would worsen'. A Soviet deployment 'would immediately arouse the international community and would invite sharply unfavourable, multipronged consequences.... [It will give o]ur mutual enemies an excuse to deploy on Afghan territory military formations hostile to you.... [O]ur troops would have to fight not only with foreign aggressors, but also with a certain number of your people'. Instead, Kosygin promised advisers and equipment.[81] Then Taraki met Brezhnev. Brezhnev reiterated the CPSU politburo position, telling him that sending Soviet ground forces 'would only play into the hands of enemies—yours and ours'.[82]

An analysis of the situation by the Soviet politburo commission, dated 1 April, said the Kabul regime 'has not yet established a firm basis of support in the provincial and urban administrative political organs...', and 'the PDPA has not yet become a mass political organization.... The people have demonstrated fear, suspicion, and distrust of the PDPA leadership'. And PDPA leaders, 'displaying their political inflexibility and inexperience, rarely heeded' Soviet advice. The commission also said that:

> the use of Soviet troops in repressing the Afghan counterrevolution would seriously damage the international authority of the USSR and would set back the process of disarmament. In addition, [it] would reveal the weakness of the Taraki government and would widen the scope of the counter-revolution both domestically and abroad....

The report concluded that the USSR should continue helping to improve the Afghan army and urging a broadening of the regime's political base.[83]

On 26 March Soviet cargo planes began delivering light tanks and armoured personnel carriers, plus 25 military helicopters, including a weapon new to Afghan forces: the latest, deadliest, and most expensive Soviet helicopter gunship, the MI-24 Hind. An Asian military attache in Kabul understood that Soviets flew and serviced the complicated MI-24s,[84] but this was not clear. The head of Soviet military advisers in Afghanistan, Lt.-Gen. Lev N. Gorelov, reported on 14 April that Amin, on Taraki's instructions, also asked that 15 or 20 combat helicopters with Soviet crews be sent secretly for use 'should the situation worsen...'. Marshal Nikolai V. Ogarkov, the chief of the Soviet general staff, said '[t]his should not be done'. Asked a month later if Soviet troops would enter Afghanistan, Amin denied having 'so far raised this issue with them'.[85]

Weapons deliveries were followed by a visit to Kabul of the general responsible to the CPSU for Soviet military discipline, morale, and loyalty, Alexei A. Yepishev. During the 'Prague spring' of 1968, he had assessed the situation in Czechoslovakia and returned home advocating Warsaw Pact intervention. Yepishev arrived in Kabul on 5 April with six other generals, and stayed for a week. They found that '[t]he low level of political training, the extreme religiousness and downtrodden nature of the masses of soldiers, and the social heterogeneity of the servicemen' enabled opponents of the regime to demoralize the army.[86] Soon after, the USSR ordered home 'all women and children of Soviets working outside Kabul' rather than risk more Herat episodes, and it sent in hundreds of additional Soviet military advisers.[87]

Spreading Rebellion

The situation worsened, with 'massive anti-government armed actions' in seven provinces in May 1979, an army rebellion in Jalalabad in June, an uprising of Hazaras in Kabul on 23 June, a mutiny of army troops at the ancient Bala Hissar fortress overlooking Kabul on 5 August, and numerous smaller uprisings. In the countryside, some entire army units joined the resistance with their weapons, and desertions cut other units to a third or a quarter of normal strength.[88] As the situation deteriorated, the CPSU politburo commission of Gromyko, Andropov, Ustinov, and Ponomarev recommended that 'a parachute battalion disguised in the uniform (overalls) of an aviation-technical maintenance team' be sent to Bagram air base. The politburo agreed.[89] On 7 July, a 600-man battalion from the nearest Soviet strike force, the elite 105th Guards Airborne Divison stationed at Ferghana in Uzbekistan, 'was clandestinely transferred' to Bagram in order to guard this key military communications and logistical centre for the Kabul region.[90] But Taraki and Amin wanted fighting troops. On 19 and 20 July they asked visiting CPSU secretary Ponomarev that 'approximately two' Soviet divisions—between 14 000 and 26 000 men, depending on the type of divisions—be sent to Afghanistan. They were rebuffed. However, from Kabul, Ambassador Puzanov, the senior Soviet military adviser, Gorelov, and the KGB representative, Lt.-Gen. Boris S. Ivanov, continued to urge a Soviet military role. Their fifth such message to Moscow since 6 May was a 12 August request for several battalions—1200 or more men—to guard Bagram and Bala Hissar.[91]

As resistance spread and intensified in Afghanistan during the spring and summer of 1979, the regime met it with 'mass arrests, shooting of undesirables,...and shooting of Muslim clergy', a Soviet expert related.[92] In March or April, between 1200 and 1700 men of Kerala, a village in Konar province, were rounded up by the army, accused of helping the resistance, and massacred. A month or two later, all the men in a northern village near government posts recently attacked by *mujahideen* were rounded up and drowned in the Amu Darya. In both cases Soviet advisers accompanied the Afghan soldiers and reportedly ordered or approved the killings. Many similar horror stories were described by survivors.[93] The increasing atrocities swelled the flow of refugees to Pakistan and Iran that had begun within days of the Saur *coup*. By the end of 1979 Pakistan estimated that it was sheltering 400 000 Afghan refugees.[94]

CHANGING PERCEPTIONS

Although the CPSU politburo's position in reaction to Herat was clear and sensible, Moscow's understanding of the Afghan situation increasingly came to depend on wrong preconceptions and bad information. In the spring of 1979, according to KGB officials, Moscow ordered that all intelligence be analysed in Kabul, signed jointly by the ambassador, chief military adviser, and senior KGB and GRU officials, and sent to the CPSU politburo. Divergent opinions on the spot led, however, to 'a dwindling flow of intelligence to Moscow'. Even worse, 'the abundant "negative information" put politburo members in a bad mood.... Moscow demanded more "positive information"'. Despite reality, good news came to make up 'almost 95 per cent of our reports'. Apparently separate from these joint reports, 'the CPSU central committee emissaries' in Kabul also had a channel to Moscow, and they were more listened to than the KGB, said one KGB official with perhaps more concern for shifting blame than for honesty.[95]

In mid-August, as Soviet media were backing into cautious distancing of the USSR from the Afghan problem, the politburo commission summoned Gorelov and Ivanov to Moscow. They met with the three politburo members as well as chief of general staff Ogarkov and a first deputy foreign minister, Georgi M. Korniyenko. Committing Soviet troops to Afghanistan was not considered, according to Gorelov's later account. He told the meeting that, 'despite the demoralizing processes, the Afghan army would be capable of defending the gains of the April revolution on its own after it was reorganized...'. But, Gorelov said, Ivanov disagreed on 'the combat capability of the Afghan army and on other complex processes underway in the PDPA. Unfortunately, Ivanov's opinion and that of his [KGB] colleagues seemed more convincing to our political leadership at that time...'.[96]

Gorelov's remarks, which did not explain the KGB position, were published in 1989 as part of a media effort by the Soviet armed forces to absolve themselves of blame for the Afghanistan involvement. The KGB resisted this effort. According to former KGB general Oleg D. Kalugin, another meeting was held in August at an unspecified level. His boss, Kryuchkov, told the meeting that 'Andropov is against our military involvement'. But, Kalugin said, the head of military intelligence, GRU General Pyotr I. Ivashutin, 'insisted on intervention'.[97] Regardless of what the GRU's attitude might have been, the balance of available evidence suggests that the military was less willing to intervene than the KGB.

The CPSU decided on 15 August to send to Kabul the deputy defence minister who commanded Soviet ground forces. He was 71-year-old Ivan G. Pavlovskiy, the planner and commander of the 1968 invasion of Czechoslovakia. His 20-man mission, which arrived secretly in Kabul on 17 August, was supposed to coordinate operations of Soviet military advisers and the Afghan army and to organize military aid, Pavlovskiy said later. Other sources said he was authorized to propose the complete reorganization of the Afghan army, using as a threat the withholding of Soviet aid if this were not done. Amin asked him on 25 August for the dispatch of Soviet troops, but Pavlovskiy had been told by Ustinov before leaving Moscow to tell Afghan officials that 'in no case' would Soviet forces be sent to Afghanistan. Pavlovskiy's mission was originally expected to stay for only about 25 days, but in a rapidly changing and worsening situation it remained until 22 October.[98]

Paralleling the growth of Soviet involvement were several ineffectually vague American warnings against Soviet interference in Afghanistan. President Carter delivered one of them to Brezhnev in Vienna on 17 June 1979: 'There are many problems in Iran and Afghanistan, but the United States has not interfered in the internal affairs of those nations. We expect the Soviet Union to do the same.' Brezhnev—whose interpreter later said he was becoming senile and scarcely able to comprehend what Carter was saying—denied a Soviet role in the Saur *coup* and expressed the hope that the United States would join the USSR in discouraging attacks on the Kabul regime.[99]

THE REGIME AND THE SOVIETS

The Herat explosion led to changes in both the Kabul regime and the Soviet role. On 27 March, Amin replaced Taraki as prime minister while continuing to be foreign minister. Taraki remained president and became the head of a new High Council for the Defence of the Homeland. Although the common perception was that Amin was now running the government, with Taraki reduced to a figurehead, Puzanov said Taraki continued to chair cabinet sessions—to Amin's great annoyance.[100] By late May the United States heard suggestions 'that the Soviets are already moving forward with plans to engineer replacement of the present Khalqi leadership..., perhaps with the exiled Parchamist leaders including...Karmal...'. But a Soviet official in Kabul said that 'at this time' there was no apparent alternative leadership.[101]

Soviet Ambassador Puzanov and his Dari-speaking deputy, Yuriy K. Alekseyev, advised Taraki and Amin to moderate domestic policies and broaden the regime's base by bringing new people into government. The Soviets also sought PDPA unity, with an end of 'repressions in the party as well as the arrests and executions', Puzanov said later. 'Taraki and Amin agreed with me, but nothing actually changed'. In July Ponomarev and his deputy, Rostislav A. Ulyanovskiy, made the first of three visits to Kabul. They urged upon the regime a four-point programme: creation of local organs of power to link workers and 'national patriotic forces' with the regime, writing a national constitution, 'consolidation of all forces objectively interested in democratic transformations', and 'the strengthening of legality and law and order...'. But, Puzanov said, '[u]nfortunately, [the regime] managed to carry out only a small amount' of this.[102]

Amin—whom Puzanov considered 'cunning and deliberate...the evil destiny of the April revolution'—manœuvered to keep Soviet officials from dealing with Taraki. While praising Taraki publicly, Amin criticized him privately, 'especially with Soviet advisers,...question[ing his] competence [and] stressing his weaknesses as an organizer...'.[103] Amin told Puzanov on 21 July that Taraki was 'concentrating the leadership in his own hands, [but] cannot to a sufficient extent control the execution of commands'.[104] Soviet officials came to see Amin as the obstacle to their efforts in saving the regime from its own mistakes. They wanted to replace him with a more conciliatory head of government, while leaving Taraki as the symbolic chief of state. But Amin apparently was aware of Soviet manœuvering and also believed Taraki was conspiring against him with four members of the Soviet-trained military clique: Sarwari, the top political policeman; Watanjar, the defence minister; Sher Jan Mazdooryar, who as interior minister had at least nominal control of the regular police; and Gulabzoy, the communications minister.[105]

Accounts of this period differ, but Amin's colleagues later said he forced a showdown in a PDPA politburo meeting on 28 July, blamed Taraki for governmental failures, and won effective control of the armed forces.[106] Cabinet changes strengthened Amin's supporters and undermined his opponents while 'fuel[ing] the latent discontent in both factions of the PDPA over...Amin's...ever greater personal power', a Soviet observer said. Watanjar, Gulabzoy, and other central committee members 'began openly criticizing Amin' at party meetings 'for his dictatorial ways...'. They tried to get Taraki to remove or demote him, '[b]ut Taraki was misled by Amin's vigorous efforts to build up his [Taraki's] personality cult...'.[107]

TARAKI IN MOSCOW

With the situation in Kabul growing more Byzantine while Soviet concern mounted, Taraki stopped in Moscow on the way home from a nonaligned summit meeting in Havana for 'a friendly meeting in the Kremlin...'. Only Taraki, Brezhnev, Gromyko, and Brezhnev's foreign affairs adviser, Andrey M. Aleksandrov-Agentov, were listed in the 10 September meeting. Protocol would normally have required inclusion of Shah Wali, the Afghan foreign minister who had accompanied Taraki to Havana. He apparently was excluded because he was Amin's man, but he was later reported to have learned what happened and told Amin.

Brezhnev reportedly appealed to Taraki to get rid of Amin or at least limit his powers. Taraki refused, saying he had 'boundless confidence in...[his] loyal pupil and associate'. Daoud had made the mistake of not grooming a successor, Taraki added, but he was grooming Amin.[108] An alternate, if not directly contradictory, report said Taraki was very disturbed by Amin's degree of control in Kabul. This version said Taraki 'noted that Amin was not conducting the policy on which they had agreed at the very beginning of the revolution, and this could lead to dangerous consequences'.[109] Brezhnev later told a Western visitor that he had warned Taraki that Amin was plotting to destroy him.[110] A second point of dispute was Taraki's reminder to Brezhnev of Afghan requests for help from Soviet troops. Brezhnev rebuffed him, reportedly reiterating that '[t]he appearance of our soldiers...would probably turn some of the Afghan people against the revolution...'.[111] A point of agreement between Taraki and Brezhnev was the need to broaden the Kabul regime's base in an effort to limit public opposition. Reports by some sources that Brezhnev had Taraki meet Karmal in Moscow in a reconciliation effort were denied by other sources and seem unlikely.[112]

TARAKI'S FALL

According to confused and conflicting accounts of this period, when Taraki returned to Kabul on 11 September he was surprised to be greeted by Amin. Taraki reportedly had been involved in a plot for the political police, AGSA, headed by Sarwari, to kill Amin as he was driving to the airport. But Sarwari's deputy and nephew, Aziz Ahmad Akbari, told a Soviet adviser of the plot and then, on his advice, informed Amin, who avoided an ambush.[113]

At a cabinet meeting soon after Taraki's return, Amin demanded the dismissal of Sarwari, Watanjar, Mazdooryar, and Gulabzoy from the cabinet because he suspected them of plotting with the Soviets against him, as well as guarantees that Taraki would not plot against him. Taraki refused, but Amin took 'advantage of Taraki's indecisiveness and his inability to take any swift and effective measures', according to the CPSU. On 14 September Amin dismissed the four without Taraki's sanction.[114] Taraki summoned Amin to the presidential palace, the old Arg. Amin was wary, but Puzanov—under instructions from Moscow to try to get the two men to cooperate[115]—assured him it was safe to go. Puzanov, Pavlovskiy, Gorelov, and Ivanov were waiting at the palace to act as intermediaries. When Amin, with an armed escort, entered the building where Taraki lived and worked, presidential guards fired at him down a staircase, reportedly under orders from Sarwari and Watanjar to shoot anyone trying to approach Taraki's quarters. Amin escaped uninjured, rounded up a small military force, went back, fought a sharp, short battle, captured Taraki, and imprisoned him in the palace.[116]

Sarwari, Watanjar, Mazdooryar, and Gulabzoy took refuge in the Soviet embassy and were later smuggled out to the USSR—'in nailed-down boxes', one account said.[117] This seemed to confirm that they had tried to get rid of Amin with the backing, perhaps even instigation, of Moscow. The failure created the worst possible result for the Soviet Union. Amin had been freed of any moderating influences from Taraki while his suspicion and hatred of the Soviets had been reinforced. Puzanov advised Moscow that Taraki was finished, and 'the stake must be made on Amin'. Gorelov and his deputy military adviser for political affairs, Zaplatin, hugged and kissed Amin, but Moscow's protocol congratulations on his new jobs was bare of 'unnecessary praises and overtures', the CPSU noted privately.[118] Gromyko sent a message to Soviets in Kabul on 15 September saying that 'it is deemed expedient not to refuse to deal with Amin...[but] everything possible must be done to restrain Amin from engaging in repression against Taraki's supporters...'. Soviet military and security advisers should continue to 'carry out their direct functions of preparing for and conducting combat operations against rebel formations...', Gromyko added.[119] By the late summer of 1979 no significant order was issued by either the Afghan armed forces or civilian ministries until countersigned by Soviet advisers.

AMIN IN POWER

Except for extra tanks guarding the radio station and several unexplained explosions, Kabul remained normal.[120] Then at

8 p.m. on 16 September, Kabul Radio announced that an 'extraordinary session' of the PDPA central committee had discussed a request by Taraki—who just five days earlier had appeared at the airport in robust health —'that he be relieved of his party and government positions due to health reasons and physical incapacity which render him unable to continue his work'. The committee 'approved his request by a majority vote. In his place, Comrade Hafizullah Amin...was appointed as the secretary general of the PDPA'. The committee also passed a resolution that was circulated secretly to party members denouncing the 'unprincipled behavior and terrorist actions of Nur Mohammed Taraki and the gang of four' and expelling all five from the PDPA. After the central committee meeting, many of the same people reconvened as the revolutionary council, approved Taraki's request to be relieved of government posts, and named Amin as president.[121]

Amin had said in an interview on 9 September that 'our decisions are not made by an individual but are made collectively...'.[122] But after overthrowing Taraki, Amin tried to blame him for all problems and public discontent. 'From now on', he said in speeches on 17 and 18 September, 'Afghanistan will not be ruled by any one person'. Without naming Taraki, Amin blisteringly criticized 'those arrogant ones who were on the seat of power, who engaged in tyrannical acts and swallowed the fruits of other people's hard work...'.[123] Amin's jealousy, as well as his resentment over not getting the credit he felt he deserved for bringing the PDPA to power and then running the government, were clear. Revenge was sweet.

When journalists asked about Taraki on 23 September, Amin said he 'is definitely sick...[and] doctors treat him...'. The Soviet embassy offered to have him treated in the USSR but was rebuffed. On 10 October *The Kabul Times* reported that Taraki 'died yesterday morning of serious illness, which he had been suffering for some time...'.[124] The following January Karmal's government said that on 8 October Amin ordered Taraki killed. The chief of the palace section of the former AGSA, which Amin had renamed *Kargari Astekhbarati Muassasa* (Workers' Intelligence Bureau), or KAM, and two lieutenants tied Taraki up on a bed and suffocated him with a cushion.[125] When told of Taraki's death, Brezhnev broke down in tears, according to Gromyko. '[I]t was too much for Brezhnev to bear. He was simply beside himself,' Gromyko said years later. 'Taraki's murder has to be taken into account when considering the steps taken by the Soviet Union in Afghanistan.' Another Soviet version said Brezhnev took the murder 'personally. To those closest to him he said that he had been given a slap in the face, to which he had to respond. And his response was' the invasion.[126]

Although Amin insisted to American diplomats that relations with Moscow were 'very cordial and friendly',[127] the truth was otherwise. Keeping East German leader Erich Honecker—and probably other bloc leaders—advised of developments, the CPSU said 'one cannot be uncritical of many of Amin's methods and activities, in particular his extreme lust for power, ruthlessness in his relations with former colleagues, [and] forming opinions and making decisions singlehandedly'. Brezhnev commented on 4 October that 'we are not pleased by all of Amin's methods and actions'.[128] Amin's anger with the Soviets surfaced on 6 October. Foreign Minister Shah Wali invited all Communist ambassadors except the Chinese one to a meeting. Vasily S. Safronchuk, the Soviet adviser to the Afghan foreign ministry, represented Puzanov, who was showing Moscow's displeasure with the new regime by boycotting official events. Wali told the ambassadors that Watanjar and the other three missing officials had begun conspiring against Amin in the spring and had arranged several unsuccessful attempts on his life. Wali accused Puzanov of complicity in an abortive attempt to purge Amin on 14 September. He said Puzanov denied knowing where the four missing men were while hiding them in his embassy—as proven by intercepted phone calls. Wali added that Amin had been invited to Moscow to discuss the situation but had refused to go.[129] Wali later asked Moscow to recall Puzanov. He was replaced on 1 December by Fikryat A. Tabeyev, the 51-year-old CPSU first secretary of the USSR's predominately Muslim Tatar region. Tabeyev was told not to send reports back to Moscow, where on-the-spot assessments were no longer wanted.[130]

INTERNAL TIGHTENING

After seizing power, Amin moved quickly to tidy up some loose ends. He had an imprisoned former royalist prime minister, Nur Ahmed Etemadi, executed as an act of revenge and a warning to the Soviets not to think of alternative leaders. He also ordered the death of Badakhshi, a PDPA founder and later defector who had been captured in the summer of 1978.[131] But Amin also talked of ameliorating policies for which he had been primarily responsible but could now conveniently blame on Taraki. He initially replaced Sarwari as head of the brutal political police, KAM, with Sarwari's nephew Akbari, who had warned Amin of the 11 September plot. But, in the Afghan tradition of trusting relatives more, he replaced Akbari in October with his own nephew and son-in-law, Assadullah Amin.[132]

Kabul radio began announcing releases from the crowded prisons. Karmal's regime later charged that 'only a few scores from several thousands of political prisoners were set free while thousands more were shoved into Pul-i-Charki prison daily'.[133] On 8 October Amin commuted Qadir's and Keshtmand's death sentences for alleged plotting in 1978 to 15 years' imprisonment, and Rafi's 20-year sentence was reduced to 12 years.[134] On 16 November the interior ministry began posting lists of persons who, it said, had died in prison from April 1978 to September 1979, the period that could be blamed on Taraki. Public readings of names, said to number 12 000, were halted after emotional scenes of women weeping and men screaming.[135] The number of Afghans killed by the Taraki and Amin regimes is lost in inadequate records and deliberately hidden atrocities. Najibullah's police chief made public in 1989 a list of 11 000 political prisoners killed during the 20 months, some of them reportedly by Amin's own hand.[136] Western estimates of deaths run from 35 000 or 50 000 officials, intellectuals, 'and other potential non-Communist leaders', to a count of 50 000 or 100 000 that included villagers, and to an estimate of 250 000 by one resistance source.[137] Afghan official estimates of the number of PDPA members among those killed ranged from 1000 to 4500,[138] but Soviet media never put this higher than 500.

While Amin improved government operations—starting work on a constitution, writing economic plans, making gestures to appease conservative Islamic elements, and other ventures—the CPSU politburo commission took a dim view of his moves. In a 29 October report it described Amin as 'an ambitious, cruel, treacherous person' and said he was trying to purge the PDPA and government of all potential opponents—'the scale of repressions in the party, army, state apparatus, and civic organizations has widened...'. Andropov said in early December 'the party, the army, and the government apparatus...were essentially destroyed' by Amin's repressions. The politburo commission found that between Amin's seizure of power and his downfall 'more than 600 members of the PDPA, military personnel, and other persons suspected of anti-Amin sentiments were executed without trial or investigation'.[139]

AMIN'S FOREIGN RELATIONS

The commission's 29 October report also said Amin was seeking to pursue a 'more balanced' foreign policy, meaning a policy of less dependence on Moscow. 'Amin's behaviour in his relations with the USSR more and more distinctly reveals that he is insincere and two-faced.' What American diplomats considered routine and not very productive meetings with Amin were interpreted in KGB reporting from Kabul as raising 'the possibility of a change in the political line...pleasing to Washington'.[140]

Amin tried to improve relations with Pakistan, which Kabul and Moscow blamed for the spreading civil war because of *mujahideen* training camps and supply facilities there. In his first speech as president, Amin said he hoped President Ziaul Haq and his *de facto* foreign minister, Agha Shahi, would visit Kabul as soon as possible to eliminate misunderstandings, and Amin also appealed for talks with Iran.[141] Amid continued Afghan accusations of Pakistan's role in the civil war, Zia decided that sending Shahi to Kabul would be seen as a sign of weakness and might demoralize the Afghan resistance, whose cause he supported emotionally while trying to keep any commitment publicly vague.[142]

After Wali said on 6 October that Amin had refused an invitation to visit Moscow, Amin's attitude toward dealing with the Soviets changed. When General Zaplatin, the chief Soviet political adviser to the Afghan army, was going to Moscow for consultations at some unspecified date in October, Amin gave him a personal letter 'with five wax seals' to deliver to Brezhnev. Amin 'asked to be heard', Zaplatin said. 'It seemed to him, and not without reason, that non-objective information was getting to Moscow. Alas, [Soviet leaders] did not want to speak with him at such a crucial, critical juncture.' During the consultations, Zaplatin and his boss Gorelov told Ustinov, Ogarkov, Yepishev, and others 'that Amin had no respect for the Soviet Union...'.[143] Rebuffed by Brezhnev and facing a deteriorating military and economic situation, Amin sought other support. By early December he was sending messages to Pakistan that Zia described as frantic.[144]

Amin did not have the option of a divorce from Moscow, of becoming 'an Asian Tito', contrary to some later suggestions. He lacked public support. His civil ministries were being run by 1500 or more Soviet advisers. Between 3500 and 4000 Soviet military officers and technicians ran the armed forces, which had lost an estimated half of its pre-*coup* 8000 officers and non-commissioned officers by October 1979, to purges or defections.[145] Pavlovskiy reported that '[t]he combat morale and fighting elan of the troops, the state of military discipline, and the army's willingness to act are still low'.[146] Soviet writers said later that, 'By the end of 1979, civil war had spread to a sizeable part of the country...'.[147]

The *mujahideen* were growing stronger. They were receiving 'limited financial and material support' from Saudi Arabia, at least $250 000 from Libya, and some help from Iran and Egypt. Pakistan provided weapons and other aid, contrary to formal denials. Starting with a July decision, the United States helped *mujahideen* propaganda and provided non-military supplies. Beginning in November, the supplies included field hospitals and communications equipment. Up to the Soviet invasion, however, neither the United States nor China was willing to risk antagonizing Moscow by arming fighters against the Soviet-backed regime.[148]

As the situation deteriorated, on 3 December Amin asked Col. Gen. S. Magometov, who had replaced Gorelov as chief Soviet military adviser, to send Soviet interior ministry troops 'which, together with our people's militia, could provide security and restore order in the northern regions' while two Afghan army divisions were redeployed.[149] But by then Moscow had lost interest in dealing with Amin.

NOTES

1. *DRA Annual, 1979*, p. 43. Anwar, *Tragedy*, p. 94, says six were arrested; *New Times*, No. 35, 1978: 29, says seven.
2. Barnett R. Rubin, 'Afghanistan: The Fragmentation of a State and Chances for Reconstruction', paper, Austin, Texas, 20 October 1989, p. 7.
3. *DRA Annual, 1979*, pp. 43-4.
4. Ghaus, *Fall*, p. 197; interviews with Afghan exiles, 1980; Louis Dupree, 'Red Flag over Hindu Kush, Part 2: The Accidental Coup, or Taraki in Blunderland', *AUFS/A* 45 (1979); 6; Anwar, *Tragedy*, p. 88; Morozov, 'Our Man, 2', p. 33.
5. First published as an analytical conclusion (Bradsher, *Afghanistan and the Soviet Union*, p. 75), this was also the view of Gankovskiy, including in a talk in Washington, 6 February 1990, and other Soviet sources.
6. Gankovskiy, Washington, 6 February 1990; Col. V. G. Safronov, 'Afghanistan: Results and Conclusions; As It Was (A Historian's Commentary)', *Voyenno-Istoricheskiy Zhurnal*, May 1990, pp. 66-71, in JPRS, *Soviet Union, Military Affairs* [hereafter *JPRS-UMA*], No. 91-005, 13 February 1991, pp. 126-32 [cited hereafter as Safronov, 'As It Was']. Karmal said there was no plan to overthrow Daoud, Parchami leaders opposed armed action, and 'not one of the Parchamis was let in on the coup plan'; *Trud*, 24 October 1991, 1, in *JPRS-UIA-91-027*, 27 November 1991, p. 54. Lyakhovskiy and Zabrodin, 'Secrets, Part 1', said Qadir equivocated.
7. *DRA Annual, 1979*, pp. 27-9, 736; Dupree, 'Red Flag, 2,'; Kabul Radio, 12 May 1978, in *FBIS/ME*, 15 May 1978, pp. S1-4; Havana Radio, 21 May 1978, in *FBIS/ME*, 22 May 1978, pp. S1-3; Tanjug from Kabul, 6 May 1978, in *FBIS/ME*, 9 May 1978, pp. S1-3; *New York Times*, 3 May 1978, p. 1; *New York Times Magazine*, 4 June 1978, p. 50; *Asiaweek*, 9 June 1978, pp. 7-9; Lyakhovskiy and Zabrodin, 'Secrets, Part 1'.
8. *DRA Annual, 1979*, pp. 27-8 (reproduced from an early May 1978 publication), and p. 55 (reproduced from a late May 1978 pamphlet); *Die Zeit*, 9 June 1978, in *FBIS/ME*, 9 June 1978, pp. S1-5; Havana Radio, 21 May 1978, in *FBIS/ME*, 22 May 1978, pp. S1-3.
9. Kabul Radio, 27 April 1978, in *FBIS/ME*, 28 April 1978, p. S1, and 1 May 1978, pp. S1-2; Dupree, 'Red Flag, 2', p. 12; US Embassy Kabul, cable 3234, 27 April 1978.
10. US Embassy Kabul, cable 3242, 27 April 1978; Kabul Radio, 29 April 1978, in *FBIS/ME*, 1 May 1978, pp. S1-2.

11. Kabul Radio, 27 June 1990, in *FBIS/NE*, 3 July 1990, p. 43.
12. Kabul Radio, 30 April 1978, in *FBIS/ME*, 1 May 1978, pp. S1-2.
13. Ibid.; *DRA Annual, 1979*, pp. 3-4; US Embassy, Kabul, cable 3619, 6 May 1978, in *Spynest*, Vol. 29, p. 63; Anwar, *Tragedy*, p. 112.
14. *DRA Annual, 1979*, p. 2; Ghulam Muradov, *Oriental Studies in the USSR (No. 3), Afghanistan: Past and Present* (Moscow, 1981), p. 196. Karmal's anti-Amin version is in *Trud*, 24 October 1991, pp. 1, 4, in *JPRS-UIA-91-027*, 27 November 1991, pp. 54-5.
15. E.g., letter to author from Abdul Rashid Jalili, 14 August 1997.
16. *Komsomolskaya Pravda*, 21 September 1991, p. 3, in *JPRS-UPA-91-043*, 18 October 1991, p. 5; telephone interview with Kalugin, Washington, 11 September 1997.
17. Puzanov to the Soviet foreign ministry, 31 May 1978, in *CWIHPB*, Nos. 8-9: 133.
18. *DRA Annual, 1979*, pp. 5-6; Puzanov's report, *CWIHPB*, Nos. 8-9: 133. For varying versions, see Anwar, *Tragedy*, p. 111; Arnold, *Afghanistan's Two-Party*, pp. 198-201; Anthony Hyman, *Afghanistan Under Soviet Domination, 1964-83* (New York, 1984), p. 81.
19. Morozov, 'Our Man, 1', p. 39; pamphlet in *DRA Annual, 1979*, pp. 31-59.
20. Odd Arne Westad, 'Prelude to Invasion: The Soviet Union and the Afghan Communists, 1978-1979', *International History Review*, February 1994, pp. 53-4; Anwar, *Tragedy*, pp. 113-15; Vasili Safronchuk, 'Afghanistan in the Taraki Period', *International Affairs*, January 1991, pp. 87-8; Louis Dupree, 'Red Flag Over the Hindu Kush, Part V: Repressions, or Security Through Terror Purges, I-IV', *AUFS/A*, No. 28, 1980: 3-4.
21. Morozov, 'Our Man, 1', p. 39; *New Times*, No. 12, 1990: 8-10.
22. Puzanov's report to CPSU, 18 June 1978, in *CWIHPB*, Nos. 8-9: 134.
23. Kabul Radio, 8 July 1978, in *FBIS/ME*, 8 and 21 July 1978, pp. S4 and S4.
24. *Pravda*, 19 January 1980, p. 5, in *FBIS/SU*, 23 January 1980, p. D1.
25. Kabul Radio, 17 August 1978, in *FBIS/ME*, 18 August 1978, p. S1. Ulyanovskiy, 'Afghan Revolution', p. 14, says from the July 1978 purge of Parcham until the December 1979 Soviet invasion 'around ten mass purges were carried out in the army'.
26. Kabul Radio, 28 November 1978, in *FBIS/ME*, 13 December 1978, p. S4.
27. Kabul Radio, 18 and 23 August 1978, in *FBIS/ME*, 21 and 24 August 1978, pp. S1 and S1; *Washington Post*, 7 November 1978, p. A17; Dupree, 'Red Flag, Part V', p. 5.

28. Confessions of Qadir, Rafi, and Keshtmand in *DRA Annual, 1979*, pp. 1321-67.
29. Ibid., pp. 6, 566-73, 1321-67; Kabul Radio, 28 November 1978, in *FBIS/ME*, 13 December 1978, pp. S1-7; Arnold, *Afghanistan's Two-Party*, p. 70.
30. Morozov, 'Our Man, 2', p. 33.
31. *DRA Annual, 1979*, pp. 572-3; US Embassy Kabul, cable 9163, 16 November 1978.
32. Kabul Radio, 9 May 1978, in *FBIS/ME*, 10 May 1978, p. S1; Kabul Radio, 4 May 1978, in *FBIS/ME*, 4 May 1978, p. S1; *Die Zeit*, 9 June 1978, in *FBIS/ME*, 9 June 1978, pp. S1-5; *Washington Post*, 7 November 1978, p. A17; Puzanov to Soviet foreign ministry, 31 May 1978, in *CWIHPB*, Nos. 8-9: 133.
33. *Kabul Times*, 4 August and 19 April 1979, pp. 1 and 1.
34. Aleksandr Y. Bovin in *Moscow News*, No.16, 1980, p. 7.
35. *Literaturnaya Gazeta*, 20 September 1989, p. 14, in *JPRS-UMA-89-023*, 4 October 1989, p. 41.
36. Jimmy Carter, *Keeping Faith: Memoirs of a President* (New York, 1982), p. 256.
37. Gankovskiy, Washington, 6 February 1990.
38. Cyrus Vance, *Hard Choices: Critical Years in America's Foreign Policy* (New York, 1983), pp. 384, 386.
39. Agha Shahi, *Pakistan's Security and Foreign Policy* (Lahore, 1988), p. 4.
40. *Krasnaya Zvezda*, 12 October 1989, p. 2, in *JPRS-UMA-89-025*, 27 October 1989, p. 9.
41. Interview with senior US diplomats in Kabul at the time, 1980; House of Commons, 'Afghanistan: The Soviet Invasion and Its Consequences for British Policy' (London, 1980), p. 6; *Washington Post*, 6 May 1978, p. A15.
42. *Vechernaya Moskva*, 26 July 1989, p. 4, says 28 April, but Puzanov's report to the foreign ministry refers to a 29 April meeting, in *CWIHPB*, Nos. 8-9: 133.
43. Tass from Moscow, 3 May 1978, in *FBIS/SU*, 4 May 1978, p. J1.
44. Andrei Kozyrev and Andrei Shumikhin, 'East and West in the Third World', *International Affairs*, March 1989: 65-6.
45. G. A. Fedorov, et al., *Marxism-Leninism on War and the Army* (Moscow, 1961 and 1977 editions), quoted by William F. Scott and Harriet Fast Scott, 'Soviet Projection of Military Presence and Power, Vol. II, A Review and Assessment of Soviet Policy and Concepts on the Projections of Military Presence and Power' (McLean, Va., 1979), pp. 9, 45-7; A. I. Sorokin, ed., *V. I. Lenin on the Defence of the Socialist Fatherland* (Moscow, 1977), quoted by Scott and Scott, 'Soviet Projection', p. 76.

46. *Izvestiya*, 6 February 1980, p. 5, in *FBIS/SU*, 8 February 1980, p. A4.
47. V. M. Kuldish, ed., *Military Force and International Relations* (Moscow, 1972; English edition, Arlington, 1973), pp. 103, 105.
48. Moscow Television, 27 December 1991, in *FBIS/SU*, 31 December 1991, p. 4.
49. Morozov, 'Our Man, 1', pp. 38-9.
50. US Embassy Kabul, cable 3805, 10 May 1978, in *Spynest*, Vol. 29: 64.
51. State Department, cable 194166, 1 August 1978, in *Spynest*, Vol. 30: 21; Carter, *Keeping Faith*, p. 196; Zbigniew Brzezinski, *Power and Principle: Memoirs of the National Security Advisor, 1977-1981* (New York, 1983), p. 212; US Embassy Tehran, cable 4062, 30 April 1978.
52. *Vechernaya Moskva*, 26 July 1989, p. 4 (emphasis added).
53. Kabul Radio, 25 May 1978, in *FBIS/ME*, 8 June 1978, pp. S2-3; *DRA Annual, 1979*, pp. 67, 73-5.
54. Amnesty International, *The Disappeared* (London, 1979), pp. 64-5; Jeri Laber and Barnett R. Rubin, *'A Nation Is Dying'*: *Afghanistan Under the Soviets 1979-87* (Evanston, 1988), pp. 5-6.
55. CPSU to East German leader Erich Honecker, in *CWIHPB*, Nos. 8-9: 135.
56. Tass from Kabul, 26 April 1980, in *FBIS/SU*, 28 April 1980, p. D3; Kabul Radio, 27 June 1990, in *FBIS/NE*, 3 July 1990, p. 44.
57. Lt. Col. A. Oliynik, 'The Sending of Troops to Afghanistan: Participants in the Events Tell and Documents Attest to How the Decision was Made' [hereafter Oliynik, 'Sending of Troops'], *Krasnaya Zvezda*, 18 November 1989, pp. 3-4, in *JPRS-UMA-90-004*, 8 February 1990, pp. 74-9; *Vechernaya Moskva*, 26 and 29 July 1989, pp. 4 and 4.
58. Kabul Radio, 2 August 1978, in *FBIS/ME*, 17 August 1978, pp. S1-4; Budapest Radio, 11 December 1980, in *FBIS/SA*, 12 December 1980, pp. C1-2.
59. Kabul Radio, 27 June 1990, in *FBIS/NE*, 3 July 1990, p. 44.
60. Rashid, 'Final Report', pp. 8-12; Girardet, *Afghanistan*, pp. 113-14; Richard F. Strand, 'The Evolution of Anti-Communist Resistance in Eastern Nuristan', in Shahrani and Canfield, *Revolutions & Rebellions*, pp. 77-93; David Busby Edwards, 'Origins of the Anti-Soviet Jihad', in Farr and Merriam, *Afghan Resistance*, pp. 32-3; Roy, *Islam and Resistance*, pp. 98-109.
61. *Die Zeit*, 9 June 1978, in *FBIS/ME*, 9 June 1978, pp. S1-5.
62. *DRA Annual, 1979*, pp. 62-70.

63. Kabul Radio, 30 [*sic*] November 1984, in *FBIS/SA*, 9 November 1984, p. C4, and 7 January 1980, in *FBIS/ME*, 9 January 1980, p. S2; Safronchuk, 'Afghanistan in the Taraki Period', pp. 87-8.

64. Kabul Radio, 10 September 1979, in *FBIS/ME*, 12 September 1979, p. S8.

65. Decrees in *DRA Annual, 1979*.

66. Bakhtar from Kabul, 27 April 1989, in *FBIS/NE*, 1 May 1989, pp. 36-7; *Pravda*, 18 February 1980, in *FBIS/SU*, 21 February 1980, pp. D3-4; Kabul Radio, 28 April 1980, in *FBIS/SA*, 29 April 1980, pp. C1-3.

67. Oliynik, 'Sending of Troops'.

68. *Kabul Times*, 15 July 1979, p. 1; *Novoye Vremya*, 11 April 1980, p. 15, in *FBIS/SU*, 21 April 1980, pp. D6-9; Bakhtar from Kabul, 27 April 1989, in *FBIS/NE*, 1 May 1989, p. 36.

69. Moscow Radio, 11 September 1988, in *FBIS/SU*, 12 September 1988, p. 12; *Ogonek*, No. 30, 1988: 25-7.

70. *Novoye Vremya*, 11 April 1980, pp. 5-7, in *FBIS/SU*, 21 April 1980, pp. D6-9; *Pravda*, 17 October 1980, pp. 2-6, in *FBIS/SU*, 21 October 1980, pp. D4-11; *Sovetskaya Rossiya*, 27 April 1989, p. 3, in *FBIS/SU*, 3 May 1989, p. 23.

71. Tass from Moscow, 5 December 1978, in *FBIS/SU*, 6 December 1978, pp. J10-13; FCO, 'Soviet Bloc Network of Friendship Treaties' (London, 1980).

72. *FBIS Trends*, 13 December 1978, p. 6; *Za Rubezhom*, 26 February 1981, p. 6, in *FBIS/SU*, 12 March 1981, pp. P8-10; Moscow Radio, 5 December 1978, in *FBIS/SU*, 5 December 1978, p. J2.

73. Department of State, cable 304356, 1 December 1978, in *Spynest*, Vol. 29: 73-5.

74. State Department, 'The Kidnapping and Death of Ambassador Adolph Dubs, Summary of Report of Investigation' (Washington, 1979); CIA reports, 16 and 23 February 1979, made public 11 June 1984; Vasili Safronchuk, 'Afghanistan in the Amin Period', *International Affairs*, February 1991: 81.

75. *New York Times*, 23 February 1979, p. 3; US Embassy Kabul, cable 2052, 18 March 1979, in *Spynest*, Vol. 29: 79.

76. Ulyanovskiy, 'Afghan Revolution'; Gankovskiy, Washington, 6 April 1988; *Za Rubezhom*, No. 30, 1982: 12-13, in *FBIS/SU*, 29 July 1982, pp. D1-3.

77. Oliynik, 'Sending of Troops', says the first such camp in Pakistan opened in January 1979. See *Washington Post*, 2 February 1979, p. A23, and *New York Times*, 16 April 1979, p. 1.

78. *Financial Times*, 23 June 1989, p. 6; *Pravda*, 16 April 1989, p. 5, in *FBIS/SU*, 17 April 1989, p. 15; Oliynik, 'Sending of Troops'; *Vechernaya Moskva*, 28 July 1989, p. 4; *Dagens Nyheter*, 16 February

1986, p. 13, in *FBIS/SA*, 21 February 1986, p. C2 (quoting the rebellion's leader, Ismael Khan, as saying 'some 24 Soviet advisers were killed'); Radek Sikorski, *Dust of the Saints: A Journey to Herat in Time of War* (London, 1989), pp. 230-31 (quoting Ismail Khan as saying 68 or 69 Soviets were killed, three or four of whom were skinned alive); *CWIHPB*, Nos. 8-9: 142 (quoting Kosygin as saying 'We have 24 advisers in Herat'—a figure that apparently omitted dependents).

79. Moscow Television, 14 July 1992, in *FBIS/CE*, 17 July 1992, pp. 30-31.

80. *Sovetskaya Rossiya*, 3 August 1991, p. 4, in *FBIS/SU*, 8 August 1991, p. 38; Oliynik, 'Sending of Troops'; *Washington Post*, 15 November 1992, p. A32.

81. *CWIHPB*, Nos. 8-9: p. 147.

82. *CWIHPB*, No. 4, Fall 1994: 74.

83. *CWIHPB*, No. 3, Fall 1993: 67-9.

84. *CWIHPB*, No. 4: 75; *Washington Post*, 28 March and 10 May 1979, pp. A16 and A33.

85. Oliynik, 'Sending of Troops'; *CWIHPB*, Nos. 8-9, 151; *Kabul Times*, 16 May 1979, p. 1.

86. *Krasnaya Zvezda*, 25 April 1979, p. 3 in *FBIS/SU*, 1 May 1979, pp. D1-3.

87. US Embassy Kabul, cable 4888, 25 June 1979, in *Spynest*, Vol. 29: 129.

88. *Economist*, 11 August 1979, p. 53; *Washington Post*, 7 August 1979, p. A13; Oliynik, 'Sending of Troops'; *Vechernaya Moskva*, 29 July 1989, p. 4.

89. *CWIHPB*, Nos. 8-9: 152-3.

90. Oliynik, 'Sending of Troops.'

91. Oliynik, 'Sending of Troops'; *CWIHPB*, Nos. 8-9: 153; *Komsomolskaya Pravda*, 27 December 1990, p. 3, in *JPRS-UMA-91-006*, 4 March 1991, pp. 62-3; *Sovetskiy Voin*, No. 23, 1989: 6-8, in *JPRS-UMA-90-005*, 15 February 1990, p. 51.

92. Gankovskiy in *Izvestiya*, 5 May 1989, p. 5, in *FBIS/SU*, 10 May 1989, p. 33.

93. Laber and Rubin, '*A Nation Is Dying*,' pp. 6-7; *Liberation*, 27 December 1984, pp. 16-18, in *JPRS-NEA-85-018*, 5 February 1985, pp. 148-9.

94. J. Bruce Amstutz, *Afghanistan: The First Five Years of Soviet Occupation* (Washington, 1986), p. 224; Nancy Hatch Dupree, 'The Demography of Afghan Refugees in Pakistan', in Hafeez Malik, ed., *Soviet-American Relations with Pakistan, Iran and Afghanistan* (London, 1987), p. 368.

95. Morozov, 'Our Man in Kabul, Part 3', *New Times*, No. 40, 1991, p. 39; Oleg Kalugin with Fen Montaigne, *The First Directorate: My 32 Years in Intelligence and Espionage Against the West* (New York, 1994), p. 234.

96. Oliynik, 'Sending of Troops'; *Znamya*, April 1991, pp. 219-20 (which dates the meeting as late September).

97. *Moscow News*, 1 July 1990, p. 13; Kalugin, *First Directorate*, p. 233.

98. *Vechernaya Moskva*, 28 July 1989, p. 4; Oliynik, 'Sending of Troops'; *CWIHPB*, Nos. 8-9: 154, 158; CIA cable, Director 516886, 19 September 1979, in *Spynest*, Vol. 30: 162-3; *Sovetskaya Rossiya*, 20 December 1989, p. 6, in *JPRS-UMA-90-007*, 23 March 1990, p. 125.

99. Carter, *Keeping Faith*, pp. 254-6; Viktor Sukhodrev in *Ogonyok*, No. 9, 1989.

100. US Embassy Kabul, cable 7281, 2 October 1979, in *Spynest*, Vol. 30: 108; *DRA Annual, 1979*, pp. 593, 614, 619.

101. State Department briefing memorandum, 'Soviet-Afghan Relations: Is Moscow's Patience Wearing Thin?', 24 May 1979.

102. US Embassy Kabul, cable 4888, 25 June 1979, in *Spynest*, Vol. 29: 128; *Vechernaya Moskva*, 26 July 1989, p. 4.

103. *Vechernaya Moskva*, 26 and 28 July 1989, pp. 4 and 4; *Far Eastern Economic Review*, 23 January 81, pp. 28-9; Safronchuk, 'Afghanistan in the Taraki Period', p. 83.

104. *CWIHPB*, Nos. 8-9: 153.

105. US Embassy Kabul, cables 5459, 5493, and 5627, 18, 22, and 25 July 1979, in *Spynest*, Vol. 29: 179-81, 192-4, and 200-204; Anwar, *Tragedy*, pp. 157-65; *Washington Post*, 9 October 1979, p. A11; Alexandre Dastarac and M. Levant, 'What Went Wrong in Afghanistan', *Le Monde Diplomatique*, February 1980: 6-7, in *JPRS-Near East/North Africa-2093*, 21 March 1980.

106. Anwar, *Tragedy*, pp. 162-3; Tass from Kabul, 28 July 1979, in *FBIS/SU*, 30 July 1979, p. D1.

107. Safronchuk, 'Afghanistan in the Amin Period', p. 83.

108. Safronchuk, interview, Austin, Texas, 20 October 1989; Safronchuk, 'Afghanistan in the Amin Period', p. 85.

109. *Literaturnaya Gazeta*, 20 September 1989, p. 14, in *JPRS-UMA-89-023*, 4 October 1989, p. 42.

110. Armand Hammer, as quoted by US diplomats, 1980. Morozov, 'Our Man, 4', p. 32, supports this account.

111. *Literaturnaya Gazeta*, 20 September 1989, p. 14, in *JPRS-UMA-89-023*, 4 October 1989, p. 46.

112. *MERIP Reports*, No. 89, July-August 1980: 16; *Economist*, 22 September 1979, p. 60; Dastarac and Levant, 'What Went Wrong'; Anwar, *Tragedy*, p. 168.

113. Dastarac and Levant, 'What Went Wrong'; Morozov, 'Our Man, 4', p. 32; Lyakhovskiy and Zabrodin, 'Secrets, Part 2', *Armiya*, No. 6, 1992: 57-66; Anwar, *Tragedy*, pp. 166-7.

114. Ibid., pp. 169-71; *CWIHPB*, Nos. 8-9: 156; Kabul Radio, 11 and 14 September 1979, in *FBIS/ME*, 12 and 15 September 1979, pp. S3 and S1; *Economist*, 22 September 1979, p. 60; US Embassy Kabul, cable 7281, 2 October 1979, in *Spynest*, Vol. 30: 108; Morozov, 'Our Man, 4', p. 33.

115. *CWIHPB*, Nos. 8-9, p. 154. The CPSU Politburo instructions noted that 'we cannot take it upon ourselves to arrest Amin with our own battalion force, since this would be a direct interference in the internal affairs of Afghanistan and would have far-reaching consequences. Indeed, this is practically unfeasible'.

116. Safronchuk, 'Afghanistan in the Amin Period', pp. 85-6, 89-90; Morozov, 'Our Man, 4', p. 34; *Literaturnaya Gazeta*, 20 September 1989, p. 14, in *JPRS-UMA-089-023*, 4 October 1989, p. 42; Dastarac and Levant, 'What Went Wrong'; US Embassy Kabul, cable 6914, 16 September 1979; US Embassy cable 7281, 2 October 1979, in *Spynest*, Vol. 30: 110; Anwar, *Tragedy*, pp. 171-2; Kabul Radio, 8 December 1979, in *FBIS/ME*, 11 December 1979, pp. S1-6; *Vechernaya Moskva*, 29 July 1989, p. 4. The sources differ on details.

117. *Izvestiya*, 5 May 1989, p. 5, in *FBIS/SU*, 10 May 1989, p. 33; Morozov, 'Our Man, 4', pp. 34-5; *Son Atyechestva*, 3 January 1992, pp. 6-7, in *Afghanistan Forum*, No. 21, p. 3.

118. Morozov, 'Our Man, 4', p. 35; *Pravda*, 18 September 1979, p. 1, in *FBIS/SU*, 19 September 1979, p. D1; *CWIHPB*, Nos. 8-9: 156.

119. *Komsomolskaya Pravda*, 27 December 1990, p. 3, in *JPRS-UMA-91-006*, 4 March 1991, p. 63. See also *CWIHPB*, Nos. 8-9: 154-5.

120. *Economist*, 22 September 1979, p. 60; interviews with diplomats, 1980-81.

121. Kabul Radio, 16 and 17 September 1979, in *FBIS/ME*, 17 and 18 September 1979, pp. S1-2 and S6; Karachi Radio, 17 September 1979, in *FBIS/ME*, 18 September 1979, p. S6.

122. Kabul Radio, 14 September 1979, in *FBIS/ME*, 19 September 1979, pp. S5-7.

123. Kabul Radio, 17 and 18 September 1979, in *FBIS/ME*, 18 and 25 September 1979, pp. S1-5 and S5-10.

124. Kabul Radio, 26 September 1979, in *FBIS/ME*, 27 September 1979, pp. S1-5; US Embassy Kabul, cable 7318, 3 October 1979, in *Spynest*, Vol. 30:113; *Kabul Times*, 10 October 1979.

125. Tass from Kabul, 5, 14, and 18 January 1980, in *FBIS/SU*, 7, 15, and 21 January 1980, pp. D3, D4, and D8-9.

126. *Observer*, 2 April 1989, p. 23; *Literaturnaya Gazeta*, 20 September 1989, p. 14, in *JPRS-UMA-89-023*, 4 October 1989, p. 43. Oliynik, 'Sending of Troops', denies this linkage.

127. US Embassy Kabul, cable 7218, 27 September 1979, in *Spynest*, Vol. 30: 89-91; US Embassy Kabul, cables 7726 and 8117, 28 October and 21 November 1979.

128. *CWIHPB*, Nos. 8-9: 156.

129. US Embassy Kabul, cables 7444 and 7784, 11 and 30 October 1979; House of Commons, 'Afghanistan', p. 42; *Economist*, 3 November 1979, pp. 52-3; Safronchuk, 'Afghanistan in the Amin Period', pp. 89-90 (which differs on details). Early accounts of this period, including this author's, exaggerated Safronchuk's importance as a result of his being quoted in diplomatic reporting from Kabul.

130. *Economist*, 3 November 1979, pp. 52-3; Kabul Radio, 19 November and 1 December 1979, in *FBIS/ME*, 20 November and 3 December 1979, pp. S4 and S1; Safronchuk, 'Afghanistan in the Amin Period', pp. 94-5; Georgiy A. Arbatov, *Zatyanuvsheyesya Vyzdorovleniye (1953-1985 gg): Svidetelstvo Sovremennika* (Moscow, 1991), p. 229.

131. *New York Times*, 17 September 1979; US Embassy Kabul, cables 6936, 7502, and 7784, 17 September, 15 and 30 October 1979; Adamec, *Biographic Dictionary*, pp. 34-5.

132. Anwar, *Tragedy*, pp. 166-7; Arnold, *Afghanistan's Two-Party*, p. 94.

133. *Kabul New Times*, 3 January 1980.

134. *New York Times*, 9 October 1979, p. 8.

135. *Amnesty International Report 1980* (London, 1980), p. 177.

136. US Embassy Kabul, cable 7218, 27 September 1979; *New York Times*, 9 September 1989, p. A15, and 2 December 1889, p. 4; *Amnesty International Report 1980*, p. 179.

137. *Orbis*, Spring 1989: 274-5; Roy, *Islam and Resistance*, p. 95; M. Centlivres-Demont et al., 'Afghanistan: La Colonisation Impossible' (Paris, 1984), p. 199, cited by Alexander Alexiev, 'The United States and the War in Afghanistan', RAND P-7395 (Santa Monica, January 1988).

138. Kabul Radio, 30 October 1985, in *FBIS/SA*, 7 November 1985, p. C4; Kabul Radio, 9 January 1980, in *FBIS/ME*, 10 January 1980, pp. S3-4.

139. Commission report in *Journal of South Asian and Middle Eastern Studies (JSAMES)*, Winter 1994: 55; *CWIHPB*, Nos. 8-9: 157-60.

140. Interviews with diplomats, 1981; *JSAMES*, Winter 1994: 54; *CWIHPB*, Nos. 8-9: 157, 159. In the spring of 1979, the CIA surveyed Afghanistan for possible sites for intercepting electronic signals from Soviet Central Asian missile tests, replacing those lost when the Shah of Iran fell, but the United States later turned to China for monitoring sites; Robert M. Gates, *From the Shadows:*

The Ultimate Insider's Story of Five Presidents and How They Won the Cold War (New York, 1996), p. 132; *CWIHPB*, Nos. 8-9: 130, 132.

141. Kabul Radio, 17 September 1979, in *FBIS/ME*, 18 September 1979, pp. S1-5.
142. Related by an official who was involved but declined to be identified.
143. *Vechernaya Moskva*, 29 July 1989, p. 4. Kuldip Nayar, *Report on Afghanistan* (New Delhi, 1981), p. 43, says Amin made a brief trip to Moscow 'in early December', but there is no evidence for this, and circumstantial evidence indicates it is wrong.
144. *Indian Express*, 13 February 1980, p. 6, in *FBIS/ME*, 21 February 1980, pp. S1-2.
145. Radio Liberty Research, RL17/80, 2 January 1980; CIA station Kabul, report NHK-4132, 30 October 1979, in *Spynest*, Vol. 30: 155; *Economist*, 17 November 1979, pp. 68-9; AFP from Islamabad, 8 November 1979, in *FBIS/ME*, 9 November 1979, pp. S1-2.
146. *CWIHPB*, Nos. 8-9: 158.
147. *Izvestiya*, 23 December 1988, p. 5, in *FBIS/SU*, 23 December 1988, p. 25.
148. State Department, cable 266505/01, 11 October 1979, in *Spynest*, Vol. 30: 142; US Embassy Tripoli, cable 1185, 29 July 1979, in ibid., Vol. 29: 215; US Embassy Tehran, cable 5246, 21 May 1979, in ibid., Vol. 29: 114; CIA station Islamabad, report NPR-2117, 30 October 1979, in ibid., Vol. 30: 148-9; US Embassy Kabul, cable 6016, 7 August 1979, in ibid., Vol. 30: 3; Brzezinski, *Power and Principle*, pp. 427, 429; Gates, *From the Shadows*, p. 146; Saeeduddin Ahmad Dar, ed., *Selected Documents on Pakistan's Relations with Afghanistan 1947-1985* (Islamabad, 1986), pp. 192-97; *Washington Post*, 15 February 1980, p. 1; *New York Times Magazine*, 6 April 1980, p. 28.
149. Oliynik, 'Sending of Troops'.

CHAPTER 3

MOSCOW'S DECISION

During nine months of 1979, from the Kremlin leadership's refusal to get involved in the Herat uprising until the invasion of Afghanistan, in Moscow opinion shifted slowly toward making the USSR's first military deployment outside the Soviet bloc created by World War II. Without careful analysis, Soviet leaders decided on the basis of instincts developed by years of using force rather than diplomatic finesse, of looking to foreign gains rather than domestic costs, of assuming that Communist power must never retreat in the Cold War. They were afraid the Kabul regime was about to collapse; they were unwilling for ideological or security reasons to let this happen. The Soviet public was not consulted. Only years later could Najibullah say, 'Soviet and Afghan leaders have courageously acknowledged the error of the decision to send Soviet troops into Afghanistan'.[1]

The decision was taken against a background that in the 1970s encouraged Soviet expansionism. 'The world was turning in our direction,' according to Ponomarev's deputy.[2] The American defeat in Vietnam combined with Soviet successes in helping leftist regimes attain power in Angola and Ethiopia, to encourage adventuristic seizing of Third World opportunities to extend Moscow's influence. The immediate context of the decision was events that reduced Moscow's incentives to avoid actions which might endanger East-West relations. One was the flare-up in September 1979 of American hostility over the Soviet military brigade in Cuba and then the immediate return to normal relations by the Carter administration. Some American officials thought this back-down, more than any other single factor, led Soviet leaders to think they could safely risk international reaction to the invasion. A second key event was the seizure of American hostages in Iran on 4 November. The worldwide focus on Tehran, and the possibility that the United States might use force there, offered possible cover for Soviet action in the same way the Anglo-French invasion of Suez distracted attention from the USSR's crushing of Hungarian freedom fighters in 1956.[3] And the second round of strategic arms limitations talks, SALT II, had stagnated.

KABUL'S REQUESTS FOR TROOPS

Moscow said after the invasion that the Afghan government had asked it to send troops, but its accounts confused the number of requests, and archival material shows that the requests varied from small units to a division or two—but nothing like the size of the invasion force. A committee of the parliamentary Supreme Soviet that in 1989 investigated the invasion decision, said, 'Documentary evidence has established that since March 1979 the Afghan government had, on more than 10 occasions, asked for Soviet troops detachments to be sent into the country...'. Mikhail S. Gorbachev wrote in 1987 that Kabul asked 11 times 'before we assented...'. Moscow's last military supervisor of the Soviet Army's presence in Afghanistan said in 1989 there were '12 or 13 appeals'.[4] Most Soviet accounts published shortly after the invasion in an effort to justify it said 14 requests were made, but some said 16, and a defence ministry account later said 18. Some accounts said requests began in 1978, others said March 1979. Some said both Taraki and Amin made requests, others named only Taraki.[5] Karmal first said Taraki made 14 requests and Amin made none, but later said the PDPA central committee and the revolutionary council forced Amin to make three requests[6]—

although Amin's control of both groups makes force unbelievable.

One result of Kabul's requests for troops was a KGB evaluation of how the Afghan people would react to the Soviet Army's presence. Thirty KGB commandos were sent to Kabul in late October, and in early November they fanned out across the country in two-man teams to assess public opinion. This 'Z group' reported that '[s]ending Soviet troops into Afghanistan means war, and there is no way to win it without exterminating the entire nation', one of the commandos said later.[7] But if that was their report at the time, rather than a later gloss on something less clear, they were ignored.

Attempts to Remove Amin

In the autumn of 1979 the KGB also began to examine 'various methods of eliminating' Amin, such as a sniper's bullet or a land mine, but 'all this was rejected for various reasons', according to a Soviet writer.[8] Or was it? In late November a shadowy Soviet general, presumably from the KGB, arrived in Kabul. PDPA activists and some military men reportedly made plans to replace Amin that were 'to be carried out in the middle of December'. According to a Soviet military writer, the Soviets '*learned* that between December 13 and 16 there would be a *coup* against Amin by his enemies'.[9] This could hardly have been organized without KGB involvement—at the least inspiration, probably direction. Karmal had been brought to Moscow from his Czechoslovak exile in October. KGB boss Andropov ordered him, with five other members of a new Afghan government that Kremlin ideologist Mikhail A. Suslov had chosen, to fly to Bagram air base. They arrived there on 13 December, ready to rush down to Kabul and take over when Amin was ousted. The next day, Soviet military commanders preparing for the invasion were told that Amin had been deposed.

'But when the operation to kill Amin failed, Babrak was hurriedly brought back again to the Soviet Union,' the military writer said.[10] There was shooting in the presidential palace on 17 December. The only person reported hit was Amin's nephew Asadullah, the head of KAM, who was flown to the USSR for medical treatment.[11]

Soviet publicists asserted that in December 1979 a *mujahideen* offensive was impending, 'the Afghan army was demoralized and [incapable] of preserving the integrity of the country..., the state was almost in ruin..., power had fallen from the grip of the Kabul government..., [and the regime] would have had literally a few hours left to live' if the Soviet Army had not arrived.[12] This was subsequently admitted to have been exaggerated. The commander of the 105th Airborne, Maj.-Gen. I. F. Ryabchenko, said figures used by Soviet officials in 1979 for *mujahideen* strength 'were patently too high. I believe that someone deliberately inflated the amount. Possibly to accelerate entry of the [Soviet] troops.... [I]t was later determined that it was impossible for [the *mujahideen*] to strike in the end of December'.[13]

THE SOVIET DECISION-MAKING STRUCTURE

Accepting inflated figures, which Ryabchenko implied came from the KGB, the Soviet leadership felt it had to do something to preserve its client Communist state. Such a feeling did not brook a rational decision-making process. The bureaucracy was not asked to produce papers analysing policy alternatives or possible repercussions. Members of the self-perpetuating leadership acted from their world view and Communist philosophy, as well as on the basis of 'departmental interests', Eduard A. Shevardnadze said later.[14] Also, none of the cynical men in the inner circle wanted to appear less than tough as the succession to the sick Brezhnev approached.[15]

The 1989 Supreme Soviet investigation—which was rigged to condemn the invasion decision—found the decision was made by politburo commission members Andropov, Ustinov, and Gromyko, plus the sick and reportedly senile Brezhnev.[16] Brezhnev was later described as being at the time unable to sustain an intelligent conversation for more than 20 or 30 minutes and incapable of making political decisions on his own.[17] Andropov, Ustinov, Gromyko, and alternate politburo member Ponomarev agreed on the invasion before a 12 December 1979 meeting of the CPSU politburo in Brezhnev's Kremlin office, and Brezhnev concurred. At the meeting they presented their conclusion to seven other full politburo members. One of them, Brezhnev's personal aide Konstantin U. Chernenko, wrote out in longhand a 'top secret' decree 'on the situation in "A"'. It authorized Andropov, Ustinov, and Gromyko to carry out the decision, keeping the politburo informed. Brezhnev signed the document. Then, to spread responsibility, he had the full members present sign it across the top. The three full members with posts outside Moscow who missed the meeting added their signatures on 25 and 26 December, as the invasion was underway, but the remaining full member at the time, the hospitalized Prime Minister Kosygin, never did sign.[18]

Bureaucratic Interests

The decision can be seen as a result of convergent 'departmental interests' in an oligarchic state. What was for one politburo member a primary reason for action might have been secondary for another, who had his own primary reason, but their various reasons reinforced one another. A diplomatic report said Gromyko personally favoured proving to pro-Soviet neutrals that the USSR was true to its promises, and he later breathed fiery defiance of Washington's hostile reaction to the invasion.[19] Andropov's KGB was responsible for the sensitive Central Asian border and for controlling internal dissension in Moscow's Islamic colonial empire. His earlier skepticism apparently gave way partly out of a desire to avoid victorious Islamic anti-Communism in Afghanistan, where his KGB was playing a major role in supporting and seeking to direct the regime. Andropov's support also reportedly was strongly urged by Ustinov. Ustinov, a civilian political boss of the military, was so receptive to the need for maintaining commitments to clients and other political considerations that he overrode objections of his professional soldiers.

Gromyko, as quoted by his son, said Brezhnev decided whom to invite to discussions on Afghanistan. In addition to the four named by the Supreme Soviet, Gromyko said two other politburo members, Kosygin and ideologist Suslov, and an unidentified few others 'discussed this problem behind the doors of the general secretary's [Brezhnev's] office, which actually were closed...'.[20] This apparently refers to discussions before 12 December. The roles of Kosygin and Suslov remain unclear. Kosygin's health was failing, and he was not mentioned in official reports from 17 October until after 12 December. His son-in-law later implied that Kosygin thought the decision was wrong,[21] which would account for his never signing the invasion decree. Suslov's involvement—or, rather, his failure to leave any tracks—was more curious. Suslov was listed as a decision-maker not only by Gromyko but also by others claiming access to inside information, including former politburo member Pyotr E. Shelest and former politburo alternate Boris N. Yeltsin.[22] Indeed, it would have been out of character for Suslov, the old Stalinist supervisor of CPSU and governmental foreign affairs, not to have played a role in trying to hold Afghanistan. But, using Ponomarev as his front man, Suslov deliberately kept to the background of what he believed was a no-win situation, according to a senior CPSU official.[23]

Non-voting alternate politburo members other than Ponomarev, as well as CPSU secretaries, were only told of the decision '[s]everal days before it was implemented...'. Shevardnadze said he and Gorbachev, who were alternate members at the time, were presented with a *fait accompli*.[24] Brezhnev's main adviser on foreign affairs, Aleksandrov-Agentov, said he only learned that Soviet troops were in Kabul and Karmal had replaced Amin when he asked Andropov how to answer accumulated telegrams from Amin requesting military aid.[25] This statement, while unbelievable, interestingly implies that Andropov's KGB had assumed primary responsibility for Afghan policy.

The Supreme Soviet investigation found that 'the decision to send in troops was made in violation of the USSR Constitution...'. It named Article 73, section 8, which said 'questions of peace and war, defence of sovereignty, protection of the state frontiers and territory of the USSR, organization of defence, and direction of the armed forces...shall be subject to the jurisdiction of [the USSR's] highest agencies of state power and administration'. These are the Supreme Soviet and its presidium, but they 'did not examine the question of sending troops to Afghanistan'. The report added that, if the decision had been submitted to the full presidium or the Supreme Soviet, 'in accordance with the established practice at that time...it would most likely have been approved'—an understatement about bodies that rubberstamped CPSU leaders' decisions.[26] Brezhnev reportedly rejected Gromyko's recommendation to get Supreme Soviet approval.[27]

Defending the Decision

In the late 1980s denigration of Brezhnev for his 'period of stagnation', primary blame was put on him for the wrong and illegal decision to invade Afghanistan. In defending the decision against international outrage in 1980, however, Soviet spokesmen represented it as a collective action of the broad leadership. But it was not until 23 June 1980 that the

CPSU central committee met and formally endorsed the invasion. Reporting to the first CPSU congress after the invasion, on 23 February 1981, Brezhnev said without specific reference to Afghanistan that the politburo 'carefully studied in advance' questions submitted to it, and 'all decisions were adopted in *a spirit of complete unanimity*'. [28] Earlier, he was paraphrased as saying the Soviet leadership had 'weighed the pros and cons [of invading],...questioned the matter at length,...[and] had some hesitations...[but they] had to prevent a collapse' of the Kabul regime.[29]

How 'carefully studied' was the decision, how closely 'weighed the pros and cons'? As war escalated in the mid-1960s in distant Vietnam, Soviet leaders followed policy advice of their diplomats and area experts.[30] Afghanistan, both closer and becoming a problem in a perceptually changed era, was different. Numerous foreign affairs experts, specialists on Afghanistan, military leaders, and others who logically should have been consulted insisted later that they had not been, or their advice had been ignored. Some Soviets lamented the paucity of people who had a deep understanding of Afghan affairs. The head of the Soviet Academy of Sciences' Institute of Oriental Studies, the putative main repository of expertise on Afghanistan, said later the decision was made 'without a real understanding of...the situation in Afghanistan...', and a military scholar agreed.[31] The foreign ministry reportedly set up a study group in the summer of 1979 that strongly advised against military involvement, but it was ignored. By October Gromyko had quit discussing Afghanistan with his deputies, presumably because he did not want to hear arguments differing from his fixed opinion.[32] Puzanov said that, when he returned to Moscow in November after seven years as ambassador in Kabul, officials 'were not even interested in my opinion about the situation...or the expediency of sending troops there'.[33]

PLACING, OR EVADING, BLAME

The scramble to escape blame for the invasion decision that peaked in 1989 and 1990 produced more assertions than clarity. Conflicting views within the various institutions involved, especially the military and the KGB, combined with highly selective memories to obscure the opinions and policy recommendations available to the Brezhnev clique. Advice from Soviet officials in Kabul apparently was conflicting when it was not simply reduced to the 'positive information' wanted in Moscow. A KGB official asserted self-servingly that information from CPSU advisers to the PDPA, headed by Semyon M. Veselov, 'was given more credit [in Moscow] than information from the KGB intelligence (which did not, on many occasions, reach the country's top echelons of power)'.[34]

The Soviet military's vociferous denial of responsibility included insistence that it advised against the invasion. Both the head of army advisers in Kabul, Gorelov, and his deputy who headed advisers to the Afghan army's political administration, Zaplatin, said Soviet 'military advisers did not ask for' the dispatch of Soviet troops.[35] Soviet ground forces commander Pavlovskiy said he reported after his nine-week survey 'that there was no need to send our troops...'.[36] Chief of staff Ogarkov, his first deputy, Sergei F. Akhromeyev, and their chief of operations, Valentin I. Varennikov, reportedly opposed the move.[37] The military's chief political commissar, Yepishev, and a deputy, Maj.-Gen. Dmitriy A. Volkogonov, were said to have spoken to Ustinov against the move.[38] Such assertions long after the event evoked sarcastic questions in Moscow about the generals' unwillingness or inability in 1979 to stand up to their civilian bureaucrat boss.[39] But the Soviet army was too thoroughly cowed by the CPSU to challenge political decisions.

The KGB had by the mid-1980s begun circulating stories that it always knew the invasion was a bad idea. But a leading Soviet specialist on the subject, Vladimir Snegirev, concluded that '80 per cent of the responsibility...belongs to people from the KGB. And one of the key figures, undoubtedly, was V. A. Kryuchkov',[40] the head of KGB foreign intelligence who had helped set up the PDPA regime and supervised it closely. Aleksandr Morozov, a deputy to the KGB's boss in Kabul, Ivanov, also made Kryuchkov the main villain.[41] One report said the KGB 'manufactured conspiracies' by the United States to make Afghanistan an anti-Soviet outpost, replacing Iran after the shah's fall, and thus played on Brezhnev's fears.[42] An anonymous KGB colonel said KGB officers in Afghanistan reported 'that troops cannot be sent in...[because that] would bring about bloodshed and antagonize loyal Afghans', but Andropov was telling CPSU leaders that the Afghans 'were awaiting us there almost with open arms'. The colonel asserted that the invasion would not have occurred 'in the absence of Andropov's *purposeful* disinformation of the politburo'.[43] And a defender of Brezhnev contended that the decision could not have been taken 'despite the opinion of both military and civilian specialists...without Andropov's participation, since he was the conduit of all intelligence information on the situation in Afghanistan, and on the intentions of the United States, Pakistan, and China'.[44]

Whatever the truth of various inputs to the decision, Soviet leaders could pick those reports that reinforced their ideological, emotional, institutional, or other inclinations. According to some accounts, the decision was for Brezhnev primarily an emotional reaction to Amin's murder of Taraki. Gromyko was quoted as saying that 'Brezhnev was simply shaken by the murder of Taraki, who not long before had been his guest', and told close associates he had to respond to this slap in the face.[45]

BASIC CONSIDERATIONS

With Afghanistan considered in the autumn of 1979 to be 'on the verge of disintegration',[46] considerations behind the invasion decision fall into several categories: concern about repercussions of the collapse of a client regime on Soviet interests elsewhere, apprehension about possible danger to Soviet Central Asian borderlands, worries about ideological purity and consistency, and the facilitating factor of already deteriorating East-West relations. There was also concern about the safety of the thousands of Soviet citizens in Afghanistan. More broadly, the decision can be seen as a logical outcome of a Soviet political system that emphasized the need to maintain control in any situation, to hold onto any political power opportunity, to keep up strong defences and forward positions because of a seige mentality, to spend on competition for influence abroad rather than on problems at home.

The perception that the USSR had to be seen as supportive of the PDPA in order to hold the loyalty and support of other clients was stronger in Moscow than in client capitals, although it echoed in the Third World for years. Conservative Soviet leaders were not prepared to risk an implication of weakness. The memory of Nikita S. Khrushchev's being criticized at the time of his 1964 ouster for failing adequately to support Cuba in the 1962 missile crisis argued against exposing any similar vulnerability in future Kremlin politics, especially with the succession to Brezhnev looming ahead.

The loudest part of immediate Soviet justifications for the invasion was the need to defend the USSR's security. *Pravda* on 31 December 1979 blamed local resistance in Afghanistan on 'internal reaction,...forces that are losing power and privileges', but shifted the focus to accusing imperialism of trying to take advantage of this. The fall of Iran's shah had created cracks

in the notorious "strategic arc" that Americans have been
building for decades close to the southern borders of the Soviet
Union. In order to mend these cracks, [the United States sought
to bring Afghanistan under its control, but] our country...will
not allow Afghanistan's being turned into a bridgehead for
preparation of imperialist aggression against the Soviet Union.[47]

Once composed, this tune was fully orchestrated by Soviet
spokesmen. Brezhnev said there was a 'real threat that
Afghanistan would lose its independence and be turned into
an imperialist military bridgehead on our southern border'.
Asserting later, 'We had no choice but to send troops', he
claimed that plans 'to create a threat to our country from
the south have failed'.[48] As criticism mounted of what the
West saw as Soviet aggression, Moscow more shrilly insisted
it had acted to prevent aggression by others against
Afghanistan and potentially against the USSR.

Occasional, terse Soviet references to religious and ethnic
problems in Central Asian republics and a handful of reports
from the region about continued hostility to Russian colonial
rule—for example, a 1978 Tajik riot against Russians in
Dushanbe—suggest another aspect of concern about the
Afghan border. With religious fervor already spreading from
the Iranian revolution against the shah, there was
apprehension over the vulnerability of border republics to
infection if Afghanistan lost its buffer role by throwing off
its new Communist rulers.[49] A year after the invasion, the
KGB boss for Muslim Azerbaijan charged that American
intelligence 'services are trying to exploit the Islamic
religion—especially in areas where the Muslim population
lives—as one factor influencing the political situation in our
country'.[50]

Politburo member Victor V. Grishin explained the
invasion in ideological terms: 'Socialist internationalism
obliged us to help the Afghan people defend the April
revolution's gains'.[51] Andropov merged ideological and
defensive reasons, calling the invasion 'a lofty act of fidelity

to the principle of proletarian internationalism, necessary for the defence of our homeland'.[52] The editor of *Izvestiya* said in 1988 'supporting the socialist regime [in Afghanistan had been] a holy mission'.[53] The 1989 Supreme Soviet committee's report said the invasion decision 'was undoubtedly affected by the excessive ideologization of Soviet foreign policy activity which had occurred over a period of many years under the direct influence of the ideological tenets that held sway at the time'.[54]

Raw Materials and Strategy?

Some Afghan exiles and Westerners hypothesized that considerations in the invasion decision were gaining access to Afghan raw materials and strategic positioning for Soviet forces. However, Afghanistan's undeveloped iron ore, copper, uranium, oil, and other natural resources had little value in the foreseeable future for a USSR starved of the investment capital needed for exploitation, and Moscow made no significant effort to tap them.

Nor did the Soviets try to develop a military posture in Afghanistan enabling them to threaten areas beyond it. Nonetheless, many Western commentators focused on the fact that the invasion moved Soviet military forces closer to Persian Gulf oil routes and the Arabian Sea. This raised the question of whether the move was primarily a defensive one to protect the Central Asian border and preserve a Marxist protege regime, or an offensive one to use Kabul's weakness as an excuse to advance the Soviet strategic position in the Middle East and South Asia. For many, the answer became less an assessment of the evidence than a mirror of long-held attitudes about the nature of the Soviet system and its foreign policy. The foreign affairs committee of Britain's House of Commons found 'no evidence that the invasion...was part of a Soviet grand strategy' but noted 'the opportunistic trend of Soviet tactics'.[55] American scholar

George F. Kennan said that 'in the immediate circumstances [the Soviet] objective was primarily defensive'. But historian Richard E. Pipes said the invasion was 'clearly not designed as an end in itself.... I see their entire design as offensive and not defensive'.[56] The United States Defence Intelligence Agency agreed: 'The key motivation that propelled Moscow's move was to bring its long-standing strategic goals closer within reach. Control of Afghanistan would be a major step toward overland access to the Indian Ocean and to domination of the Asian subcontinent.'[57] China also concurred, saying the invasion 'was designed to pave the way for [a Soviet] strategy of southward expansion'.[58] But the weight of testimony in the 1988 and 1989 Soviet examinations of the invasion decision indicated that defensive thinking had been more important in 1979. Soviet generals never considered Afghanistan to be on the way to anywhere.

Against the reasons that seemed to propel the USSR into Afghanistan, there were negative considerations of political and diplomatic costs as well as financial ones. Anecdotal evidence suggests that Soviet leaders did not evaluate the costs with any care. Financially, the politburo did not seem to count rubles, only results, as it bankrupted the country. Politically and diplomatically, there were reasons for the politburo to think it could order an Afghan action with little more international cost than the USSR had paid for propping up regimes in Angola and Ethiopia over ineffective Western objections. The Carter administration had publicly denied itself the kinds of retaliation for Soviet bad conduct that Moscow had most reason to dislike: a halt to negotiations to limit the strategic arms race that the Kremlin knew it could ill afford and feared it might lose, and restrictions on grain sales to the USSR. Besides, relations with Washington were already poor, did not seem likely to sink much lower regardless of action in Afghanistan, and were unlikely to improve soon even without such action. '[T]he downward spiral of US Soviet relations had released the brakes on

Soviet international behaviour,' Secretary of State Cyrus Vance commented later.[59]

Moscow apparently felt that any outrage over Afghanistan would quickly pass. It also believed that any loss of goodwill that an invasion might cause in the Third World might be more than offset by respect for Soviet power, its willingness to use it, and for proving loyal to a friendly regime in trouble.

THE TIMING OF THE DECISION

According to later statements by key Soviet players, considerations of 'committing our troops' to Afghanistan arose sometime between the August 1979 meeting of the politburo commission and October, when Gorelov and Zaplatin were summoned to Moscow to meet with Ustinov, Ogarkov, and others. In the interim, Amin had deposed Taraki, the Afghan army had further weakened from defections and insurrections, and the *mujahideen* had strengthened. Pavlovskiy said that, when he returned from Kabul on 3 November, a proposal to send 75 000 troops to 'stabilize the situation in Afghanistan' was under consideration, but Ustinov 'did not want to listen...[to my] opinion that there was no need for us to commit our forces...'.[60]

The Soviet Army's Turkestan military district, which abutted on most of the Afghan border, was a backwater. In early 1979, the district's only combat-ready division was the 105th Airborne at Ferghana. Western intelligence reports said that beginning in October 'tens of thousands' of reservists, mostly central Asians, were mobilized to bring two of the region's motorized infantry divisions up to strength, and some 8000 vehicles and other equipment were commandeered from the civilian economy. Ryabchenko, the 105th commander, said that on 7 October one of his regiments was 'unexpectedly' ordered to begin training with these infantry divisions.[61] In November a satellite communications ground station appeared at Termez, the Soviet railhead for the ferry crossing of the Amu Darya on the main route into Afghanistan. This indicated the establishment of a special military headquarters linked to the defence ministry in Moscow. Termez became the point from which Marshal Sergei L. Sokolov, Ustinov's first deputy defence minister, commanded the invasion. His chief of staff was Army General Varennikov, newly appointed as a deputy defence minister. On 12 or 13 December, Lt.-Gen. Yuriy V. Tukharinov, the first deputy commander of the Turkestan military district, was named commander of the newly created Soviet 40th Army, composed of all forces committed to Afghanistan.[62]

On 29 November, troops from the 105th Airborne began flying into Bagram to strengthen the battalion that had been there since July. Three battalions—about 2500 soldiers— were at Bagram by 6 December, and on that day the CPSU politburo decided also to send into Afghanistan a 500-man GRU special forces (*spetsnaz*) unit 'in uniforms which do not reveal its belonging to the USSR armed forces'. Between 8 and 10 December a 600-man armoured unit joined the 105th battalions at Bagram, and ten days later it moved north to secure the highway through the Salang Pass tunnel on what was to become one of the two main overland routes for the invasion. By 12 December a 105th battalion had been seen at Kabul airport.[63] In late November or early December, the *mujahideen* seized Feyzabad, capital of Badakhshan province on the Soviet border, and Soviet warplanes flying from the USSR reportedly supported the Afghan army's unsuccessful effort to retake it.[64]

According to a Soviet general staff officer, 'During the first days of December 1979...Ustinov informed a narrow circle of officials in the ministry of defence of a possible decision by the political leadership to employ our troops in Afghanistan'. On 10 December, the officer said, Ustinov ordered the general staff to make ready an airborne division plus planes to carry it and 'to raise the readiness status of two motorized rifle divisions in the Turkestan military district'[65]—apparently not meaning the two divisions already being readied. Between 11 and 15 December, 280 transport planes gathered in the Moscow area and in Central Asia, and tactical fighter aircraft were shifted from bases deep in the USSR to airfields near the Afghan border. Two other airborne divisions from the Soviet Army's elite strike forces were placed on alert, the 103rd at Vitebsk in Belorussia and the 104th at Kirovabad in Azerbaijan.[66] The general staff issued more than 30 directives on Ustinov's orders, but no documentation was found in defence ministry archives later when the invasion had been officially repudiated.

Zaplatin was summoned urgently to Moscow again on 10 December. The next day he found Ogarkov and Yepishev 'extremely disturbed about the situation in Afghanistan'. Ustinov told Zaplatin that 'we must make a decision' and showed him a report from an unidentified source that seemed to justify action. Zaplatin contended that the person who sent it—the implication was a KGB officer—'had been deluded' and that it was possible to work with Amin, contrary to the opinion of some Soviets in Kabul.[67] But Ustinov was beyond reassurance. The day after that, 12 December, Ustinov along with Andropov and Gromyko got the politburo to endorse their invasion plan.

Almost no one outside the involved military units was told about the venture until Ustinov called together senior defence ministry officials and announced the decision on 24 December.[68] On the same day he and Ogarkov signed an order to move troops into Afghanistan 'for purposes of providing international assistance to the friendly Afghan people and for creating conditions conducive to the prevention of possible anti-Afghan actions on the part of bordering states'.[69] Ryabchenko said he was given an order that '[t]his is not to be an invasion or an occupation; we are to render assistance to friendly Afghanistan in the struggle against the counterrevolution....[I]t is necessary to cut off the flow of weapons, ammunition, and equipment from Pakistan and Iran'.[70]

The Soviet general staff told Ustinov—who reportedly commented that the *mujahideen* would throw down their arms and run when faced with the Soviet Army—that the 75 000 men originally planned to go into Afghanistan could not 'stabilize the situation' but would instead increase the rebellion and turn it against Soviet troops. The general staff therefore proposed that the troops 'be stationed in separate garrisons [and] not become involved in combat operations under any pretext', Pavlovskiy recalled.[71] 'According to the initial plan,' Varennikov said, Soviet troops 'would help the local population to protect themselves against the [*mujahideen*] gangs and give them help with food and all essential goods'[72]—which, although not carried out, was the Soviet propaganda line for all that the troops did in the first few years of the war. When its garrison plan proved unrealistic, the general staff lacked any operational concept beyond using forces trained and equipped for conventional warfare against Western Europe or China—not for combating guerrillas—to secure towns and communication routes.

The 'prevailing feeling among the troops' sent into Afghanistan was 'that they were to be there only a short time and should be home by 23 February [1980] at the latest', one Soviet journalist recalled.[73] Another said 'Soviet diplomats, military men, and politicians, as well as our Afghan friends,...expected peace to come in a year, or a year and a half at the very most'.[74] *Izvestiya* 's foreign affairs commentator, Aleksandr Y. Bovin, said he 'thought that within three or four months we would fulfill our duty, help the government stabilize itself, defeat the foreign counter-revolution, and return home'.[75] In Kabul, Soviet Ambassador Tabeyev expressed confidence that Afghanistan would be completely peaceful and orderly by September 1980.[76]

NEEDED: A COVER STORY

One important element was still missing: a cover story. The Soviet general staff was told that an agreement had been reached for Kabul Radio to announce 'to all the world' that Afghanistan had asked for Soviet troops to be sent to its help.[77] This did not happen, possibly because of the failure of the mid-December plot to eliminate Amin that had taken Karmal briefly to Bagram. It was difficult for Moscow to fabricate a plausible alternative to Amin. He had murdered, banished into exile, or otherwise eliminated just about any alternative leader. The situation called for the invention of some group of Afghans who could be clothed in a claim to legitimacy, described as having removed their evil president, installed in power, and used to ask for Soviet help as a legal response to a treaty obligation.

The Soviet Union had plenty of experience in manufacturing cover stories. The Bolsheviks had recreated the tsarist empire as the USSR by using small groups of local supporters in, for example, the Transcaucasus and Bukhara, who claimed to speak for the masses in asking that troops be sent in to consolidate Bolshevik power and supervise accession. Moscow used a local front group to gain control of Mongolia in 1921. After failing to take over Finland with a bogus front group in 1939 because the Finns fought back, the Soviets succeeded with the technique in 1940 in Estonia, Latvia, and Lithuania. Moscow concocted a 'Hungarian Revolutionary Worker-Peasant Government' to appeal for the Soviet Army to crush the Hungarian 'freedom fighters' in 1956, and a claimed—but never produced—'letter of invitation' from Prague was used to justify the 1968 invasion of Czechoslovakia.[78]

The obvious principal for an Afghan cover story was Babrak Karmal, as Suslov had decided before the abortive mid-December plot. But the story of Karmal's role in the invasion became so muddled and contradictory that Soviet propagandists did not bother to claim documentary evidence of an Afghan invitation comparable to the bogus invitations cited in the Hungarian and Czechoslovak cases. For a while Karmal claimed that he had heroically crossed the Durand Line and lived underground in Kabul to rally resistance to Amin. He variously dated this clandestine return as August 1979, as 14 October or later that month, as mid-November, or as some vaguely later time closer to the invasion.[79] A decade later Karmal admitted that he learned of the Soviet invasion '[j]ust before it began' and was flown into Afghanistan behind the troops. He reportedly was wearing a Soviet military uniform.[80]

After Soviet soldiers had seized Kabul Radio, it broadcast on 28 December that the PDPA politburo had met that day and unanimously elected Karmal as general secretary, and a revolutionary council meeting the same day had named him president.[81] But when foreign governments, outraged by the invasion, questioned the legitimacy of Karmal's assumption of power, he backdated his accession to before the invasion. Karmal claimed that a majority—or the unanimous membership—of the PDPA central committee and the revolutionary council had tried Amin, decided to execute him, and elected Karmal to Amin's three jobs of committee general secretary, council (and national) president, and prime minister—even though, by one count, only two central committee members then in Kabul later sided with Karmal.[82] This purported decision supposedly forestalled Amin's evil intentions. They were variously described as planning a 29 December anti-Communist crackdown in cooperation with resistance groups and slaughtering millions of Afghans, or fleeing abroad to live comfortably on money 'savagely plundered [from] our toiling people'.[83] No evidence was offered for any of this.

Karmal also contradicted himself on whether Amin had asked for Soviet troops. One unbelievable version was that the central committee and revolutionary council forced Amin to make the request, but this was done 'without my personal knowledge...and without an opportunity [for me] to bring influence to bear', Karmal said in March 1980. In 1991, he insisted that 'I was strongly against the Soviet presence here. I did not invite them here...'.[84] Soviet bloc countries were told that Moscow 'responded to the request of the *newly formed* Afghanistan leadership', while other countries were told 'the leadership of the state of Afghanistan has applied to the Soviet Union for help and assistance against external aggression'.[85] The CPSU politburo even lied to other party officials, telling them 'forces were found in Afghanistan' to rise up against Amin and form new PDPA and government leaderships, which then asked for military aid.[86]

CHRONOLOGY OF AN INVASION

In early December, Ryabchenko visited Kabul with a small group of his 105th Airborne officers to study the terrain. After he had given the remaining troops at Ferghana just 24 hours' notice of their mission, some of them began flying into Kabul airport.[87] The first planes landed at 11 p.m. on 24 December—a time at which Western governments had slowed for Christmas, but an ordinary Monday night for Communists and Muslims. Soon after, other 105th troops as well as 103rd and 104th Airborne units began landing at the Soviet-built military air bases at Bagram and at Shindand, 65 miles south of Herat, and at the American-built Qandahar airport. The airlift into Kabul continued around the clock for two days, with one IL-76 crashing into the Hindu Kush mountains north of Kabul, killing 33 men.[88] 'Afghans at the airport were shocked to see the Russians arriving in uniform and toting weapons,' a Western witness reported. 'I saw some weeping.'[89]

The deployments into Afghanistan had been worked out with Maj.-Gen. Babajan, chief of operations for the Afghan armed forces, during his visit on 24 December to Termez, where Marshal Sokolov was directing Soviet operations. The next morning, Tukharinov, the new 40th Army commander, flew by helicopter from Termez to Konduz, where Amin's brother Abdullah was administering northern Afghanistan. Tukharinov discussed with him 'the disposition of our troops'.[90] At 5 p.m. on 25 December, as night fell, the 360th Motorized Infantry Division began crossing the Amu Darya from Termez on especially constructed pontoon bridges. To the west, another infantry division entered Afghanistan from Kushka on 29 December to occupy Herat and Shindand, while in the east a smaller unit crossed the upper Amu river into Badakhshan.[91] The 360th's destination was Konduz, but the following evening it was redirected to get to Kabul by 5 p.m. on 27 December. Advance units crossed the icy Hindu Kush and reached Kabul on schedule. A road accident on the 25th killed eight Soviet soldiers, and 12 more 360th soldiers died in the Soviet-built Salang tunnel, apparently from asphyxiation because the ventilation system designed for conventional engines' exhausts could not handle diesel fumes from armoured vehicles.[92] Including the IL-76 crash victims, 53 Soviets had died before the shooting started.

The redirection of the 360th indicated that Sokolov had last-minute doubts that the 5000 airborne troops assembled in Kabul by the morning of 27 December would be sufficient to overcome resistance. But the scope for armed opposition had been reduced by Soviet advisers. Repeating a trick used in the 1968 invasion of Czechoslovakia, they had Afghan soldiers turn in live ammunition and take blanks for a training exercise, remove batteries from some tanks 'for winterization', and take the firing pins from other tanks' guns 'for repair'.[93]

The attitude and actions of Amin during this period are hard to understand. While cooperating with preliminary deployments in mid-December, Amin sensed danger. Without public explanation he moved on 19 December from the Arg in downtown Kabul, which had proven so indefensible in the Saur coup 20 months earlier, to the Tajbeg palace in the Darulaman complex seven miles

southwest of the centre of Kabul. Amin's most trusted
Afghan guards accompanied him, and loyal troops held the
main Darulaman buildings.[94] On 26 December, Amin
ordered the 4th Armoured Brigade at Pul-i-Charki
garrison—Watanjar's old unit—immediately to join his
defences at Darulaman. Its commander said later that he
stalled.[95] Amin appeared on television the same day looking
dishevelled, and some diplomats thought he appeared
strained in a photograph published on 27 December, a
Thursday. A Soviet report said he told luncheon guests on
the 27th that he was 'in constant telephone contact with
Gromyko...[on] how best to formulate for the world the
information about the Soviet military aid being rendered to
us'.[96] At 2:30 p.m., after government offices had closed in
preparation for the Friday day of prayers, Amin received at
the People's Hall in Darulaman what Kabul Radio described
as a courtesy call from the Soviet minister of communications, Nikolai V. Talyzin, who had arrived in Kabul three
days earlier 'on an official and friendly visit'.[97] His call was
Amin's last reported activity—and the last Soviet courtesy.
At some time that day, Soviet agents in Amin's personal
entourage tried unsuccessfully to poison him.[98]

The Takeover

At about 7 that evening, an explosion knocked out the
Kabul telephone system. By 7:15, 105th Airborne troops
had captured the interior ministry, headquarters for internal
police. Two Soviet Army officers appeared at Kabul Radio
with Watanjar, who had returned from the USSR in the
Soviet airlift the night of 24-25 December along with
Sarwari, Gulabzoy, and others. Watanjar announced that
the 'traitor Amin' was being ousted. The station's guards
resisted, foiling a Soviet plan to block broadcasts.[99] About
the same time, a 105th battalion, some of the KGB 'Z
group' commandos who had been in Afghanistan since

October, and a KGB 'A group' commando squad that arrived on 23 December, combined forces to attack Amin's redoubt at the Tajbeg palace in Darulaman. Some 300 presidential guards resisted with help from a tank battalion and up to 2000 infantrymen.[100]

PROCLAIMING A CHANGE

While guards at both Kabul Radio and Tajbeg palace were holding out, a Soviet transmitter at Termez began broadcasting on the frequency of Kabul Radio, which continued normal programming. Overpowering Kabul, Termez broadcast at 8:45 p.m. what Western intelligence analysts later said was a tape-recorded statement by Karmal, who was then in Tashkent and did not appear publicly in Kabul until 1 January.[101] Karmal addressed those who 'have been subjected to intolerable violence and torture by the bloody apparatus of Hafizullah Amin and his minions, these agents of American imperialism.... The day of freedom and rebirth...has arrived. Today the torture machine of Amin...has been broken...'.[102]

Fighting continued in downtown Kabul, especially around the radio station, until about 10:30 p.m., with a number of casualties on both sides. Finally, at 2:40 a.m. the real Kabul Radio broadcast a brief announcement that it said came from the revolutionary council's secretariat. Without explaining what had happened, it named Karmal, who was identified as general secretary of the PDPA central committee, as the council's president, and thus president of Afghanistan. Named as vice presidents were Sarwari and Keshtmand, who had been in prison. Other members of the council presidium were Qadir, who had also been imprisoned at Pul-i-Charki, and Watanjar, plus Lt. Col. Gol Aqa. Fifteen minutes later an announcement in the name of the Afghan government said it 'earnestly demands that the USSR render urgently, political, moral, and economic assistance, including military aid, to Afghanistan. The government of the USSR has accepted...'. Twenty minutes after that, at 3:15 a.m., came an announcement 'by the revolutionary tribunal', whose composition and authority were never further identified. 'The revolutionary tribunal has sentenced to death Hafizullah Amin for the crimes he has committed against the noble people of Afghanistan.... The sentence...has been carried out.'[103]

Amin went down fighting. Westerners in Kabul, including a military attache who trailed a Soviet assault team toward Darulaman, said no Afghans were involved in the Tajbeg attack, which did not overcome stout resistance until the middle of the night.[104] The 105th's Ryabchenko bitterly blamed 'the one who organized the operation', apparently meaning the KGB 'Z group' leader, Col. G. I. Boyarinov, for failing to warn Soviet troops of what they might encounter, or to arrange 'mutual recognition and interaction signals' with other Soviet forces. This failure cost 'unjustified [Soviet] losses', Ryabchenko said.[105] As Soviet troops fought their way into the palace, meeting fierce room-to-room resistance, Boyarinov stepped outside to call for reinforcements, forgetting his own orders not to let anyone leave alive, and was killed by Soviet gunfire.[106] Amin was killed by grenade fragments, but then a Russian attacker, after comparing the body with a photo to confirm identification, 'shot him point blank' just to be sure. Between two or three and a dozen Soviets were killed in the assault, and 'quite a lot' were killed two days later when the team holding Tajbeg palace were mistakenly fired on by relieving Soviet troops, apparently from the 360th division.[107]

Both Karmal's and Soviet spokesmen insisted in early 1980 that Amin had been eliminated by Afghan action, that it was 'merely a coincidence' that he 'was removed at the time' Soviet troops arrived. Sarwari and Gulabzoy claimed that they commanded Afghan troops who stormed Tajbeg palace. But Soviets who had been involved said later that Sarwari cowered in a Soviet armoured personnel carrier until taken to see Amin's body.[108]

Karmal said later, 'During the 27 December *rebellion* some of [Amin's] followers were killed—three or four people—because they were putting up resistance', and about 200 had been imprisoned.[109] The death toll from fighting around Kabul that continued into the morning of 28 December was never announced. Diplomats' guesses of Soviet casualties began at 25 killed and 225 wounded and went upward, some much higher, while Afghan losses were presumed to have been considerably larger.[110]

Soviet Explanations

The first full, authoritative Soviet statement on the situation was published by *Pravda* on 31 December. It said the USSR had decided to grant Afghanistan's 'insistent request...[for] immediate aid and support in the struggle against external aggression...and to send to Afghanistan a limited Soviet military contingent that will be used exclusively for assistance in rebuffing the armed interference from the outside. The Soviet contingent will be completely pulled out of Afghanistan when the reason that necessitated such an action exists no longer'. Denying that the country was being occupied by Soviet troops or that the troops were involved in internal affairs, the article added that 'patriotic forces in Afghanistan...rose not only against foreign aggression but also against the *usurper*. Relying on the support of the people, they removed Amin'.[111] Taraki and Karmal were not considered usurpers.

Was it an invasion if both Taraki and Amin asked for help from Soviet troops, if Amin and his brother Abdullah knew troops were arriving but did not publicly complain? The USSR never backed up assertions of requests with documentary evidence, any letter or diplomatic message, any official Afghan invocation of the 5 December 1978 treaty.

Is it an invasion to arrive ostensibly to support a government but actually to destroy it and install another one? In a 1989 *mea culpa* for having justified the 1979 action, *Izvestiya* commentator Bovin wrote that, because the action 'began...with the destruction of the head of the legitimate government,...it is immoral to refer to the request of this government [for Soviet troops]. And the request from the Karmal government was made after the fact and has no legal force'.[112] Soviet writers later used the term 'invasion'.

WORLDWIDE OUTRAGE

The invasion outraged the non-Communist world. Some United Nations members that normally tried to avoid being counted against Moscow—whose acquiescence in Soviet policies out of fear or self-interest the Kremlin had long assumed—voted for the Soviet Army to leave Afghanistan. Only after the Soviet Army had withdrawn did Moscow admit the outrage. Varennikov said the invasion 'affected the prestige of our state. We opposed ourselves to the world community'. Moscow Radio said, 'The Afghan adventure cost us...political losses on a huge scale. The world regarded us as an aggressor...'. And Najibullah admitted 'the bitter and harsh reality...[of] the hostility of the international community and world public opinion' that isolated Afghanistan, 'in particular among the Islamic countries and member countries of the nonaligned movement'.[113]

The United States led the worldwide reaction. 'We are the other superpower on earth', President Carter said, 'and it became my responsibility...to take action that would prevent the Soviets from [accomplishing] this invasion with impunity'. In 'the sharpest message of my presidency' to Brezhnev, on 28 December Carter called the invasion 'a clear threat to peace...[that] could mark a fundamental and long-lasting turning point in our relations'. He urged Brezhnev 'to withdraw your forces and cease interference in

Afghanistan's internal affairs'. Brezhnev replied that the Soviet Army had been invited to protect Afghanistan from outside threat and would leave when the threat was eliminated. Carter called this 'obviously false,...devious, ...[and] completely inadequate and completely misleading'. He added, 'My opinion of the Russians...[and] of what the Soviets' ultimate goals are...has changed more drastically in the last week than even...the previous time I've been in office'.[114] In the bitter exchanges that followed, the KGB forged material to support a Soviet media line that Amin had been a CIA agent, but this charge was eventually dropped because an intensive KGB search failed to turn up any evidence.[115]

While recognizing that it might not be possible to get the USSR to withdraw its troops for a long time, Carter directed American officials to 'make Soviet involvement as costly as possible'. He was convinced that, unless he took a strong stand, 'we will face additional serious problems with invasions or subversion in the future'.[116] Afghanistan seemed to prove the point long argued by Carter's national security adviser, Zbigniew Brzezinski, and some other advisers: the Soviet Union was an aggressively expansionist power that was ignoring the supposed limits of détente and only understood counterforce. The invasion decided a bureaucratic struggle that had been going on in Washington over whether to take tougher stands against Moscow. Noting the toughening policy, the Soviet government on 6 January accused the United States of using the invasion as a pretext to worsen relations.[117]

The Carter administration adopted Brzezinski's view that the effect of the invasion was 'not a local but a strategic challenge'[118] with dangers for the whole region. Administration apprehensions built up to a ringing statement in Carter's State of the Union address to Congress on 23 January 1980, which became known as 'the Carter doctrine', that American armed forces would meet any 'attempt by any outside force to gain control of the Persian Gulf region...'.[119]

However, as already noted, the Soviets never made preparations for using Afghanistan as a base to project power onward. In any event, a Soviet attack toward the Gulf region would have been logistically easier from the Caucasus than through Afghanistan.

Penalyzing Moscow

Carter said he wanted to impose 'severe political consequences' for the invasion, and the National Security Council agreed on 2 January on some 26 specific actions.[120] They included delaying ratification of an already dormant SALT II treaty, curtailing Soviet fishing privileges in US waters, restricting high-technology sales, withholding grain sales, and boycotting the 1980 summer Olympics in Moscow. The short-term Western evaluation was that none of these actions hurt the USSR much, partly because other countries filled the trade gaps.[121] But Moscow reacted angrily. A Brezhnev statement published by *Pravda* on 13 January accused Carter of 'trying to speak to us in the language of the cold war...[and] deal[ing] a blow at the orderly international law system of relations among states...'.[122] By cutting Soviet-American trade almost in half, the sanctions revitalized a Soviet internal debate over emphasizing autarky or seeking the benefits of foreign trade. When Gorbachev came to power in 1985, according to Shevardnadze, one element of an 'extremely gloomy' situation was that 'American sanctions imposed because of our involvement in Afghanistan were having their effect'.[123]

Other Countries' Reactions

Pakistan, which had inherited the old British Indian apprehension of potential foes on the Northwest Frontier, expressed on 29 December grave concern over the 'far-reaching negative consequences' of the invasion and called for a Soviet withdrawal.[124] At the same time, the Soviet action revived Pakistan's relations with the United States. In August 1978 the Carter administration had halted aid to Pakistan because it was believed to be trying to make nuclear weapons, and in March 1979 Pakistan had announced its withdrawal from a 1950s American-led anti-Soviet alliance, the Central Treaty Organization, in order 'to soften the edge of Soviet-Pakistani relations...'. Relations slumped even lower when a Pakistani mob, incited by rumours of American involvement in an incident in the Islamic holy city of Mecca, burned the United States embassy in Islamabad in November 1979 while President Zia's security forces reacted with studied deliberateness.[125]

But the spectre of rampant Soviet imperialism changed Washington's attitude toward Zia's government in a way that became crucial to aid for the Afghan resistance. On 30 December 1979, Brzezinski publicly reaffirmed a 1959 United States commitment to 'take such appropriate action, including the use of armed force, as may be mutually agreed' in case of Communist aggression against Pakistan—subject to American 'constitutional procedures', which meant congressional approval. On 4 January Carter said, 'Along with other countries, we will provide military equipment, food, and other assistance to help Pakistan defend its independence and its national security against the seriously increased threat it now faces from the north'.[126] Seeking support for his confrontations with India and domestic political enemies as well as with the Soviets, Zia bargained this into a 15 September 1981 agreement for the Reagan administration to provide $3.2 billion worth of help over six years beginning 1 October 1982, half for military aid, half economic aid. A followup six-year US aid programme was worth $4.02 billion.[127]

The Soviet Union had long claimed similar interests and sympathetic attitudes with most Islamic and nonaligned countries, cultivating their support against the West. The

United States now tried to turn the invasion into these countries' opposition to Moscow, but for most of them little outside encouragement was needed. Among Islamic countries, those not directly involved in the Arab-Israeli conflict showed the strongest and most lasting concern over Muslim Afghanistan. On 29 January 1980, 35 Islamic nations meeting in Islamabad strongly condemned 'the Soviet military aggression against the Afghani people', called for a Soviet withdrawal, and said Muslim countries should not recognize the Karmal regime.[128] The Soviet use of officially controlled spokesmen for the USSR's Muslim peoples as propagandists in the Islamic world suffered a setback, and most important Islamic countries boycotted a long-planned international Islamic conference in Tashkent in September 1980. Saudi Arabia played a prominent role in Islamic condemnation, primarily as a backer of Pakistan. Iran protested that the Soviet military move was an act against all Muslims and called for Moscow to 'immediately remove its army from Afghanistan'.[129]

The invasion of a founding member of the nonaligned movement caused distress in that grouping. Cuba feared the increase in Soviet-American tension might endanger it. Dependent on Soviet aid, however, it tried loyally but with little success to use its role as the movement's current chairman to suppress nonaligned criticism of Moscow. Cuba also sought to get Afghanistan and Pakistan to negotiate a political settlement that other countries would guarantee.[130] At a meeting of the nonaligned movement's foreign ministers in New Delhi in February 1981 to consider the worsening international climate, India offered a resolution that did not call for the withdrawal of foreign troops from Afghanistan. Instead, a Pakistani amendment was adopted that expressed 'particular concern' over Afghanistan and 'urgently called' for a withdrawal.[131] What an Indian critic called India's 'sad mix of the cynical and the short-sighted' in favouring the USSR played into Pakistan's hands by making it easier for the United States to ignore Delhi's objections to rearming

Islamabad in the context of aiding the Afghan *mujahideen*. Indian military leaders eventually became concerned as Pakistan rearmed, despite India's continuing military preponderance, while Indian diplomats found themselves isolated in the nonaligned camp. China applauded Carter's tough reaction and improved relations with the United States because of a strengthened common perception of a dangerous Soviet Union.

Although the invasion was generally criticized in Western Europe, there was reluctance to react strongly. In a recession, few nations were eager to restrict trade with the USSR. In 1980 West Germany increased its exports to the Soviet Union by 31 per cent while boycotting the Olympics.[132] There was a musty European echo of 1938 in the unwillingness to relinquish hopes for good East-West relations 'because of a quarrel in a faraway country between people of whom we know nothing'.[133] A United States Congress subcommittee declared that 'the reactions of the allies have been found wanting'. A *mujahideen* leader complained that French journalists who earlier had accused American presidents visiting Paris of criminal actions in Vietnam did not even raise the subject of Afghanistan when Soviet leaders visited.[134]

Reactions came together at the United Nations. The General Assembly passed on 14 January 1980 a resolution calling for the immediate, unconditional, and total withdrawal from Afghanistan of unspecified foreign troops. The vote was an unusually overwhelming defeat for the USSR, 104 to 18, with 18 abstentions.[135] At its next regular session, the General Assembly began what became annual autumn calls for an immediate withdrawal. Even some Communist countries and Communist parties in the West were reluctant to support the Soviet action, despite Moscow's pressure on them.

SOVIET RESPONSES

Responding to widespread hostility, the Soviet Union attempted to justify the invasion, acted defiant, and attempted to reassure world opinion. Justifications hung on the contention that a popular new Afghan regime was under attack primarily from outside forces. A Soviet journal explained the doctrinal reasoning in a way that expanded the 1968 'Brezhnev doctrine' of Moscow's claiming the right to use force to preserve the Soviet bloc.

> The history of the revolutionary movement confirms the moral and political rightness of...rendering material aid including military aid, all the more so when it is a case of blatant, massive outside intervention [by others].... To refuse to use the potential which the socialist countries possess would mean in fact avoiding fulfilling an international duty.... [T]o fail to come to Afghanistan's aid would have meant handing over the Afghan revolution and peoples to be torn to pieces by the class enemies, imperialism, and feudal reaction.[136]

Izvestiya commentator Bovin explained that '[n]on-interference is a good thing, but the principles of international law do not exist in a vacuum.... History and politics cannot always be fit in legal formulas. There are situations when non-intereference is a shame and a betrayal. Such a situation developed in Afghanistan'.[137] A Soviet journal produced what in Soviet Communist ideology was the clinching argument: an appropriate quotation from Lenin. Rather than 'leave the Afghan revolution in the lurch, prey to the counter-revolution', it said, the USSR 'proceeded from the behests of Lenin, who wrote, back in 1915: 'the socialist state would if need be, help the oppressed classes of other countries "using even armed force against the exploiting classes and their states"'.[138] Brezhnev's denunciation of American sanctions warned, 'They will hit back at their initiators, if not today then tomorrow'.[139] *Pravda* reacted to Carter's State of the Union message by saying American leaders 'obviously are unwilling to make their policy in keeping with the United States' real weight in the present-day world'. There is a new correlation of forces, the CPSU organ said, and attempts 'to somehow influence the Soviet Union and its foreign policy...will suffer a fiasco'.[140]

There was little immediate reaction inside the USSR. Andropov's KGB had crushed the dissident movement since it protested the Czechoslovak invasion 11 years earlier. Another reason was the depiction of the invasion as protecting a sensitive Soviet border. Perhaps a third reason was general public apathy, carefully cultivated by the suppression of reports that the Soviet Army had gotten into a real war rather than the civic relief operation described in the media. But Andrey D. Sakharov, the father of the Soviet hydrogen bomb and later dissident winner of the Nobel Peace Prize, publicly denounced the invasion. On 22 January 1980, he was exiled from Moscow by the KGB in an attempt to silence him.[141] And across the USSR, a virtual silence did settle over the Afghanistan venture until years later, when the pain became too great to be ignored.

NOTES

1. Moscow Television, 24 December 1991 and 25 August 1990, in *FBIS/SU*, 27 December 1991 and 27 August 1990, pp. 5 and 38.
2. Karen N. Brutents, quoted by Odd Arne Westad, *CWIHPB*, Nos. 8-9: 21.
3. Interviews with American officials, 1980-81; *FBIS Trends*, 15 November through 12 December 1975, pp. 1ff.
4. Moscow Television, 24 December 1989, in *FBIS/SU*, 28 December 1989, p. 72; Mikhail Gorbachev, *Perestroika: New Thinking for Our Country and the World* (New York, 1987), p. 177; General Valentin I. Varennikov in Sovetskiy Patriot, 27 December 1989, pp. 1-2, in *JPRS-UMA-90-007*, 23 March 1990, p. 123.
5. *Izvestiya*, 1 January 1980, p. 4, in *FBIS/SU*, 4 January 1980, pp. D7-10; Moscow Radio, 22 March 1980, in *FBIS/SU*, 25 March 1980, p. D1; Oliynik, 'Sending of Troops'; Tass from Moscow,

23 April 1980, in *FBIS/SU*, 24 April 1980, p. D1; AFP from Islamabad, 28 September 1980, in *FBIS/SU*, 1 October 1980, p. D6; Kabul Radio, 11 May 1981, in *FBIS/SA*, 12 May 1981, p. C1-4.

6. *Al-Ahali*, 15 January 1986, pp. 6-7, 10, in *FBIS/SA*, 23 January 1986, p. C5; Kabul Radio, 11 January 1980, in *FBIS/ME*, 14 January 1980, p. S5; *Der Spiegel*, 31 March 1980, pp. 139-46, in *FBIS/SA*, 2 April 1980, pp. C1-9.

7. *Rossiyskaya Gazeta*, 3 June 1992, p. 4, in *FBIS-R/CE*, 22 June 1992, pp. 14-19.

8. *Komsomolskaya Pravda*, 21 September 1991, p. 3, in *JPRS-UPA-91-043*, 18 October 1991, pp. 53-4.

9. Interviews with Western officials, 1980; *Kommunist*, March 1980: 75; *Son Atyechestva*, 3 January 1992, pp. 6-7 (emphasis added).

10. Ibid.; *Komsomolskaya Pravda*, 21 September 1991, p. 3, in *JPRS-UPA-91-043*, 18 October 1991, p. 53; *Sovetskiy Voin*, No. 23, 1989: 6-8, in *JPRS-UMA-90-005*, 15 February 1990, p. 51; Pavel Demchenko, 'How It Began in Afghanistan', *Ekho Planety*, November 1989: 28; *Voyenno-Istoricheskiy Zhurnal*, No. 11, 1993, in *JPRS-UMA-94-005*, 9 February 1994, 47.

11. FCO, 'Afghanistan: Soviet Occupation'; *New York Times*, 2 January 1980, p. 1.

12. Ulyanovskiy, 'Afghan Revolution', p. 14; *Literaturnaya Gazeta*, 7 September 1988, p. 14; Moscow Radio, 15 July 1988, in *FBIS/SU*, 19 July 1988, p. 13.

13. *Sovetskiy Voin*, No. 23, 1989: 6-8, in *JPRS-UMA-90-005*, 15 February 1990, p. 52.

14. Moscow Television, 24 December 1991, in *FBIS/SU*, 27 December 1991, p. 5.

15. Remarks, Sergei Tarasenko and Anatoly Chernyaev, Princeton, 27 February 1993.

16. Georgiy A. Arbatov, *The System: An Insider's Life in Soviet Politics* (New York, 1992), p. 197; Moscow Television, 24 December 1989, in *FBIS/SU*, 28 December 1989, p. 73.

17. *Literaturnaya Gazeta*, 15 June and 14 September 1988, pp. 2 and 13-14, in *FBIS/SU*, 16 June and 19 September 1988, pp. 47 and 66-76; *Observer*, 31 May 1992, p. 1; *International Affairs*, No. 7, 1988: 15; *Ogonek*, No. 9, 1989; Moscow Radio, 9 October 1992, in *FBIS/CE*, 23 October 1992, p. 6.

18. *Krasnaya Zvezda*, 17 October 1992, p. 1; Oliynik, 'Sending of Troops'; remarks, Anatoly Chernyaev, Princeton, 27 February 1993; Moscow Radio, 9 October 1992, in *FBIS/CE Supplement*, 23 October 1992, pp. 6-7.

19. Interview with a senior US diplomat then in Moscow, 1981; Moscow Radio, 18 February 1980, in *FBIS/SU*, 19 February 1980, p. R7.
20. *Literaturnaya Gazeta*, 20 September 1989, p. 14, in *JPRS-UMA-89-023*, 4 October 1989, pp. 43-4.
21. *Argumenty i Fakty*, No. 46, 1990: 5-6, in *FBIS/SU*, 26 November 1990, p. 62.
22. *Argumenty i Fakty*, No. 18, 1989; AP from Moscow, 11 March 1989; *New York Times*, 30 March 1988, p. A11; ITAR-Tass from Moscow, 8 October 1992.
23. Interview, Anatoly Chernyaev, Princeton, 27 February 1993.
24. *Washington Post*, 15 November 1992, p. A32; ITAR-Tass from Moscow, 17 October 1992, in *FBIS/CE*, 19 October 1992, p. 4; *Izvestiya*, 23 March 1989; *Pravda*, 2 July 1988 and 24 October 1989, pp. 7 and 2-4, in *FBIS/SU*, 6 July 1988 and 24 October 1989, pp. 16 and 45.
25. *Vechernaya Moskva*, 28 July 1989, p. 4; *Izvestiya*, 26 April 1990, p. 3.
26. Moscow Television, 24 December 1989, in *FBIS/SU*, 28 December 1989, p. 73. Varennikov said, in *Sovetskiy Patriot*, 27 December 1989, pp. 1-2, in *JPRS-UMA-90-007*, 23 March 1990, p. 125, that Article 121 was also violated. It says that when the Supreme Soviet is not sitting its presidium shall declare war 'in the event of the need to fulfill international treaty obligations for mutual defence from aggression'.
27. *Literaturnaya Gazeta*, 20 September 1989, p. 14, in *JPRS-UMA-89-023*, 4 October 1989, p. 43.
28. Tass from Moscow, 23 June 1980, in *FBIS/SU*, 24 June 1980, p. R4; Moscow Radio, 23 February 1981, in *FBIS/SU Supplement*, 24 February 1981, p. 47 (emphasis added).
29. Paris Radio, 18 January 1980, in *FBIS/Daily Report, West Europe*, 21 January 1980, p. K1.
30. Ilya V. Gaiduk, 'The Vietnam War and Soviet-American Relations, 1964-1973: New Russian Evidence', in *CWIHPB*, Nos. 6-7: 254.
31. *New Times*, No. 19, 1989: 21-23; Yevgeniy M. Primakov on Moscow Radio, 1 July 1988, in *FBIS/SU*, 6 July 1988, p. 23; *Argumenty i Fakty*, No. 39, 1989: 4-5, in *FBIS/SU*, 6 October 1989, pp. 16-17.
32. According to a Soviet deputy foreign minister, Andropov and Ustinov browbeat Gromyko into agreeing to an invasion despite universal opinion against it in the foreign ministry; Georgiy M. Kornienko, *Kholodnaia voina: svidetel'stvo ee uchastnika* (Moscow, 1995), Chapter 8.

33. Safronchuk, interview, Austin, Texas, 20 October 1989; Aleksandr A. Bessmertnykh, interview, Princeton, 27 February 1993; *Vechernaya Moskva*, 28 July 1989, p. 4.
34. *New Times*, No. 40, 1991: 39.
35. *Vechernaya Moskva*, 29 July 1989, p. 4.
36. *Literaturnaya Gazeta*, 20 September 1989, p. 14, in *JPRS-UMA-89-023*, 4 October 1989, p. 44.
37. *Sovetskaya Rossiya*, 15 November 1989, p. 4, in *FBIS/SU*, 21 November 1989, p. 103; Ogonek, No. 12, 1989; Moscow Television, 14 July 1991, in *FBIS/SU*, 17 July 1991, p. 45.
38. *Sovetskaya Rossiya*, 14 March 1989.
39. *Pravda*, 15 September 1989, p. 3, in *FBIS/SU*, 21 September 1989, p. 86; *International Affairs*, No. 3, 1990: 88-9.
40. *Komsomolskaya Pravda*, 21 September 1991, p. 3, in *JPRS-UPA-91-043*, 18 October 1991, p. 53.
41. Morozov, 'Our Man, 3', p. 39.
42. Eric Miller, 'Beyond Afghanistan: Changing Soviet Perspectives on Regional Conflicts', Centre for Naval Analyses (Alexandria, Va.), January 1991, p. 3.
43. *Sobesednik*, No. 36, September 1990: 6-7, in *FBIS/SU*, 14 September 1990, p. 39 (emphasis added).
44. *Rabochaya Tribuna*, 13 December 1990, pp. 1-2.
45. *Literaturnaya Gazeta*, 20 September 1989, p. 14, in *JPRS-UMA-89-023*, 4 October 1989, pp. 43-4.
46. Ulyanovskiy, 'Afghan Revolution', p. 15.
47. *Pravda*, 31 December 1979, in *FBIS/SU*, 31 December 1979, pp. D7-10.
48. *Pravda*, 13 January 1980, p. 1, in *FBIS/SU*, 14 January 1980, pp. A1-6; Tass from Moscow, 23 June 1980, in *FBIS/SU*, 24 June 1980, p. R4.
49. *Moskovskiye Novosti*, No. 31, 1990.
50. *Bakinskiy Rabochiy*, 19 December 1980, p. 3, in *FBIS/SU*, 7 January 1981, pp. R1-3.
51. *Moskovskaya Pravda*, 6 February 1980, pp. 2-3, in *FBIS/SU*, 14 February 1980, p. R22.
52. *Pravda*, 12 February 1980, p. 2, in *FBIS/SU*, 15 February 1980, pp. R4-6.
53. Ivan D. Laptev in *Tokyo Shimbun*, 23 March 1988, p. 9.
54. Moscow Television, 24 December 1989, in *FBIS/SU*, 28 December 1989, p. 72.
55. House of Commons, 'Afghanistan', p. 35, also pp. 24-5, 81, 86.
56. US Senate, budget committee, hearings record, 26 February 1980, pp. 5, 10, 37, also 182-3.

57. DIA 'Intelligence Commentary', 7 January 1980, quoted by Steven R. Galster, 'Rivalry and Reconciliation in Afghanistan: What Prospects for the Accords?', *Third World Quarterly*, October 1988: 1520.
58. Beijing Radio, 15 January 1986, in *FBIS/China Report*, 21 January 1986, p. F1.
59. Vance, *Hard Choices*, p. 388.
60. *Vechernaya Moskva*, 28 and 29 July 1989, pp. 4 and 4; Oliynik, 'Sending of Troops'. Pavlovskiy was officially described as being in Afghanistan from 17 August to 22 October (*CWIHPB*, Nos. 8-9: 158); it is unclear where he was until 3 November.
61. Mark Urban, *War in Afghanistan* (London, 1988), pp. 38-9; Oliynik, 'Sending of Troops'; *Sovetskiy Voin*, No. 23, 1989: 6-8, in *JPRS-UMA-90-005*, 15 February 1990, pp. 51-2.
62. Urban, *War*, pp. 39-41; Oliynik, 'Sending of Troops'; *Sovetskaya Rossiya*, 20 December 1989, p. 6, in *JPRS-UMA-90-007*, 23 March 1990, p. 125; *Krasnaya Zvezda*, 24 December 1989, p. 4, in *JPRS-UMA-90-005*, 15 February 1990, p. 55.
63. Chronologies, State Department and House of Commons; *Washington Star*, 13 December 1979, p. A10; Moscow Television, 14 July 1992, in *FBIS/CE*, 17 July 1992, p. 31; *CWIHPB*, Nos. 8-9: 159.
64. *Washington Post*, 7 December 1979, p. A29.
65. Oliynik, 'Sending of Troops'.
66. Chronologies, State Department and House of Commons; Anthony A. Cardoza, 'Soviet Aviation in Afghanistan', *Proceedings*, No. 113/2/1008 (Annapolis), February 1987: 85; *Komsomolskaya Pravda*, 27 December 1990, p. 3, in *JPRS-UMA-91-006*, 4 March 1991, pp. 63-4.
67. *Vechernaya Moskva*, 29 July 1989, p. 4.
68. Ibid.; *Komsomolskaya Pravda*, 27 December 1990, p. 3, in *JPRS-UMA-91-006*, 4 March 1991, p. 64.
69. Oliynik, 'Sending of Troops'.
70. *Sovetskiy Voin*, No. 23, 1989: 6-8, in *JPRS-UMA-90-005*, 15 February 1990, p. 52.
71. Oliynik, 'Sending of Troops'; Lyakhovskiy and Zabrodin, 'Secrets, Part 2'. Some general staff officers recommended sending in six or eight times as many soldiers; Mahmut Gareyev, 'The Afghan Problem: Three Years Without Soviet Troops', *International Affairs*, March 1992: 17.
72. *Ogonek*, 18 March 1989: 6-8.
73. *Sovetskiy Voin*, No. 23, 1989: 6-8, in *JPRS-UMA-90-005*, 15 February 1990, p. 53.
74. *International Life*, No. 8, 1988: 15.

75. *Trud* (Sofia), 15 February 1989, p. 1, in *FBIS/SU*, 16 February 1989, p. 29.
76. *Sovetskiy Voin*, No. 23, 1989: 6-8, in *JPRS-UMA-90-005*, 15 February 1990, p. 53.
77. *Voyenno-Istoricheskiy Zhurnal*, No. 11, 1993, in *JPRS-UMA-94-005*, 9 February 1994, p. 46.
78. For sources, see Bradsher, *Afghanistan and the Soviet Union*, pp. 169-73.
79. *Mlada Fronta*, 1 September 1980, in *FBIS/SA*, 8 September 1980, p. C3; Kabul Radio, 11 January 1980, in *FBIS/ME*, 14 January 1980, p. S3; *Kabul New Times*, 14 January 1980, p. 1; *Current*, 16 February 1980, p. 10; *Der Spiegel*, 31 March 1980, pp. 139-46, in *FBIS/SA*, 2 April 1980, pp. C1-9.
80. *Trud*, 24 October 1991, pp. 1, 4, in *JPRS-UIA-91-027*, 27 November 1991, pp. 55-6; *Son Atyechestva*, 3 January 1992, pp. 6-7, in *Afghanistan Forum*, pp. 21, 3.
81. Tass from Kabul, 28 December 1979, in *FBIS/SU*, 28 December 1979, p. D5.
82. *Patriot*, 7 February 1980, pp. 1, 7, in *FBIS/ME*, 12 February 1980, pp. S1-3; Anwar, *Tragedy*, p. 194.
83. Ibid., pp. 196-7; Kabul Radio, 21 January 1980, in *FBIS/ME*, 22 January 1980, pp. S1-5; Bakhtar from Kabul, 17 February 1981, in *FBIS/SA*, 18 February 1981, pp. C9-15.
84. *Der Spiegel*, 31 March 1980, pp. 139-46, in *FBIS/SA*, 2 April 1980, pp. C1-9; AFP from Kabul, 21 July 1991, in *FBIS/NE*, 24 July 1991, p. 44; *Trud*, 24 October 1991, pp. 1, 4, in *JPRS-UIA-91-027*, 27 November 1991, p. 55.
85. Politburo instructions, in *JSAMES*, Winter 1994: 64-5 (emphasis added).
86. Ibid., p. 74.
87. *Sovetskiy Voin*, No. 23, 1989: 6-8, in *JPRS-UMA-90-005*, 15 February 1990, p. 52. Soviet accounts differ; see also Lyakhovskiy and Zabrodin, 'Secrets, Part 3'.
88. Ibid.; chronologies, State Department and House of Commons.
89. *Washington Post*, 27 December 1979, p. A12.
90. *Voyenno-Istoricheskiy Zhurnal*, No. 11, 1993, in *JPRS-UMA-94-005*, 9 February 1994, p. 48; *Krasnaya Zvezda*, 24 December 1989, p. 4, in *JPRS-UMA-90-005*, 15 February 1990, p. 56; *Sovetskaya Rossiya*, 20 December 1989, p. 6, in *JPRS-UMA-90-007*, 23 March 1990, p. 125.
91. *Krasnaya Zvezda*, 24 December 1989, p. 4, in *JPRS-UMA-90-005*, 15 February 1990, p. 56; *Sovetskaya Rossiya*, 20 December 1989, p. 6, in *JPRS-UMA-90-007*, 23 March 1990, p. 125.

92. Urban, *War*, p. 46; *Sovetskiy Patriot*, 27 December 1989, pp. 1-2, in *JPRS-UMA-90-007*, 23 March 1990, p. 127; *Izvestiya*, 14 November 1989, p. 6 (which says 64 Soviet servicemen and 112 Afghans died on 3 November 1982 when a collision caused vehicles to get stuck in the Salang tunnel and fill it with carbon monoxide).

93. BBC, 1 January 1980, in *FBIS/ME*, 2 January 1980, pp. S11-12; *Quotidien de Paris*, 1 October 1984.

94. Kabul Radio, 20 December 1979, in *FBIS/ME*, 21 December 1979, pp. S1-2; FCO, 'Afghanistan: Soviet Occupation'; BBC, 1 January 1980, in *FBIS/ME*, 2 January 1980, p. S11.

95. Moscow Radio, 16 January 1980, in *FBIS/SU*, 17 January 1980, p. D8.

96. *Argumenty i Fakty*, No. 44, 1990: 2, in *FBIS/SU*, 8 November 1990, p. 14.

97. Kabul Radio, 24 and 27 December 1979, in *FBIS/ME*, 27 and 28 December 1979, pp. S1 and S1.

98. Accounts vary, some saying a cook, some a doctor, tried to poison Amin; *Argumenty i Fakty*, No. 44, 1990: 2, in *FBIS/SU*, 8 November 1990, p. 14; *Komsomolskaya Pravda*, 21 September 1991, p. 3, in *JPRS-UPA-91-043*, 18 October 1991, p. 54; Anwar, *Tragedy*, pp. 187-8; Nayar, *Report*, p. 6; *Time*, 22 November 1982, p. 34.

99. *Quotidien de Paris*, 1 October 1984; Anwar, *Tragedy*, p. 190.

100. FCO, 'Chronology of Events Since April 1978', 1980; *Sovetskiy Voin*, No. 23, 1989: 6-8, in *JPRS-UMA-90-005*, 15 February 1990, p. 53; *Rossiyskaya Gazeta*, 3 June 1992, p. 4, in *FBIS-R/CE*, 22 June 1992, p. 19; Moscow Television, 22 December 1992.

101. US State Department, cable 333161, 28 December 1979; *Quotidien de Paris*, 1 October 1984; *Moscow News*, No. 31, 1990: 7.

102. Tass, ostensibly from Kabul, 27 December 1979, in *FBIS/SU*, 28 December 1979, pp. D1-2; AFP from Tehran, 27 December 1979, in *FBIS/ME*, 28 December 1979, pp. S2-4.

103. Kabul Radio, 27 December 1979 (GMT time), in *FBIS/ME*, 28 December 1979, pp. S1-2.

104. Sources interviewed in 1980. However, Anwar, *Tragedy*, p. 190, describes a fairly short fight, and Moscow Television, 22 December 1992, said '[t]he palace was seized in 40 minutes'. For criticism of contradictory accounts, see *Moskovskaya Pravda*, 13 February 1993, p. 7, in *FBIS-R/CE*, 26 March 1993, p. 9.

105. *Sovetskiy Voin*, No. 23, 1989: 6-8, in *JPRS-UMA-90-005*, 15 February 1990, p. 53; *Rossiyskaya Gazeta*, 3 June 1992, p. 4, in *FBIS-R/CE*, 22 June 1992.

106. Ibid.; *Time*, 22 November 1982, p. 34; *Komsomolskaya Pravda*, 21 September 1991, p. 3, in *JPRS-UPA-91-043*, 18 October 1991, p. 54.

107. Ibid.; *Argumenty i Fakty*, No. 44, 1990, p. 2, in *FBIS/SU*, 8 November 1990, p. 14; *Rossiyskaya Gazeta*, 3 June 1992, p. 4, in *FBIS-R/CE*, 22 June 1992, p. 19; Moscow Television, 22 December 1992; Lyakhovskiy and Zabrodin, 'Secrets, Part 3'; *Kommersant-Daily*, 6 July 1996, p. 20. These accounts differ.

108. Anwar, *Tragedy*, p. 190; *New Times*, No. 47, 1990: 15; *SSHA: Ekonomika, Politika, Ideologiya*, July 1989: 44-9, in *JPRS-USA-89-014*, 29 November 1989, p. 13; *Izvestiya*, 5 May 1989, p. 5, in *FBIS/SU*, 10 May 1989, p. 33.

109. *Der Spiegel*, 31 March 1980, pp. 139-46, in *FBIS/SA*, 2 April 1980, pp. C1-9 (emphasis added). Emine Engin, *The Revolution in Afghanistan* (n.p. [Istanbul?], 1982), p. 101, says Amin 'was killed together with 97 comrades' but gives no source; this curious book seems more ideological than factual.

110. Interviews with diplomats, 1980-81. One mystery was the unusually curt obituary in *Pravda* on 3 January 1980 for a Soviet first deputy minister of the interior, Lt.-Gen. Viktor S. Paputin, who died 28 December 1979. A CPSU bureaucrat who had been promoted to a senior policeman's position, he had supervised training of Afghan police. He arrived in Kabul about 29 November for apparently routine meetings, including one with Amin on 2 December, and flew back to Moscow on 13 December 'after a series of friendly talks'. His death stimulated Moscow rumors that he had been involved in the invasion or even the assault on Tajbeg palace, that he had killed himself for failure to arrange the quiet removal of Amin before the invasion, or that he was under pressure from Brezhnev's corrupt (and later imprisoned) son-in-law, Yuri M. Churbanov, who became a first deputy interior minister two months after Paputin died. Paputin was later acknowledged to have committed suicide, but it remained 'difficult to judge whether this action...was dictated by his trip to Kabul or by something else'; *Pravda*, 3 January 1980, p. 6, in *FBIS/SU*, 9 January 1980, p. R7; *Pravda*, 15 December 1989, p. 8; *Radio Liberty Research*, RL62/80, 1980; Kabul Radio, 30 November, 2 and 13 December 1979, in *FBIS/ME*, 3 and 14 December 1979, pp. S1-2 and S1-2; *Vechernaya Moskva*, 29 July 1989, p. 4; US Embassy Moscow, cables 94 and 1395, 3 and 25 January 1980.

111. *Pravda*, 31 December 1979, in *FBIS/SU*, 31 December 1979, pp. D7-10 (emphasis added).

112. *SSHA: Ekonomika, Politika, Ideologiya*, July 1989: 44-9, in *JPRS-USA-89-014*, 29 November 1989, p. 13.

113. Moscow Radio, 26 Dec 1989, in *FBIS/SU*, 27 December 1989, p. 11; Moscow Radio, 22 June 1990; Kabul Radio, 27 June 1990, in *FBIS/NE*, 3 July 1990, p. 45.

114. *Presidential Documents* 16 (14 January 80): 41; Carter, *Keeping Faith*, p. 472; *New York Times*, 1 January 1980, p. A4.

115. *Der Spiegel*, 31 March 1980, pp. 139-46, in *FBIS/SA*, 2 April 1980, p. C5; US Congress, House Permanent Select Committee on Intelligence, 'Soviet Active Measures' (13 July 82); *Komsomolskaya Pravda*, 21 September 1991, p. 3, in *JPRS-UPA-91-043*, 18 October 1991, p. 54; Morozov, 'KGB and the Afghan Leaders', p. 36.

116. Vance, *Hard Choices*, p. 389; Carter, *Keeping Faith*, p. 473.

117. Tass from Moscow, 6 January 1980, in *FBIS/SU*, 7 January 1980, pp. A1-4; *FBIS Trends*, 16 January 1980, p. 2.

118. US Congress, House subcommittee on Europe and the Middle East, 'NATO After Afghanistan' (1980), p. 7.

119. *Presidential Documents* 16 (28 January 80):197.

120. *Presidential Documents* 16 (14 January 80): 41; Brzezinski, *Power and Principle*, p. 431.

121. CRS, 'Afghanistan: Soviet Invasion', pp. 28-9; Carter, *Keeping Faith*, pp. 474-7.

122. *Pravda*, 13 January 1980, p. 1, in *FBIS/SU*, 14 January 1980, pp. A1-8.

123. Eduard Shevardnadze, *The Future Belongs to Freedom* (New York, 1991), pp. 80-81.

124. FCO, 'Afghanistan: Response to Soviet Intervention' (1980), pp. 1-2.

125. Robert G. Wirsing, 'Pakistan and the War in Afghanistan', *Asian Affairs*, Summer 1987; 57-75; Thomas Perry Thornton, 'Between the Stools?: U. S. Policy Towards Pakistan During the Carter Administration', *Asian Survey*, October 1982; 959-77.

126. 'Issues and Answers,' ABC News, 30 Dec 1979; *Presidential Documents* 16 (14 January 80): 27.

127. *Washington Post*, 16 September 1981, p. A7; Thomas P. Thornton, 'The New Phase in U. S.-Pakistani Relations', *Foreign Affairs*, Summer 1989: 151.

128. Text in Shahi, *Pakistan's Security*, pp. 327-30.

129. FCO, 'Afghanistan: Response to Soviet Intervention'.

130. Prensa Latina from Havana, 22 April 1993; FCO, 'Cuban Setbacks in the Non-Aligned Movement' (1980); CPSU politburo documents in *CWIHPB*, Nos. 8-9: 167-70.

131. AFP from New Delhi, 13 February 1981, in *FBIS/SA*, 17 February 1981, pp. A16-17.

132. *New York Times*, 12 Dec 1980, p. A11; House of Commons, 'Afghanistan', p. 13.
133. British Prime Minister Neville Chamberlain, 27 September 1938, about a crisis with Germany over Czechoslovakia, quoted in Winston S. Churchill, *The Second World War: The Gathering Storm* (Boston, 1948), p. 315.
134. US Congress, House subcommittee on Europe and the Middle East, 'NATO After Afghanistan', p. 1; *Nouvelles d'Afghanistan*, June 88: 9-10.
135. FCO, 'Afghanistan: Chronology'; text, Shahi, *Pakistan's Security*, pp. 334-6.
136. *Novoye Vremya*, 18 January 1980, pp. 8-10, in *FBIS/SU*, 23 January 1980, pp. BB1-5.
137. *Moscow News Weekly*, No. 16, 1980: 7.
138. *New Times*, No. 17, 1980: 23.
139. *Pravda*, 13 January 1980, p. 1, in *FBIS/SU*, 14 January 1980, pp. A1-8.
140. *Pravda*, 29 January 1980, p. 1, in *FBIS/SU*, 29 January 1980, pp. A1-5.
141. *Ogonek*, No. 8 (19 February 89): 30-31, in *JPRS-UPA-89-032*, 19 May 1989, pp. 33-8; Moscow Television, 2 June 1989, in *FBIS/SU*, 5 June 1989, p. 20.

CHAPTER 4

SITTING ON BAYONETS

Soviet leaders hoped their army's presence in Afghanistan would calm the country, producing public acceptance of a PDPA regime; but instead it had opposite effects. Bovin wrote later in *Izvestiya* that 'foreign interference engendered patriotism; the arrival of "infidels" set religious intolerance in motion'. Najibullah eventually conceded that, 'when Soviet contingents were here, the people did not sympathize with the government'.[1] Civil war turned into a national war against foreign invaders and their local puppets. Years of confused Soviet searching for Afghan policy and personnel adaptations that might still the uproar only proved the old adage of military rule: 'You can do a lot of things with bayonets, but you can't sit on them.'

The Afghan army and people were initially stunned by the bloody seizure of control by Soviet troops who had entered the country unopposed. Aside from scattered fighting beginning 27 December, the army's spreading reaction was desertion. By the end of 1980 it had dwindled, from a strength before the 1978 *coup* of some 100 000 men, to about 30 000, according to Western intelligence estimates, and only 10 000 to 15 000 of those were trusted by the Soviets to be effective fighters. Most deserters took their weapons. By late summer 1980 Soviet advisers with the remaining Afghan units withdrew from their possession anti-tank and anti-aircraft weapons to prevent their being used against Soviet forces.[2]

Public demonstrations against Soviet occupation began in Qandahar on 31 December and spread to a five-day strike in

Kabul in late February 1980. Leaflets quoted the Quran on not accepting orders from infidels. A demonstration by Kabul students on the second anniversary of the Saur *coup* was met with gunfire that 'left 156 boys and girls killed and hundreds of civilians wounded', a resistance source said. The regime said 620 persons were arrested—at least 20 of them reportedly grammar school children. Those released later told of being beaten and tortured with electrical devices. Both the February and April demonstrations in Kabul were said to have been organized by the Maoist Shola.[3] The people of Herat marked the first anniversary of their March 1979 uprising with demonstrations, and the city was reported out of Soviet control in an upsurge of urban guerrilla warfare in early August and again later. Agitation was also reported from Qandahar, Jalalabad, and Shindand.[4]

KARMAL'S APPEALS

Moscow hoped to rally the Afghan people behind Karmal, the old spellbinding orator of the constitutional period a decade earlier. Karmal's speeches on Kabul Radio from 28 December through the celebrations on 1 January of the fifteenth anniversary of the PDPA's founding—apparently taped elsewhere, before he arrived in the capital—emphasized moderation. One theme was restoring freedoms lost under Amin, 'this bloodthirsty spy of US imperialism, oppressor, and dictator'. Karmal said the new government 'will safeguard freedom and genuine inviolability of the person, freedom...[and] a total amnesty...for political prisoners, genuine democracy,...[and] favorable and safe conditions for the return of' refugees.[5]

Another theme was a broad-based government. 'Our immediate task...is not the introduction of socialism,' Karmal declared. Instead, the regime will try to strengthen and develop 'the progressive social and political foundations' of the government. '... [A] broad front will be created of all the national and democratic forces under the leadership of the [PDPA].... All democratic freedoms will be guaranteed....'[6] A third theme was 'a peaceful foreign policy, a policy of positive and active neutrality'. Karmal said Kabul had no differences with Tehran, and he called 'for the elimination of all differences with the Pakistani leaders' but then, contradictorily, reiterated Afghan calls for self-determination for Pakistan's Pushtun and Baloch ethnic groups. He advocated 'disinterested friendship' with China. He added that, so long as there was outside interference, '[we] shall ask for further assistance from the USSR and...from Vietnam, victorious Cuba, Ethiopia, Angola, and the victorious Palestinian Arab people and others'.[7]

Prisoner Releases

Admitting that '[r]evolutionary rules and legality [had been] trampled upon', the regime began releasing survivors of political imprisonment under Taraki and Amin. The first group included Keshtmand, Rafi, Qadir, Taraki's widow, and Sarwari's wife, as well as other PDPA members, religious leaders, and other, non-political figures.[8] By mid-January the government claimed to have freed 10 000 persons from Pul-i-Charki prison, and Karmal said later that 15 000 persons had been freed nationwide 'in the first few hours' of his takeover. At the same time, different persons were imprisoned, including Shah Wali and 17 others associated with Amin.[9] However, the United States State Department said, '[t]he number actually released was far smaller' than 10 000 and included common criminals, while Amnesty International said 'independent sources in Kabul estimated that between 3000 and 4000 prisoners had been released from...Pul-i-Charki...'. There were angry, sometimes violent scenes as relatives learned that prisoners had been killed or were still being held. As mentioned earlier, the Najibullah regime made public in 1989 a list of 11 000 political prisoners who it said had been killed in Taraki's and Amin's times.[10]

SECOND PHASE OF THE REVOLUTION

Karmal's conciliatory rhetoric ushered in what was heralded as 'the new or second phase of the Saur revolution'.[11] The differences were to be the modification of Taraki's over-simplified Marxism into an ideology less hostile to the Afghan people's Islamic beliefs, spreading a properly Leninist view through education, and creation of governmental and public organizations to mobilize and control the uneducated masses.

Karmal faced several problems in staffing his new regime. Old personal rivalries between PDPA faction members, freshly embittered by the murder of Amin, limited cabinet collegiality. The scarcity of capable, experienced people 'who were loyal to the command of the revolution'[12] was another problem. A third was the reluctance of non-party people to serve foreign rulers. As a result, the regime's roster seemed to be a Soviet-dictated compromise. Karmal's first deputy premier was the senior surviving Khalqi, Sarwari. The second deputy premier in charge of economic planning was a Parchami, Keshtmand, who reportedly had been personally tortured by Sarwari after being arrested for the alleged 'Eid plot' in 1978, while another Parchami told of attending PDPA meetings with a Khalqi who had torn out his fingernails.[13] Gulabzoy, the second-ranked Khalqi, was named interior minister with control of militia forces and the regular police; but the politically more sensitive secret police were put under a Parchami, Najibullah. The new foreign minister, Shah Mohammad Dost, was a career diplomat suspected of having been recruited by the Soviets years earlier while serving in the Afghan embassy in Washington.[14] Rafi became defence minister, Watanjar minister of communications, and Mazdooryar transportation and tourism minister. Qadir got a sinecure on the presidium of the revolutionary council, while Nur got a more meaningful seat on the reconstituted PDPA politburo. Politburo seats also went to Ziray, the slippery politician known as 'Quicksilver' who was the only person to serve in the party's leadership under Taraki, Amin, Karmal, and Najibullah, and to Panjshiri who, one Soviet account suggests, had been a party to Moscow's plan to poison Amin.[15]

An 11 January 1980 decision to include non-party people in the revolutionary council was not carried out, but the cabinet included three former officials under Daoud. One was Jallalar, who had long been suspected of being a Soviet agent.[16] Except for Karmal's mistress, Ratebzad, who became education minister as well as a politburo member, all the senior people were men. While the Communists improved the social status of women, particularly in Kabul, they did little to practice real equality. Najibullah said in 1987 that women 'virtually do not exist in the leadership or middle circles' of the PDPA, their role in public life was 'still trivial', and even though 43 per cent of personnel in education were women 'there are no women in leading [educational] positions'.[17]

SOVIET ADVISERS IN CHARGE

By mid-1980, Soviet advisers were estimated to number 6000 to 8000, and a 1987 estimate was 9000 in the Afghan civilian bureaucracy alone.[18] 'Karmal listens very attentively to the advice of our comrades', Ponomarev told the CPSU politburo on 17 January 1980.[19] But Karmal later expressed a different perspective. Soviet 'advisers were everywhere.... I was not a leader of a sovereign state. It was an occupied state where [the Soviets] in fact ruled'.[20] A CPSU politburo meeting on 13 November 1986 implicitly confirmed this by discussing several points on which the Afghan leadership could be allowed to make its own decisions.[21]

PDPA documents were freely changed by Soviet advisers before being circulated, assignments and promotions were decided by the Soviets, foreign policy statements were written by them, and Soviet journalists ran Afghan media, with some articles written in Moscow and sent to Kabul for translation.[22] In 1987, a Soviet Army lieutenant counter-manded an order from the Afghan interior minister in front of Western diplomats, and members of an Afghan delegation to a World Bank conference told friends they had to follow the orders of their Soviet advisers.[23]

Among Soviet advisers, KGB personnel were dominant. 'Hundreds of KGB officers', including more than ten generals, served as advisers, according to a Soviet specialist. '[A]lmost all affairs...were handled by V. A. Kryuchkov's men, and by him personally.' The KGB boss in Kabul, *rezident* Vilior Osadchy, gave instructions directly to Karmal. KGB officials even rehearsed Najibullah on how to answer journalists' questions and sometimes put orders to him in writing.[24] Najibullah later described cabinet meetings in the early 1980s. Each minister had a Soviet adviser. 'As the conference goes on the debate gets higher and the advisers move closer to the table, while the Afghans move away, and finally the Soviets are left to quarrel among themselves.' He added, the 'large number of advisers...caused...a spirit of stagnation, laziness, irresponsibility, and corruption inside the party'.[25]

A Soviet ambassador to Kabul, Yuliy M. Vorontsov, admitted later, 'We were always doing things for them our way, expecting them to just stand by and watch'. A Soviet general, Boris V. Gromov, said Afghan officials 'mainly adopted a parasitic position. Through their entire demeanor and behavior the Afghan leaders let us understand what we should all do for them'. General Varennikov complained of Afghan incompetence and indifference, saying 'some advisers often found it easier to do things themselves than to get their Afghan colleagues to fulfil the task set'.[26]

But Varennikov also noted that many advisers 'were disastrously lacking in knowledge of oriental affairs'. Criticizing the Brezhnev era, he added, 'The dogmatism of the period of stagnation could not but affect their thinking and actions'.[27] A Soviet writer said advisers were 'not always carefully select[ed] and train[ed] with a view to specific features of [Afghanistan], its customs, culture, and the people's lifestyle. Sometimes our specialists unthinkingly endeavor[ed] to transfer artificially to Afghan soil Soviet experience...'. Many spent years leading 'an isolated life inside the Soviet colony' without studying 'the local languages, history, and customs...'.[28] Najibullah agreed: 'The advisers' level of competence was...not always up to the requirements of the situation.' This reportedly 'shattered [the] idealism' of junior PDPA members.[29]

A Soviet reporter summed up the situation in early 1989 with the remark that '[n]ot everyone wants to admit it, but the fact that the war has gone badly is not Afghanistan's fault. They were carrying out our policies'.[30] Karmal emphasized this point when asked in 1982, 'Do you disagree with the Soviet Union on any matter of policy or principle?' 'Not at all', he dutifully replied.[31] And in 1987 Najibullah was asked, 'Are there any differences between the USSR and Afghanistan on how to resolve the Afghan problem?' 'No, none whatsoever', he said. 'There is complete unanimity of views between us.'[32]

KARMAL'S FAILURE

Soviet officials soon found that, rather than rallying support, Karmal 'evoke[d] profound hatred in many people due to the role he played in December 1979'.[33] By February 1980 the angry public demonstrations and the increase of *mujahideen* opposition made the Soviets consider trying to drop him in a deal to win foreign acceptance of the regime.[34] Varennikov complained later that Karmal 'always listened carefully to the proposals that were put to him' but did nothing. 'Karmal did not deserve trust from his own comrades in arms, from the people, or from our advisers'. He did not learn from his blunders, and 'he did not know how to work, or he did not consider it necessary to do so'.[35]

Karmal quickly developed severe self doubt, began drinking heavily, and looked shaky at his few public appearances. He denied reports of a suicide attempt but enigmatically said later that he tried twice 'to resign but could not as the Afghan leadership had fled the country'.[36] Moscow decided there was no alternative leader who might unify the country and escape the stigma of fronting for hated foreigners. The public signal that the Soviets had decided to stick with Karmal was his meeting with top leaders in the Kremlin on 16 October 1980. Admitting in his Moscow speeches having made mistakes, and abjectly praising Brezhnev, Karmal seemed intent on proving that he had learned his lesson and would loyally do better in the future. His remarks on return home indicated that he had been sharply lectured on the need to overcome his regime's shortcomings.[37]

By the spring of 1980 the Soviets had begun trying to stabilize a situation that was proving politically, economically, and militarily more complex and costly than they had expected. Military changes are discussed in Chapter 6. Safronchuk, who had been called home in early December 1979 because there were no prospects of improving Amin's foreign relations, was sent back to Kabul in late March 1980 with orders to start international negotiations to settle the conflict.[38] His work is discussed in Chapter 8.

The third effort was to institutionalize the PDPA and government. Both had worked irregularly without public explanations. The new PDPA central committee, at its first meeting in April, adopted party by-laws, issued 'theses' that critiqued mistakes since April 1978, and laid out a temporary party programme.[39] The revolutionary council followed up by issuing without discussion a 6000-word 'Basic Principles of the Democratic Republic of Afghanistan' as a temporary constitution, the first since Daoud's because Amin's was never completed. This proclaimed the government to be 'the reflection of the ideals and defender of the interests of the toilers and all the people of the country...'. Without mentioning 'socialism' or 'Marxism', but imitating what Article 6 of the 1977 Soviet constitution said about the CPSU, it declared the PDPA to be 'the leading and guiding force of the society and state'—thus legalizing party dictatorship. While claiming nonalignment, it said Afghanistan 'will broaden and strengthen its all-round traditions, friendship, and cooperation with the USSR...'.[40]

The CPSU subsidized the expansion of the PDPA in an effort to have its members penetrate every aspect of Afghan life, to steer every kind of organization with orders transmitted by party insiders, on the Soviet pattern. Government employees, professionals, and others were coerced to join the PDPA.[41] Some who refused to join were fired from such government jobs as teaching, and members were paid up to four times as much as others.[42] Premium pay, presumably, was linked to government subsidies for the PDPA in the way that the Soviet state secretly subsidized the CPSU.

PDPA Membership Claims

Inconsistent claims of growing PDPA membership were issued regularly as political assertions of public acceptance, hence legitimacy. The party, which variously claimed 15 000 or 18 000 members in April 1978 but probably had only 4000 or so, dwindled in the internecine strife after that.[43] By early 1982, 60 000 members were claimed, only 20 per cent of them 'workers and peasants'.[44] By late 1984 the claim was 120 000, and it continued to rise steadily to a peak of 205 000 members in 1988, of whom more than 150 000 were in the armed forces. Then claims began to decline. Najibullah said in June 1990 there were 'more than 173 000 members' and 'almost 40 000' had been killed.[45] Foreign estimates of the number of hard-core PDPA activists ranged from 3000 to 15 000.

In early 1980 the PDPA had begun trying to leaven its bourgeois, bureaucratic membership with some of the workers and peasants that it claimed to represent. Karmal conceded in 1981 that the party had few of them.[46] After a 1986 claim that 34 per cent of party members were 'workers, peasants, and craftsmen', the emphasis swung to the proportion of members 'defending the country', which Najibullah put at 65 per cent. By 1988 more than 60 per cent of all military personnel including 75 per cent of the officers were reported to be PDPA members.[47]

The strong military element meant a youthful party profile. The party founded a Democratic Youth Organization of Afghanistan (DYOA) as a junior auxiliary modelled after the CPSU's Young Communist League, or Komsomol.[48] The PDPA's youth and inexperience meant a need for training in the Soviet way of running a country through a hierarchically organized party. A PDPA Institute of Social Sciences was created just four days after the Soviet invasion, to train members according to 'behests of great Lenin', Najibullah said.[49] Moscow also summoned some Afghan leaders to the USSR for special training. None the less, Najibullah complained in 1987 that some senior officials had insufficient professional and political qualifications.[50]

Party Dictatorship

Afghans proved apt pupils of Lenin's dictatorial system as administered for them by Soviet advisers. 'Due to known reasons', Najibullah said in 1987 without explaining them, 'electing secretaries of the party organizations, party committees, and the activists of social organizations has not yet taken place in our party'. Top-down control by designating those in charge helped explain his complaint that local party units were 'passive and...unable to assume responsibility for their region and villages'.[51] Najibullah admitted in 1990 that meetings of the PDPA central committee, which in theory made basic decisions, were scripted in advance. He implied that this was done by Soviet advisers.[52]

Karmal claimed in 1985, 'Party organizations have been created and are active in all provinces, cities, in the majority of districts and subdistricts,...and in *most* villages'. Soviet reports of the speech changed this to a more realistic 'in *many* villages'.[53] Karmal backed away from his claim two months later, admitting the PDPA network in villages 'has remained weak.... It is necessary...to creat[e] a broad network of primary organizations where the workers live, particularly in the villages'. But almost four years later PDPA organizations existed in only 900 of Afghanistan's approximately 15 000 villages.[54] Noting 'the complexity' of working among villagers, Najibullah said in 1988, 'Party members have not gone out resolutely into the countryside but [have] hidden themselves in' towns.[55] The CPSU politburo was told in 1986 that the population under Afghan government control numbered only three million in towns and two million in the countryside.[56]

PARCHAMI-KHALQI INFIGHTING

Efforts to build up and improve the PDPA were corroded by endemic hostility between Parchamis and Khalqis. The Taraki-Amin vendetta against Parcham and then Karmal's revenge on Khalq caused 'a weakening of the party (and correspondingly of state organs and the army), a decline in its influence, and the alienation of the masses from the new power', Bovin wrote.[57] Under Karmal 'the PDPA was being torn apart by violent and irreconcilable internal discord', one Soviet journal said.[58] Another said that Soviet advisers, 'who often did not understand the complicated social and tribal structure...and the basic alignment of political forces', were unable to control factionalism. Worse, they 'fell under the influence of their own "advisers", becoming even more ardent Khalqists or Parchamists than Afghans themselves'.[59] Intensely nationalistic Khalqis resented not only their loss of power but also Parchami dependence on the Soviets. Violent clashes between the factions were reported by April 1980.[60] By that summer many assassinations were being attributed to factional rivalry rather than to the *mujahideen*, and there were reports that Khalqis who did not desert to the guerrillas helped them from inside the regime.[61]

Cracking down, the regime announced in June the execution of Amin's brother Abdullah and nephew Assadullah, those involved in murdering Taraki, former Khalqi ministers of communications, border affairs, and planning, and others.[62] Thousands of other Khalqis were held in Pul-i-Charki prison, where Soviet troops reinforced Afghan guards and Soviet advisers were present during interrogations under torture.[63] The senior surviving Khalqi, Sarwari, flew to Moscow in June 1980 ostensibly for medical treatment but, according to some accounts, because Karmal demanded that the Soviets remove him. Without returning to Kabul, he arrived on 15 August in Ulan Bator, banished to the ambassadorship to Mongolia. In June 1981 he was stripped of his PDPA politburo seat and in July 1986 he lost his central committee membership.[64] The next most senior Khalqi, Gulabzoy, lost much of his power as interior minister in a government reorganization in July 1980 that gave Parchamis better control over personnel matters.[65]

But what Moscow Radio called a 'blood feud' between the two factions continued. Major *coup* plots by Khalqi military officers were reported in June, July, and October 1980, February 1981, and later, but thwarted by what apparently was primarily Soviet action.[66] Gunfights in the presidential palace were reported in June 1981 and September 1985; and in June 1983, factional fighting raged for three days in the army's 25th Division. Some of the many other clashes arose because the member of one faction who 'took a ministerial post or was appointed the commander of a[n army] division...[began] expelling the members of the [other] feuding group', a Soviet journal said.[67] Ziray said factionalism caused 'the assassination of Parchamis and Khalqis', and a Soviet magazine said it 'includ[ed] the physical elimination of political rivals'.[68]

Plans in early 1982 to hold the PDPA's first congress since the founding one in 1965 were changed because of violence over delegate selection and apparent Parchami fears that Khalqis might outvote them in choosing a new leadership. The meeting on 14 and 15 March 1982 was instead turned into a party conference, which meant no leadership elections were required.[69] Najibullah later warned 'that defiance of unity is treachery against our friendship with the Soviet Union...'. He said Khalqi-Parchami infighting had 'damaged our party to the same degree as our declared enemies have done'.[70]

Both factions developed sub-factions. Some Khalqis defended Amin's actions, while others denounced him, and tension existed between followers of Sarwari and Gulabzoy. Parcham was even more fractured. Karmal and Keshtmand were considered rivals, the latter drawing on support from his Hazara Shi'ite community. On 11 June 1981 Keshtmand was appointed chairman of the council of ministers, or prime minister, without any announcement of Karmal's relinquishing the post.[71] After Najibullah replaced Karmal as PDPA leader in 1986, a clique of Karmal's followers began what were denounced as 'anti-party activities' against Najibullah.[72]

PDPA WEAKNESSES

The Afghan government was also weakened by incompetence and corruption. Many officials were more interested in getting rich than serving the masses on whose behalf they claimed to rule. '...[T]he revolution ended for some of them on the day they received everything from the revolution—position and personal comfort', Najibullah noted.[73] The shortage of capable people willing to work for a puppet regime meant that loyalty took precedence over ability and honesty. Another problem was that, taking advantage of wartime laxity, many Soviet advisers set bad examples by illegal transactions so they could take home Western consumer goods that continued to flow into Afghanistan throughout the war. A third problem was that in Afghan society a person's first duty is to his relatives and clansmen, not to some abstract party or government. Nepotism is traditional, even honourable. Karmal opposed centuries-old practices when he called on the PDPA in 1985 to 'fight seriously against...tribal and local family issues, nepotism, personal favouritism,...and factionalism'.[74] Neither he, with his mistress and his half-brother in the Parchami leadership, nor his intermarried senior comrades practised what they preached.

Throughout the 1980s, Afghan leaders catalogued and castigated official shortcomings, calling for reform. Year after year the criticisms were almost the same—to no effect. Karmal said in April 1980 that it was necessary to eliminate 'lawlessness, disobedience, embezzlement, bureaucracy, pilferage of public property, chauvinism, and so forth'.[75] After the stiff lecture from Soviet leaders in Moscow in October 1980, he told party activists that 'previous service or relationships...[or] an instance of heroism or other service' were no longer enough. They would now be judged on their 'struggle against the counter-revolution...[and] on the successful fulfillment of the duties which the party puts forward in the political, economic, and social fields'. All party and government officials would also be judged by their 'eternal friendship and solidarity with' the CPSU, Karmal added.[76]

Nothing changed, nothing was done. A foreign correspondent found in late 1984 that 'a "new class" of careerists and profiteers has emerged...[and] an evil spirit of totalitarian temptation haunts' Kabul.[77] After repetitious scoldings of the party, Karmal said in August 1985, 'We should launch an irreconcilable struggle against misappropriation, corruption, embezzlement, wasteful expenditure, bribery, and oppression', but he did not explain why no campaign had been launched earlier.[78] In his last major published speech as PDPA general secretary, Karmal indicated in April 1986 that nothing had changed in 'corruption, giving and taking bribes, [and] embezzlement...'.[79]

When Najibullah became general secretary, he quickly echoed the same complaints. Officials were abandoning village jobs to live in cities, and they were sheltering their sons from military service, he noted. Although he claimed in June 1987, 'We have started a serious struggle against embezzlement and bribe taking...',[80] little changed. Limited steps to discipline malefactors usually just meant shifting them to new jobs, there to continue their bad practices.[81] In May 1990 the problem was still 'embezzlement, misuse and plundering of public properties,...trafficking and abuse of drugs,...bribe-taking,...economic sabotage, deceiving of youths,...blackmailing and intimidation', and many other offences.[82] A PDPA politburo member told a Soviet newspaper in June 1990, 'The PDPA leaders include thieves and bribe-takers, and there were plenty of abuses', but the party still lacked 'the determination to deal with' them.[83]

For years Moscow media censored mention of PDPA factional fighting, made only vague references to other regime problems, and even published rosy opposites of truths that Afghan leaders were telling their own people. After Karmal was replaced by Najibullah, however, Soviet media began quoting the latter's strictures. At first this just indicated a new leaf had been turned. But, as Moscow began to back out of its Afghan quagmire, it became a way of letting the Afghans damn themselves as not deserving continuing Soviet military support. Later Moscow media added their own harsh judgements to justify the withdrawal of the Soviet Army.

APPEALING TO THE MASSES

Soviet advisers resumed with Karmal the efforts they had begun with Taraki to put a wider foundation under the narrow ruling clique in an effort to win public support for the regime. This was part of the recommendations that the CPSU politburo commission made on 27 January 1980, along with seeking PDPA unity, appealing to Afghan Muslim clergy, and 'setting up of normal economic life...'.[84] Karmal told Kremlin leaders in October 1980 that party and state leaders were organizing meetings of various social, economic, ethnic, tribal, and religious groupings 'to support the party and government...'.[85] Trade unions were created that the PDPA politburo said had the first task of explaining official policies to workers and organizing them to defend the revolution, with only the final task listed as 'the defence of workers' interests and rights'.[86] Imitating Soviet practice, the PDPA affiliate Democratic Youth Organization of Afghanistan (DYOA) established a Young Pioneers organization to indoctrinate schoolchildren.[87] However, Karmal complained in November 1984 that the DYOA was failing to indoctrinate young people properly, so that they were 'falling prey to the propaganda and deeds of the enemy', and the politburo found in 1988 that the DYOA's 'patriotic military training' was weak.[88] Organizations for artists, journalists, and writers and poets were also created, plus a Democratic Women's Organization of Afghanistan (DWOA) under the leadership of Anahita Ratebzad, and a Union of Peasants' Cooperatives.

After 'the entire structure of public organizations [had] in effect been created from scratch', as *Pravda* noted,[89] and after some delays, some dozen new groups were brought together under the umbrella of a National Fatherland Front (NFF). The NFF was established on 15 June 1981 'to mobilize, in pursuance of PDPA policy,...all noble people of Afghanistan to take active and conscious part' in achieving official goals. In a carefully scripted procedure, 940 delegates elected Ziray as chairman of the NFF national committee and adopted a constitution that said the PDPA was 'the guiding force of the [NFF] and the whole society of Afghanistan'. It added that the NFF's 'patriotic duty' was to 'protect and expand the valuable treasures of friendship and cooperation between the peoples of Afghanistan and the Soviet Union'.[90]

NFF officials, who were mostly minor government functionaries masquerading as regional leaders or members of the 1960s parliaments who had lost their importance, became targets for *mujahideen* assassination or dropped out under guerrilla threat. Although NFF membership claims reached 'nearly a million', Najibullah said in 1987, 'So far, we do not have [NFF constituent] organizations in whose creation the people are interested'.[91] After Ziray had been replaced in March 1985 as NFF leader by Abdul Rahim Hatef, a supposedly neutral old political figure from 1960s parliaments, and the name had been changed in January 1987 to the National Front of the Democratic Republic of Afghanistan, the organization admitted to having failed to play its assigned role.[92] A secretary of the front said that in 1990 people 'were somewhat justified in believing that...[it was] a false front [for the PDPA]. That is why [it] was politically ineffective'.[93]

Denial of Communism

Another aspect of Karmal's 1980 attempt to build popular support, or at least avoid alienating people, was denying that his regime was Communist—or socialist, which in the

Soviet world usually meant the same thing. His regime avoided the earlier use of Communist terminology, which *Pravda* noted had been 'incomprehensible to simple people...[and had] not only undermined the masses' enthusiasm but also their trust in the leadership'.[94] Disavowals of Marxism strengthened as the PDPA's failures became clearer. Najibullah pretended in 1989 that '[t]he programme and composition of the PDPA have never been Communist'.[95] Trying in 1990 to escape what was becoming the worldwide discrediting of Communism, Najibullah argued that 'the creation of the PDPA was not on the basis of any ideological need but on the basis of the historic necessity of the struggle to salvage society from backwardness', and the party's policy brought it 'under the influence of a specific ideology...[that] set up great obstacles for the creation of a broad national base...'.[96]

Denying Communism was accompanied by emphasizing Islam. Karmal and his Soviet advisers hoped that the way to remove or at least reduce opposition to the regime was to end the PDPA's long hostility to religion. Barialay said that in Taraki and Amin's period the regime had been 'impatient and often used force against religious leaders, whom it regarded without exception as opponents of progress'. But now, he said, we realize 'that the thinking of the predominately illiterate population is still being formed mainly by the mullahs'.[97] A Soviet observer noted, 'It was under the banner of Islam that the counter-revolution developed'.[98]

Karmal issued a declaration in January 1980, guaranteeing freedom of religion,[99] but many religious leaders reportedly were imprisoned for the February demonstrations. In April the PDPA promised 'full freedom and rights of Muslims, the clergy, and noble and patriotic *ulemas* .... Their religious activities in the social, economic, and cultural spheres will be supported'—activities in the political sphere being implicitly banned. Over Khalqi protests, Taraki's red national flag was replaced with the old royal colors of black, red, and

Islamic green plus a state emblem containing religious symbolism.[100] In June, amid public displays of piety, Karmal asserted that the Soviet invasion 'date of 27 December represents the intervention of God Almighty. That the USSR is helping us is also an act of God'.[101]

A 'chief board on Islamic questions' attached to the revolutionary council and a 'supreme council of the *ulemas* and clergy of Afghanistan' were created in imitation of the Soviet system for bringing under bureaucratic control a religion that lacked a clerical hierarchy, with trappings of support for religion: more than 16 000 religious leaders were given small state salaries, and more than 2000 mosques reportedly built.[102] However, Islam was 'acknowledged verbally but not taken into account in practice', according to a Soviet observer.[103] Such efforts therefore failed to turn religion to regime advantage. The *mujahideen* had already seized the religious advantage from people seen as atheistic Communists tied to Soviet infidels. The *mujahideen* regarded official mullahs as they did collaborationist NFF officials, and assassinated many of them, too.[104]

Lack of Majority Support

Karmal conceded in November 1985 that the PDPA lacked majority support.

> In encouraging the party toward a new approach in regard to the expansion and consolidation of the social bases of the revolutionary power of the people, we always recall the instruction of Lenin, who said: With patience and calmness and with the correction of past mistakes, the party *will decisively obtain a majority* among the masses of the people and, with patience, will create relations which will make it capable of leading the masses in all circumstances.

Karmal added that 'the party should speedily change its tactics', bringing more non-party people into the government, because '[t]he fate of the revolution depends on whether or not we can expand and broaden the social base of the people's power'.[105] After replacing Karmal, Najibullah noted more guardedly, 'It would be incorrect to say that the people of Afghanistan completely trust us and have confidence in us'.[106] Moscow recognized that the PDPA never won a broad backing of 'the people' in whose name it claimed to rule. In a CPSU politburo meeting on 13 November 1986, a speaker went unchallenged when he asserted that '[w]e have lost the battle for the Afghan people. The government is supported by a minority of the population'.[107]

RULE BY FORCE

Soviet advisers knew that lack of regime popularity required stern alternatives. In the best Stalinist fashion, they set out to develop a more efficient political police system. Amin's KAM was purged and reborn on 11 January 1980 as *Khadimat-e Atal'at-e Dowlati*, or State Information Service, known from its Dari initials as KhAD.[108] While Najibullah was put in nominal charge, it was controlled by the KGB. A Soviet journal said KhAD's KGB advisers 'used the tools of Stalin's great terror—secret denunciations, anonymous spies, "confessions" extracted by torture, secret trials for tens of thousands and public show trials for a few, unannounced executions and long prison terms'.[109] KhAD was also taught to assassinate *mujahideen* leaders, penetrate hostile or simply neutral groups, foment trouble in Afghan refugee camps abroad, mount terror operations in Pakistan, and other things.[110]

Within a few years KhAD grew to between 15 000 and 20 000 personnel, and by 1989 it numbered an estimated 25 000. Men joined for exemption from military conscription, ten times as much pay as government clerical workers, and access to liquor, prostitutes, and extortion money. There was, however, little evidence of ideological commitment.[111] Following the model of the KGB's 'Kremlin division', KhAD included a fully equipped military division to protect the Parchami leadership from Khalqi coup attempts, which it did in 1990.[112] Shortly after Najibullah turned over leadership of KhAD to his deputy, Maj.-Gen. Ghulam Faruq Yaqubi, in order to concentrate on PDPA work, the organization was on 9 January 1986 promoted to being the ministry of state security, *Wazarat-e Amaniat-e Dowlati*, or WAD from its initials,[113] but it continued to be generally known as KhAD.

A Soviet representative to Kabul's special revolutionary court, which provided a pretence of legality for predetermined sentences, said the Afghan situation 'practically repeated ours, point by point, of the 1937-38 years' of Stalin's purges. In many Afghan cases, he said, a 'man had confessed to a crime that had not been committed'.[114] A Soviet journalist reported in 1991 indications that 'since the end of the 1970s the Afghan [political police] have killed tens of thousands of people'.[115] Interior ministry forces and regular army troops, as well as their Soviet advisers, and the Soviet Army itself, also routinely engaged in barbaric activities. Victims described 'a pattern of human rights violations that is among the worst in recent history', according to Asia Watch, a Western human rights organization.[116]

Human Rights Violations

The inhumanity of regime and Soviet actions was overwhelming, horrifying, depressing—and well-documented. Fahima Nasery, a 31-year-old schoolteacher, was arrested in 1981 for distributing *shabnahmas* calling for the public to support the resistance. She was tortured with electric shocks, battered, and forced to live in bloody cells with rats. Sentenced to 13 years in prison, she was released in a year, after her family bribed a senior KhAD official.[117] After being held for six years on charges of helping the *mujahideen*, Arifa reported that 'interrogators were getting confessions from women prisoners by burning them with cigarettes and hanging them upside down...'.[118] Shafaq Tarialai, a former Afghan army officer who joined the resistance, was beaten, given electric shocks, and hung by his feet. He reported that Russian and Afghan interrogators tore out fellow prisoners' fingernails and killed one by literally tearing his body apart.[119] There are innumerable such accounts, many of them mentioning Soviet participation in the horrors of Afghan prisons.[120] How many people were imprisoned, how many executed, will never be accurately known. One of Afghanistan's leading scholars, Kabul University historian Mohammad Hassan Kakar, who was held in Pul-i-Charki from 1982 to 1987, estimated that at least 150 000 persons had been jailed and 50 000 executed.[121]

The Soviet Army was responsible for a whole separate category of atrocities. Illiterate peasants from widely separated parts of Afghanistan told similar stories without prompting or consultation with each other. *Mujahideen* activity near a village often led to retaliatory Soviet attacks on unarmed people with a savagery that went beyond merely killing them. Children were tortured and killed in front of their parents, women kidnapped and repeatedly raped before being killed, pregnant women ripped open, and other barbarous ventings of Soviet hatred, frustration, and anger were inflicted upon a defenceless peasantry. One study listed in first-person detail 8152 cases of regime and Soviet atrocities in villages through 1983.[122] Villages along roads were razed to eliminate possible shelter for ambushes, while more remote villages were bombed, raked with aerial gunfire, and sown with air-dropped land mines. Some were sprinkled with what appeared to be toys. 'I thought it was a bird, a toy bird', said 4-year-old Sabra. When she picked it up, it blew off her fingers and burned her head.[123]

It became a savage war on both sides. One study by exiled Afghans said the Kabul regime and the resistance were equally guilty of violating human rights. The *mujahideen* also tortured and killed prisoners, and their Peshawar offices maintained private prisons with the apparent acquiesence of Pakistani authorities.[124] Organized groups and undisciplined local guerrillas were savage in a primitive tradition that lacked Kabul's or Moscow's claims to modern, civilized governmental standing but were none the less terrible for that. The *mujahideen* usually took primitive vengence on Soviet prisoners and Afghan officers or PDPA members, while treating Afghan conscripts more leniently.[125] Soviet soldiers heard stories of comrades' being sexually mutilated and blinded before being killed, and of 'undershirting'—slitting a living man's skin around the waist and peeling it off over his head.[126] Such stories probably fuelled the Soviets' own savagery in a circle of violence.

United Nations Report on Atrocities

Reports of official atrocities in Afghanistan gained new credence from a 1985 study under neutral auspices. The United Nations Commission on Human Rights named a special rapporteur 'to examine the human rights situation in Afghanistan...'. He was Felix Ermacora, an Austrian law professor and member of parliament. Refused entry to or cooperation from Afghanistan, Ermacora interviewed refugees and others for a February 1985 report. It found the regime guilty of

> gross violations of human rights...[in which] many lives have been lost, many people have been incarcerated in conditions far removed from respect for human rights and fundamental freedoms, many have been tortured and have disappeared, [and] humanitarian norms have been flouted .... [The fighting] has given rise to...willful killing, including murder; torture and inhuman treatment; denial of a fair trial; arbitrary arrest and

execution of sentences; [and] taking of hostages.... [There have been] reprisals, indiscriminate bombardment, non-respect for hospital zones, [and] maltreatment of prisoners....

Following the UN General Assembly's practice of not naming the USSR in resolutions calling for a troop withdrawal from Afghanistan, Ermacora did not name it in his report. But he said the presence of foreign troops was 'one of the main causes of the present human rights situation'.[127]

The USSR sought to discredit not only the report but also its author, whose earlier criticisms of Chile, Israel, and South Africa—that coincided with Soviet foreign policy objectives—Moscow had found honest and objective.[128] Criticism from Moscow and Kabul intensified when Ermacora updated his report in February 1986 by, among other things, accusing Soviet and Afghan troops of 'systematic brutality' against civilians.[129] In 1987 the Kabul regime and its Soviet advisers changed their tactics, inviting Ermacora in for an escorted, controlled look at the situation. Although he found human rights violations, he also thought there had been improvements, which drew criticism from the *mujahideen* and Pakistani authorities.[130] Ermacora continued to monitor conditions, saying in 1989 that the human rights situation 'remains a matter of deep concern even after the withdrawal of the Soviet troops'.[131]

REGIME EDUCATION

By 1985, according to one estimate, more than 90 per cent of 'Afghans with a higher education from Western or other non-Communist universities have either been killed or have disappeared into prisons or else have fled to Western countries'.[132] The regime tried to educate a new generation of Afghans that would, Karmal said, accept their country's place in the Soviet world.[133] Education was Russified, the teaching of the English language replaced with compulsory Russian, more Soviet textbooks adopted, Marxism courses given eight hours of the 30-hour school week. But with schools seen as Communist indoctrination centers and attacked by angry villagers, 89 per cent of them had closed by 1984, and by 1986 more than 2000 teachers 'have been martyred', the regime said. Karmal complained that '[t]he quality of teaching...remained low...', with only 40 per cent of teachers having 'higher educational and vocational training'.[134] In 1988 illiteracy was officially reported to be increasing, despite a literacy programme.[135]

Afghanistan's premier educational centre, Kabul University, had some 750 teaching staff in 1978. Within a few years 276 had fled abroad, 36 had been executed, and six were in prison. Many were replaced with Soviets or with Afghans whose qualifications were more political than academic. The student body dropped from 14 000 to 6000, mostly girls plus some males whose families' PDPA connections meant they had no incentive to study.[136] Najibullah complained that many graduates did not work 'in fields for which they were educated, as a result of friendship, nepotism, tribal links, and bribes', but instead had comfortable office jobs.[137]

Afghan students also went to the USSR and other Communist countries, more often as a result of nepotism than of merit. Najibullah said in 1987 there were 'more than 10 000 Afghan students in the Soviet Union', adding that 'a majority...are weak in their studies'.[138] The Soviet people became increasingly hostile to these students as the hardships and deaths of Soviet soldiers in Afghanistan became better known. Some students were beaten, a few murdered.[139] Under a programme for war orphans between the ages of 7 and 10 to receive ten years of Soviet education, 870 children left Afghanistan in November 1984. Although Afghan and Soviet officials said the programme had by 1989 included only 1800 orphans, charges that 10 000 or more children had been kidnapped for brainwashing in the USSR

circulated in Peshawar and the West.[140] In 1993 about 2000
Afghan children were reported stranded in former Soviet
republics, including 113 orphans in Uzbekistan and 170
orphans in Tajikistan.[141] Some 11 000 other Afghan children
had by 1988 spent brief periods in Soviet Pioneer camps
that were combination vacation places and indoctrination
centers. Two resistance commanders reported capturing boys
as young as 8 who had been trained in the Soviet Union as
spies and assassins.[142]

AN APPEARANCE OF PUBLIC PARTICIPATION

Ermacora's 1985 report criticized the failure to respect the
April 1980 'basic principles' provision for holding a *loya
jirgah* as the 'highest organ of state power'. In apparent
reaction, the regime began trying to create an illusion of
consulting the public. Kabul announced on 12 April 1985
the summoning of a *loya jirgah*. The very next day it said
'elections for *jirgah* representatives had already been held in
13 of the 29 provinces'. On 20 April elections by
unexplained procedures were said to be complete, and a 23
April opening day was announced. The 2000 delegates
dutifully endorsed regime policies without the debate that
had historically marked *loya jirgahs*.[143] The *mujahideen* later
killed some provincial participants.

Lesser *jirgahs* followed, reportedly under Soviet direction.
A gathering was held in Kabul from 14 to 16 September
1985, of some 3700 representatives of Pushtun and Baloch
tribes from both sides of the Durand Line, including tribes
in Pakistan.[144] The regime had for years been trying to win
over these tribes because of their strategic position astride
mujahideen supply routes. Karmal's minister for frontier and
tribal affairs, Fayz Mohammed, sought to buy tribal loyalty
in the time-honoured way using money bags, but he was
killed in September 1980 by tribesmen who sent word that
the Pushtun code of hospitality did not apply to stooges of

Russian infidels.[145] Later, KhAD under Najibullah—whose father had been an agent of Daoud's, working for Pushtunistan—took responsibility for trying to win tribal support, with a Soviet general at Jalalabad controlling the effort. But Karmal conceded 'shortcomings and defects' in dealing with tribes, and Najibullah said government departments violated 'signed protocols with tribes'.[146]

Karmal openly tried to bribe the tribes at the September 1985 *jirgah*. '... [H]uge sums have been allocated for the economic development of tribal areas', he said, but 'materializing all these objectives' required tribal cooperation with regime defence efforts and not allowing the *mujahideen* to use their territories. The delegates dutifully endorsed regime positions, including defending Afghan borders against 'counter-revolutionary terrorist bands from abroad'.[147] Pakistani authorities were alarmed by Kabul's recruiting of support from their tribal territory and the traditional handing out of guns after the *jirgah*.[148] Islamabad was even more angered by a *jirgah* in Kabul on 9 and 10 April 1986, of 1750 representatives of 'independent Pushtun tribes'— meaning those in Pakistan—that declared 'irreconcilable enmity' with Pakistani authorities.[149] But the practical effects of buying delegates for such propaganda exercises seem to have been slight.

With the same implausible haste that the *loya jirgah* 'elections' had been announced and held, the regime announced on 10 August 1985 that Karmal had signed a decree for local elections to begin the next day.[150] The PDPA politburo issued guidelines for 'appointing the candidates' so as to get a desirable social mix, and advised that 'elections should be held with spectacular ceremonies'.[151] Press photos and articles indicated that mostly small, unspectacular gatherings consisted almost entirely of men raising their hands in favour of unopposed candidates.[152] Even a Soviet reporter, no stranger to sham elections, found these elections to have 'a rather peculiar character...because of the military-political situation which remains difficult and because of the many national traditions and practices'.[153] Voting by stages around the country ended on 17 September 1986, with 85 per cent of voters said to have participated in those unspecified areas 'under revolutionary rule'.[154] Najibullah soon admitted that new local councils 'have not yet become true organs of action', and the 14 200 elected officials 'have not been given real authority and have not been enlisted to solve serious problems'. Some people, he added in obvious reference to unelected PDPA officials, 'do not want new people to have power...[because] they are worried about losing their own authority and privileges'.[155]

Soviet Pressure

Behind the windowdressing of *jirgahs* and elections lay Soviet pressure. New Kremlin leader Gorbachev was beginning to want to get rid of the Afghan burden, as discussed in Chapter 9. Gorbachev told Karmal in October 1985, 'We must think together about withdrawing the Soviet force from Afghanistan'. Karmal, knowing his regime was unviable without Soviet troops, reacted negatively.[156] When Karmal told an interviewer that the idea of bringing former King Zahir Shah and one of his officials into the government 'will never be discussed', a Soviet reprint of the interview omitted that remark.[157] Moscow media began to urge on Kabul a 'positive dialogue...[with] those who so far stick to positions hostile to the revolution...'.[158]

Under Soviet pressure, Karmal announced a ten-point reconciliation programme on 9 November 1985. He said 'authority will not be monopolized by the PDPA...[and] credible representatives of the people who can reflect the interests of various strata and groups in our society' would be brought into the leadership. Promising 'principled and flexible compromise in accord with the national interests of the country', he invited Afghans abroad to return 'without prejudice and distinction...'.[159] Lacking any enthusiastic response, Moscow kept prodding the regime. *Pravda*, which conceded that '[f]ar from all people in Afghanistan, even among working sections of the population, accepted the April revolution', said a 'positive dialogue' with opponents was needed, and '[r]econciliation presupposes known compromises'.[160]

There was little compromise in Kabul's appointment on 26 December 1985 of 14 senior officials, including a deputy prime minister, in a supposed widening of the government's political base. Although nine of them were identified as not being PDPA members, most had already held lower-ranking regime positions; they were collaborators being given more prominence. In an apparent rebuke that used a term which would become a policy theme, *Pravda* said on 3 January 1986 that 'achieving *national reconciliation*...[requires] certain compromises...[and] the recruitment of new political allies and friends'.[161] On 16 January the revolutionary council more than doubled its size with 79 new members, 54 of whom were listed as non-party—most of them collaborators in regime jobs. The National Fatherland Front's leadership added 33 members.[162]

The *jirgahs*, local elections, and governmental broadening had no effect on the Afghan situation. With all power still in the hands of the PDPA and, behind it, Soviet advisers, regime support was not effectively widened. Najibullah said later the broadening policy was 'carried out with a conservative method, doubt, and lack of courage' in order to preserve the PDPA's monopoly of power. 'Despite the presentation of incorrect figures, which became part of the habits of the central and local party and government authorities, state sovereignty was not practically expanding', he added.[163] A Soviet writer later accused Karmal of not taking 'vigorous steps to put [the policy of broadening support] into practice...'.[164] Having failed in 1980 to reconcile and pacify the country, and now having failed in the new efforts in 1985 to revitalize the regime, Karmal had become a liability for his Soviet masters.

NOTES

1. *Izvestiya*, 23 December 1988, p. 5, in *FBIS/SU*, 23 December 1988, p. 25; Kabul Television, 15 January 1992.
2. *Voyenno-Istoricheskiy Zhurnal*, No. 11, 1993, in *JPRS-UMA-94-005*, 9 February 1994, p. 51.
3. Girardet, *Afghanistan*, pp. 177-80; Anwar, *Tragedy*, p. 208; National Committee, *Russia's Barbarism*, I, unnumbered; State Department, 'Country Reports on Human Rights Practices', 2 February 1981, p. 931.
4. Rashid, 'Final Report', p. 87.
5. Tass from Kabul, 29 and 30 December 1979, in *FBIS/SU*, 31 December 1979, pp. D1-5 and D1-5; Kabul Radio, 1 January 1980, in *FBIS/ME*, 2 January 1980, pp. S1-5.
6. Ibid.; Tass from Kabul, 29 December 1979, in *FBIS/SU*, 31 December 1979, p. D2.
7. Ibid.; Tass from Kabul, 30 December 1979, in *FBIS/SU*, 31 December 1979, p. D4; Kabul Radio, 1 January 1980, in *FBIS/ME*, 2 January 1980, pp. S1-5.
8. Kabul Radio, 17 April 1980, in *FBIS/SA*, 22 April 1980, p. C3; Moscow Radio, 29 December 1979, in *FBIS/SU*, 31 December 1979, pp. D5-6.
9. *L'Humanite*, 11 July 1980, p. 8, in *FBIS/SA*, 18 July 1980, pp. C1-3; *Kommunist*, No. 5, 1980: 71-8; *Times of India*, 11 February 1981, p. 1, in *FBIS/SA*, 23 February 1981, pp. C1-2.
10. State Department, 'Country Reports', 2 February 1981, p. 931; *Amnesty International Report 1980*, p. 180; AFP from Kabul, 11 and 12 January 1980, in *FBIS/ME*, 14 January 1980, pp. S13-15 and S13-15; *New York Times*, 9 November 1989, p. A15.
11. Kabul Radio, 17 April 1980, in *FBIS/SA*, 22 April 1980, p. C3.
12. Ibid.
13. Arnold, *Afghanistan's Two-Party*, p. 181; FCO, 'Afghanistan Report', July 1980.
14. Ghaus, *Fall*, p. 190.
15. Arnold, *Afghanistan's Two-Party*, pp. 188-205; *Argumenty i Fakty*, No. 44, 1990: 2, in *FBIS/SU*, 8 November 1990, pp. 13-14.
16. Kabul Radio, 13 June 1981, in *FBIS/SA*, 15 June 1981, p. C9. The *Kabul New Times* said 78 of the 191 important governmental appointments made by May 1980 went to non-party people; Anwar, *Tragedy*, p. 215.
17. Kabul Radio, 14 June 1987, in *FBIS/SA*, 19 June 1987, pp. C1 and P2; Kabul Radio, 18 October 1987, in *FBIS/NE*, 23 October 1987, p. 36.

18. AFP from Islamabad, 10 June 1980, in *FBIS/SA*, 10 June 1980, p. C1; FCO, 'Sovietisation of Afghanistan'; FCO, 'Afghanistan Report', June and August 1980; *U. S. News and World Report*, 2 March 1987.

19. *CWIHPB*, Nos. 8-9: 163.

20. *Trud*, 24 October 1991, pp. 1, 4, in *JPRS-UIA-91-027*, 27 November 1991, p. 56.

21. *CWIHPB*, Nos. 8-9: 178-80.

22. *Komsomolskaya Pravda*, 21 September 1991, p. 3, in *JPRS-UPA-91-043*, 18 October 1991, p. 53; *Die Welt*, 20 August 1984; *New York Times Magazine*, 24 March 1985, pp. 53-5; *International Affairs*, February 1990, p. 21.

23. State Department briefing, 10 February 1988.

24. *Komsomolskaya Pravda*, 21 September 1991, p. 3, in *JPRS-UPA-91-043*, 18 October 1991, p. 53; Morozov, 'KGB and the Afghan leaders', p. 35; *Washington Post*, 12 November 1989, p. D4.

25. *International Affairs*, February 1990, p. 21; Kabul Radio, 27 June 1990, in *FBIS/NE*, 3 July 1990, p. 45.

26. *Daily Telegraph*, 6 May 1989, p. 10; *Sovetskaya Rossiya*, 15 November 1989, p. 4, in *FBIS/SU*, 21 November 1989, p. 104; *Ogonek*, 18 March 1989, pp. 6-8, 30-31.

27. Ibid.

28. *Literaturnaya Gazeta*, 14 October 1987, p. 14, in *FBIS/SU*, 27 October 1987, p. 36.

29. *Pravda*, 26 April 1989, p. 4, in *FBIS/NE*, 26 April 1989, p. 45; Anwar, *Tragedy*, p. x.

30. *New York Times*, 8 February 1989, p. A6.

31. BBC Television, 22 March 1982, in *FBIS/SA*, 23 March 1982, pp. C3-4.

32. *Muslim*, 26 February 1987, p. 8, in *FBIS/SA*, 10 March 1987, p. C2.

33. *Izvestiya*, 15 June 1991, p. 7, in *FBIS/SU*, 18 June 1991, p. 16.

34. *Voyenno-Istoricheskiy Zhurnal*, No. 5, 1990: 66-71.

35. *Ogonek*, 18 March 1989, pp. 6-8.

36. Safronchuk, interview, Austin, Texas, 20 October 1989; *Trud*, 24 October 1991, pp. 1, 4, in *JPRS-UIA-91-027*, 27 November 1991, p. 53; *Daily Telegraph*, 22 January 1980, p. 4; AFP from Kabul, 21 July 1991, in *FBIS/NE*, 24 July 1991, p. 44.

37. Kabul Radio, 19 October 1980, in *FBIS/SA*, 22 October 1980, p. D3; *Pravda*, 17 and 18 October 1980, pp. 2 and 2, in *FBIS/SU*, 21 and 22 October 1980, pp. D4-11 and D1; Kabul Radio, 14 November 1980, in *FBIS/SA*, 17 November 1980, pp. C1-7.

38. Safronchuk, interview, Austin, Texas, 20 October 1989.

39. Kabul Radio, 17 April 1980, in *FBIS/SA*, 22 April 1980, pp. C1-9.

40. Kabul Radio, 19 April 1980, in *FBIS/SU*, 23 April 1980, pp. C1-13.
41. AFP from Kabul, 19 October 1991, in *FBIS/NE*, 21 October 1991, p. 52; State Department, 'Country Reports on Human Rights Practices for 1983', (Washington), February 1984, pp. 1190, 1194.
42. Kerry M. Connor, 'The Movement of Afghan Refugees to Peshawar', in Farr and Merriam, *Afghan Resistance*, p. 171; *Afghanistan Information Centre Monthly Bulletin*, November-December 1984, p. 7.
43. Kabul Radio, 30 [3] November 1984, in *FBIS/SA*, 9 November 1984, p. C6; Kabul Radio, 18 October 1987, in *FBIS/NE*, 23 October 1987, p. 33; Arnold, *Afghanistan's Two-Party*, p. 100; Anwar, *Tragedy*, pp. 104-07.
44. Ul'yanovskiy, 'Afghan Revolution'.
45. Kabul Radio, 30 [3] November 1984, in *FBIS/SA*, 9 November 1984, p. C6; Kabul Radio, 15 May 1988, in *FBIS/NE*, 17 May 1988, p. 42; Kabul Radio, 27 June 1990, in *FBIS/NE*, 28 June 1990, p. 35.
46. Anwar, *Tragedy*, p. 214.
47. *Pravda*, 12 July 1986, p. 5, in *FBIS/SU*, 17 July 1986, p. D2; Kabul Radio, 31 December 1989, in *FBIS/NE*, 4 January 1990, p. 38; *Argumenty i Fakty*, 2 July 1988, p. 4, in *FBIS/SU*, 14 July 1988, p. 19.
48. *Pravda*, 27 September 1980, p. 5, in *FBIS/SU*, 28 September 1980, pp. D3-11.
49. Bakhtar from Kabul, 24 June 1986, in *FBIS/SA*, 25 June 1986, p. C1.
50. Kabul Radio, 18 October 1987, in *FBIS/NE*, 23 October 1987, p. 35.
51. Ibid.; Kabul Radio, 10 July 1986, in *FBIS/SA*, 15 July 1986, p. C5.
52. Kabul Radio, 23 March 1990, in *FBIS/NE*, 30 March 1990, p. 28.
53. Kabul Radio, 10 January 1985, in *FBIS/SA*, 14 January 1985, p. C4; *Pravda*, 12 January 1985, p. 4, in *FBIS/SU*, 16 January 1985, p. D4; *Krasnaya Zvezda*, 11 January 1985, p. 3, in *FBIS/SU*, 14 January 1985, p. D1 (emphasis added).
54. Kabul Radio, 27 March 1985, in *FBIS/SA*, 3 April 1985, p. C4; *Agitator*, No. 17, 1988: 47-9, in *JPRS-UIA-88-018*, 23 November 1988, p. 77. Kabul Radio, 13 March 1987, in *FBIS/SA*, 16 March 1987, p. C2, claimed PDPA units covered 2,000 villages.
55. *Pravda*, 26 April 1988, p. 4, in *FBIS/SU*, 26 April 1988, p. 18.
56. *CWIHPB*, Nos. 8-9: 180.
57. *Izvestiya*, 23 December 1988, p. 5, in *FBIS/SU*, 23 December 1988, p. 25.
58. *Voyenno-Istoricheskiy Zhurnal*, No. 5, 1990: 66-71.
59. *New Times*, No. 12, 1990: 8-10.

60. PTI from Kabul, 10 and 14 April 1980, in *FBIS/SA*, 10 and 14 April 1980, pp. C1 and C9.

61. FCO, 'Afghanistan Report', July 1980; FCO, 'Afghanistan Chronology'; Arnold, *Afghanistan's Two-Party*, p. 112.

62. Kabul Radio, 8 and 14 June 1980, in *FBIS/SA*, 9 and 16 June 1980, pp. C1-3 and C1-3.

63. State Department, 'Country Reports on Human Rights Practices, 1980', pp. 929-30; FCO, 'Afghanistan Report', September 1980.

64. Montsame from Ulan Bator, 15 August 1980, in *FBIS/SA*, 25 August 1980, p. C5; Kabul Radio, 12 and 13 June 1981, 10 July 1986, in *FBIS/SA*, 15 June 1981 and 11 July 1986, pp. C1-5 and C3.

65. Kabul Radio, 20 July 1980, in *FBIS/SA*, 21 July 1980, pp. C1-5.

66. Moscow Radio, 11 September 1988, in *FBIS/SU*, 12 September 1988, p. 12; State Department, 'Afghanistan: A Year of Occupation' (Washington, December 1980); interviews with State Department officials, 1981; Arnold, *Afghanistan's Two-Party*, p. 113.

67. *Economist*, 20 June 1981, p. 36; State Department, 'Afghanistan: Six Years of Soviet Occupation' (Washington, December 1985), p. 9; Zalmay Khalilzad, 'Moscow's Afghan War', *Problems of Communism*, January-February 1986: 7; *New Times*, No. 12, 1990: 8-10.

68. Kabul Radio, 19 October 1987, in *FBIS/NE*, 29 October 1987, p. 38; *Ogonek*, No. 30, 1988: 25-7.

69. Kabul Radio, 14 and 15 March 1982, in *FBIS/SA*, 15 and 16 March 1982, pp. C1-3 and C1-3; State Department, 'Afghanistan: Three Years of Soviet Occupation', (Washington, December 1982), pp. 6-7.

70. Kabul Radio, 10 July 1986, in *FBIS/SA*, 15 July 1986, p. C4; Kabul Radio, 18 October 1987, in *FBIS/NE*, 23 October 1987, p. 38.

71. Kabul Radio, 12 and 13 June 1981, in *FBIS/SA*, 15 June 1981, pp. C1-5 and C9. Kakar, *Afghanistan*, says (p. 182) Keshtmand was an Isma'ili Gadee who associated himself with the Hazaras for political reasons.

72. Kabul Radio, 19 October 1987, in *FBIS/NE*, 29 October 1987, pp. 37 and 39.

73. Kabul Radio, 10 July 1986, in *FBIS/SA*, 15 July 1986, p. C2.

74. Kabul Radio, 22 November 1985, in *FBIS/SA*, 4 December 1985, p. C6.

75. Kabul Radio, 29 April 1980, in *FBIS/SA*, 30 April 1980, p. C1.

76. Kabul Radio, 14 November 1980, in *FBIS/SA*, 17 November 1980, pp. C1-7.

77. *Die Zeit*, 28 December 1984, p. 3.

78. *Kabul New Times*, 12 August 1985, p. 2.
79. Kabul Radio, 2 April 1986, in *FBIS/SA*, 7 April 1986, pp. C1-5.
80. Kabul Radio, 12 May 1987, in *FBIS/SA*, 22 May 1987, p. C3; *Literaturnaya Gazeta*, 14 October 1987, p. 14, in *FBIS/SU*, 27 October 1987, p. 34; Kabul Radio, 28 June 1987, in *FBIS/NE*, 2 July 1987, p. P5.
81. Kabul Radio, 14 June and 18 October 1987, in *FBIS/NE*, 19 June and 23 October 1987, pp. P10 and 35; AFP from Islamabad, 28 August 1989, in *FBIS/NE*, 29 August 1989, p. 3.
82. Kabul Radio, 21 May 1990, in *FBIS/NE*, 23 May 1990, p. 29.
83. *Komsomolskaya Pravda*, 13 June 1990, p. 3, in *FBIS/SU*, 19 June 1990, p. 19.
84. *CWIHPB*, Nos. 8-9: 164.
85. *Pravda*, 17 October 1980, p. 2, in *FBIS/SU*, 21 October 1980, pp. D3-11.
86. FCO, 'Sovietization of Afghanistan'.
87. *Mlada Fronta*, 18 February 1981, p. 3, in *FBIS/SA*, 6 March 1981, p. C2.
88. Kabul Radio, 18 November 1984, in *FBIS/SA*, 20 November 1984, p. C1; Kabul Radio, 10 March 1988, in *FBIS/NE*, 11 March 1988, p. 57.
89. *Pravda*, 31 January 1981, p. 4, in *FBIS/SU*, 5 February 1981, pp. D3-6.
90. Tass from Kabul, 29 December 1980, in *FBIS/SU*, 30 December 1980, pp. D2-3; Bakhtar from Kabul, 15 and 16 June 1981, in *FBIS/SA*, 19 June 1981, pp. C16-19, C1, and C4-15.
91. Kabul Radio, 7 November 1985 and 15 January 1987, in *FBIS/SA*, 8 November 1985 and 20 January 1987, pp. C1 and C3.
92. State Department, 'Afghanistan: Six Years', p. 10; Kabul Radio, 15 January 1987, in *FBIS/SA*, 20 January 1987, p. C 6; Kabul Radio, 3 February 1986, in *FBIS/SU*, 4 February 1986, pp. D3-4.
93. *Al-Hurriyah*, 29 April 1990, pp. 35-40, in *JPRS-NEA-90-035*, 28 June 1990, p. 36.
94. *Pravda*, 18 February 1980, p. 6, in *FBIS/SU*, 21 February 1980, pp. D3-4.
95. Bakhtar from Kabul, 18 November 1989, in *FBIS/NE*, 22 November 1989, p. 36.
96. Kabul Radio, 27 June 1990, in *FBIS/NE*, 3 July 1990, p. 55.
97. Budapest Radio, 11 December 1980, in *FBIS/SA*, 12 December 1980, pp. C1-2.
98. *Voprosy Filosofii*, No. 8, 1980: 60-71, in *FBIS/SU Annex*, 6 October 1980, pp. 1-12.
99. Kabul Radio, 25 January 1980, in *FBIS/ME*, 28 January 1980, pp. S1-2.

100. Kabul Radio, 17 and 19 April 1980, in *FBIS/SA*, 22 and 23 April 1980, pp. C6 and C2.
101. Kabul Radio, 18 June 1980, in *FBIS/SA*, 20 June 1980, pp. Cl-6.
102. AFP from Islamabad, 10 July 1980, in *FBIS/SA*, 10 July 1980, pp. C3-4; Kabul Radio, 19 September 1981, in *FBIS/SA*, 22 September 1981, pp. C2; Chantal Lobato, 'Islam in Kabul: The Religious Politics of Babrak Karmal', *Central Asian Survey*, Vol. 4, No. 4: 112-13.
103. *Ogonek*, 18 March 1989, pp. 6-8, 30-31.
104. IISS, 'Strategic Survey 1985-86', p. 131.
105. Kabul Radio, 22 November 1985, in *FBIS/SA*, 4 December 1985, pp. C2, C7 (emphasis added).
106. Kabul Radio, 29 May 1986, in *FBIS/SA*, 2 June 1986, p. C1.
107. *CWIHPB*, Nos. 8-9: 180.
108. Kabul Radio, 11 January 1986, in *FBIS/SA*, 14 January 1986, p. C1.
109. *New Times*, No. 8, 1990: 15.
110. State Department, 'Afghanistan: Four Years of Soviet Occupation', (Washington, December 1983), pp. 5-6; Mackenzie, 'Brutal Force', pp. 8-17; Fullerton, *Soviet Occupation*, pp. 119-22.
111. State Department, 'Country Reports on Human Rights Practices for 1989' (Washington, 1990), p. 1320; Lee O. Coldren, 'Afghanistan in 1985: The Sixth Year of the Russo-Afghan War', *Asian Survey*, February 1986, pp. 238-9.
112. *Argumenti i Fakty*, No. 30, 1990.
113. Kabul Radio, 11 January 1986, in *FBIS/SA*, 14 January 1986, p. C1.
114. *Trud*, 3 March 1992, p. 3, in *FBIS/CE*, 20 March 1992, p. 102.
115. *Komsomolskaya Pravda*, 29 June 1991, p. 4, in *FBIS/SU*, 12 July 1991, p. 13.
116. Asia Watch, 'Afghanistan: The Forgotten War' (New York, February 1991).
117. *Insight*, 5 December 1988, pp. 8-17.
118. Midia (a resistance press service), Peshawar, 4 March 1990.
119. Laber and Rubin, 'A Nation Is Dying', pp. 84-5.
120. E.g., ibid.; annual reports of the State Department, 'Country Reports on Human Rights Practices'; annual reports of Amnesty International (London) and its special reports on Afghanistan; reports of Asia Watch (New York); the Independent Counsel on International Human Rights, 18 November 1987, in *Afghan Jehad*, January-March 1988: 36-49; author's interviews.
121. Telephone interview, Mohammad Hassan Kakar, 12 June 1990.

122. National Committee for Human Rights in Afghanistan, *Russia's Barbarism in Afghanistan*, Vols. 1-3 (Peshawar, October 1984, July 1985, February 1986).

123. *Free Afghanistan Report* 8 (September 1985): 1.

124. *Sunday Times*, 12 February 1989, p. A15; Asia Watch, *Afghanistan: The Forgotten War: Human Rights Abuses and Violations of the Laws of War Since the Soviet Withdrawal* (New York, 1991), pp. 21-7, 42-55; Afghan League of Human Rights, report, June 1993, Peshawar.

125. Asia Watch, *Afghanistan: Forgotten War*, p. 69.

126. *Newsweek*, 20 February 1989, p. 27; *Argumenty i Fakty*, 30 December 1989, pp. 4-5, in *FBIS/SU*, 9 January 1990, p. 121.

127. Felix Ermacora, 'Report on the situation of human rights in Afghanistan', United Nations document E/CN.4/1985/21, 19 February 1985, pp. 48, 28, and 50.

128. Tass from New York, 4 December 1985, in *FBIS/SU*, 5 December 1985, p. CC5; *Krasnaya Zvezda*, 13 December 1985, p. 3, in *FBIS/SU*, 18 December 1985, pp. D2-5; *Christian Science Monitor*, 1 March 1985, p. 7; *Die Welt*, 26 April 1985.

129. *New York Times*, 27 February, 12 November, and 21 November 1986, pp. A9, A8, and A1.

130. Felix Ermacora, 'Report on the situation of human rights in Afghanistan', United Nations document A/42/667, 23 October 1987, p. 27; *Le Point*, 12 October 1987.

131. Quoted in *Afghan Jehad*, October 1988-December 1989: 38.

132. Sayd B. Majrood, 'Past and Present Education in Afghanistan—A Problem for the Future', in Huldt and Jansson, *Tragedy*, p. 87.

133. Kabul Radio, 30 October 1985, in *FBIS/SA*, 7 November 1985, pp. C5-6.

134. Batinshah Safi, 'Afghan Education During the War', in Huldt and Jansson, *Tragedy*, p. 113; Sayed Mohammad Yusuf Elmi, 'The Impact of the Sovietization on Afghan Education and Culture', in Majrooh and Elmi, *Sovietization*, pp. 90-91; *Les Nouvelles d'Afghanistan*, October-November 1984: 13-15; Kabul Radio, 7 October, 2 April, and 7 October 1986, in *FBIS/SA*, 10 October, 7 April, and 10 October 1986, pp. C3, C4, and C2-3.

135. Kabul Radio, 7 June 1988, in *FBIS/NE*, 9 June 1988, p. 45.

136. Elmi, 'Impact of Sovietization', pp. 79-81; Girardet, *Afghanistan*, pp. 140-5; Bakhtar from Kabul, 16 June 1986, in *FBIS/SA*, 17 June 1986, pp. C1-2.

137. Bakhtar from Kabul, 30 November 1987, in *FBIS/NE*, 3 December 1987, p. 59.

138. Kabul Radio, 8 November 1987, in *FBIS/SU*, 10 November 1987, p. 43.

154   AFGHAN COMMUNISM AND SOVIET INTERVENTION

139. *Wall Street Journal*, 17 March 1986, p. 21; *Komsomolskaya Pravda*, 5 January 1989, p. 1, in *FBIS/SU*, 6 January 1989, pp. 23-4; *Moscow News*, 15 January 1989, p. 13.
140. State Department, 'Afghanistan: Five Years of Soviet Occupation', (Washington, December 1984), p. 5; Tass from Kabul, 16 August 1989, in *FBIS/SU*, 17 August 1989, p. 13; *Sovetskaya Rossiya*, 13 January 1990, p. 5, in *FBIS/SU*, 18 January 1990, p. 23; A. Rasul Amin, 'The Sovietization of Afghanistan', in Rosanne Klass, ed., *Afghanistan: The Great Game Revisited* (New York, 1987), p. 324.
141. Interfax from Moscow, 18 March 1993, in *FBIS/CE*, 18 March 1993, p. 61.
142. Bakhtar from Kabul, 27 August 1988, in *FBIS/NE*, 30 August 1988, p. 43; Antoine LaFont, 'My Testimony from Afghanistan', *Central Asian Survey*, November 1983: 123; ZDF Television, 3 October 1984, in *FBIS/SA*, 5 October 1984, pp. C3-4.
143. State Department, 'Afghanistan: Six Years', p. 10. See also *FBIS/ SA* for this period.
144. State Department, 'Afghanistan: Six Years', p. 10; Bakhtar from Kabul, 14 September 1985, and Kabul Radio, 16 September 1985, in *FBIS/SA*, 16 and 20 September 1985, pp. C1, C1-3.
145. *Za Rubezhom*, 10 January 1986, pp. 12-13, in *FBIS/SU*, 24 January 1986, p. D7; interviews with Afghan exiles, 1981.
146. Kabul Radio, 30 March and 22 November 1986, in *FBIS/SA*, 3 April and 25 November 1986, pp. C2 and C4.
147. Kabul Radio, 14 and 16 September 1985, in *FBIS/SA*, 19 and 20 September 1985, pp. C6 and C2.
148. AFP from Islamabad, 6 November 1985, in *FBIS/SA*, 7 November 1985, p. F1.
149. Kabul Radio, 9 April 1986, in *FBIS/SA*, 11 April 1986, pp. C1-2.
150. Kabul Radio, 10 August 1985, in *FBIS/SA*, 12 August 1985, p. C1; Bakhtar from Kabul, 22 July 1985, in *FBIS/SA*, 24 July 1985, p. C1.
151. Bakhtar from Kabul, 10 February 1986, in *FBIS/SA*, 12 February 1986, pp. C2-3.
152. Kabul Radio, 11 August 1985, in *FBIS/SA*, 13 August 1985, p. C5; *Kabul New Times*, pp. 12, 14, 17, and 20 August 1985, p. 1.
153. Moscow Television, 11 August 1985, in *FBIS/SU*, 14 August 1985, p. D1.
154. Kabul Radio, 13 and 22 November 1986, in *FBIS/SA*, 19 and 25 November 1986, pp. C1 and C2; *Kabul New Times*, 5 November 1986, p. 1.
155. Kabul Radio, 10 and 21 July 1986, in *FBIS/SA*, 15 and 23 July 1986, pp. C3 and C1-2.
156. Pyadyshev, 'Najibullah', p. 19.

157. Kabul Radio, 13 October 1985, in *FBIS/SA*, 18 October 1985, p. C2; *Za Rubezhom*, 6 December 1985, p. 8, in *FBIS/SU*, 13 December 1985, pp. D4-7.
158. *Pravda*, 22 December 1985, p. 5, in *FBIS/SU*, 24 December 1985, p. D1.
159. Kabul Radio, 9 November 1985, in *FBIS/SA*, 12 November 1985, pp. C1-6.
160. *Pravda*, 22 December 1985, p. 5, in *FBIS/SU*, 24 December 1985, p. D1.
161. *Pravda*, 3 January 1986, p. 5, in *FBIS/SU*, 6 January 1986, p. D6 (emphasis added).
162. Kabul Radio, 17 January 1986, in *FBIS/SA*, 21 and 22 January 1986, pp. C1-3 and C1-4; *Pravda*, 18 January 1986, p. 4, in *FBIS/SU*, 22 January 1986, p. D1.
163. Kabul Radio, 27 June 1990, in *FBIS/NE*, 3 July 1990, pp. 45-6.
164. *New Times*, 4 May 1987, p. 20.

CHAPTER 5

NEW COP ON THE BEAT

The Soviet willingness to stick with Karmal for six years despite his failure to rally popular support was typical of the Brezhnev era's stolid persistence in policies with little questioning of their validity and its continuation of uninspired officials in the same jobs for decades. But new attitudes toward a multitude of old problems that Gorbachev brought to the Soviet leadership in March 1985 numbered Karmal's days. The failure of the *jirgahs*, local elections, and governmental broadening to build support for the regime at the expense of the *mujahideen* meant that a new approach was needed.

Gorbachev told a CPSU politburo meeting on 20 March 1986 that 'Karmal is very much down in terms of health and in terms of psychological disposition', and a comrade added, 'Karmal tells himself that he cannot cope with his functions'. *Izvestiya* explained later that, '... disappointed in Babrak Karmal but still anticipating at least a drawn outcome to the war', Moscow decided to replace him.[1]

Instead of choosing a neutral figure who might appeal to non-party Afghans at the risk of antagonizing PDPA members, or switching from Karmal's Parcham faction to the Khalqi leader Gulabzoy, the Soviets decided they needed someone who would carry out their orders with tough efficiency. The obvious man was Najibullah, the hard, dynamic boss of KhAD. In that job he had been the protege of Kryuchkov, the KGB's overseer of Afghan affairs, who apparently played a key role in the change. Najibullah later suggested another consideration in his selection. He said that, when Gorbachev told Karmal in October 1985 that they must think of a Soviet military withdrawal, Najibullah told other Afghans in the delegation that Karmal had been wrong to react negatively. A Soviet version of this story said that a Soviet observer noted at the time that Najibullah 'was perhaps the only one [in the delegation] to acquiesce in the proposed step'.[2]

CHANGING LEADERS

On 21 November 1985, the PDPA central committee named Najibullah a party secretary; he was already a politburo member. His KhAD deputy, Yaqubi, was promoted from candidate to full member of the central committee.[3] When Yaqubi became the head of KhAD two weeks later, Najibullah was free to concentrate on his expanded party duties of supervising military and security affairs, including both KhAD and Gulabzoy's interior ministry troops, and 'party organizational matters'.[4] The latter duty was, as Stalin had shown in the 1920s, the best way to the top in a Leninist system because it enabled one to put allies and clients into key jobs.

Karmal, accompanied by Najibullah and others, attended the 27th congress of the CPSU in late February and early March 1986. In his report to the congress that is discussed further in Chapter 9, Gorbachev said the USSR 'would like in the near future' to withdraw its forces from Afghanistan—as soon as 'outside interference' had ended—and Moscow had already worked out a timetable with Kabul.[5] But in his brief address to the congress, Karmal emphasized the need for Soviet support and said nothing about a withdrawal.[6] Signifying the tense relationship, Karmal was the only head of a ruling Communist party invited to the congress who was not granted a private audience with Gorbachev or any other CPSU politburo member.

Less than a month after returning to Kabul, Karmal flew to Moscow again on 30 March. No reason was publicly announced, and the Soviets did not acknowledge his presence. Only after he had returned home on 1 May did Kabul Radio report that he had had 'medical checkups in the Soviet Union'.[7] Gorbachev summoned Karmal to his CPSU central committee office and told him he should turn over leadership to Najibullah. '... [D]azed, he obseqiously begged Gorbachev to change his mind, promising to perform his duties in a more correct and active way,' but Gorbachev 'was inexorable', according to a participant in the meeting.[8]

During Karmal's absence from Kabul, demonstrations, probably organized by Ratebzad, called for him to remain in power. The main speaker at Kabul's celebrations of the Saur *coup* anniversary, Defence Minister Nazar Muhammad, did not mention the missing Karmal, and *Pravda* marked the occasion with an unusually critical review of Afghan events.[9]

The day after Karmal returned to Kabul, the PDPA central committee began meeting while Soviet troops and tanks took positions around the capital to prevent trouble. Kryuchkov was reportedly in Kabul to supervise developments.[10] Late on the night of 4 May, Kabul Radio reported that Karmal had asked the committee to accept his resignation as general secretary 'due to my perception of my responsibilities and because of health reasons, and after a careful assessment of my possibilities and of the issues and international problems...'. The committee voted unanimously to accept the resignation 'because of health reasons'. But the committee also 'wished [Karmal] success in his duties as president of the...revolutionary council and member of the PDPA...politburo',[11] which he was obviously healthy enough to retain. After the deaths of Daoud, Taraki, and Amin, Karmal became the first Afghan to survive leaving the top job since the king was deposed in 1973. He left with his comrades' formal thanks. Moscow was silent.

Criticisms of Karmal

Keshtmand, who presided at the central committee session, nominated Najibullah as general secretary. One of Najibullah's 'outstanding qualities', Keshtmand said, was 'his belief in collective and consultative leadership and his respectful approach to the views of party comrades and members of the central committee'. This implied criticism of Karmal echoed Amin's accusation that the deposed Taraki had practised one-man rule. Najibullah later added to the rebuke. He said 'problems demand that the role of collectivism should be enhanced...', and he would be more successful than Karmal by 'keep[ing] to the party's guidelines'.[12] Najibullah said in June that the PDPA had made 'the necessary decisions' to separate the top party and state jobs, but within 17 months he had taken the presidency also, and there was no more talk of collectivism.[13]

Karmal kept up normal public appearances—despite numerous reports of his heavy drinking—while sounding almost pathetically grateful for having been allowed to keep a figurehead presidency. Najibullah conceded that new PDPA factionalism had been created, blaming those who 'saw a danger to their private interests' with the fall of their patron.[14] Parcham split on some questions between those still loyal to Karmal and Najibullah's supporters. Students demonstrated for Karmal eight times within the first week of his demotion, and other protests continued sporadically for months.[15] Najibullah reacted by moving against Karmal's main supporters. His half-brother Barialay was first placed under house arrest, then imprisoned for some two years, and expelled from the PDPA central committee.[16] Ratebzad, who reportedly organized the student demonstrations, was stripped of the leadership of the women's movement that she had created in the 1960s and ousted from the PDPA central committee.[17] As his supporters were fired from key jobs and some were arrested, Karmal was rumoured to have protested fruitlessly to the Soviets that they were being persecuted.[18]

A Temporary President

The CPSU politburo discussed the still-troublesome Karmal on 13 November 1986. It decided that he had to be removed in a way that would preserve his relations with Moscow.[19] On 20 November, amid tightened security, the PDPA central committee convened to hear Najibullah read a letter from Karmal. It asked the party and revolutionary council to accept 'my resignation for the obvious reasons that I mentioned previously, and in the present special conditions, from my party and state posts'. The failure to spell out a health reason or explain the 'special conditions' were peculiar, but Najibullah denied that the letter had been dictated to Karmal. The central committee unanimously agreed to Karmal's giving up his politburo seat and the national presidency, and it gave him a rent-free house and a pension ten times the average for disabled soldiers or survivors of those killed fighting the *mujahideen*.[20]

The revolutionary council immediately rubberstamped the PDPA decision. It named Mohammed Chamkani as acting president until the writing of a new constitution was completed. A Pushtun from Paktia province who did not belong to the PDPA, at least openly, Chamkani had been a member of parliament in the constitutional period and later a provincial governor. He was the regime's figurehead chairman of the September 1985 tribal *jirgah* and had become a vice president of the revolutionary council when it was expanded in January 1986.[21]

Still Karmal was trouble. Rumours in December 1986 said security men kept him from receiving visitors and he turned down an ambassadorship in Eastern Europe[22]—which would have been a repeat of his 1978 banishment. A large demonstration by his supporters on the 1987 anniversary of the Saur *coup* apparently stimulated action. After reports that he was under house arrest, Tass said on 4 May 1987 that, 'in accordance with the recommendation of doctors and upon an invitation, [Karmal] left for the Soviet Union today for treatment and rest...'. *Izvestiya* later described this as a medical pretext to get rid of him.[23] His departure triggered further factional strife.

TOUGH NEW LEADER

The replacement of Karmal with Najibullah was a generational change. Karmal was 57 years old, a veteran of leftist struggle since about the time the 38-year-old Najibullah was born. It was as a member of Karmal's Parcham faction that Najibullah was exiled to the ambassadorship to Iran in 1978. When summoned home that autumn to face treason charges, he absconded with the embassy's money and lived in Yugoslavia, returning home with the Soviet invasion.[24] Najibullah fit the Soviet-assigned role of KhAD boss. Big, burly, with 'an imposing, indeed intimidating, physical presence', the formidable man of constitutional era demonstrations proved a brutal policeman. A number of Pul-i-Charki survivors said Najibullah personally executed prisoners. His favourite technique reportedly was to beat them to the floor and then stomp them to death.[25]

With brutality went political flexibility. Asked five months after becoming general secretary to identify policy differences with Karmal's regime, he replied, 'No, I cannot. Our strategy has not changed. Concerning tactics, our tactics have become more flexible'. And, as quoted earlier, he professed 'complete unanimity of views' with the USSR.[26] Flexibility extended to his name. When he became general secretary he insisted on being known only as Najib. The once devout youth explained that his school and PDPA friends had abbreviated Najibullah by dropping the Islamic suffix 'of God'.[27] But, as appealing to the religious Afghan people became part of his effort to build support, he went back to Najibullah in October 1987, although evading questions of whether he was personally religious.[28]

Najibullah ensured his domination of the PDPA central committee by packing it with supporters at a 10 July 1986 meeting.[29] Fifteen months later Najibullah said that in doubling the committee's size the politburo 'failed to provide strict control over the selection of new members. As a result, a number of mistakes were made, and inevitably a number of party members were [later] expelled from the central committee'.[30] On 30 September 1987, Najibullah also tightened control over the government. At a revolutionary council meeting, Keshtmand thanked Chamkani for his services as acting president but said the PDPA politburo had decided 'that under the present complicated situation' a permanent president was needed. '... [O]nly a representative of the PDPA central committee can hold this position...[b]ecause the PDPA is the only overt political party today.' The politburo had selected Najibullah, whom the council elected unanimously. Chamkani was moved down to first vice president.[31]

NATIONAL RECONCILIATION

As PDPA leader, Najibullah felt Soviet pressure to improve on Karmal's three 1985 initiatives to rally support for the regime. Najibullah conceded on 20 November 1986 that only 'true patriots and long-standing friends of the revolution [had] joined the leadership organs' in Karmal's supposed broadening of the government, but said 'people who are still neutral' should be recruited.[32] He and his Soviet advisers turned to national reconciliation, a concept that Gorbachev publicly advocated on 28 July 1986. The Soviet leader explained it as 'expanding the social base of the April national democratic revolution, right up to the point of creating a government involving participation by political

forces who have been outside the country but who are ready
sincerely to participate in the nationwide process of
constructing a new Afghanistan'.[33]

Najibullah said on 22 September 1986, 'We have formed
an extraordinary commission for national reconciliation' to
receive those willing to renounce their opposition and
observe regime laws.[34] The lack of any concessions made
that sound grudging of Soviet pressure rather than
conciliatory. But Najibullah claimed complete agreement
with Soviet leaders on national reconciliation, after Kremlin
talks on his first official visit to Moscow since taking over
the Afghan leadership, from 11 to 13 December 1986.
Gorbachev, while not repeating previous Soviet leaders'
statements that the Afghan revolution was irreversible,
assured Najibullah that the USSR 'will not abandon our
southern neighbour in a difficult situation'.[35] Later events
indicated he also pressed Najibullah to give national
reconciliation enough substance to create the possibility of
eroding resistance support. Soon after the visit, *Izvestiya*
echoed an American line from Vietnam, saying 'the main
battle under way in Afghanistan today is not taking place on
the battlefield; it is the battle for the hearts and minds of
Afghans...'.[36]

As Najibullah explained national reconciliation to the
PDPA central committee, its key points were a ceasefire
beginning 15 January 1987, a general amnesty and an
invitation for refugees to come home, and the 'creation of a
government of national unity with the participation
of...various political groups, moderates, and monarchists,
and the leaders of armed anti-state groups who are active
abroad...'. However, Najibullah made it clear that the PDPA
would keep power. The aims of reconciliation included 'the
complete implementation of the PDPA action
programme...and the consolidation of a regime friendly with
the Soviet Union', he said.[37]

A 277-member national reconciliation commission met
on 3 January 1987. Najibullah told it that the *mujahideen*

were 'traitors and filthy vultures...in the service of sworn enemies of our people: reactionary imperialists and neocolonialists ..., [but] we are even ready to talk to [these]...dangerous people'.[38] Asked later who would lead the armed forces under a national unity government, he replied, 'The PDPA, which is entrusted with the general political leadership of society, will...'.[39] The ceasefire, whose terms benefited the regime, did not become effective as resistance leaders based in Peshawar scorned the whole national reconciliation package.

National reconciliation created 'panic and pessimism...fear and concern' among PDPA members, some of whom had trouble 'understand[ing] the meaning of peaceful negotiations and political dialogue', Najibullah admitted later.[40] In June 1987 he said, 'The policy...is more difficult and more complex than we imagined', and in October he warned that its implementation was being hampered by PDPA members who 'are not ready to compromise with the opposition for fear of losing their position...'. The policy had stimulated factionalism that 'will be regarded as treachery' and severely punished, Najibullah said ineffectually.[41] Contrary to Kabul's claims, *Pravda* said national reconciliation had 'not broken old prejudices...[or found] proper understanding among forces hostile to' the regime.[42]

Appearances of Sharing Power

A law to regulate a multi-party political system, published on 6 July 1987, contained a lot of qualifications worded vaguely enough to make possible broadly restrictive interpretations by PDPA officials.[43] Najibullah later counted a dozen parties, including four or five in a 'leftist democratic bloc',[44] but a Soviet commentator pronounced the bloc a failure because of PDPA domination. A member of one party in the bloc said the whole multi-party structure was cosmetic because the only parties tolerated were ones that would toe the PDPA line.[45]

On 14 July 1987, Najibullah offered the armed opposition, exiles, supporters of former king Zahir Shah, and others, the jobs of vice president, deputy prime minister, head of the supreme court, a dozen ministerial posts, and several other ostensibly important government positions; and the prime minister's job was offered later. But real power lay in the presidency and such key ministries as defence, security, interior, and foreign affairs, none of which was offered. The resistance quickly rejected the offer.[46] Najibullah admitted in October that the whole multi-party concept was hollow by reassuring worried PDPA members that 'this party...does not and will not give away power. It only refrains from wielding a monopoly of power to broaden the party from the viewpoint of composition, credibility, and prestige'.[47]

A NEW CONSTITUTION

The attempt to give the regime a new look culminated in a constitution to replace the April 1980 'basic principles'. A draft was published on 15 July 1987. To adopt it and elect a new president, the revolutionary council designated 1350 delegates for a *loya jirgah* who met in Kabul on 29 November 1987. Najibullah assured the delegates that the multi-party system 'does not mean the surrender of positions' held by the PDPA. Thus comforted, and despite the shooting outside, the *loya jirgah* approved the constitution on 30 November and unanimously elected an unopposed Najibullah as president.[48]

The new constitution[49] changed the country's name from the Democratic Republic of Afghanistan to a less Soviet-sounding, Republic of Afghanistan. It recognized the PDPA's leading role but allowed other parties, a provision that *Pravda* had an awkward time explaining to its readers in the single-party Soviet state.[50] Calling a *loya jirgah* 'the highest manifestation of the will of the people', the constitution took the name of that traditional gathering of leaders, who acted by consensus, to use for a body to meet irregularly and make decisions by majority vote. The president, who would decide when to convene the *loya jirgah*, was to be elected by it to a seven-year term. He was supreme commander of the armed forces, approved all laws, convened 'when so required' a cabinet that was responsible to him, approved appointments and pensions for judges, senior officials, and military officers, declared emergencies and mobilizations, switched vice presidents as he saw fit, and generally dominated everything. A meaninglessly weak legislative power was assigned to a two-house national assembly named the *meli shura*, with a fully elected lower house, the *wolasi jirgah*, and a partly elected, partly appointed senate, the *sena*. After visiting Afghanistan in early 1988, Ermacora reported to the United Nations that this constitution, which he said was not devised by a 'free act of self-determination', did not adequately safeguard human rights or guarantee a multi-party system.[51]

Pretence of Elections

National assembly elections were abruptly scheduled on 19 March 1988 to be held from 6 to 15 April—in violation of a law requiring three months' notice. The regime claimed 1547 000 Afghans in 8666 villages cast secret ballots, but observers reported many irregularities, including a lack of secret ballots and publication of candidate lists only after polls had opened.[52] Najibullah, who 14 months earlier had said it was 'totally unrealistic' to think of the PDPA's losing elections,[53] engaged in reverse rigging to ensure that members of other parties and independents won seats for show purposes. Publicly identified PDPA members filled only about a quarter of the 184 elected seats in the *wolasi jirgah* and 51 elected to the *sena*, while some seats were 'reserved for the opposition' and left empty.[54]

On 26 May 1988, shortly after the Soviet Army began withdrawing from Afghanistan and the regime was worried about surviving without its foreign shield, the PDPA politburo thanked Keshtmand for serving as prime minister for seven years and made him a party secretary. Najibullah named as prime minister Mohammad Hassan Sharq.[55] An old leftist aide to Daoud, Sharq was not a PDPA member and therefore was supposed to have a broad, conciliatory appeal. But he was widely believed to be a KGB agent and had been the regime's ambassador to India, and since June 1987, a deputy prime minister.[56] The revolutionary council held its final meeting, also on 26 May, and went out of business as the constitution came into effect.[57] The *meli shura* began its first session on 30 May. Sharq announced on 7 June a cabinet with 11 old regime servants as supposedly new faces, while key jobs were filled with familiar PDPA faces. After failing to get a prominent resistance commander or respected retired general to become defence minister, Najibullah settled, in August, for the Khalqi army chief of staff, Col. Gen. Shahnawaz Tanai.[58]

THE ECONOMIC SITUATION

The Afghan economy 'has been destroyed by the war', *Pravda* observed in 1988, and 'cannot meet the basic needs of its population', another Soviet newspaper said later.[59] 'Presently, Afghanistan is mostly leaning on the gratis assistance and favourable credits of the friendly countries', with the war 'devouring two-thirds of the government's material resources', the prime minister, Fazl Haq Khaliqyar, said in May 1990.[60]

'The major part of our production enterprises, pastures, electric power, and water supply systems were totally destroyed', Najibullah said in 1989. 'The accursed war has converted the green lands to unharvested fallow ground filled with weeds.'[61] Khaliqyar, noting that '[t]raditionally, Afghanistan is an agricultural country', said that, 'unfortunately, the greatest of all damage was inflicted on this sector of the economy, affecting peasants and livestock holders'.[62] A survey of the war's effect on agriculture found that between 1978 and 1986 a third of farms were abandoned, the area cultivated by working farms declined by 30 per cent, and overall agricultural production fell 55 per cent, while farmers lost 70 per cent of their sheep and goats and 40 per cent of their draught oxen.[63] Najibullah said that, 'because there is no raw material [from agriculture], the factories do not function'.[64]

In a country that never had accurate statistics, the Soviet embassy in Kabul estimated in 1988 the destruction was 'over $10 billion'.[65] Keshtmand said in February 1990, when he was back as *de facto* prime minister, that 'losses suffered by the country's economy' were estimated at more than 700 billion Afghanis[66]—$12.7 billion at the then official exchange rate. Other, differing, figures were also published. No one really knew how to put a price on the ruin of a country.

Economic disruptions fuelled inflation. A deputy prime minister said in 1988 that 'prices are too high and are often beyond the means of ordinary Afghans'.[67] In Kabul, whose population approximately tripled to some two million, some 70 per cent of the children admitted to hospitals in 1989 suffered from malnutrition or deficiency diseases.[68] A physician said in 1989 that his government salary of 5000 Afghanis a month had not risen in five years, but rice had recently gone from 300 Afghanis a kilogram to 1000, meat from 100 to 800 Afghanis a kilogram, eggs from 5 to 35 Afghanis apiece.[69] Most government enterprises operated at a loss, but the regime fed inflation by covering deficits as well as war costs with Soviet-printed money.[70] Another inflationary factor was counterfeit Afghanis introduced by the CIA 'in order to wreck the Kabul regime's economy and allow the *mujahideen* to buy weapons and ammunition', according to American sources.[71]

Soviet Economic Aid

Soviet economic aid sustained the Kabul regime from shortly after the PDPA came to power until the end of 1991, when the USSR broke up. Moscow provided between 80 and 90 per cent of all foreign aid received during the war years.[72] An official of Moscow's Institute for Oriental Studies commented in 1980 that in economic terms Afghanistan had become another backward republic of the USSR whose deficits and development expenses had to be met by Moscow.[73] A Standing Intergovernmental Commission for Economic Cooperation became the mechanism for the Soviet economic planning organization, Gosplan, to take over effective control of the limited degree of centralized economic management possible in wartime Kabul—mostly just making decisions on what goods to supply and how to distribute them.[74] 'We have,' the Afghan commerce minister said in 1988, 'the enormous amount of Soviet economic aid to thank for the fact that we have been able to survive at all during these last few years'.[75] Under Moscow's pressure, its East European allies also supplied some aid, and such non-bloc countries as Yugoslavia and India ran small aid projects.[76]

The amount of Soviet economic aid to Kabul—military aid costs are discussed in Chapter 7—is obscured by traditional Soviet secrecy as well as the complex bookkeeping of Moscow's command economy that hid true costs. Even Soviet officials were uncertain.[77] According to American calculations, in almost a decade—from the invasion to the Soviet troop withdrawal—$3.311 billion worth of economic aid was promised and most was probably delivered.[78] An Afghan report said almost half the economic aid from 1978 to 1985 was a gift, but in early 1990 the Soviet finance ministry listed Afghanistan as owing 3.055 billion rubles, officially equal to $4.888 billion, for both economic and military aid. *Izvestiya* commented, 'We should not count seriously on...being repaid soon...'. As of 1 January 1996, the Russian comptroller's office said, Afghanistan owed $8.228 billion. The increase was not explained.[79]

As the USSR's own economic problems became more obvious in the late 1980s, Soviet public hostility toward aid to Afghanistan began to be publicized, and Afghan waste and corruption became an issue. Najibullah admitted in 1987 that Soviet grants 'are not being justly distributed..., [and] hoarding and bribery ha[ve] been transformed into a source of wealth for individuals'.[80] Soviet media told of 'irresponsibility and disorganization of the Afghan administrative apparatus', of 'individual bureaucrats [who] grew rich on the free aid being supplied by our country', and of outright theft. They also complained that Soviet aid was often unlabelled, so Afghan recipients did not appreciate who was helping them.[81]

In addition to economic ties between the Afghan and Soviet national governments, Soviet republics, *oblasts* (provinces), and cities began in 1987 to make direct economic, cultural, trade union, and other ties with Afghan provinces and towns.[82] Such ties apparently were intended to relieve the bureaucratic and financial burden on Moscow, permit more direct and specialized supervision of project implementation, and bypass the corruption and inefficiency of Kabul to get aid to the Afghan grass roots. Some provincial ties and central government economic relations as well were intended to strengthen private enterprise in Afghanistan.[83] Despite attempts to set up rural cooperatives and state farms as part of the PDPA's naive effort to socialize the economy, more than 99 per cent of agricultural output came from private farmers. Keshtmand said in early 1990 that private business contributed 78 per cent of the country's gross national product, with 60 per cent of foreign trade and 85 per cent of domestic trade in private hands.[84] Private businessmen—a high proportion of them Hindus and Sikhs whose families had moved to Afghanistan decades earlier from British India—were the victims of what a Soviet commentator called 'unjustified repressions', and Sharq said they 'suffered enormous damage'.[85] None the less, they bought carpets, dried fruit, and other traditional products in villages beyond government control, paid various taxes or bribes to the *mujahideen* and Afghan forces to move their goods, and sent them abroad, bringing back food and consumer goods that were essential for the fractured economy. They also ran the bazaar stalls where ordinary Afghans shopped, and they changed money for regime and Soviet officials.[86]

Throughout the 1980s, ordinary Afghans suffered and adjusted, a few people got rich, the new elite of PDPA leaders bullied and gave wild parties,[87] politics changed and adapted, and the war went on.

NOTES

1. *CWIHPB*, Nos. 8-9: 178; *Izvestiya*, 16 September 1991, p. 5, in *FBIS/SU*, 17 September 1991, p. 13.
2. Pyadyshev, 'Najibullah', p. 19.
3. Kabul Radio, 21 November 1985, in *FBIS/SA*, 22 November 1985, p. C1. At the same time, Panjshiri lost his politburo seat and Abdul Qadir was replaced as a candidate politburo member by new Defence Minister Nazar Muhammad.
4. Kabul Radio, 5 December 1985 and 4 May 1986, in *FBIS/SA*, 6 December 1985 and 5 May 1986, pp. C2 and C2. This paralleled the move of Andropov from heading the KGB to the CPSU secretariat in May 1982, as Brezhnev's health was waning, before succeeding him.
5. Moscow Television, 25 February 1986, in *FBIS/SU Supplement*, 26 February 1986, p. O31.
6. *Pravda*, 1 March 1986, p. 11, in *FBIS/SU*, 19 March 1986, pp. O14-15.
7. Kabul Radio, 1 May 1986, in *FBIS/SA*, 2 May 1986, p. C1.

8. Anatoly F. Dobrynin, *In Confidence: Moscow's Ambassador to America's Six Cold War Presidents (1962-1986)* (New York, 1995), pp. 442-3.

9. Kabul Radio, 23 April 1986, in *FBIS/SA*, 28 April 1986, p. C1; *Pravda*, 27 April 1986, p. 5, in *FBIS/SU*, 30 April 1986, pp. D3-4.

10. BBC, 6 May 1986, in *FBIS/SA*, 7 May 1986, p. C1; *Trud*, 24 October 1991, pp. 1, 4, in *JPRS-UIA-91-027*, 27 November 1991, p. 57.

11. Kabul Radio, 4 May 1986, in *FBIS/SA*, 5 May 1986, pp. C1-2.

12. Ibid.; Bakhtar from Kabul, 14 May 1986, in *FBIS/SA*, 16 May 1986, p. C1; *Der Spiegel*, 23 June 1986, pp. 104-06, in *FBIS/SA*, 27 June 1986, p. C1; Kabul Radio, 10 July 1986, in *FBIS/SA*, 15 July 1986, p. C1.

13. Bakhtar from Kabul, 20 June 1986, in *FBIS/SA*, 23 June 1986, p. C1. When the CPSU ousted Nikita S. Khrushchev in 1964, it decided that no one should hold both his jobs as party leader and as prime minister—the effective head of the Soviet government, while the president has little power. But after weakening Kosygin's prime ministerial authority, Brezhnev added a strengthened presidency to his party leadership in 1977.

14. Kabul Radio, 18 October 1987, in *FBIS/NE*, 20 October 1987, pp. 44-5.

15. *New York Times*, 12 May 1986, p. A7; Karachi Radio, 10 June 1986, in *FBIS/SA*, 11 June 1986, p. F1; *Le Monde*, 15 November 1986.

16. *Nepszabadsag*, 7 September 1989, p. 6, in *FBIS/NE*, 14 September 1989, p. 39; Kabul Radio, 17 October 1987, in *FBIS/NE*, 19 October 1987, p. 44.

17. Kabul Radio, 6 August and 22 November 1986, in *FBIS/SA*, 12 August, 25 and 26 November 1986, pp. C2, C3, and C1; Kabul Radio, 10 June and 17 October 1987, in *FBIS/NE*, 11 June and 19 October 1987, pp. P1 and 44.

18. Tanjug from Islamabad, 12 November 1986, in *FBIS/SA*, 13 November 1986, pp. C1-2.

19. *CWIHPB*, Nos. 8-9: 178-80.

20. Kabul Radio, 20 and 22 November 1986, 13 May 1987, in *FBIS/SA*, 21 and 26 November 1986, 19 May 1987, pp. C1, C2, and C3.

21. CTK from Kabul, 20 November 1986, in *FBIS/SA*, 21 November 1986, p. C3; *Pravda*, 28 March 1986, p. 4, in *FBIS/SU*, 2 April 1986, p. D3; Kabul Radio, 17 January 1986, in *FBIS/SA*, 22 January 1986, p. C1.

22. Xinhua from Islamabad, 10 December 1986, in *FBIS/SA*, 10 December 1986, p. C1.

23. *Le Monde*, 20 May 1987, p. 6; Tass from Kabul, 4 May 1987, in *FBIS/SU*, 5 May 1987, p. D1; *Izvestiya*, 15 June 1991, p. 7, in *FBIS/SU*, 18 June 1991, p. 16.

24. Mackenzie, 'Brutal Force', p. 14; Pyadyshev, 'Najibullah', p. 22; *Danas*, 29 August 1989, pp. 50-52.

25. *New York Times*, 2 December 1987, p. A9; *New York Times Magazine*, 29 December 1991, p. 23; Paris Radio, 29 May 1988, in *FBIS/NE*, 1 June 1988, p. 34.

26. Kabul Radio, 21 October 1986, in *FBIS/SA*, 24 October 1986, p. C3; *Muslim*, 26 February 1987, p. 8, in *FBIS/SA*, 10 March 1987, p. C2.

27. *Pravda*, 5 October 1987, p. 5, in *FBIS/SU*, 5 October 1987, p. 31.

28. *Der Spiegel*, 23 June 1986, pp. 104-106, in *FBIS/SA*, 27 June 1986, p. C2; Kabul Radio, 21 October 1986, in *FBIS/SA*, 24 October 1986, p. C2.

29. Kabul Radio, 10 July 1986, in *FBIS/SA*, 11 July 1986, pp. C1-3.

30. Kabul Radio, 18 October 1987, in *FBIS/NE*, 23 October 1987, pp. 33.

31. Kabul Radio and Bakhtar from Kabul, 30 September 1987, in *FBIS/NE*, 1 October 1987, p. 32.

32. Kabul Radio, 22 November 1986, in *FBIS/SA*, 25 November 1986, p. C2.

33. Moscow Television, 28 July 1986, in *FBIS/SU*, 29 July 1986, pp. R18-19.

34. Kabul Radio, 23 September 1986, in *FBIS/SA*, 24 September 1986, p. C1.

35. Bakhtar from Kabul, 31 December 1986, in *FBIS/SA*, 5 January 1987, p. C1; *Pravda*, 14 December 1986, p. 2, in *FBIS/SU*, 15 December 1986, p. D4.

36. *Izvestiya*, 27 December 1986, p. 4, in *FBIS/SU*, 29 December 1986, p. D1.

37. Bakhtar from Kabul, 31 December 1986, in *FBIS/SA*, 5 January 1987, pp. C2-3.

38. Kabul Radio, 3 January 1987, in *FBIS/SA*, 5 January 1987, pp. C7-9.

39. Kabul Radio, 18 January 1987, in *FBIS/SA*, 21 January 1987, pp. C7-8.

40. Kabul Radio, 18 October 1987 and 27 June 1990, in *FBIS/NE*, 20 October 1987 and 3 July 1990, pp. 44 and 46.

41. Kabul Radio, 14 June and 18 October 1987, in *FBIS/NE*, 19 June and 20 October 1987, pp. P2 and 44.

42. *Pravda*, 26 April 1987, p. 5, in *FBIS/SU*, 1 May 1987, p. D1.

43. Kabul Radio, 8 July 1987, in *FBIS/NE*, 9 July 1987, pp. P1-2.

44. Bakhtar from Kabul, 1 September 1988, in *FBIS/NE*, 2 September 1988, p. 40; Bakhtar from Kabul, 12 July 1986, in *FBIS/SA*, 16 July

1986, p. C2; Kabul Radio, 18 January 1987, in *FBIS/SA*, 21 January 1987, p. C6; Kabul Radio, 18 October 1987, 28 January and 26 March 1988, in *FBIS/NE*, 23 October 1987, 29 January and 28 March 1988, pp. 30, 55, and 39-40.

45. *Ogonek*, No. 30, 1988: 25-27; AFP from Kabul, 14 September 1990, in *FBIS/NE*, 14 September 1990, p. 39.
46. Bakhtar from Kabul, 14 July 1987, in *FBIS/NE*, 16 July 1987, pp. P1-2; State Department, 'Afghanistan: Eight Years', p. 13.
47. Kabul Radio, 18 October 1987, in *FBIS/NE*, 23 October 1987, p. 44.
48. Kabul Radio, 30 November 1987, in *FBIS/NE*, 1 and 3 December 1987, pp. 47 and 58; AFP from Kabul, 30 November 1987, in *FBIS/NE*, 30 November 1987, pp. 47-50; Bakhtar from Kabul, 30 November 1987, in *FBIS/NE*, 1 December 1987, p. 47; *New York Times*, 30 November 1987, p. A8.
49. Text, Kabul Radio, 2 December 1987, in *FBIS/NE*, 4 December 1987, pp. 47-57.
50. *Pravda*, 17 October 1987, p. 4, in *FBIS/SU*, 28 October 1987, pp. 31-3.
51. State Department, 'Afghanistan: Soviet Occupation and Withdrawal', p. 14.
52. Tass from Kabul, 15 April 1988, in *FBIS/SU*, 18 April 1987, pp. 45-6; Kabul Radio, 19 March and 21 April 1988, in *FBIS/NE*, 21 March and 22 April 1988, pp. 42 and 51.
53. *Die Zeit*, 13 February 1987, pp. 3-4, in *FBIS/SA*, 12 February 1987, p. C1.
54. Kabul Radio, 29 March, 14 and 21 April 1988, in *FBIS/NE*, 31 March, 15 and 22 April 1988, pp. 43, 45, and 50-51; Bakhtar from Kabul, 26 April, 8 and 9 May 1988, in *FBIS/NE*, 28 April, 9 and 13 May 1988, pp. 49, 53, and 31-7.
55. Kabul Radio, 26 May 1988, in *FBIS/NE*, 27 May 1988, p. 42.
56. *Afghan Jehad*, June-August 1987: 6; State Department, 'Afghanistan: Soviet Occupation and Withdrawal', p. 8.
57. Kabul Radio, 26 May 1988, in *FBIS/NE*, 27 May 1988, pp. 43-4.
58. Bakhtar from Kabul, 18 June 1988, in *FBIS/NE*, 20 June 1988, pp. 39-40; State Department, 'Afghanistan: Soviet Occupation and Withdrawal', p. 8.
59. *Pravda*, 20 January 1988, p. 6, in *FBIS/SU*, 26 January 1988, pp. 34-5; *Komsomolskaya Pravda*, 14 June 1990, p. 3, in *FBIS/SU*, 19 June 1990, p. 15.
60. Kabul Radio, 21 May 1990, in *FBIS/NE*, 23 May 1990, p. 29; *Kabul Times*, 31 September 1990, p. 1.

61. *Rabotnichesko Delo,* 11 April 1989, pp. 1, 5, in *FBIS/NE,* 14 April 1989, p. 46; Kabul Radio, 19 February 1989, in *FBIS/NE,* 21 February 1989, p. 60.
62. Kabul Radio, 21 May 1990, in *FBIS/NE,* 23 May 1990, p. 29.
63. Swedish Committee for Afghanistan, in *Afghan Jehad,* April-June 1988: 95-6; *Economist,* 4 June 1988, p. 30.
64. Kabul Radio, 25 December 1989, in *FBIS/NE,* 29 December 1989, p. 46.
65. Tass from Kabul, 8 August 1988, in *FBIS/SU,* 9 August 1988, p. 22.
66. Kabul Radio, 4 February 1990, in *FBIS/NE,* 8 February 1990, p. 48.
67. *Izvestiya,* 11 November 1988, p. 5, in *FBIS/SU,* 16 November 1988, p. 26.
68. *Daily Telegraph,* 17 May 1989, p. 11; *Washington Post,* 26 July 1989, p. A19.
69. *Dialogue,* 29 September 1989, p. 7.
70. Kabul Radio, 15 March 1988, in *FBIS/NE,* 22 March 1988, pp. 54-5.
71. Robert D. Kaplan, *Soldiers of God: With the* Mujahidin *in Afghanistan* (Boston, 1990), p. 23; *Washington Post,* 4 May 1987, p. C15; Tim Weiner, *Blank Check: The Pentagon's Black Budget* (New York, 1990), p. 160.
72. Kabul Radio, 15 March 1988, in *FBIS/NE,* 22 March 1988, p. 52; *Al-Watan,* 22 August 1989, p. 15, in *FBIS/NE,* 31 August 1989, p. 44.
73. FCO, 'Sovietisation of Afghanistan'.
74. *Vechernaya Moskva,* 26 July 1989, p. 4; *Pravda,* 1 October 1986, p. 5, in *FBIS/SU,* 3 October 1986, p. D1.
75. Jallalar in *Hufvudstadsbladet,* 23 May 1988, p. 12, in *FBIS/NE,* 10 June 1988, p. 45.
76. *Washington Times,* 21 March 1990, p. A8; *Pravda,* 1 September 1985, p. 5, and Tass from Moscow, 30 January 1987, in *FBIS/SU,* 17 September 1985 and 2 February 1987, pp. D3 and D1.
77. Moscow Television, 3 August 1890, in *FBIS/SU,* 6 August 1990, p. 28.
78. CIA, 'Handbook of Economic Statistics, 1990' (Washington, 1990), p. 181.
79. Bakhtar from Kabul, 30 March 1985, in *FBIS/SA,* 1 April 1985, p. C1; *Izvestiya,* 2 March 1990, p. 3, in *FBIS/SU,* 5 March 1990, pp. 83-4; *Rossiyskaya Gazeta,* 28 December 1996, p. 13.
80. Kabul Radio, 18 October and 6 November 1987, in *FBIS/NE,* 23 October and 10 November 1987, pp. 42 and 37.
81. Moscow Radio, 21 December 1988, in *FBIS/SU,* 29 December 1988, p. 24; *Pravda,* 26 September and 31 January 1988, pp. 7 and 5, in *FBIS/SU,* 28 September and 3 February 1988, pp. 34-5 and 30;

Moscow Television, 3 February 1988 and 22 January 1989, in *FBIS/SU*, 4 February 1988 and 23 January 1989, pp. 22 and 36.

82. State Department, 'Afghanistan: Soviet Occupation and Withdrawal', p. 15.

83. *Sovetskaya Rossiya*, 17 March 1988, p. 3, in *FBIS/SU*, 21 March 1988, p. 29; Tass from Kabul, 6 April 1988, in *FBIS/SU*, 7 April 1988, p. 12.

84. *Kabul Times*, 11 January 1991, p. 1; Kabul Radio, 4 February 1990, in *FBIS/NE*, 8 February 1990, p. 48.

85. Kabul Radio, 1 June 1986, in *FBIS/SA*, 3 June 1986, p. C1; Moscow Radio, 21 December 1988, in *FBIS/SU*, 29 December 1988, p. 24; *Izvestiya*, 5 August and 3 September 1988, pp. 5 and 5, in *FBIS/SU*, 10 August and 6 September 1988, pp. 16 and 32; Kabul Radio, 19 February 1989, in *FBIS/NE*, 21 February 1989, p. 59.

86. *New York Times*, 14 July 1985 and 15 May 1987, pp. 1 and A6; *Dawn Weekly Economic and Business Review Supplement*, 7 December 1985, p. 3, in *FBIS/SA*, 13 December 1985, pp. F1-2.

87. *New York Times*, 21 April 1989, p. A8; *New Times*, 27 November 1990, p. 29; AFP from Kabul, 28 December 1988, in *FBIS/NE*, 28 December 1988, p. 43.

CHAPTER 6

MUHAJERIN AND *MUJAHIDEEN*

The conflict during Afghanistan's Communist period caused an uncounted number of deaths, scarcely told suffering and hardship, and the displacement of millions of people. It changed the nature of Afghan life by destruction, the movement of refugees, and the introduction of new political players and perceptions—unleashing yet further death and destruction. The human costs of this period can never be adequately chronicled. No summary account can do justice to the injustices caused by politics, ideology, religion, ethnicity, local traditions and rivalries, and personal power lusts. The reports are seemingly endless of wanton violence, casual carnage, and primitive revenge.

ESTIMATES OF AFGHAN DEAD

In a country whose population was only vaguely known, there was no accurate way to number the dead. Most *mujahideen* leaders, regime officials, Soviet spokesmen, and Western relief agencies used estimates of 1.3 million to 1.5 million Afghan dead between the Saur *coup* and the Soviet troop withdrawal in 1989. As the Najibullah regime was collapsing three years and much more fighting later, both United Nations representative Benon Sevan and Moscow Radio said two million Afghans had been killed, but the figure used by the new *mujahideen* government in Kabul was 1.5 million for the entire fourteen-year Communist period. Estimates of Afghan wounded and maimed varied from 500 000 to two million.[1] Soviet casualties are discussed in Chapter 8.

Most estimates were derived from a survey in August 1987 of 1300 refugee families in Pakistan whose distribution approximated the whole Afghan population. It found that some 9 per cent of the pre-war Afghan population had been killed up to then. Depending upon estimates of the pre-war figure, that meant between one and 1.5 million dead, with a probable figure of 1.25 million. The study also found that about 435 000 persons had been incapacitated.[2] An Afghan demographer who criticized the survey as having a sampling bias put the number killed from 1978 to 1987 at an improbably precise 876 825.[3]

CREATING REFUGEES

Soviet and regime attacks on villages sent survivors fleeing into towns or across the Pakistani or Iranian borders. Ermacora quoted witnesses as saying massacres of villagers 'were part of a deliberate policy...to force the people to take flight'. He suggested this was intended to deprive the resistance 'of a base of support within the population'.[4] Many refugees left relatively quiet areas for economic or political reasons, from fear of regime conscription, or simply in panic after the Soviet invasion.[5] As they moved toward the borders, many were bombed, shot at, and sprinkled with anti-personnel mines. But Kabul and Moscow insisted the refugees were just nomads who came and went regularly, or they were wealthy opponents of 'the revolution', those deluded or coerced by counter-revolutionaries, or victims of Amin.[6] Instead of the Western term 'refugee', those who flee to safety, the resistance called them *muhajerin*: religious migrants who move or seek aloofness in order to defend or preserve the Islamic faith. The term came to apply primarily to those who went abroad rather than internal refugees.

The number of internal refugees at the end of the 1980s was usually estimated—or guessed—at about two million.[7] There was little more precision in the numbers used for external refugees, although authorities in Pakistan and Iran as well as United Nations officials cited figures with confidence. By the late 1980s Pakistan said it had 3.1 million registered Afghan refugees and 400 000 unregistered ones, but its figures were criticized as inflated in order to exaggerate its relief effort.[8] Confusion, bureaucratic ineptitude, corruption in ration distribution, secrecy and political controls in refugee camps, and other factors obscured true numbers. Even looser Iranian figures were confused by migratory Afghan labourers. By 1988 the United Nations High Commissioner for Refugees (UNHCR) reported 2.35 million in Iran, most of them fending for themselves rather than receiving care in special camps.[9]

If the very uncertain and perhaps exaggerated UNHCR figures of some 5.5 million refugees abroad are added to the estimate of two million internal refugees, then the war had displaced half the estimated 15 million pre-war population. When the estimate of 1.5 million dead is added, the very imprecise but nonetheless appalling conclusion is that 60 per cent of Afghanistan's people lost their lives or their homes.

REFUGEES ABROAD

In Pakistan 'the single largest concentration of refugees in the world'[10] focused on about 380 'refugee tented villages', known as RTVs, although many Afghans lived outside the official refugee system. Pakistani authorities continued to use the term RTV to deny the permanence of the problem, but residents quickly turned tent camps into Afghan villages of mud-brick houses and mud-walled compounds. Small shops expanded into large bazaars as some camps planned for 10 000 grew to towns of 100 000 or more persons. Women and children under 15 years of age made up three-quarters of the residents; the camps were obviously rest and recreation centres for *mujahideen*. The humanitarian, nonpolitical UNHCR uncomfortably abided by Pakistan's rules for registering guerrilla fighters as refugees but withdrew relief services from camps that became men-only military training centres.

Life in the camps was hard. Sanitation was poor but health standards were fairly good under the circumstances. A combined Pakistani and UNHCR programme provided basic foods, and other aid came from Western governments and private voluntary organizations. There was corruption on both sides: refugees exaggerated their numbers to get more rations, while Pakistani officials stole from the aid.[11] But considering the scope of the problem in a developing country, Pakistan's response was notably successful.

Refugee camps were initially organized and regulated by the 'white beards' who had played that role back in their villages. They were displaced by 'ration *maliks*', younger Afghans who knew how to fiddle the system to get more aid. Young *mujahideen* commanders on breaks from fighting across the Durand Line became symbols of camp authority, and with them came the complications of resistance politics. Men dominated the camps. For many rural Afghan women, life in exile opened new horizons through contacts with people and things previously unknown. But it closed the horizons of many urban women, particularly better educated ones who had become accustomed to Daoud's 1959 relaxation of restrictive customs—particularly Pushtun, and in many cases non-Islamic, ones. These women were forced into unwanted seclusion and isolation as the war's threat to Afghan customs caused some men to become insistent upon observing them.[12] The contrast with the Kabul regime, which emphasized modern opportunities for women, was sharp.

With guerrilla fighters making periodic visits to the camps where their wives waited, the refugee community in Pakistan had 'a fertility rate that may well be the highest in recorded history'.[13] The UNHCR and relief agencies under its auspices ran some camp schools. Schools were also operated by Middle Eastern interests and resistance organizations. The latter influenced the selection of teachers for UNHCR schools, so that political affiliation came to count more than educational qualifications. Most schools were for boys. The principal of one said, 'The prime duty of our teaching staff is to instill in [Afghan boys] the spirit of *jihad*'.[14]

A poll of 2287 men and 155 women in 106 Pakistani refugee camps in July 1987 showed that 71 per cent wanted former king Zahir Shah as their spokesman.[15] This was unacceptable to the Islamists and also to Pakistani authorities, who had fostered the Islamists since 1973 because they were enemies of the old royal family that agitated for Pushtunistan. The Islamists repeatedly denounced the king as the man who had opened the doors to Communism in Afghanistan and rejected any role for him in the country's future.[16] Pakistan refused to let Zahir Shah visit the country and denied his supporters access to the refugees or the *mujahideen*.[17] The poll was dismissed as unscientific and prejudiced. The respected refugee professor who published it, Sayed Bahaouddin Majrooh, was murdered. Gulbuddin Hekmatyar, who was widely suspected of ordering the murder, reportedly warned that those who backed the king would share Majrooh's fate.[18] Nonetheless, a number of independent observers in touch with refugees found a strong belief that the king represented the peaceful 'good old days', which created hope that he could somehow resolve the refugees' problems.[19]

REFUGEE AND RESISTANCE POLITICS

Pakistan saw an opportunity in Afghan turmoil to steer the resistance along political lines that fit its long-term goal of having a friendly, even subservient government in Kabul.

This required shaping the *mujahideen* politically. Too many factions—one observer counted 137 by March 1980—would be hard to control. Pakistani officials therefore chose to work through leaders whom they knew. The primary group was Afghan Islamists who were close to President Zia's supporters in the politically similar Pakistani *Jamaat-i Islami* and to Pakistani military intelligence, ISI. Secondarily, there were traditional Afghan notables known to Pakistani officials.

The two main Pakistan-based opponents of the PDPA, Rabbani and Hekmatyar, and others, united on 24 September 1978 into a movement headed by Mohammad Nabi Mohammadi, who as a recent arrival from Afghanistan was a neutral figure with no faction of his own. But Rabbani's Jamiat and Hekmatyar's Hezb soon felt they were losing support to Mohammadi. Unity evaporated, with Mohammadi keeping many clerical supporters and evolving his own party, *Harakat-e Inqilab-e Islami* (Islamic Revolutionary Movement). Soon after, in 1979, Mohammed Yunus Khales left Hekmatyar's Hezb to create his own party, which became known as *Hezb-Khales*. Then Sibghatullah Mojaddedi created the *Jebh-e Nejat-e Melli* (National Liberation Front) and Ahmad Gailani established *Mahaz-e Melli Islami* (National Islamic Front [of Afghanistan], known to Westerners as NIFA). This brought the main Peshawar parties to six.[20]

Saudi Arabia used promises of aid in 1979 to try to get the parties to cooperate.[21] After the Soviet invasion, a Saudi representative played a key role in getting some parties to set up a united front for the January 1980 meeting of Islamic countries to condemn the USSR.[22] The front's chairman was Abdul Rasul Sayyaf, who had just emerged from a Kabul prison and was therefore considered neutral in *mujahideen* power struggles. Hekmatyar refused to be considered an equal of the other five parties, however, and on 18 March 1980 they announced an alliance without him.[23] Disagreement over what kind of future Afghanistan they were seeking proved disruptive. In addition, the five parties found Sayyaf too dictatorial and too possessive of Saudi and Gulf money for their cause. The alliance dissolved in January 1981 amid angry charges of corruption and abuses of power by Sayyaf. Like Mohammedi, he kept vestiges of the alliance as his own party, *Ittihad-e Islami* (Islamic Union, or Unity). Now there were seven Peshawar groups. Pakistan froze the number there and required all refugees to be certified by one of the seven in order to draw rations. Certification was intended to avoid duplicate aid distribution, winnow out Communist infiltrators, and enhance Pakistan's influence.[24]

Pakistan's selection of *mujahideen* leaders, paralleled and reinforced by the channelling of most military aid to the resistance through the seven, established a controversial framework for the political struggle between Kabul and the *mujahideen*. It did not, however, give the seven popular legitimacy for the same reason that Soviet sponsorship denied legitimacy to the PDPA regime. All were creatures of foreigners. The Zia government, rather than any representative group of Afghans, anointed the leaders that Islamabad would continue to try to foist upon Afghanistan throughout the anti-Communist war and even after. The leaders did not reflect the Afghan religious, political, or ethnic spectrum. Islamists held a disproportionate role, while Shi'ites were ignored. Deliberately left out were important elements from the anti-Communist political scene, not least the technocrats who had served the king. Except for one Tajik, the seven leaders were Ghilzai or Eastern Pushtuns.

When the Carter administration began to take interest in helping the resistance, Pakistan selected *mujahideen* leaders for a meeting with a special CIA envoy in Peshawar in May 1979.[25] Thereafter, ISI controlled virtually all foreign military aid to reach the resistance through Pakistan, which was the main access because of Iran's anti-Western attitude and focus on its war with Iraq. Under Zia, ISI came to dominate policy-making on Afghanistan.[26] Its attitude that the problem had to be solved by military means, to the advantage of the Islamists, distressed the Pakistani foreign ministry, which sought a politically broader negotiated solution to the Soviet presence and civil war.[27]

THE PESHAWAR SEVEN

The competition between Hekmatyar's Hezb and Rabbani's Jamiat that had begun in 1977 worsened during the war. Many saw it as a Pushtun-Tajik conflict, although both parties crossed ethnic lines. These two Islamist groups became in many ways the most important resistance units, Hezb because of ISI favouritism and Jamiat because of its commanders Massoud and Ismail Khan. These and the other five Peshawar parties, all of them Sunni Muslim, drew their strengths primarily from ethnic, tribal, regional, group, family, or personal connections in a classic Afghan way of building support.[28] Such ties were more important than views about a future government. The groups were not political parties in the Western sense. They lacked ideologies, and they did not seek to build mass support or to advocate coherent policies in an effort to achieve popularity. Indeed, they often seemed to scorn popularity, preferring the machinations of competitive cliques. They also scorned exiled Afghans who sought to think ahead and make plans for a post-Communist period.

The leader most noted for his machinations, as well as for challenging traditional Afghan conventions of leadership and support structures, was **Hekmatyar**. His party was Leninist in both its dictatorial nature and its ruthless drive to achieve power in whatever amoral way was expedient. As a Ghilzai Pushtun who had grown up in the Tajik north, cut off from Pushtun tribal networks, Hekmatyar appealed with spellbinding oratory to others from geographic pockets of ethnic minorities and to detribalized youths from the state educational system. The latter were also the original recruiting target for the PDPA. Both the Communists and Hekmatyar sought to banish the traditional Afghan system of government by tribal, territorial, and ethnic notables. Both alienated not only those notables but also masses of followers who were comfortably accustomed to the old system. Their difference was in the PDPA's Soviet Marxist theory of an egalitarian society versus a government on Islamic lines as defined personally by Hekmatyar. 'The religious leader must simultaneously be the political leader,' he said,[29] defying the Afghan tradition that village mullahs were subservient to the larger landholders.

Pakistan's favouritism toward Hekmatyar was partly a result of backing from Hussain Ahmad, leader of the Pakistani Jamaat that Zia used for domestic political support. Ahmad took advantage of this leverage to solidify official backing for Hekmatyar, whom he saw as capable of establishing in Afghanistan the kind of rigorously Islamic state that Ahmad sought in Pakistan. Hekmatyar's lack of a tribal or ethnic power base made him need this support and hence open to guidance. But he was not easy to handle. Once, when he flouted Pakistani guidance, Zia ordered ISI to warn him 'that it was Pakistan who made him an Afghan leader, and it is Pakistan who can equally destroy him if he continues to misbehave'. The rebuke had 'little noticeable effect'.[30]

ISI spread the word early in the war that Hekmatyar commanded the largest guerrilla organization, the best-organized and militarily most effective group. This was always doubtful, but any degree of truth in it resulted from ISI's forcing refugees to cooperate with him on threat of losing rations and its giving Hezb the weapons that attracted guerrilla adherents. Little was heard, however, of Hekmatyar's followers fighting Kabul's troops or Soviet forces. Instead, his faceless commanders—Hekmatyar dominated all Hezb publicity—were widely accused of provoking turf battles with other parties' fighters and robbing their supply convoys while conserving their own arms and energies for the struggle for power after the PDPA fell.[31] He was widely accused of ordering the assassination of competing *mujahideen* commanders and challenging public figures such as Majrooh, of running secret prisons in Pakistani refugee camps where opponents were tortured and murdered, of other ruthless actions—all of which he glibly denied.[32] While respected for his intelligence, his grasp of detail, and his ability to inspire others, Hekmatyar was feared for his single-minded determination to achieve personal control in the ruins of Afghanistan.

Rabbani's Jamiat was a looser organization originally built around religious leaders from both state and private Islamic schools. While seeking a state based on religion, it was less hostile to conventional secular Afghan modes of exercising authority than Hezb, more willing to accept a multi-party system than Hekmatyar's autocratic belief in a single religious party. Jamiat had enough Pushtun and Uzbek adherents to make a convincing case that it was not just an expression of separatism by its primary following of Tajiks. Unlike Hekmatyar, the mild and sometimes indecisive Rabbani did not feel threatened by such strong personalities as Massoud and Ismail Khan.

Khales, born in 1919 or 1920, was the oldest Peshawar leader and the only one who regularly left Pakistan to join his followers in combat. An eastern Pushtun, educated in Afghan and Pakistani religious schools, he split with Hekmatyar primarily because he believed in wide-ranging cooperation for the sake of their cause and could not accept Hekmatyar's demands for personal control or hostility toward those who rejected it. Khales also accused Hekmatyar of avoiding combat. A number of traditional religious leaders followed Khales. His adherents included some of the more effective commanders, such as Abdul Haq in the Kabul area and Jalaluddin Haqqani in Paktia. Some saw Khales as a beloved figurehead, while Haq's family ran Hezb-Khales as a political front for a military organization, but Haq later distanced himself from the party's increasingly fundamentalist character.[33]

The fourth Islamist party, Ittihad, became **Sayyaf**'s personal vehicle for Saudi Arabian financial support to the resistance. A member of the Kabul University Islamist group, Sayyaf had been imprisoned by Daoud in 1973 or 1974 and was only released in the post-invasion amnesty. Fluent in classical Arabic from studies in Mecca, Sayyaf identified with the puritanical Wahhabi form of Islam in official favour in Saudi Arabia, which scorned Afghanistan's more ecumenical and Sufi-influenced form. Sayyaf's adaptability made him a channel for the money and influence of Saudi Wahhabis as well as Muslim Brotherhood members in other Arab countries. This money bought some support inside Afghanistan, particularly among Sayyaf's fellow Ghilzai Pushtuns immediately north of Kabul, but his party lacked a natural base and remained small.

Of the three parties built on traditional Afghan ties rather than religious revivalism, the Harakat of Nabi **Mohammadi** was in 1979 considered to be the largest, although estimates of parties' sizes were necessarily vague. A Ghilzai Pushtun born in 1921, Mohammadi ran an influential Islamic school during the 1960s and was an outspokenly anti-Communist member of the second parliament. His clerical appeal united tribal leaders, village mullahs, and some other religious leaders in the Pushtun south and east into a personal network. For a time Harakat also had some Tajik, Uzbek, and Turkmen adherents, but most of these joined Jamiat or the regime. Fallen to minor political and military importance by the mid-1980s, Harakat was a focus of stories about *mujahideen* corruption that circulated in Peshawar.

The other two traditionalist leaders, Mojaddedi and Gailani, came from Afghan families of religious renown. Both claimed Arab ancestry but had close family ties with Ghilzai Pushtuns. **Mojaddedi**'s family led the Naqshbandi Sufi brotherhood in southern Afghanistan. It had long vouched for the religious legitimacy of Afghan kings and mediated crises between the throne and Pushtun tribes. His Jebh party had some Pushtun followers in the southeast, but was never a major guerrilla force.

Gailani's status as a hereditary saint in, and leader of, the Qadiri Sufi brotherhood made him a religious adviser to Zahir Shah and later to Daoud. A Westernized businessman as well, he preferred the European clothing of Kabul's elite to the traditional Afghan garb of his fellow leaders, thus earning from the foreign press the scathing label 'Gucci guerrilla'. Gailani's Mahaz united Pushtun tribal chiefs and old regime elites. Never strong militarily, it had several notable commanders, such as Amin Wardak and Abdul Latif. More effective in working with Western journalists than the other parties, Mahaz did a service to the resistance as a whole by publicizing its cause.

Aside from the fact that Pakistan rather than the Afghan people chose the seven leaders and parties, four other points about them were important. First, none spoke exclusively for a single ethnic element, despite each one's primary focus on Ghilzai or eastern Pushtuns or on Tajiks. Personal ties were more important than ethnic, ideological, or other factors. Second, all had adherents around the Durrani Pushtun centre of Qandahar, but none directly represented the Durranis—just as that traditionally ruling branch of Pushtuns had been shut out of the predominately Ghilzai PDPA. Third, despite cross-cutting factors that blurred the picture, the traditionalists in general represented the old elite that wanted to re-establish its influence through tribal leaders, landlords, a technocratic bureaucracy, maybe even a monarchy. Despite evidence of grassroots support for this, the Islamists opposed it. They sought to remake the system to their advantage, capturing the old elite's privileges in a religion-based government able to cope with a modern technological world. And fourth, the Peshawar seven represented only the Sunni Muslim majority of Afghans. The Shi'ite minority, mostly in the central Hazarajat region, found no place in the parties anointed by Islamabad, nor did the small Isma'ili Muslim element. This Pakistani shortsightedness enabled Tehran to develop competitive influence, although some Afghan Shi'ites refused to follow their Shi'ite co-religionists in Iran.

THE SHI'ITE RESISTANCE

By the summer of 1979, Khalqi influence had been driven from the Hazarajat by at least 37 different factions. Left pretty much on their own, and bitter toward Sunni opponents of the regime because Shi'ites had borne the brunt of the failure of the June 1979 Kabul uprising, the factions fought for power, land reform, and other issues. The struggle for control going on in Iran was reflected among militant Afghan factions, and by the autumn of 1984 Iranian-oriented parties dominated the Hazarajat. Its people were caught between Islamic radical, traditionalist, and other influences.[34]

Some Hazaras who rejected Iranian influence supported the *Harakat-e Islami* (Islamic Movement) led by Muhammad Asef Mohseni. Described by a Pushtun as 'the most prestigious living Afghan Shi'ite religious chief',[35] Mohseni came from Qandahar's sizeable Shi'ite community and paralleled that city's Durrani Sunni support for Zahir Shah. Harakat's main following was among Qandahar and Kabul Shi'ites. Oriented away from the Hazarajat's internal struggles, it was the most active Shi'ite group in fighting the Soviets and the PDPA. Operating primarily from Quetta in Pakistan, Mohseni rejected Pakistani efforts to have Harakat absorbed by one of the Peshawar parties, but he maintained contacts with them as well as the Iranians.

Aside from the main Sunni and Shi'ite *mujahideen* groups, and separate from the numerous small guerrilla units that protected their immediate localities, there were several other elements in the constantly shifting Afghan guerrilla picture. Maoist survivors of the late 1960s and early '70s in competition with Khalq and Parcham were important in

some urban areas up to about 1984. *Setem-i-Melli* fought
Taraki and Amin but joined Karmal's regime. The small,
scattered Isma'ili Muslim communities ended up supporting
Kabul until a key group deserted in 1992.[36]

LACK OF RESISTANCE UNITY

The Sunnis, unable or unwilling to work with the Shi'ites or
Isma'ilis, were incapable of cooperating among themselves.
Repeated attempts to unify the Peshawar seven failed.
Foreign efforts, particularly by Islamic nations, to offer the
resistance moral if not material support were confused by
the lack of any single effective voice for the *mujahideen*.
The Islamists' rejection of the traditionalists' desire to use
Zahir Shah as a unifying figure was one obstacle to their
acting like an exile alternative to the Kabul regime. Another
was Pakistan. It disliked the old Afghan royal family, did not
want any one united power centre to obstruct ISI's
manipulation of guerrilla groups, feared that an exile
government might establish itself in the Pushtun-inhabited
frontier area in a way that would challenge Pakistani
authority, and was apprehensive of provoking the USSR.[37]
The Saudis used their influence to block any direct
involvement by Zahir Shah, even though in June 1983 the
former king, then 68 years old, broke the virtual silence of
his Roman exile to offer himself as a unifying figurehead
with 'no ambitions, least of all to restore the monarchy'.[38]

Several factors finally came together to make greater unity
of the seven desirable. They included greater Soviet military
pressure, increased American military aid, and the resulting
need for better coordination both militarily and in
international political representation. On 29 March 1985,
President Zia invited the seven Peshawar leaders to dinner
and served them an ultimatum: form an alliance that would
represent the resistance collectively.[39] As a result, the seven
announced on 16 May 1985 the formation of a single

organization, *Ittehad-e Islami Mujahideen Afghanistan* (Alliance of Islamic Religious Warriors of Afghanistan). Under a rotating leadership, the alliance claimed to speak for the whole resistance even though Shi'ites and others were not represented. However jockeying for power continued among the seven.[40]

THE GROWING NARCOTICS TRADE

The war removed what few restraints there had been on growing opium poppies in Afghanistan and the frontier areas of Pakistan. By 1981-2 the region was supplying more than half the heroin reaching Europe and the United States. The United Nations said that in 1990 Afghanistan alone was the world's largest producer of opium resin that was turned into heroin at illegal Pakistani factories.[41] For some *mujahideen*, narcotics were a way of financing the fight. For others, drug profits became an end in themselves, with local warlords more interested in making money than in a *jihad*. Some ISI officers and other officials 'with access to the highest political circles' in Pakistan were accused of involvement in the narcotics trade from Afghan resistance areas and the Pakistani frontier. The ISI pipeline that funneled foreign weaponry through Pakistan to the *mujahideen*, reportedly worked in reverse to export narcotics.[42] Afghan regime officials also profited from the narcotics trade. An official Kabul newspaper said in 1990 that 'the heroin trade [was] engaged in by high-ranking individuals in the government of Afghanistan [who used] Afghan refugees as dealers in smuggling narcotics between Afghanistan and Karachi...'.[43]

FOREIGNERS IN THE RESISTANCE

The war attracted support from Muslims from many lands. The most notable foreign element, politically and financially although not in military accomplishments, became Arabian puritanism. Adherents of the strict, Saudi-based Wahhabi sect of Islam had for decades been been making small missionary efforts in Afghanistan, Pakistan, and India. American scholar Louis Dupree had noted that most beliefs of Afghan Islam 'relate to localized, pre-Muslim customs'.[44] Wahhabis felt that '[u]n-Islamic customs and traditions have found their way into [the] lives' of Afghans, and they hated sufism and the use of Persian religious literature, which they considered corrupted.[45] Wealthy Wahhabis in Saudi Arabia and the Gulf states perceived the Afghan war as an opportunity to propagate their version of Islam. They opened schools in refugee camps and financed relief programmes. Sayyaf was for a time their front man. But for many Afghans, they were almost as feared and hated as the Communists for attacking Afghan beliefs and customs. As *mujahideen* volunteers, Wahhabis were more disruptive of other resistance elements than effective against Soviets or regime forces.[46]

Foreign Muslims were drawn to the Afghan war. Estimates of their number were between 15 000 and 35 000.[47] Many wanted a chance to participate in a *jihad*, but some were more interested in gaining military experience than in fighting Afghan or Soviet Communists. Men who learned guerrilla skills in the Afghan war were by the 1990s fighting non-Muslims from Bosnia through Kashmir to Burma and the Philippines. Others were leading fundamentalist challenges to moderate Muslim governments across the Arab world, from Algeria and Tunisia through Egypt and Jordan to Indonesia. Still others were accused of terrorism, from bombings of the World Trade Centre in New York in 1993 to Filipino airliners in 1995. Even after Kabul's Communist regime fell in 1992, Muslim radicals continued to arrive for military training in special Afghan camps. The United States said Afghanistan was in 1993 'a breeding ground for terrorist activities around the world...'.[48]

NOTES

1. *New York Times*, 27 November 1988 and 9 June 1989, pp. 21 and A30; Reuter from Kabul, 21 May 1992; Moscow Radio, 20 April 1992, in *FBIS/SU*, 21 April 1992, p. 8; Kabul Radio, 28 April 1993, in *FBIS/NE*, 30 April 1993, p. 39.
2. Marek K. Sliwinski, 'The Decimation of a People', *Orbis*, Winter 1989: 39-55; *Afghan Jehad*, September-December 1987: 39-48. The margin of error was a wide plus or minus 15 per cent, indicating uncertain methodology.
3. Noor Ahmad Khalidi, 'Afghanistan: Demographic Consequences of War, 1978-1987', *Central Asian Survey*, Vol. 10, No. 3: 106.
4. Ermacora, 'Report', 1985, pp. 30, 27.
5. Grant M. Farr, 'The Effect of the Afghan Refugees on Pakistan', in Craig Baxter, ed., *Zia's Pakistan: Politics and Stability in a Frontline State* (Boulder, 1985): 96; interviews with Afghan exiles, Peshawar, 1987-8.
6. *Al-Ahali*, 15 January 1986, pp. 6-7, in *FBIS/SA*, 23 January 1986, p. C2; *Pravda*, 22 July 1985, in *FBIS/SU*, 25 July 1985, pp. D3-4.
7. Marek K. Sliwinski, 'On the Routes of '*Hijrat*' [exodus]', *Central Asian Survey*, Vol. 8, No. 4: 85; *Christian Science Monitor*, 31 August 1990, p. 10.
8. State Department, 'World Refugee Report', (Washington, January 1992); Wirsing, 'Pakistan and the War', p. 62.
9. State Department, 'Afghanistan: Soviet Occupation and Withdrawal', p. 17.
10. US Committee for Refugees, 'Afghan Refugees: Five Years Later' (Washington, D. C., January 1985): 4.
11. Dupree, 'Afghanistan in 1983', p. 233; *Washington Post*, 9 November 1987, p. A25; *Christian Science Monitor*, 3 January 1986, p. 7; Marvin G. Weinbaum, 'The Politics of Afghan Resettlement and Rehabilitation', *Asian Survey*, March 1989: 298.
12. Kathleen Howard-Merriam, 'Afghan Refugee Women and Their Struggle for Survival', in Farr and Merriam, *Afghan Resistance*, pp. 103-26; State Department, 'Country Reports on Human Rights Practices for 1989' and '... for 1990' (Washington, D. C., 1990 and 1991): pp. 1325-6 and 1365-6.
13. International Rescue Committee, in *Afghan Jehad*, April-June 1988: 98.
14. *New York Times*, 27 March and 12 June 1988, pp. 16 and 14.
15. *New York Times*, 4 and 24 December 1987, pp. A39 and A35.
16. E.g., INRA from Islamabad, 8 March 1987, in *FBIS/SA*, 9 March 1987, p. C2; *Afghan Jehad*, June-August 1987: 8-9.

17. Barnett R. Rubin, US House of Representatives, Foreign Affairs Committee, hearing, 7 March 1990, p. 5; *Washington Post*, 17 April 1988, p. C2.
18. *New York Times*, 19 March 1988, p. 4.
19. Conversations in Peshawar, Islamabad, and Washington with refugees, aid workers, scholars, journalists, and others, 1987-90.
20. State Department, 'Afghanistan: Eight Years', p. 8; Afghan exiles. For party charters, see *Afghan Jehad*, January-March 1988 and April-June 1988.
21. US Embassy Jidda, cable 7548, 6 October 1979, and CIA analysis in State Department, cable 266505/1, 11 October 1979, in *Spynest*, Vol. 30: 114 and 143.
22. *Far Eastern Economic Review*, 29 February 1980, p. 22.
23. Riaz M. Khan, *Untying the Afghan Knot: Negotiating Soviet Withdrawal* (Durham, 1991), p. 70; Roy, *Islam and Resistance*, p. 122.
24. Dupree, 'Demography', pp. 370-71.
25. Rubin, House Foreign Affairs Committe, hearing, 7 March 1990, p. 5.
26. *New York Times*, 12 June 1988, 26 February and 26 May 1989, pp. 14, 15, and A3; Mohammad Yousaf, *Silent Soldier: The Man Behind the Afghan Jehad* (Lahore, 1991).
27. *Pakistan Times*, 31 January and 1 February 1989, p. 1.
28. In addition to sources cited below, the following is drawn from talks with Afghans in Washington, Peshawar, and Islamabad, 1983-90; State Department, 'Afghanistan: Eight Years', p. 8; *Afghan Jehad*, January-March 1988 and April-June 1988; Roy, *Islam and Resistance*.
29. *Die Welt*, 24 June 1987, p. 7, in *JPRS-NEA-87-092*, 16 October 1987, p. 48.
30. Yousaf, *Silent Soldier*, p. 101.
31. *New York Times*, 19 March 1988, p. 4; *Wall Street Journal*, 11 February 1988, p. 31; Radek Sikorski, 'Missing in Nuristan', *Spectator*, 9 January 1988, pp. 14-15.
32. *New York Times*, 19 March 1988, p. 4; Asia Watch, 'Afghanistan: The Forgotten War', pp. 64-5; State Department, 'Country Reports on Human Rights Practices for 1990', pp. 1361-2.
33. Kaplan, *Soldiers of God*, p. 87; Roy, *Islam and Resistance*, 2nd edition, pp. 221-2.
34. Lorentz, 'Anatomy of an Entanglement'; Roy, *Islam and Resistance*, pp. 141-8; Girardet, *Afghanistan*, pp. 196-201; Rashid, 'Afghan Resistance', pp. 217-21; State Department, 'Afghanistan: Six Years', p. 7.
35. *Le Monde*, 17 October 1984, p. 7.
36. Roy, *Islam and Resistance*, pp. 118-19, 138, 104.

37. Riaz Khan, *Untying*, p. 73.
38. *Le Monde*, 22 June 1983, p. 7, in *FBIS/SA*, 24 June 1983, pp. C1-2.
39. Private communication to the author from an exiled Afghan technocrat in Islamabad, 30 March 1985; Riaz Khan, *Untying*, p. 80.
40. *New York Times*, 17 May 1985, p. A12; *Washington Post*, 4 September 1985, p. A28.
41. State Department, 'International Narcotics Control Strategy Report', (Washington, 1984), pp. 4, 7-8; AFP from Islamabad, 29 November 1991, in *FBIS/NE*, 2 December 1991, p. 63.
42. Marvin G. Weinbaum, 'War and Peace in Afghanistan: The Pakistani Role', *Middle East Journal*, Winter 1991: 76; Yousaf, *Silent Soldier*, pp. 85-6.
43. *Heywad*, 8 April 1990, pp. 1-2, in *JPRS-NEA-90-041*, 3 August 1990, p. 14.
44. Dupree, *Afghanistan*, p. 104.
45. *Arab News*, 14 September 1985, p. 9; Olivier Roy, 'The Mujahidin and the Preservation of Afghan Culture', paper, Arlington, Va., 25-6 September 1986; Roy, 'Modern Political Culture and Traditional Resistance', in Huldt and Jansson, *Tragedy*, p. 112.
46. *Washington Post*, 2 March 1989, p. A42; *New York Times*, 19 August 1990, p. 14.
47. *New York Times*, 28 March and 11 August 1993, pp. 14 and A8; *Rossiyskaya Gazeta*, 17 August 1993, p. 7, in *JPRS-USR-93-111*, 25 August 1993, p. 65.
48. Secretary of State Warren Christopher, CNN interview, 28 May 1993.

CHAPTER 7

A 'VERY STRANGE' WAR

In a conflict that they entered without proper training or equipment, the Soviet armed forces had a hard and ultimately unsuccessful learning experience. Their morale and discipline suffered, although their ability to survive the war was never in doubt. The Afghan regime's armed forces were even less prepared, and they suffered the psychological strain of fighting under foreign control with ultimate survival very much in doubt. Most *mujahideen* fought for the inspiring combination of religion and protection of home, family, and age-old traditions. Their cause initially made up for lack of training and equipment, and as they acquired these through Pakistan, the resistance forces became unbeatable.

In a guerrilla war, an unbeatable resistance means that the conventional army suffers defeat simply by failing to master the situation, even though it is not driven from the field. Soviet marshals, whose frames of reference were World War II and possible war in central Europe or north China, understood this. '... [T]hat war in Afghanistan is very strange,' said the commander of Warsaw Pact forces, Marshal Viktor G. Kulikov. He added, 'It is very difficult to defeat a people determined to defend itself'.[1] The most senior Soviet officer to serve in Afghanistan, Marshal Sergei F. Akhromeyev, observed, 'We suffered a defeat' there. But it was a defeat of only a small part of the USSR's total military capabilities—a failure more than a battlefield defeat.[2]

THE LIMITED CONTINGENT

The Soviet invasion force was publicly named the *Ogranichenniy Kontingent Sovetskogo Voyska v Afganistane* (Limited Contingent of Soviet Troops in Afghanistan), or OKSVA. Moscow translated *ogranichenniy* as 'limited', rather than its usual meaning of small or insignificant, to indicate that a major military involvement was not intended. Not until it had been withdrawn was the QKSVA's main element publicly identified by its Soviet defence ministry name, the 40th Army. The contingent also included air force units and such special forces as KGB border guards, who manned a zone up to 100 kilometers (62 miles) into Afghanistan from the Soviet border.

The invasion force quickly came up to about 85 000 men, with another 30 000 supporting them from just across the Soviet border. Initially, a high proportion was Uzbeks, Tajiks, and Turkmen reservists, but as their normal 90-day call-up period ended they were replaced with conscripts who mirrored the Soviet ethnic balance better.[3] Few conscripts wanted to go to Afghanistan, but many career officers asked to go for the same reason that Americans officers volunteered for Vietnam: combat experience is the best qualification for promotion. Except for the few who had been involved in Third World conflicts, Soviet soldiers had not had such experience for more than a generation. 'Grey-haired commanders found themselves under fire for the first time in the Afghan foothills,' a Soviet military writer observed. '... [I]t was only there, in the Hindu Kush, that the commanders—some of them with an academic background—finally became soldiers.'[4]

Adjusting the Force Size

The invasion force was adjusted to local needs, with the return to the USSR beginning in June 1980 of 10 000 men whose tanks, missile batteries, and other heavy equipment was useless.[5] But, overall, the OKSVA grew slowly, despite senior Soviet officers' opinion that a military solution was impossible and Ustinov's reported conversion by early 1981 to the view that the army should be withdrawn.[6] The force reached between 115 000 and 120 000 men in 1985. In addition there were 30 000 to 50 000 men just across the Soviet border, engaged in logistical, air power, and sometimes tactical ground support. A Soviet officer said the force was limited to 120 000 men by the constraints of Afghanistan's infrastructure.[7] The United States Defence Department analysed the limit as being

> in accordance with [the force's] constrained mission: to protect the government from resistance forces and keep the insurgency at a tolerable level; to enable the Afghan armed forces to take over the combat burden gradually; to forego significant attacks against the *Mujahedin* across the borders of Pakistan or Iran; and to keep Soviet personnel casualties and equipment losses low.[8]

In his speech on 28 July 1986 that foreshadowed national reconciliation, Gorbachev said that by the end of 1986 one tank regiment, two motorized rifle regiments, and three anti-aircraft regiments would return home as a step toward a political settlement. In an apparent reference to American satellite reconnaissance, he said the withdrawal would be done 'in such a way that all those for whom this step may be of interest may be easily convinced of this'.[9] By 31 October, six regiments totalling some 8000 men had crossed into the USSR—where they caused a medical 'catastrophe...[by bringing] serious infectious diseases: epidemic hepatitis, typhoid fever, malaria'.[10] The three anti-aircraft regiments left no gap since they had never played a military role. The tank regiment had been understrength and unused, and it was padded out with tanks sent into Afghanistan just to be withdrawn ceremonially. The key elements were the two motorized rifle regiments, the kinds of units that did the actual fighting. The United States Defence Intelligence Agency (DIA) reported that, within days of Gorbachev's speech, 'the Soviets began to move additional [motorized rifle] units into' Shindand and Konduz. The motorized rifle regiments already at those garrisons, which had better equipment than the new arrivals, went into the field. Then the new arrivals withdrew to the USSR amid publicity, and the original regiments returned to garrison. DIA said 'the United States has clear and convincing evidence' that the claimed withdrawal was 'a sham, and deceptive'.[11]

In 1991 General Varennikov said '546 200 Soviet citizens...served in the complement of Soviet troops in...Afghanistan from 1979 to 1989'.[12] General Boris V. Gromov said in 1993 that 525 000 served in the 'limited contingent', plus 90 000 border guards and 5000 Soviet interior ministry troops, a total of 620 000, of whom 546 000 participated in combat operations.[13]

Command Structure

At only four divisions, the 40th Army was a forward headquarters—its staff located in the Tajbeg Palace at Darulaman, rehabilitated after Amin was killed there—for the Turkestan Military District based at Tashkent, which handled its logistics. But in fact the OKSVA was controlled by an 'operations group' of the Soviet defence ministry's general staff that was stationed secretly in Kabul. This group ran Soviet combat operations, organized and supervised the Afghan armed forces, and played a role in political and economic affairs. Specialized lower echelons of the Soviet armed services, such as artillery, also tried to have a voice, creating 'cumbersome and overlapping forms of command and control...[that] caused confusion', a Soviet study said later.[14]

The invasion commander, Marshal Sokolov, was the first head of the 'operations group', and the last was Sokolov's deputy in the invasion, Varennikov. Soviet commanders' names were kept secret, however, until the withdrawal. Then, the last 40th Army commander, the 'youthful,...slender, handsome, blue-eyed' Lt.-Gen. Boris V. Gromov, became the most publicized hero of the USSR's entire Afghan involvement.[15] But Gromov later admitted 'moments when I was not honest as far as objectives given to me were concerned. I lied. I told lies, including slightly untrue reports sent to Moscow. I did all this only to save peoples' lives'.[16]

Varennikov said the initial Soviet 'mission was to...establish garrisons and thus stabilize the situation.... [W]e did not intend to involve ourselves in combat activities'.[17] The 40th Army eventually had forces stationed at 315 places around Afghanistan.[18] These deployments were supposed to protect key cities, military installations, and logistical routes, thus freeing the Afghan army to deal with the *mujahideen*. But this defensive stance periodically required offensive operations to keep guerrillas from building up threats in sensitive areas. When not out of garrison on operations, the Soviets were threatened by sniper fire and mortar attacks. 'There is no rear in Afghanistan', a Soviet journalist found. 'The front line is everywhere.'[19]

Adjusting to the Situation

The Soviet Army was not prepared for this new, unexpected kind of warfare. The elusive guerrillas were unlike foes expected to be met frontally on the plains of central Europe or Manchuria. The Soviets had scarcely studied their own World War II mountain warfare or post-war fights against Ukrainian and Baltic guerrillas, or comparable experiences of other armies. Ignoring the lessons that such a study might have taught, their army was road-bound and vulnerable to ambush. A hero of Afghan combat complained that Soviet forces 'fell into such lethargy after the Second World War' that training was poor, 'not correspond[ing] to the requirements of modern battle', and officers and soldiers were able to deal only with the expected. A major who was crippled in Afghanistan said a majority of Soviet dead had died because they had not received proper training for combat.[20]

Gromov said 'there were shortcomings in the implementation of our tasks.... [W]e frequently made decisions without having a sufficiently good idea about the enemy's forces and resources and without paying sufficient attention to his specific tactics'.[21] Incompetence was costly. On one occasion, '[m]any soldiers froze to death in the mountains' because their commanders got drunk and forgot about them, an officer recalled.[22] A military journal described 'callous and thoughtless leaders...[who] approached...their duty obligations with criminal irresponsibility'.[23] Below the officer ranks in an army that lacked career sergeants, there were 'almost no veterans.... Young people are fighting and [taking] unwarranted risks which older men would not permit...'.[24]

Inadequate Equipment

Soldiers' personal equipment proved as ill-adapted to this kind of war as the training. Conscripts suffered from the lack of hats to shield their faces from the harsh sun at temperatures above 40 degrees Celsius (104F), and from sleeping bags inadequate for temperatures lower than 30 below (-22F). Hiking boots were scarce and did not last long, so some 'soldiers bought themselves running shoes out of their own meager pay'. They were forced to pay for bloody uniforms that were cut off their wounds.[25] Weaponry was improved during the war, although the logistical system worked badly and field maintenance was poor. Helicopters, without which 'the war in Afghanistan would have been simply impossible', one Soviet commentator said,[26] were upgraded to cope with the heat and high altitudes. Artillery was adapted for mountain warfare and used 'in flexible and innovative ways', while newer and better models of armoured vehicles, warplanes designed for accurate ground attack, and other equipment were slowly introduced.[27]

Diets were poor, sanitation and health care primitive, diseases epidemic. Some 42 per cent of all Soviet soldiers who served in Afghanistan contracted viral hepatitis, 20 per cent had influenza or other acute infectious respiratory diseases, 14 per cent suffered from dysentery or other acute intestinal diseases, and typhoid or paratyphoid, malaria, typhus, measles, diphtheria, and other sicknesses were common. An official veterans' committee said more than 52 per cent of all Soviets who served in Afghanistan 'caught infectious diseases'. *Voyenno Meditsinskiy Zhurnal* (*Military Medical Journal*) said that, for every Soviet soldier who died in hospital while being treated for combat wounds, more than eight died during treatment for infectious diseases. Men wounded in battle were poorly tended, and evacuation arrangements were inadequate.[28]

Nonetheless, many Soviet soldiers performed heroically. 'One in every four of our servicemen has had orders and medals conferred on him,' Gromov said in 1988, and a defence minister later said 'nearly 200 000 had been decorated'. The USSR's highest military award, Hero of the Soviet Union, which is given for both combat heroism and senior military leadership, was awarded to 76 men. Three went to the men who assaulted Darulaman on 27 December 1979, including the commander who was killed. He was one of 26 posthumous heroes, and others included men who, '[w]ith their last grenades,...blew up the enemy surrounding them and themselves, too'.[29] Such commanders as Sokolov, Akhromeyev, and Gromov were made heroes, although the death toll provoked bitter Soviet questions about 'people who have received hero stars but not answered for the price at which those stars were attained'.[30] Stories circulated that some hero stars were given for bogus reasons. While 'many decorations have simply been lost', ordinary soldiers felt Moscow was 'stingy with medals', as a wounded veteran put it. Indeed, in World War II the USSR awarded approximately one hero star for every 2000 combatants, while in Afghanistan the ratio was one per 15 000.[31]

Soldiers' Problems

Many Soviet soldiers were the opposite of heroes. Officially, they committed 6412 crimes in Afghanistan, including 714 murders, but that apparently included few of the numerous atrocities against the Afghan people.[32] Weapons and other military equipment were bartered for narcotics, and 'cases of monstrous corruption' were reported. At least two Soviet staff generals sold weapons and unspecified 'services...to the opposition...'.[33] KGB officers became personally wealthy by shipping home uninspected baggage with gems, furs, and imported electronic equipment as part of 'a real "gravy train"', for which no one was punished.[34] After the Soviet military withdrawal, some 2500 soldiers were in Soviet prisons for crimes in Afghanistan, mostly against Soviet property. They were granted amnesty on 28 November 1989.[35] There were also unconfirmed reports of one or two mutinies by Soviet Central Asian troops stationed in Afghanistan. One account said Tajik and Uzbek soldiers fought Russians at the Dasht-e Abdan garrison on 12 September 1985, leaving more than 200 dead and the base destroyed.[36] A veteran said there was no brotherhood among soldiers, only common fear.[37]

Scarcity of the usual Soviet narcotics—vodka and other alcohol—caused the cheap and plentiful supplies of Afghan drugs to be used by a majority of troops to deal with the stress of combat as well as the harsh living conditions and boredom. In a survey of men who had served in Afghanistan, 55.6 per cent said hashish was available, 22.2 per cent named heroin as accessible, and 11.1 per cent said LSD was also available.[38] '[S]oldiers did not always take [drugs] in combat situations,' a Soviet lecturer said, 'but this did happen...[in order to] ease nervous stress prior to combat operations, during night-time guard duty close to bushman positions, and other circumstances'.[39]

An old problem in the Soviet armed forces that worsened in Afghanistan was known as *dedovshchina*, a term usually translated too mildly as 'hazing'.[40] The Soviet defence ministry called it 'nonregulation inter-relationships' among soldiers. It was brutal, often sadistic, and increasingly ethnic-inspired mistreatment of new conscripts by more senior enlisted men. Some victims were crippled, some were killed, many committed suicide rather than face further beatings or male rape, some escaped by deserting to the *mujahideen*, and some killed their tormentors.[41] Officers did not want to know what was going on in the barracks so long as senior soldiers kept others in line. Military commanders tried to hide or deny the problem. But a civilian outcry against it—by mothers of conscripts, veterans, and others—focused so much bad publicity on the armed forces after Gorbachev had relaxed censorship that the armed forces began making half-hearted efforts to reduce the problem.

There is no evidence that any outsiders except Soviets fought for the Kabul regime, although the presence of troops from Cuba, Vietnam, and other Soviet allies was rumoured. The only identified personnel from such countries were civilian advisers, police trainers, and other non-combatants. Despite Soviet denials of using allied troops, many *mujahideen* believed they were involved.

THE AFGHAN ARMED FORCES

As the Afghan army dwindled to perhaps 30 000 men because of desertions, as mentioned in Chapter 4, the 'army's former military command had disintegrated to a considerable degree...[and] junior officers were promoted to command positions', a Soviet military historian said.[42] Press-gang enlistment of males from 16 to 49 years old replaced combat losses and desertions, which a Pakistani official estimated at 20 000 a year. Gromyko said in 1986 that, 'in the Afghan army, the number of conscripts equals the number of deserters'. In 1987, Najibullah claimed the armed forces numbered 127 000, including 40 000 in the army, 10 000 in the air force, plus militia, interior ministry troops known as *sarandoy*, and KhAD troops.[43] Many officers had few troops; divisions were the size of brigades, brigades the size of companies.

Some militia units played critical roles in the Kabul regime's last years. The most important was led by Abdul Rashid Dostam, a rugged, uneducated Uzbek born in 1949; and was composed primarily of Uzbeks and Turkmen from the northwest. Mercenaries who were paid with Soviet money constituted Dostam's unit, which was known as the Jowzjani militia from its origin as a local defence force in the Sheberghan area, or as the 53rd militia division. Its fearless and ruthless fighting was accompanied by spare-time looting, as well as rape, arson, and other amusements.[44] A similar unit, the 80th militia division, was composed of Tajik followers of the Isma'ili religious leader and Baghlan province governor Sayyed Mansoor Naderi, and was led by his son Jaffar Naderi.

Revolving Door Army

With the exception of a few elite units of convinced Communists who got special Soviet training, the regular army seemed to operate on a revolving door basis. Most men were dragooned into the army; many deserted as soon as possible from a system that denied some their allotted food and clothing, kept them locked in barracks, and only issued them weapons as they were thrown into combat for which they had been given hardly any training. As a result, the morale and military effectiveness of most army units was low, their casualties high. Some deserters went home, but some took their weapons and became *mujahideen*. Joining the militia became a way for resistance bands to rest, recuperate, and refit at government expense before defecting to resume the war. At many army outposts the men reached tacit agreements with the *mujahideen* to leave each other alone.

In the early years, Soviet officers, who made all the decisions and gave all the orders, assigned the Afghan army primarily to garrison duty and to advance positions in sweep operations—taking the first casualties in front of Soviet troops. But by 1983 and 1984 the Soviets decreased Afghan roles in joint operations because of ineffectiveness and unreliability. Soviet soldiers did not trust Afghan soldiers alongside them, considering them cowards who might panic and run, and Soviet commanders withheld operational secrets for fear of leaks to the resistance.[45] Najibullah said, 'Not one of our armed units went into action without Soviet support. The Afghan army didn't exist as an efficient force. Neither we nor you [Soviets] saw to making it efficient'. A Russian commentator said later that the Soviet assumption of responsibility 'resulted in the total demoralization of the national armed forces and the loss of combat capability and motivation to conduct combat operations'.[46]

MUJAHIDEEN FORCES

The number of *mujahideen* who fought the Soviets and the Kabul regime will never be known with any accuracy. This was partly a result of the sporadic, disorganized nature of the war, partly a matter of definition. Some resistance fighters became full-time professionals, some rallied for particular actions, some mostly farmed and only fought when their immediate home areas were threatened. The estimates of a

Soviet military historian are as useful as any: 'If between 1981 and 1983 active *mujahideen* formations numbered approximately 45 000 men, by 1986 they already numbered 150 000.'[47] Different Afghan defence ministers cited figures ranging from 100 000 men in 1300 groups in 1987, of whom 70 000 were 'active participants in the war', to 200 000 in 1989.[48] Resistance leaders' estimates also varied widely.

The distinction between untrained, occasional fighters and standing guerrilla forces is important. The resistance began on an improvised, disorganized basis among villagers with few weapons. Local leaders were often poorly educated mullahs or *amirs*—big landowners, tribal chiefs, or other traditional bosses. Some survived to become important commanders, such as the mullah Jalaluddin Haqqani in Paktia Province. But younger villagers tended to learn the skills of war faster and to combine them with political appeals better, so they attracted more followers. A third category of emerging leaders was young men with higher education, either those from Kabul colleges such as Massoud and Zabiullah or from the armed forces such as Ismail Khan. These educated men knew how to use other talented men to build their organizations, while traditional leaders limited their groups because they were suspicious of more sophisticated men. Most of the important *mujahideen* commanders were educated men who had been Afghan army officers—some with training in the USSR—or were trained by the Pakistanis.[49] Some 1500 commanders of separate guerrilla groups can be identified, but one observer estimated that '200 or so resourceful, independent-minded commanders...have carried the vast majority of the military operations...'.[50]

Just as rumours persisted of the Soviets' using allies and clients to help fight the war, so were there recurring stories of foreigners' fighting alongside the *mujahideen*. Moscow and Kabul charged that American, Pakistani, Chinese, French, Japanese, Egyptian, Saudi Arabian, and various other Arab nationals were involved. However, except for volunteers from the Muslim world and Pakistani ISI soldiers, there was no evidence of direct foreign involvement. Non-Muslims were not welcome. Western soldiers of fortune who went to Peshawar looking for work found themselves unwanted.

Armaments and Training

A resistance leader estimated that in the early years 80 per cent of *mujahideen* weapons and ammunition came from defections and mutinies or was captured, but this later dropped to only 30 or 35 per cent.[51] Some groups could simply buy what they wanted from Afghan or Soviet sources, or trade arms with merchants for fruit and vegetables. The massive system of arms supply through Pakistan is discussed below. As weaponry improved, so did military skills. Most *mujahideen* learned under fire; one leader estimated that only 5 to 10 per cent had had any military training.[52] Training was not always popular with Afghans who prided themselves on being natural fighters and who distrusted regular soldiers. This led to the taking of unnecessary combat risks for demonstrative or even exhibitionist purposes, compounded by the concept that *jihad* was a religious commitment not to be contaminated by professional military accomplishments. None the less, ISI trained more than 80 000 Afghans in Pakistan just from 1984 through 1987.[53] The most successful internal training programme was set up by Massoud in the Dari-speaking northeast. His network became, in early 1985, the Supervisory Council of the North, a major political as well as military factor.[54]

As the resistance strengthened, KhAD agents under KGB supervision, using family and group connections that ran across battle lines, sought to arrange for *mujahideen* bands to rally to the regime or retire from active fighting. While the results were sometimes just temporary rests for the resistance, some bands dropped out of the war. The most significant contact was between Soviet army officers and

Massoud, who refused to deal with regime officials. By the end of 1982, the Panjshir valley—Massoud's base area—had been wrecked by six Soviet offensives intended to keep it from being used to stage attacks on the vital Salang highway just to its west. Massoud needed a respite, and the 40th Army wanted to concentrate its forces elsewhere. After tense bargaining, Massoud agreed in January 1983 to a six-month truce, later extended to sixteen months before the Soviets launched their largest offensive up the valley in May 1984. Massoud used the time to revive the valley's agriculture and to improve his forces. He also sent units into adjacent valleys to help other guerrilla groups, thus undercutting regime propaganda that sought to depict him as having sold out the resistance cause.[55] Later regime efforts to make a deal with him or else discredit him were ignored. Soviet military intelligence concluded, 'The [Soviet and regime] spread of disinformation about [Massoud]'s activity contribute[d] to his having become a legendary and semi-mythical figure among the people'.[56]

In addition to authorized Soviet negotiations with Massoud, he later claimed that 'some Soviet generals were in constant contact with my people'. Asked if this meant traitors in the KGB and GRU, Massoud replied, 'Precisely. How otherwise could I have learned about almost all the strategic plans of the Soviet command, a week, sometimes a whole two [weeks], before they were to have been carried out? Then I acted, in anticipation, of course'. Some Soviets helped him because they 'understood that this campaign was unjust', and some gave him assistance for money, Massoud said.[57]

CHANGING NATURE OF THE WAR

The nature of the war changed as all three elements—OKSVA, regime forces, and resistance—adapted their tactics and shifted their expectations. A Soviet military historian wrote that the 40th Army's initial

> attempts to organize an offensive against *dushman* (bandit) detachments using large combined military units according to the rules of classical warfare and to pursue them, proved ineffectual.... The shift around 1981-1982 primarily to raid-based maneuvers and operations involving individual reinforced battalions, the large-scale execution of close and wide envelopment, and the landing of ground-assault forces by helicopter...also failed to produce the necessary results since the mobile *dushman* detachments, having perfect knowledge of the terrain, found ways and means of preventing the bulk of their forces from being pursued and routed.... All attempts made to block by military means the routes bringing fresh reserves of *mujahidin* onto the territory of Afghanistan ended in failure.... Recognition of the fact that...socioeconomic, political, and organizational and propaganda measures [should take precedence over military means] led to [the Soviet abandonment] of conducting numerous 'field' operations against individual *dushman* detachments and groups and [instead] concentrat[ing]...no less than 60 per cent of available Soviet troops...on maintaining control of strategically important regions and securing lines of communications.... The remaining units (primarily airborne troops) took part in conducting large-scale operations aimed at destroying important bases and routing bands of insurgents.... From spring 1985, there was a visible trend toward the gradual withdrawal of Soviet troops from active combat operations and a transfer of initiative to Afghan armed forces, while Soviet units were left only with the task of providing them with air, artillery, and engineer support.[58]

Varennikov agreed that 'the peak of combat operations in Afghanistan [was] in late 1984 and early 1985'.[59] Official Soviet casualty figures gave 2060 combat deaths in 1984, the highest for any one year, with 1623 in 1982 and 1552 in 1985 ranked next.[60] But there are some problems in the historian's account. It puts the largest and last Soviet offensive of the war, the drive to Khost that began in late

1987, in the category of destroying bases and routing insurgents. And it dates the trend toward gradual withdrawal a year too early, presumably in order to make it coincide with Gorbachev's becoming CPSU general secretary. However, Western analyses of the changing nature of the war are not dissimilar.

Soviet Operations

The Soviet Army's initial idea of just establishing garrisons, while the Afghan army fought the war was overturned by the February 1980 demonstrations in Kabul and an appeal by Karmal to Moscow, according to one Soviet account. In March 1980, the Soviet general staff sent Sokolov an order: 'You will commence joint operations with the [Afghan army] with the mission of eliminating armed bands of the opposition....'[61] Gromov said that in March 1980, when he was serving in a division, he realized 'it was a war', not an easy occupation, because 'major losses' began.[62]

Offensives were launched, but it was logistically impossible to occupy the whole country, and once an offensive ebbed, guerrillas returned. Akhromeyev told the CPSU politbuto in 1986, 'There is no single piece of land in this country which has not been occupied by Soviet soldiers. Nevertheless, the majority of territory remains in the hands of rebels'.[63] While fighting more or less continually in such hot areas as Qandahar and Herat, the Soviets ignored much of the country. They stopped military operations in the Hazarajat in 1981 and held only two token garrisons in central Afghanistan until 1987. By December 1987 there were no Soviet troops in twelve provinces.[64] Soviet operations radiated from the country's circular road system. Vehicles were frequently ambushed on the roads. Many stretches of the vital Salang highway and other roads became lined with burned-out Soviet and regime armour and trucks. Road surfaces were torn up by mines.

Despite superior firepower, both Soviet and Afghan troops sometimes found themselves forced to fight desperate defensive actions, usually when they blundered into ambushes because of a chronic lack of good intelligence on *mujahideen* activities. Soviet veterans told of inaccurate or mistakenly ordered bombing by their own planes and rocketing by their own helicopters that killed Soviet soldiers—the 'friendly fire' problem that many armies found not uncommon in the confusion of modern warfare. One officer said that coordination of Soviet ground troops with artillery and aerial support often broke down, 'something that cost us much in blood.'[65]

Chemical Warfare?

In the early years of the war, there were numerous reports that Soviet and regime forces were using lethal chemicals or toxins against unprotected Afghans. The United States Department of State said in 1982 that Soviet forces had killed 3000 or more in at least 36 incidents of gas warfare, and Ermacora cited evidence of poison gas in his 1985 UN human rights report.[66] Uneducated, illiterate refugees from different parts of Afghanistan told similar stories—that Soviet forces had killed people hiding in irrigation tunnels or caves with chemicals that, in some cases, caused quick putrefaction of bodies.[67] A former Soviet officer in Afghanistan said villages were attacked with chemicals that killed everyone in them; a young Soviet prisoner of the *mujahideen* gave details of chemical attacks; and a Dutch journalist filmed a Soviet helicopter spraying a village and one of the resulting dead.[68]

And yet, determined efforts by scientists and government officials from both committed and neutral countries to find physical traces that would show what kinds of fatal chemicals or toxins had been used—and that would be convincing evidence of them—were unavailing. A former British paratrooper who travelled extensively in Afghanistan as a journalist called the charges 'a complete lie'.[69] Moscow and Kabul media denied the charges. As reports of chemical warfare declined after 1982 and ceased by 1985, the question was left unresolved.

There was similar disagreement over the concept of 'scorched earth'. The term applies militarily to the deliberate, complete devastation of an area in order to deny an enemy any value from holding it. Numerous published reports said the Soviets were following a 'scorched earth' policy. However, the United States Department of State said in December 1986 that, despite 'many credible reports of deliberate Soviet/regime destruction of crops, homes, and agricultural infrastructure, it appears that the Soviets do not have a *general* scorched earth policy'. A year later it estimated that only 5 to 10 per cent 'of cultivated area has been damaged since the invasion'.[70] Most of the damage was in a belt 50 miles wide along the Durand Line. There, as well as in the Panjshir valley, the Soviets sought to deny the guerrillas popular support and shelter by destruction intended to cause depopulation. In other areas, Soviet forces cleared possible ambush sites and opened up lines of fire by destroying villages close to supply routes and cutting down age-old avenues of trees shading roads. Such actions were compounded by the destruction of villages and massacring their inhabitants in retaliation for attacks. Soviet journalists and defectors told of soldiers' being ordered to kill Afghans in cold blood, to shoot any suspicious villager, and to call in aerial attacks on houses where peasants might be sheltering guerrillas.[71] A Russian commentator said 'the use (frequently unsanctioned) of "scorched earth" tactics...resulted in the extreme animosity of the population and totally excluded the possibility of "isolating" the partisans, which is extremely vital under conditions of the absence of a solid front line'.[72]

FOREIGN WEAPONS FOR THE *MUJAHIDEEN*

The Soviet invasion triggered an increase in help already being given to the resistance, but it was not until the mid-1980s that aid took on a major military significance. A change in the attitude of foreign suppliers, primarily the United States, then meant that better weapons began coming out of a pipeline running back from Pakistan to China, to Saudi Arabia and small Persian Gulf states and Egypt, to Britain and on to America.

Some Westerners worried that military aid only encouraged people to resist an occupying army that retaliated by killing women and children but was widely presumed to be undefeatable. Was it morally right for the West to try to fight the Soviets to the last Afghan? Afghans impatiently waved off such questions. All they asked, said both actual fighters and noncombatant supporters, was help in carrying on their proud tradition of resisting outside control, of maintaining their independence. 'The Americans help us because we are killing their enemies,' said one *mujahideen* commander who was critical of CIA advice.[73] They could and would fight even without outside help, Afghans insisted and repeatedly proved.

In addition to the weapons pipeline, a parallel network of humanitarian aid developed, most notably from Western Europe in addition to weapons-supplying countries such as the United States. Western and Islamic countries also worked to build support for the *mujahideen* and condemnation for the Communists. The CIA had been covertly organizing demonstrations in South Asia and Europe against PDPA rule as early as September 1979. After the invasion, it secretly sponsored demonstrations, international conferences, press articles and television programmes, and other propaganda against the Soviets and their puppets.[74]

Pakistan's Role

President Zia's motives were mixed in making Pakistan the focus of the military aid programme. He wanted to be rid of the refugee problem, hoped to deny the USSR a consolidated base on the Northwest Frontier, and sought foreign funding to favour Afghan factions least likely to raise the Pushtunistan issue in the future or to cooperate with India. Zia also saw the situation in terms of gaining regional power and influence as well as making domestic political gains from Pakistan's religious right by backing the Afghan Islamists.[75] Apprehension about Soviet retaliation caused Zia to assert falsely that Pakistan was not permitting the training or equipping of guerrillas on its territory and would not allow them to use it as a sanctuary.[76]

Iran was not a significant channel for other countries' aid but itself provided some help to the *mujahideen*, particularly, the Shi'ites. It acted out of missionary zeal and traditional desire for influence in the Hazarajat and western Afghanistan, but some anti-Soviet feelings and broader power politics also played a role. For most of the Soviet time in Afghanistan, Iran's energies were focused on fighting Iraq. When Tehran complained to Moscow about arming Iraq, the Soviets replied that supplies would be halted if Iran would stop supporting Afghan guerrillas—which Iran refused to do.[77]

INCREASING AMERICAN AID

After the Soviet invasion, President Carter decided the United States had 'a moral obligation' to help the resistance with more than just the medical and communications supplies already being provided.[78] The first American shipment of lethal equipment arrived in Pakistan on 10 January 1980. It was mainly .303 Enfields, the almost antique rifles that were the best weapon in general use in

Afghanistan and therefore not distinguishable as foreign aid.[79] The day before, the CIA briefed the US Senate Select Committee on Intelligence on plans to send about $30 million worth of covert aid to the *mujahideen* in cooperation with other countries. There were no congressional objections.[80] By the end of the Carter administration in January 1981, the United States was spending about $60 million a year on a military aid programme involving Saudi Arabia, Egypt, China, and other countries working through Pakistan.[81]

Egyptian President Anwar Sadat said in September 1981 that the United States had arranged soon after the Soviet invasion for him to provide Soviet-type weapons for the *mujahideen*. Similar to the .303 Enfields, they were indistinguishable from weapons captured by the guerrillas or taken by defectors from the Afghan army, thus offering what diplomats called 'plausible deniability' of foreign aid.[82] At least until 1983 most American-supplied weapons originated in Egypt, although Egypt was later accused of dumping inoperative old weaponry. Egypt also trained Afghan guerrillas.[83] Israel played a role, too. Hundreds of tons of Soviet-made armaments that Israel captured in its 1982 incursion into Lebanon were sold to the United States for shipment to the *mujahideen*.[84] But over time the most important Middle Eastern backer was Saudi Arabia. It matched or even exceeded American money for military aid, while leaving the United States to make arrangements, and it also provided direct subsidies to guerrilla groups.[85]

China, whose hostile confrontation with the USSR encouraged working relations with the United States, was also active. American Defence Secretary Harold Brown arranged in Beijing in January 1980 a 'significant acceleration' in China's aid, with the United States paying to transport Chinese arms to *mujahideen* pickup points in Pakistan. Later, the United States bought Soviet-style weapons made in China for use in the aid programme.[86] British anti-tank weapons turned up in *mujahideen* hands after the Thatcher government talked of unspecified support.[87]

After Ronald Reagan became the United States president in January 1981, new officials felt more should be done for the resistance. Reagan expressed on 9 March 1981 his personal willingness to provide supplies to the guerrillas. With Zia wanting 'to keep the pot boiling, but not boil over' into a Soviet retaliatory attack on Pakistan, Reagan revived Carter's idea of aiding Pakistan enough for it to channel more aid to the *mujahideen* without being so worried about the Soviet reaction.[88] After the $3.2-billion United States aid programme to buttress Pakistan had begun in October 1982, Reagan ordered the CIA in December 1982, to begin supplying the Afghan resistance with Soviet-style bazookas, mortars, grenade launchers, mines, and recoilless rifles, and possibly also shoulder-fired anti-aircraft missiles. Most were purchased from China. Overall, however, American aid remained at the Carter administration's final level of about $60 million a year, and Saudi Arabia matched this amount.[89]

Congressional Escalation

The big expansion of American aid, with its multiplier effect of drawing in more aid from Saudi Arabia and other countries, was largely a result of the United States Congress's seizing the lead in supporting the *mujahideen*. Congress had initially gone along with Carter and Reagan administration requests for small aid allocations for a presumedly lost cause. But on 20 September 1982 a liberal Democratic senator, Paul E. Tsongas of Massachusetts, introduced a resolution cosponsored by 98 other senators calling for the administration to provide 'effective material assistance' to the *mujahideen*. The resolution added that it would be 'indefensible to provide the freedom fighters with only enough aid to fight and die, but not enough to advance their cause'.[90] CIA officials lobbied members of Congress to avoid public discussion for fear it would endanger supply lines through Pakistan, and the resolution was bottled up in the Senate Foreign Relations Committee.[91] None the less, it apparently played a role in stimulating Reagan's December 1982 order to the CIA. When Tsongas revived the resolution in October 1983, State Department officials insisted that reference to 'material assistance' be replaced with a vague statement that the United States 'encourage and support the people of Afghanistan to continue their struggle [and] support [them] effectively...in their fight for freedom'.[92] The Senate passed the resolution 97-0 on 3 October 1984. The next day the House of Representatives gave an unopposed voice vote to an identical resolution.

By then Congress was forcing on the CIA more money for the *mujahideen* than the agency sought. In the autumn of 1983, a secret amendment added $40 million to one of the US Defence Department's appropriations bills in which Afghan aid was hidden. By early 1984 the American share of the programme was running at about $80 million a year.[93] The House Appropriations Committee added another $40 million in July 1984. Three members of Congress, Republican Senators Malcolm Wallop of Wyoming and Gordon J. Humphrey of New Hampshire and Democratic Representative Charles Wilson of Texas, led the drive for more aid. 'There were 58 000 [American] dead in Vietnam, and we owe the Russians one,' Wilson said. Wilson prevailed upon the administration to begin supplying the guerrillas with 20-mm Oerlikon anti-aircraft guns designed in Switzerland for mountain warfare. Although the eleven Oerlikons that saw action failed to live up to expectations, they marked an important change from providing only Soviet-style weapons that gave Pakistan 'plausible deniability' to supplying weapons believed best adapted to Afghan conditions.[94]

Congress allocated $250 million for the 1985 fiscal year beginning 1 October 1984, more than doubling the size of the American programme and bringing total US military aid, from 1979 to late 1985, to $625 million. Afghan aid became 'more than 80 per cent of the CIA's annual expenditures for [all its] covert operations'.[95] The allocation was made in virtual secrecy while Congress was having a highly publicized fight over Reagan's efforts to get just $24 million in covert aid for anti-Communist guerrillas in Nicaragua, the 'contras'. Afghanistan, with none of the moral ambiguities that surrounded the Nicaraguan situation, was termed a non-controversial 'model case for anti-Communist action'. It became a highlight of what was called 'the Reagan Doctrine' of aiding insurgencies against Soviet-backed Third World regimes.[96] In addition to the US $250 million, *Izvestiya* calculated that Saudi Arabia and the United Arab Emirates provided another $320 million for the 1985 fiscal year, West Germany $40 million, Britain $17 million, and Japan $10 million, for total military aid to the resistance in 1985 worth $637 million.[97]

A Changed American Goal

About the time Congress voted the $250 million, a United States government study found that the *mujahideen* were being worn down by the Soviets and might be crushed. Responding to this and the congressional mood, Reagan signed in April 1985 a secret National Security Decision Directive 166. It called for United States support for efforts to drive Soviet forces out of Afghanistan 'by all means available'. The directive overrode opposition from the CIA and the State Department, predicated on fear of Soviet retaliation against Pakistan.[98] A programme that had begun just to make the USSR suffer for the invasion had changed into seeking a Soviet defeat. The change was a result of congressional prodding combined with the Reagan administration's realization of the Afghan people's determination and Pakistan's growing willingness to risk Soviet anger.

Congress's first public consideration of Afghan aid was a vote 11 July 1985 of $15 million for humanitarian relief for Kabul's opponents. In September the administration secretly sought and obtained congressional permission to add to the Afghan military aid programme between $200 million and $300 million in unspent 1985 funds in a secret Pentagon account earmarked for the CIA's use.[99] According to various American media reports—which were not always consistent—the military aid programme totalled some $470 million in the 1986 fiscal year beginning 1 October 1985, some $715 million in 1987, and approximately $600 million in the 1988 fiscal year when the Soviet military withdrawal began. This meant American military aid worth a total of $2.4 billion.[100] The final total by the end of 1991 was around $3 billion for a United States programme run by a CIA task force of fewer than 100 persons in Washington, Pakistan, and elsewhere. With Saudi matching money and other contributions that the CIA task force also managed, the *mujahideen* apparently had been allocated more than $6 billion worth of armaments, logistical support, and subsidies by the time the Kabul regime collapsed in 1992.[101]

Corruption in Military Aid

How much military aid actually reached the *mujahideen* is uncertain. Reports from Peshawar said 'extensive corruption wastes much of the growing US assistance...'.[102] Estimates published in late 1984 and early 1985 said between one-third and one-half was diverted by Pakistan, which was widely accused of keeping the best weaponry for itself and giving the resistance its obsolescent equipment, or was diverted by *mujahideen* leaders in Peshawar, some of whom maintained such bloated bureaucracies that little money was left for the guerrillas.[103] Senator Humphrey charged in

December 1984 'serious mismanagement of our aid programme, perhaps of scandalous proportions', but the CIA insisted at the time that no more than 10 per cent of the aid failed to reach the *mujahideen*. By 1986, CIA analysts reportedly told Congress that at least 20 per cent of the weapons went astray, while a study by the US National Security Agency estimated the loss at 30 per cent.[104]

Few *mujahideen* commanders admitted having received outside aid. Initial reasons might have been that they could not distinguish the Soviet-style weapons from abroad or they wanted to support Pakistan's transparent official denials of channelling aid. But the main reason was political. Proudly independent Afghans found it hard to admit any dependence on or obligation to outsiders, particularly non-Islamic foreigners, and very particularly Americans, who had long been depicted in the Islamic world as enemies because of their support for Israel. Therefore, many commanders flatly denied getting American help while receiving, through Pakistan, aid organized and partially paid for by the United States.[105] Hekmatyar, who received the most but denied it the loudest, was publicly the most anti-American. But, with his typical hypocrisy, he sent aides to Washington to lobby for more aid when deliveries began to decline as the Soviets started withdrawing.[106]

ISI'S KEY ROLE

The United States, and countries such as Saudi Arabia that worked with it to aid the *mujahideen*, allowed Pakistan to decide how to distribute that aid. That meant President Zia and the Interservices Intelligence Directorate, to whom he assigned responsibility for the programme, had more than just logistical power. ISI exercised political power to try to shape the future of Afghanistan through choosing which guerrilla groups to favour.[107] Under General Akhtar Abdur Rahman, the head of ISI from 1979 to 1987, an Afghanistan bureau of some 460 Pakistanis was run from 1983 to 1987 by Brigadier Mohammad Yousaf. Yousaf, who described himself as the 'overall guerrilla leader', said his bureau was

> charged with the day-to-day coordination of the Afghan Jihad. This department control[led] the allocation of arms and ammunition; their distribution to Mujahideen leaders and commanders; the training of Mujahideen in Pakistan; the allocation of funds from the US and Saudi Arabian governments; and the strategic planning of operations inside Afghanistan.... From 1980 until 1987, Pakistani Army teams from ISI went into Afghanistan to advise and assist the Mujahideen on operations.... [T]he CIA's tasks in Afghanistan were to purchase arms and equipment and arrange their transportation to Pakistan; provide funds for the purchase of vehicles and transportation inside Pakistan and Afghanistan; train Pakistani instructors on new weapons or equipment; provide satellite photographs and maps for our operational planning; provide radio equipment and training, and advice on technical matters when so requested. The entire planning of the war, all types of training of the Mujahideen and the allocation and distribution of arms and supplies were the sole responsibility of the ISI.... [Nonetheless,] the CIA's contributions have played a vital role. ...Without the backing of the US and Saudi Arabia the Soviets would still be entrenched in [Afghanistan]. Without the intelligence provided by the CIA many battles would have been lost, and without the CIA's training of our Pakistani instructors the Mujahideen would have been fearfully ill-equipped to face, and ultimately defeat, a superpower.[108]

Western officials, scholars, and journalists found that Pakistan aided guerrilla leaders more on the basis of their willingness to follow Islamabad's orders than their fighting effectiveness. Key ISI and Pakistani civilian officials were Pushtun (Pathan) fundamentalists who favoured Afghan Pushtun Islamists over Tajiks, other Afghan minorities, and Muslim modernizers. Referring to the Islamists, Yousaf said 'some 70 per cent of logistic support was given to the fundamentalist parties, but no single party got more than 20 per cent...[which] rankled the Americans...'.[109] Some observers thought Hekmatyar's organization received considerably more than 20 per cent even though few of his followers were prominent in the fighting.[110] Pakistan's favouritism played into Kabul's hands by stimulating fears inside Afghanistan of anti-modernist dictatorial rule in the name of Islam if such people as Hekmatyar took over, helping prolong the war after the Soviet withdrawal.

Defaulted American Influence

When the Carter administration became eager to help the *mujahideen*, policymakers scarcely considered the possibility or desirability of using that aid or direct support to Pakistan for leverage on the Afghan political aspects of the conflict. Four factors obscured a broad, long-term perspective. Washington took the position of a supplicant needing Pakistani help to oppose the Soviets, and was therefore unable to set terms. Second, the United States did not expect the Soviets ever to leave Afghanistan, so it saw no need for urging resistance political unity. If anything, disunity limited the scope of any regime military victories, restricted Kabul's ability to corrupt or bribe the opposition, and lessened the chance of some compromise that might relax pressure on Moscow. A third factor was persistent American failure to appreciate the political, ethnic, and tribal currents within the resistance. This ignorance extended to the fourth factor, a limited appreciation of the way in which Pakistan was trying to shape Afghanistan's future. While the United States hitched its policy to Pakistan's, so did most of its friends and allies, but Iran and such Middle Eastern groups as militant Wahhabis did not.

As American involvement escalated, there was limited, ineffectual reconsideration. At some point in the mid-1980s, according to Yousaf, the CIA, and senior US government officials, pressed Akhtar and myself to be allowed to decide who got the arms, how much they received, what targets the Mujahideen should attack, and demanded that American instructors train the Mujahideen. None of these things ever happened...[because direct American involvement] would have meant giving truth to Soviet propaganda that the war was not a Jihad, but an extension of US foreign policy...[and because] the CIA [was] mostly incompetent in...training, logistics, and operational matters....[111]

By the time the Soviets began leaving and Washington started focusing on the importance of *mujahideen* cooperation in a future Afghan government, it had become too late to reverse the ill effects of a decade of foreign-funded Pakistani manipulation. The roots of the post-Communist civil war for control of Afghanistan were firmly anchored. Under the circumstances in which the *jihad* had begun and foreign aid was provided, however, the United States never had a chance to control Afghanistan's future. There was no clearly missed opportunity.

IMPROVED WEAPONRY

Until 1985, Pakistan's fear of Soviet retaliation for too strong a resistance effort caused it to limit both the quantity and quality of weapons provided to the *mujahideen*.[112] The supply of Oerlikon guns and British-made Blowpipe anti-aircraft missiles—neither of which was effective—was the beginning of the change to better weaponry. But the most important single change, indeed, the closest thing to a decisive development in a long, indecisive war, was the introduction of another anti-aircraft missile. It was the American-made Stinger, a 34.5-pound, shoulder-fired missile that had entered United States Army inventories in 1981. Its heat-seeking guidance system made it a formidable weapon against the helicopters and ground attack planes that had been a major Communist advantage over the unmechanized guerrillas. 'The Stingers changed the face of the war,' a guerrilla commander said. 'After they arrived, the Soviets no longer ruled the skies.'[113] *Mujahideen* morale skyrocketed, Soviet morale plummeted.

The decision to supply Stingers was controversial. In Washington, the United States Army was afraid it did not have enough Stingers for its own needs; some officials worried about Stingers' falling into the hands of terrorists or of Soviets, who might develop countermeasures; others did not want to lose 'plausible deniability' with so obviously an American-supplied weapon. In Islamabad, President Zia rejected Stingers for several years because of deniability—with the concommitant danger of Soviet retaliation—and the possibility that terrorists would get them. Zia changed his mind in January 1986, saying '[t]his is the time to increase the pressure'. By mid-February the decision had been made for the US Defence Department to provide 400 Stingers to the CIA for the *mujahideen*.[114]

Instructors from the Pakistani army, which had been equipped with Stingers a short time earlier, began in the summer of 1986 to train men from Hekmatyar's group, although his anti-American attitude caused him later to deny having received Stingers.[115] On 26 September 1986, a Stinger team from Hezb-Hekmatyar ambushed eight Mi-24 helicopter gunships as they approached Jalalabad airport. It shot down three. Their destruction, and the downing of two more Soviet helicopters the next day, sent a chill through the Soviet high command. The defence ministry in Moscow complained that the supply of Stingers marked 'a qualitatively new stage in Washington's interference' in Afghan internal affairs.[116]

As a result of Stinger kills, Soviet ground attack planes began dropping their bombs from higher altitudes, hence less accurately. Helicopter gunships stopped loitering over targets for accurate firing, or by coming in too low for Stingers they exposed themselves to machine-gun fire, or they simply avoided many formerly vulnerable targets.

Troop-carrying helicopters were also restricted. Soviet forces therefore lost both firepower and mobility. Although the Soviet and Afghan air forces adjusted their tactics to reduce losses, they effectively lost a trump card in the war—control of the air.[117]

Early publicity said Stingers were shooting down an average of one Soviet or Afghan aircraft a day, or 1.2 a day, even two a day, although the rate fell as Communist pilots began to fly frightened.[118] A US Army study later called Stingers 'the war's decisive weapon' and said they 'changed the nature of combat.... Because [Soviet and Afghan] air interdiction was ineffective, unrestricted movement of [guerrilla] troops and supplies became the norm', and other resistance weapons could be used more effectively. The study said that in the 873 days from the introduction of the Stingers until the completion of the Soviet withdrawal, 340 firings had downed 269 aircraft—both helicopters and fixed-wing planes, both Soviet and Afghan.[119] This figure was compatible with a Russian 1993 study of war losses that said 118 planes and 333 helicopters were lost during the whole Soviet involvement in Afghanistan.[120] Kabul and Moscow said guerrillas shot down with Stingers at least nine planes and helicopters carrying civilians. Most of these were military aircraft—indistinguishable from troop carriers—that served areas unreachable on closed or ambush-interdicted roads. Communist media did not mention this point in a campaign against allegedly deliberate *mujahideen* attacks on planeloads of helpless women and children.[121]

After the Kabul regime had fallen, the United States began trying to buy back a reported 300 Stingers unaccounted for out of about 1000 supplied, so they would not get into the hands of terrorists or hostile states. With Iran and others bidding for Stingers, an initial $10 million allocated for repurchase in 1992 had to be raised the following year to $55 million as the price soared for those in the hands of impoverished former resistance fighters and various middlemen. Repurchase efforts yielded little result and much worry.[122]

Once the faucet was open for one type of technologically advanced weapon for a resistance problem, other types poured out of the American pipeline through Pakistan. They included an improved anti-tank missile, the French-German Milan; a Spanish 120-millimetre mortar with twice the range of previously supplied mortars and aiming accuracy derived from American satellite data; Chinese and Egyptian 122-millimetre rocket launchers; and the Israeli-made Lightfoot system of explosive cords to clear paths through minefields. 'Resistance access to military supplies of all types increased significantly over the past year,' the Pentagon commented in April 1988, 'and resistance military operations were correspondingly more effective'.[123] The 1993 Russian study said the Soviets lost 147 tanks and 1314 armoured vehicles in Afghanistan.[124]

HUMANITARIAN AID

Increased military aid to Afghans outside regime control was paralleled by more humanitarian aid. Medical groups such as the Paris-based *Medecins sans Frontieres* and *Medecins du Monde* opened clinics in remote parts of the country, and general purpose groups such as the Swedish and Norwegian committees for Afghanistan as well as many smaller groups began relief programmes. At the instigation of Congress, the United States government authorized in 1985, health, educational, agricultural, and other kinds of aid to war-affected parts of Afghanistan, some of which was channelled through organizations such as *Medecins du Monde*. This public American programme was never well publicized, partly because of official wariness in Washington and Islamabad of making it seem provocative, and partly because it was less exciting than the well-known but supposedly secret, arms aid. This meant that humanitarian aid was 'covert overt', while military aid was 'overt covert'.

TRYING TO INTERDICT SUPPLIES

Across the Durand Line ran more than 230 recognized passes and trails, and innumerable other places could be crossed, particularly in the southern desert.[125] Four-wheel-drive light trucks bought by the CIA-run programme took military and humanitarian supplies into southern Afghanistan, while mules—some supplied by China and the United States—horses, and even camels were used in the more mountainous north. Caravans took several weeks to reach the Panjshir Valley, longer to get to the northern areas. The inability of pack animals to carry as much as trucks, as well as the cost and other problems of animal transportation, restricted guerrillas in rougher areas more remote from Pakistan to less intensive forms of fighting, without the heavy use of ammunition as in, for example, Paktia province on the border.[126]

The Soviets had recognized at the time of the invasion the desirability of closing the Pakistani border to stop aid, but apparently rejected it as either unnecessary or impractical. But as both the quantity and quality of military supplies for the resistance increased, the Soviets put more importance on trying to choke off supply routes. Regime appeals to Pushtun tribes along the Durand Line to block access had little success. The *mujahideen* found ways around strongpoints intended to block main routes. The emphasis was therefore placed on attacking the pack animal or truck convoys.

Ambushes were set up by special Soviet combat teams—usually 40 or 50 men—who were put into guerrilla territory by helicopter and then extracted after a fight.[127] These operations stimulated the legend of the *spetsnaz*.[128] The term was used loosely for reconnaissance troops and other special forces including commandos of the Soviet Defence Ministry's Main Intelligence Directorate, or GRU, to which it properly applied. Wearing paratrooper uniforms to disguise their specialization, the GRU troops comprised about 20 per cent of Soviets directly involved in combat. The US Defence Department called *spetsnaz* 'the most effective fighting force that the Soviets have in Afghanistan'.[129]

In addition to 1200 GRU *spetsnaz* troops introduced into Afghanistan in 1979—who became plagued with 'drunkenness [and] drug addiction'—another 6000 were sent there in 1985 to try to curtail guerrilla supplies.[130] In 1986, Marshal Akhromeyev told the CPSU politburo that '50 000 Soviet soldiers are stationed to close off the border, but they are not in a position to close off all passages ...'.[131] During 1987, Soviet and Afghan forces organized 10 740 ambushes along supply routes. However, of 200 border crossings detected in August 1987, 'only half...were routed; the rest have disappeared in the mountains...', while only half of the more than 100 convoys detected in June 1988 were destroyed.[132] A Western estimate said a third of *mujahideen* weapons and ammunition deliveries in 1987 were 'destroyed by Soviet air-strikes or night ambushes'.[133] But a Soviet military historian concluded that attempts to close supply routes 'were unsuccessful. Ambush operations...did not always prove to be effective...[because of] enemy reconnaissance...[and] a well-tested [guerrilla] system of march security.... It can in effect be considered that the border remained open...'.[134]

TROUBLE ACROSS BORDERS

In December 1985, Pushtuns in Pakistan's tribal territory caused trouble for the Pakistani army and its facilitation of *mujahideen* operations. *Izvestiya* confirmed that this trouble was '[u]nder...influence [from] Afghanistan...'[135]—which meant under Soviet direction. Many Pakistani frontier people did not need to be influenced to dislike refugee squatters on their lands and other effects of the war. Pakistan crushed the trouble with such old British frontier tactics as destroying the houses of ringleaders.[136]

The war spilled over into Pakistan in other ways. These included fuelling a more violent society with more guns, increased narcotics trafficking and addiction, and greater corruption. Pakistan's acting prime minister in 1993, Moin Qureshi, said his country paid 'a very dear cost in political, social, and economic sectors' for helping the Afghan resistance. 'The entry of illegal weapons...and the menace of narcotics...have cast a bad influence on our democratic system and national institutions.'[137]

Targeting Pakistan

The Soviets tried to intimidate Pakistan with aerial and artillery strikes across the border, usually at *mujahideen* bases in refugee camps, and with terrorism, sometimes aimed at resistance facilities and followers but often directed against ordinary Pakistanis. From the beginning of 1980 through 1983, seven persons were killed in Pakistan by aircraft and artillery attacks. Then, as Pakistani aid enabled the resistance to take a greater Soviet toll, the attacks increased. They peaked in 1986, with 774 aerial and 663 ground violations of Pakistan, and in 1987, with 657 aerial and 778 ground violations. The total from 1980 through 1989 was 5329 violations, according to Pakistani figures, causing 2362 casualties, including more than 550 killed.[138] The border attacks were possibly calibrated as pressure on Pakistan in peace negotiations, discussed later. Pakistan's air force shot down several intruding planes. But Islamabad did not react directly to these border attacks. There were, however, suspicions that *mujahideen* rocket attacks on Kabul were ISI-inspired retaliation.

'Terrorist explosions' and other sabotage emanating from Afghanistan killed 890 persons and wounded 3201 in 1617 incidents in Pakistan from 1980 through 1989, with the peak in 1987. The increased planting of bombs in such places as public markets and buses can be closely correlated with the increase in quality and quantity of arms aid flowing through Pakistan to the *mujahideen*. The KGB organized this campaign that was conducted by KhAD, and later WAD, often using Pakistani mercenaries rather than Afghans, and reaching beyond frontier areas to all of Pakistan's major cities.[139]

Raids into the USSR

Fomenting cross-border trouble was a two-way game. By 1982 several *mujahideen* groups were recruiting men in Soviet Tajikistan to join the fight in Afghanistan against the same Russian colonialism that they suffered. Some small raids were conducted into Tajikistan, Uzbekistan, and Turkmenistan, including one on 3 March 1984 that an Afghan guerrilla commander said killed ten Soviet border guards.[140] In October 1984, according to Brigadier Yousaf, CIA director William J. Casey urged ISI to send propaganda material and weapons into Soviet Central Asia to encourage local uprisings. Yousaf said this led to ISI's training and dispatching hundreds of *mujahideen* on raids and sabotage missions up to 25 kilometers (15 miles) into the USSR. Cross-border attacks reached their peak in 1986.[141]

While local media in Soviet Central Asia carried some limited reports, for years Moscow chose not to give the raids national publicity. Then on 8 March 1987, one man was killed and two persons wounded by ten or twelve rockets fired across the Amu Darya into a Tajikistan town, Pyandzh, whose military airfield had been hit earlier. Soviet troops immediately made the kind of retaliatory sweep through villages on the Afghan side of the river that had followed previous attacks. But this time, after *mujahideen* reports of the incident had been picked up by Western media, Moscow reported the attack on 2 April.[142] On 9 April, some 50 guerrillas rafted across the Amu Darya and attacked a Soviet border outpost, killing two guards before being repulsed. Retaliatory sweeps reportedly killed hundreds of Afghans. On 19 April Tass reported this raid, saying the USSR 'will take every necessary measure to stop any infringements on the inviolability of [its] frontiers...'.[143]

On 25 April, the Soviet ambassador in Islamabad threatened Pakistani Foreign Minister Sahabzada Yaqub Khan with dire consequences if any further operations were conducted into Soviet territory. The ambassador implied a direct Soviet attack on Pakistan. Pakistani civilian leaders, who reportedly had not been told of ISI's role in the raids, ordered them halted immediately. Yousaf said ISI stopped planning and directing them, and told the *mujahideen* to quit, but a few more raids were reported.[144]

NOTES

1. *Danas,* 14 April 1987, pp. 47-51, in *JPRS-TAC-87-032,* 20 May 1987, p. 79.
2. *Novoye Vremya,* No. 14 (April 1991): 14-19, in *FBIS/SU,* 10 May 1991, p. 36; Dmitriy G. Yevstafyev, 'Low Intensity Conflicts and Russia's Defence Policy', *SSHA: Ekonomika, Politika, Ideologiya,* No. 3, 1993: 33-41.
3. FCO, 'Chronology'; 'The Ethnic Composition of Soviet Forces in Afghanistan', *Radio Liberty Research,* RL 20/80, 1980.
4. *Literaturnaya Gazeta,* 28 August 1985, p. 14, in *FBIS/SU,* 6 September 1985, p. D3.
5. Kabul Radio, 22 June 1980, in *FBIS/SA,* 23 June 1980, p. C1; FCO, 'Afghanistan Report' (February 1980); State Department, 'Afghanistan: A Year of Occupation'.
6. Yuri V. Gankovsky, 'The Dynamics of Russian-Afghan Relations: A View from Moscow', in Mohiaddin Mesbahi, ed., *Russia and the Third World in the Post-Soviet Era* (Gainesville, 1994), p. 360.
7. Transcript of Pentagon briefing, 30 October 1986; *Kabul Times,* 17 December 1990, p. 1; Defence Department, 'Soviet Military

Power', (Washington, April 1985), p. 129; Col. Valeriy N. Ochirov, conference, Centre for Naval Analysis, Alexandria, Va., 26-7 September 1990. The authorized limit was only 108 000 (Sergei F. Akhromeyev and Georgiy M. Kornienko, *Glazami Marshala i Diplomata* (Moscow, 1992), p. 167), but in practice this apparently was exceeded.

8. Defence Department, 'Soviet Military Power: Prospects for Change' (Washington, September 1989), p. 22.

9. Moscow Television, 28 July 1986, in *FBIS/SU*, 29 July 1986, pp. R18-19.

10. Tass from Moscow, 5 November 1986, in *FBIS/SU*, 6 November 1986, pp. D1-2; *Komsomolskaya Pravda*, 18 June 1989, p. 2.

11. Transcript of briefing, Pentagon, 30 October 1986.

12. *Krasnaya Zvezda*, 24 May 1991, p. 2, in *JPRS-UMA-91-015*, 21 June 1991, p. 16.

13. *Krasnaya Zvezda*, 6 May 1993, p. 1, in *FBIS/CE*, 6 May 1993, p. 31.

14. *Ogonek*, 18 March 1989, pp. 6-8, 30-31; *Krasnaya Zvezda*, 2 July 1989, p. 2, in *FBIS/SU*, 6 July 1989, p. 85; *Kommunist Voorozhennykh Sil*, No. 15 (August 1990): 15-20.

15. *Ogonek*, 18 March 1989, pp. 6-8; *Pravda*, 9 August 1988, in *FBIS/SU*, 10 August 1988, p. 17. In the Soviet Army, lieutenant general was a two-star rank.

16. NTV, Moscow, 12 April 1997.

17. *Sovetskiy Patriot*, 27 December 1989, pp. 1-2, in *JPRS-UMA-90-007*, 23 March 1990, p. 123.

18. AFP from Islamabad, 22 October 1988, in *FBIS/NE*, 24 October 1988, p. 58.

19. *Komsomolskaya Pravda*, 24 February 1988, p. 3, in *FBIS/SU*, 9 March 1988, pp. 21-2.

20. Moscow Television 27 January 1989; *RFE/RL Daily Report*, No. 106, 5 June 1990.

21. *Zemedelsko Zname*, 22 July 1988, p. 6, in *FBIS/SU*, 26 July 1988, p. 17.

22. *Sobesednik*, No. 40 (October 1990): 6, in *FBIS/SU*, 5 November 1990, p. 70.

23. Lyakhovskiy and Zabrodin, 'Secrets, Part 4', *Armiya*, No. 9, 1992: 64-70.

24. *Komsomolskaya Pravda*, 24 February 1988, p. 3, in *FBIS/SU*, 9 March 1988, p. 23.

25. *Kommunist Vooruzhennykh Sil*, No. 9 (May 1990): 48-55, in *JPRS-UMA-90-023*, 15 October 1990, p. 90; *SSHA: Ekonomika, Politika, Ideologiya*, No. 6, 1989, pp. 70-77, in *JPRS-USA-89-013*, 24 October 1989, p. 26.

26. *Literaturnaya Gazeta*, 15 February 1989, pp. 13-14, in *FBIS/SU*, 17 February 1989, p. 19.

27. *Washington Post*, 5 July 1989, p. A2; *Sovetskaya Rossiya*, 20 December 1989, p. 6, in *JPRS-UMA-90-007*, 23 March 1990, p. 127.

28. *Voyenno Meditsinskiy Zhurnal*, July 1991: 27-31; ITAR-Tass from Moscow, 21 April 1992, in *FBIS/SU*, 22 April 1992, p. 6; *Agitator Armii i Flota*, No. 10 (May 1989): 15-17, in *JPRS-UMA-89-017*, 13 July 1989, p. 43; *Argumenty i Fakty*, 24 December 1988, pp. 4-5, in *FBIS/SU*, 27 December 1988, p. 30.

29. Moscow Radio, 1 July 1988, in *FBIS/SU*, 6 July 1988, p. 17; Pavel Grachev on Ostankino Television, 15 February 1994; *Pravda*, 19 September 1986, p. 6, in *JPRS-UMA-86-067*, 3 December 1986, p. 39; *Kommersant-Daily*, 6 July 1996, p. 20. Mark Galeotti, *Afghanistan: The Soviet Union's Last War* (London, 1995), says (p. 56) 200153 medals and orders were awarded but does not list a source.

30. *Pravda*, 15 September 1989, p. 3, in *FBIS/SU*, 21 September 1989, p. 87.

31. *Komsomolets Uzbekistana*, 7 December 1989, p. 3, in *JPRS-UMA-90-005*, 15 February 1990, p. 54; *Pravda*, quoted in *Oregonian*, 2 December 1987. Hero medal comparison calculated from statistics in *Great Patriotic War of the Soviet Union: 1941-45, A General Outline* (Moscow, 1970): 449-50, and statistics cited above.

32. *Rabochaya Gazeta*, 6 April 1990; *Literaturnaya Gazeta*, 26 October 1988, p. 12, in *FBIS/SU*, 1 November 1988, p. 90.

33. Sergei Khovanski, 'Afghanistan: The bleeding wound', *Detente*, No. 6 (Spring 1986): 2; *Komsomolskaya Pravda*, 26 February 1991, p. 2; *Argumenty i Fakty*, No. 39 (30 September 1989): 4-5, in *FBIS/SU*, 6 October 1989, p. 17; *Trud*, 3 March 1992, p. 3, in *FBIS-R/CE*, 20 March 1992, p. 102.

34. *Sobesednik*, No. 36 (September 1990): 6-7, in *FBIS/SU*, 14 September 1990, pp. 39-40.

35. Tass from Moscow, 17 September, 28 and 29 November 1989, in *FBIS/SU*, 18 September, 28, 29, and 30 November 1989, pp. 25, 77, 72, and 51; Moscow Television, 28 November 1989, in *FBIS/SU*, 29 November 1989, p. 72.

36. *Monthly Bulletin*, No. 56, Afghan Information Centre, Peshawar, November 1985, cited by Marie Broxup, 'Afghanistan According to Soviet Sources 1980-85', *Central Asian Survey*, Vol. 7, Nos. 2/3: 203. 'Mike Winchester' (Anthony Davis), 'Muj Invade USSR', *Soldier of Fortune*, June 1990: 56-63, dates such a clash as March 1980.

37. Svetlana Alexievich, *Zinky Boys: Soviet Voices from a Forgotten War* (London, 1992).
38. *Argumenty i Fakty*, 30 July and 24 December 1988, pp. 4 and 4-5, in *FBIS/SU*, 3 August and 27 December 1988, pp. 27 and 31; *Sotsiologicheskiye Issledovaniya* 4 (July-August 1989): 56-61, in *JPRS-USS-90-001*, 1 February 1990, pp. 16-19.
39. *Literaturnaya Gazeta*, 26 October 1988, p. 12, in *FBIS/SU*, 1 November 1988, p. 90.
40. Literally, 'grandfatherliness.' The term *starikovshchina* ('old-timerliness') was also used.
41. Alexiev, 'Inside the Soviet Army,' pp. 35-44; *Washington Post*, 19 August and 19 November 1990, pp. C4 and A28; Stuart Dalrymple, 'Bullying in the Soviet Army,' *Radio Liberty Research*, RL 185/88, 29 April 1988; *Narodna Armiya*, 16 November 1988, pp. 1, 4, in *FBIS/SU*, 18 November 1988, p. 92; Borovik, *Hidden War*, pp. 121-2.
42. IISS, *Military Balance, 1977-1978*, p. 55; Safronov, 'As It Was'.
43. Mohammad Yousaf and Mark Adkin, *The Bear Trap: Afghanistan's Untold Story* (London, 1992), p. 57; Urban, *War*, p. 106; *CWIHPB*, pp. 8-9, 179; David Isby, 'The Army of the Republic of Afghanistan', *Afghanistan*, No. 8 (Winter 1988): 11.
44. 'Mike Winchester' (Anthony Davis), 'Blood Feud: Kabul in Flames as Muj Battles Muj', *Soldier of Fortune*, November 1992: 32; Anthony Davis, 'The Afghan Army', *Jane's Intelligence Review*, March 1993, p. 136.
45. Lyakhovskiy and Zabrodin, 'Secrets, Part 4'; David C. Isby, 'Soviet Strategy and Tactics in Low Intensity Conflict', in Richard H. Shultz, Jr., et al., *Guerrilla Warfare and Counterinsurgency: U.S.-Soviet Policy in the Third World* (Lexington, 1987), p. 332.
46. Pyadyshev, 'Najibullah', p. 21; Yevstafyev, 'Low Intensity Conflict'.
47. Safronov, 'As It Was'.
48. Tass from Kabul, 15 January 1987, in *FBIS/SU*, 16 January 1987, p. D6; *Izvestiya*, 8 August 1989, p. 5, in *FBIS/SU*, 9 August 1989, p. 17.
49. Conversations with Afghan exiles; Rashid, 'Final Report', pp. 16, 25-6.
50. Marvin G. Weinbaum, 'The Politics of Afghan Resettlement and Rehabilitation', *Asian Survey*, March 1989: 291.
51. Lecture, Washington, 17 November 1987.
52. David C. Isby, *Russia's War in Afghanistan* (London, 1986, p. 36).
53. Yousaf and Adkin, *Bear Trap*, p. 29.
54. State Department, 'Afghanistan: Seven Years', p. 4; Paul Castella, 'News from the Forbidden Country: the Evolving Mujahedin', *International Defence Review*, No. 4, 1989: 424.

55. Girardet, *Afghanistan*, pp. 85-7; Urban, *War*, pp. 118-19, 143-4.
56. *Izvestiya*, 30 April 1992, p. 6, in *FBIS-R/CE*, 15 May 1992, p. 9.
57. *Sobesednik*, July 1997, p. 3; Moscow Television, 5 October 1997.
58. Safronov, 'As It Was'.
59. *Ogonek*, 18 March 1989, pp. 6-8, 30-31.
60. *Pravda*, 17 August 1989, p. 6, in *FBIS/SU*, 17 August 1989, p. 14. Total casualties below.
61. Lyakhovskiy and Zabrodin, 'Secrets, Part 3'.
62. Moscow Television, 3 March 1989, in *FBIS/SU*, 6 March 1989, p. 103.
63. *CWIHPB*, Nos. 8-9, p. 180.
64. Roy, *Islam and Resistance*, p. 141; Girardet, *Afghanistan*, pp. 197-8; Isby, *War in a Distant Country*, p. 41; *Pravda*, 2 December 1987, p. 5, in *FBIS/SU*, 3 December 1987, p. 38.
65. *Trud*, 12 March 1989, p. 1, in *FBIS/SU*, 21 March 1989, p. 104; *Moscow News*, No. 30, 1989: 8-9; Borovik, *Hidden War*, pp. 119-20; *Krasnaya Zvezda*, 16 April 1989, p. 1, in *JPRS-UMA-89-017*, 13 July 1989, p. 13; Lyakhovskiy and Zabrodin, 'Secrets, Part 4'.
66. State Department, 'Chemical Warfare in Southeast Asia and Afghanistan' (Washington, March 1982), 6, and 'Chemical Warfare in Southeast Asia and Afghanistan: An Update' (Washington, November 1982); transcript, State Department news conference, 14 September 1981; Ermacora, 'Report', 1985, p. 31.
67. *Le Point*, 6 October 1986; Stuart J. D. Schwartzstein, 'Chemical Warfare in Afghanistan: An Independent Assessment', *World Affairs*, Winter 1982-3: 267-72; Fullerton, *Soviet Occupation*, pp. 110-18; Urban, *War*, pp. 56-7; interviews with refugees, 1982-7.
68. Radio Liberty, Soviet Background Notes—Unevaluated Comments by Recent Emigrants, SBN 5-89, June 1989, p. 7; Fullerton, *Soviet Occupation*, pp. 114-15; *Soldier of Fortune*, June 1989: 54.
69. Peter Jouvenal, quoted in Urban, *War*, p. 57.
70. State Department, 'Afghanistan: Seven Years', p. 14 (emphasis added); State Department, 'Afghanistan: Eight Years', p. 15.
71. E.g., Gennady N. Bocharov, *Russian Roulette: Afghanistan Through Russian Eyes* (New York, 1990), pp. 67-78; *New York Times*, 28 June 1984, p. A10; Radio Liberty Research, RL 270/84, 12 July 1984; Radio Free Europe Research, Vol. 10, No. 1 (4 January 85): 3-5; *Russkaya Mysl*, 7 March 1985, pp. 6-7.
72. Yevstafyev, 'Low Intensity Conflict'.
73. Abdul Haq, AFP from Peshawar, 17 April 1989, in *FBIS/NE*, 18 April 1989, pp. 45-6.
74. CIA station New Delhi, cable 51273, 28 September 1979, in *Spynest*, Vol. 30: 135-7; Gates, *From the Shadows*, p. 358.

75. Weinbaum, 'War and Peace,' pp. 72-3; Amin Saikal, 'The Regional Politics of the Afghan Crisis', in Saikal and Maley, *Soviet Withdrawal*, p. 55.
76. Karachi Radio, 6 and 13 January 1980, in *FBIS/ME*, 7 and 14 January 1980, pp. S17 and S9.
77. IRIB Television, Tehran, 30 April 1992, in *FBIS/NE*, 1 May 1992, p. 39.
78. *Congressional Quarterly*, 4 August 1984, p. 1903; Carl Bernstein, 'Arms for Afghanistan', *New Republic*, 18 July 81, pp. 8-10.
79. Charles G. Cogan, 'Partners in Time: The CIA and Afghanistan since 1979', *World Policy Journal*, Summer 1993: 76.
80. 'Today,' NBC Television 9 January 1980; *Washington Post*, 15 February 1980, p. A1.
81. Woodward, *Veil*, p. 79; Joseph E. Persico, *Casey: From the OSS to the CIA* (New York, 1990), p. 225; Gates, *From the Shadows*, p. 251.
82. *Washington Post*, 23 and 24 September 1981, pp. A23 and A24; Carter, *Keeping Faith*, p. 475.
83. Woodward, *Veil*, p. 269; Yousaf and Adkin, *Bear Trap*, p. 85; *New York Times*, 14 February 1980, p. 1.
84. Yousaf and Adkin, *Bear Trap*, pp. 83-4; Urban, *War*, p. 162.
85. Woodward, *Veil*, pp. 104, 372; Brzezinski, *Power and Principle*, pp. 448-50; *New York Times*, 29 August 1991, p. A28; Yousaf and Adkin, *Bear Trap*, p. 81.
86. Ibid., p. 85; *Washington Post*, 25 June 1989, p. A24.
87. Fred Halliday, 'Afghanistan: The Limits of Russian Imperialism', *New Statesman*, 5 December 1980, pp. 10-12.
88. *New York Times*, 10 March 1980, p. 1; Gates, *From the Shadows*, p. 252.
89. *New York Times*, 3 May 1983, p. 1; *Washington Post*, 25 June 1989, p. A24; James Rupert, 'Afghanistan's Slide Toward Civil War', *World Policy Journal*, Fall 1989: 784; Gates, *From the Shadows*, p. 251.
90. Richard Mackenzie, 'Afghan Front Rests on Capitol Hill', *Insight*, 11 June 1990, pp. 22-3.
91. Ibid.; Malcolm Wallop, 'U. S. Covert Action: Policy Tool or Policy Hedge?,' *Strategic Review*, Summer 1984: 10-11.
92. Ibid., *Washington Post*, 8 September 1984, p. A22.
93. *Congressional Quarterly*, 4 August 1984, p. 1903; *Washington Post*, 13 January 1985, p. A1.
94. Woodward, *Veil*, pp. 316-18; Fred Barnes, 'Victory in Afghanistan: The Inside Story', *Reader's Digest*, December 1988: 89; *Congressional Quarterly*, 4 August 1984, p. 1903; *Washington Post*, 8 September 1984, p. A22; Jack Wheeler, 'Wilson's Wrath', *Soldier of Fortune*, July 1989: 52-9; Weiner, *Blank Check*, p. 159; *Jane's*

Defence Weekly, 29 November 1986, p. 1259; Yousaf and Adkin, *Bear Trap*, p. 87.

95. *New York Times*, 28 November 1984, p. A1; *Washington Post*, 13 January 1985, p. A1.

96. *New Yorker*, 11 April 1988, pp. 80-81; *Economist*, 19 January 1985, p. 23; Stephen S. Rosenfeld, 'The Guns of July', *Foreign Affairs*, Spring 1986: 701-702.

97. *Izvestiya*, 11 June 1985, p. 5, in *FBIS/SU*, 21 June 1985, p. D6.

98. *New York Times*, 19 June 1986, p. A7; Barnes, 'Victory in Afghanistan', p. 90; *Wall Street Journal*, 16 February 1988, p. 1.

99. *Wall Street Journal*, 9 October 1985, p. 2; *New York Times*, 10 October 1985, p. A4.

100. *Christian Science Monitor*, 11 April 1986 and 8 March 1988, pp. 12 and 8; *New York Times*, 10 October 1989, p. A17; Weiner, *Blank Check*, p. 161.

101. *Washington Post*, 5 and 20 April 1992, pp. C5 and A19; *Washington Times*, 2 May 1989, p. A3; Cogan, 'Partners in Time', pp. 76-9.

102. *Wall Street Journal*, 27 December 1984, p. 16; Weinbaum 'Politics of Afghan Resettlement', p. 298; Rupert, 'Afghanistan's Slide', p. 766; Persico, *Casey*, p. 313.

103. *Sunday Times*, 10 March 1985, p. 23; *Economist*, 8 December 1984, p. 12; *Christian Science Monitor*, 26 September 1984 and 11 April 1986, pp. back page (unnumbered) and 12; *New York Times*, 15 July 1985 and 24 March 1987, pp. A3 and A14.

104. *Washington Post*, 27 December 1984, p. A6; *Chicago Tribune*, 3 February 1985, Perspective section, p. 1; Weiner, *Blank Check*, p. 153.

105. E.g., Rabbani, *Wakh*, 20 April 1984, in *FBIS/SA*, 20 April 1984, p. C2; Massoud, *Avanti*, 23-4 December 1984, p. 17; Hekmatyar, *Muslim*, 28 December 1983, p. 8, in *FBIS/SA*, 12 January 1984, pp. C1-2.

106. *Insight*, 28 March 1988, p. 35; *La Stampa*, 9 February 1988, pp. 1-2.

107. Yousaf and Adkin, *Bear Trap*, p. 102; Barnett R. Rubin, 'The Fragmentation of Afghanistan', *Foreign Affairs*, Winter 1989/90: 154.

108. Yousaf, *Silent Soldier*, pp. 16-17, 59; Yousaf and Adkin, *Bear Trap*, pp. 29, 95-6.

109. Yousaf, *Silent Soldier*, pp. 78-9.

110. *Economist*, 27 August 1988, pp. 23-6; *New York Times*, 9 February 1989, p. A8; *Washington Post*, 6 March, 10 September, and 15 October 1989, pp. A1, C1, and B7.

111. Yousaf, *Silent Soldier*, pp. 76-7.

112. Yousaf and Adkin, *Bear Trap*, p. 83; Roy, *Islam and Resistance*, pp. 122, 209.
113. *Insight*, 11 June 1990, p. 23; *Jane's Defence Weekly*, 10 October 1987, p. 785.
114. Yousaf and Adkin, *Bear Trap*, pp. 174-88; *Wall Street Journal*, 16 February 1988, p. 8; Gates, *From the Shadows*, pp. 349-50.
115. Yousaf and Adkin, *Bear Trap*, p. 177; *Al-Mustaqbal*, 25 March 89, pp. 23-4, in *FBIS/NE*, 27 March 1989, p. 44. In contrast, the militarily most effective Afghan leader, Massoud, said his forces 'were the last ones to receive' Stingers, getting only eight; Moscow Television, 5 October 1997.
116. Tass from Moscow, 4 November 1986, in *FBIS/SU*, 5 November 1986, p. D1; *Washington Post*, 12 February 1989, p. A1.
117. David Isby, 'The Lessons of Afghanistan', in Derek Leabart, ed., *The New Soviet Military Thinking* (New York, 1989); *Jane's Defence Weekly*, 25 July 1987, pp. 154-5.
118. *New York Times*, 17 December 1986 and 7 July 1987, pp. A3 and A6; *Al-Ittihad Al-Usbu'i*, 29 October 1987, p. 17, in *FBIS/NE*, 4 November 1987, p. 45.
119. *Washington Post*, 5 July 1989, p. A2.
120. Col. Gen. G. F. Krivosheyev, ed., *Grif Sekretnosti Snyat* (Moscow, 1993), pp. 399-406, cited in Garthoff, *Detente and Confrontation*, revised ed., pp. 1022-3.
121. Moscow Television, 12 June 1987 and 11 April 1988, in *FBIS/SU*, 15 June 1987 and 12 April 1988, pp. E12-13 and 24; Gorbachev, *Perestroika*, p. 177.
122. *Wall Street Journal*, 2 December 1992 and 15 January 1993, pp. A2 and A7; *New York Times*, 24 July 1993, p. 1; *Times* (London), 14 May 1994, p. 17.
123. *Washington Post*, 21 September 1987 and 12 February 1989, pp. A1 and A34; *New York Times*, 17 July 1989, p. A5; *Soldier of Fortune*, June 1989: 60; Defence Department, 'Soviet Military Power: An Assessment of the Threat, 1988' (Washington, April 1988), p. 120.
124. Krivosheyev, *Grif Sekretnosti Snyat*, pp. 399-406, in Garthoff, *Detente and Confrontation*, revised ed., pp. 1022-3.
125. Louis Dupree, 'Afghanistan in 1982: Still No Solution', *Asian Survey*, February 1983: 134; *Za Rubezhom*, 10 January 1986, pp. 12-13, in *FBIS/SU*, 24 January 1986, p. D5.
126. Rashid, 'Final Report', pp. 52, 109; Castella, 'News from the Forbidden Country', p. 423-4.
127. David Isby, 'Soviet Special Operations Forces in Afghanistan, 1979-85', Boeing Light Infantry Conference, 1985, pp. 182-97.
128. A contraction of *spetsialnoe naznacheniye*, or special purpose (forces).

129. Urban, *War*, p. 150; Isby, 'Lessons of Afghanistan'; Alexiev, 'Inside the Soviet Army', pp. 28-30, 32-3; *Krasnaya Zvezda*, 15 November 1996, p. 2; transcript of Pentagon briefing, 30 October 1986.

130. *Komsomolskaya Pravda*, 9 November 1994, p. 3, in *JPRS-UMA-94-047*, 16 November 1994, pp. 1-3.

131. *CWIHPB*, Nos. 8-9: 180.

132. *Krasnaya Zvezda*, 9 October 1987, 26 April and 8 July 1988, pp. 1, 3, and 3, in *FBIS/SU*, 23 October 1987, 26 April and 11 July 1988, pp. 22, 21, and 37.

133. IISS, 'Strategic Survey, 1987-88', p. 136.

134. Safronov, 'As It Was'.

135. *Izvestiya*, 28 January 1986, p. 5, in *FBIS/SU*, 30 January 1986, p. D2.

136. *Sotsialisticheskaya Industriya*, 27 December 1985, p. 3, in *FBIS/SU*, 3 January 1986, p. D3; *Pravda*, 28 March 1986, p. 4, in *FBIS/SU*, 2 April 1986, p. D3.

137. *New York Times*, 1 December 1991, p. 12; *Washington Post*, 29 April 1993, p. A1; Islamabad Television, 14 August 1993, in *FBIS/NE*, 16 August 1993, p. 83.

138. Arif, *Working with Zia*, p. 329.

139. Ibid., p. 330; State Department, 'Afghanistan: Eight Years', p. 21; President Zia in *Muslim*, 18 November 1987, p. 1, in *FBIS/NE*, 27 November 1987, p. 67; State Department, 'Patterns of Global Terrorism: 1987' (Washington, August 1988), pp. 1, 27, 33-5.

140. Radio Liberty Research, RL 270/84, 12 July 1984; Winchester, 'Muj Invade USSR', 61; State Department, 'Afghanistan: Three Years', p. 9, and 'Afghanistan: Eight Years', p. 5; *Les Nouvelles d'Afghanistan*, December 1984-January 1985: 9-10; *Krasnaya Zvezda*, 27 March 1990, p. 3, in *FBIS/SU*, 29 March 1990, p. 16.

141. Yousaf and Adkin, *Bear Trap*, pp. 189-200; *Washington Post*, 19 July 1992, p. A1.

142. *Pravda*, 2 April 1987, p. 6, in *FBIS/SU*, 2 April 1987, pp. D2-3.

143. *Pravda*, 19 April 1987, p. 4, in *FBIS/SU*, 20 April 1987, p. D2.

144. Yousaf and Adkin, *Bear Trap*, p. 205; Winchester, 'Muj Invade USSR', p. 61; State Department, 'Afghanistan: Eight Years', p. 5.

CHAPTER 8

EFFECTS ON THE USSR

It was the nature of the Soviet system to try to hide the war's effects on the USSR, but they silently gnawed away at Soviet society. Involvement in Afghanistan exacerbated ills long present in Soviet life: impoverishment of the overall economy in order to enhance military power, half-truths in public discourse about policies and events, favouritism rampant in a 'new class' society, evasion of military service, growing use of narcotics, and others. The war made it harder for the Communist control system to keep hidden many of the problems whose very existence was usually denied. It helped dissolve the glue that held together that control system. In short, the Afghan venture was one factor that nudged the Soviet system over the brink; it contributed in a minor way to the dramatic domestic changes that culminated in the collapse of the Soviet Union.

The Soviet public was given 'many years of propagandistic lies about what was happening in Afghanistan (and remaining silent about events is also a kind of lie)...', a Soviet historian said. 'For a long time the Soviet people were simply not told that Soviet troops were conducting military actions in Afghanistan, that soldiers and officers were dying in war.'[1] Soviet media reported sporadically on army 'training exercises' in unidentified mountainous areas, or sometimes specifically in Afghanistan. But officials denied there were combat and casualties. '...[W]hat appeared in our newspapers was the complete opposite of the truth,' a Soviet Army political officer found.[2]

A 'CLOSED SUBJECT'

When Afghanistan's political problems and the prevailing
unrest were reported, the Soviet role in fighting was
censored. It was what the Soviet bureaucracy called a 'closed
subject'. A CPSU central committee directive listed what
could be reported about 'the operation of the limited
contingent...'.[3] The word 'war' was banned, and Afghan
names were substituted for Soviet ones in any media mention
of men in combat. Soldiers were not allowed to write home
about military operations or casualties, and veterans were
given strict orders not to talk about what they had seen.[4]
This avoided having to justify to the Soviet people the cost
in men and material or to confirm foreign criticism of killing
to sustain an unpopular regime. But despite censorship,
people talked and Western broadcasts were heard. As a result,
knowledge spread in the USSR of the war's hardships, of
atrocities by both sides, and of the hatred by ordinary
Afghans for their supposed helpers and liberators.[5]

Soviet media sought to make people believe the soldiers
were in Afghanistan on essentially a civic action mission of
helping villagers plant trees, clean out irrigation ditches, and
build schools, although French scholar Olivier Roy could
find no evidence of such activities in his extensive travels
inside Afghanistan.[6] Soviet journalists, one said, 'have sinned
against the truth in our reporting on the work of Soviet
soldiers in Afghanistan', writing about 'building playgrounds
for Afghan children...[and] giving concerts' instead of the
fighting.[7]

Hiding Casualties

The sins hid casualties. Through more than eight years of
fighting, the Soviet government made no statement on
casualties. The CPSU central committee directive said media
could publish 'individual and separate facts—no more than

one a month—of Soviet servicemen sustaining injuries or loss of life in the course of...repelling rebel attacks.... Publication of individual cases of heroic activities of Soviet servicemen in the course of carrying out combat tasks is to be allowed additionally'.[8] A mother's letter in the newspaper most read by draft-age youths and servicemen, *Komsomolskaya Pravda*, on 13 June 1980 was the Soviet national media's first mention of a casualty, the wounding of a soldier. Not until 30 September 1981, by which time more than 2000 Soviet soldiers had been killed in combat, did Moscow media mention—almost in passing—a Soviet military death in Afghanistan.[9] After six years of war, as Gorbachev's new policy of openness—*glasnost*—was developing at the end of 1985, only 40 killed and 62 wounded had been reported nationally, almost all as examples of individual heroism. Some bodies were buried in Afghanistan, but most went home on a 'Black Tulip', the name given to transport planes that carried the zinc coffins.[10] Burials in the USSR were usually done in semi-secrecy. No indication of where or how a soldier died was put on his tombstone. This caused indignation. Parents could not understand why there was no public credit, even praise, for their sons' assigned duty.[11]

Military Resentment

General Gromov said later that the army 'felt...great resentment' over the political policy of denying soldiers public credit for their difficult and dangerous job.[12] A former Soviet military adviser in Afghanistan said 'it was painful' that the Soviet public 'got the impression that Soviet servicemen were engaged in everything but a war'. As a result, he added, 'Soviet people started to view the glitter of combat medals and orders not as an assessment of a serious and deadly dangerous job of soldiering but as some kind of false ostentation'.[13] Even the glitter was hidden. Medals were not awarded publicly. Only a few heroes were belatedly publicized, such as paratroop sergeant Nikolay Chepik, who was held up as a model for schoolchildren because he had saved his comrades at the cost of his own life.[14]

Heroes were publicized in sporadic waves of reports that broke on the flat sea of official silence. Soviet lads were depicted as fending off ambushes or helping Afghans resist attacks, not as taking offensive actions. Aside from scattered articles, the first wave was detectable in February 1983, three months after Yuriy V. Andropov had succeeded Brezhnev as the Soviet leader. This glimpse of the war's hardship and hazard quickly ebbed. In 1984, while Konstantin U. Chernenko was the leader, the waves came closer together, the accounts of war became a bit more realistic while still emphasizing patriotism, but the overall truth was still obscured.

Soviet officials also tried to restrict foreign coverage of the war. Until late 1986, few journalists who were not Communists or at least known sympathizers received visas to visit Kabul, and those few were carefully restricted in an effort to ensure that their impressions were favourable to the regime. Correspondents who entered Afghanistan with the *mujahideen* were called spies.[15] The Soviet ambassador in Islamabad warned in October 1984 that, 'from now on, the bandits and the so-called journalists accompanying them will be killed. And our units in Afghanistan will help the Afghan forces do it'.[16] Ten non-Communist journalists are known to have died covering the war, some at the hands of Soviet or regime forces, some killed as a result of internecine strife of the *mujahideen*.[17] The Soviets also targeted aid workers, particularly European doctors and nurses, for capture or death in an effort to isolate the Afghan people and eliminate witnesses to their suffering.[18]

Changing Coverage

After Gorbachev became the CPSU leader, Soviet television's orders to say little about the war were suddenly changed in June 1985: 'Do some reports on Soviet combat operations, quickly.'[19] Press accounts of combat deaths became more frequent, although told primarily in heroic ancedotes. Later, heroism began to fade; realism turned to horror. The widely circulated magazine *Ogonek* quoted a Soviet helicopter pilot's diary about going to the site where his comrades' helicopter had been shot down. '... I saw how creepily scorched skulls grin.... We wanted to pull the bodies out right away, but as we approached a grenade exploded five metres from us. We were splattered with charred remains. For two or three days my flying suit smelled of fried meat.'[20] Another report said a Soviet 'pilot who was shot down by a "Stinger" was hacked to pieces' in a supposedly friendly village.[21]

Some media restrictions remained. When the United States secretary of state, George P. Shultz, was interviewed on Moscow Television on 15 April 1987, the translation stopped when Shultz said the Afghans 'don't want you there. They want peace with you, but they don't want you occupying their country'.[22] Afghan admissions of regime failures and weaknesses were still often deleted from Soviet reports.[23]

CONSCRIPTION CORRUPTION

A factor in Soviet attitudes toward the Afghan war was the inequality in choosing which young men were to fight and die. Favouritism and corruption had long existed in what was theoretically a system of universal male military service. They grew as knowledge of Afghan hardships and hazards spread. A bribe for an exemption cost from 2000 to 3000 roubles ($3200 to $4800)—a year or more of average salary.[24] A man whose elder son was killed in Afghanistan, and who resented others' use of favouritism to keep their children out of the war, rejected his wife's pleas to pay a bribe to keep their younger son from duty there. After the second son was also killed, neighbours regarded him as 'a scoundrel for grudging' the bribe.[25]

By 1986 Soviet media began to admit that the sons of important people did not serve in Afghanistan, or, if sent there, were protected from danger.[26] *Pravda* conceded in 1987 that 'people say that the war in Afghanistan would have ended by now if leaders' children had been sent there in addition to the sons of workers, *kolkhoz* [collective farm] members, and members of the intelligentsia. But they are apparently being kept safe and not being sent to the war'.[27] Actually, another paper said, the children and grandchildren of the Soviet intelligentsia were as scarce in Afghanistan as those of 'high-ranking leadership officials...'.[28]

The war's unpopularity and especially the inequities of manning it led to some outright defiance of conscription. Some Muslims from Tajikistan and Kirghizia preferred prison to serving in Afghanistan.[29] A protest by Caucasian Muslims who refused to go fight fellow Muslims in Afghanistan reportedly was put down by force of arms, with dead and wounded on both sides. Parents' demonstrations against sons' being sent to Afghanistan were also reported from the Caucasus, Ukraine, and other areas.[30]

VETERANS' PROBLEMS

A second domestic policy that affected attitudes toward the war was official indifference, even hostility, toward returning veterans. As the war was supposed to be unseen, so too were those who fought it. One veteran found 'a blind wall of incomprehension' from an uninformed public.[31] *Komsomolskaya Pravda* first tackled the problem by describing in early 1984, the indifference, incompetence, and bureaucratic lethargy encountered by a 23-year-old soldier who had been paralyzed by a sniper's bullet. Although the 'guilty parties have been severely punished...[for] the disgraceful heartless attitude toward' the soldier,[32] this example had little effect. Three years later the widespread 'indifference and callousness' were shown by a doctor who rejected appeals for help from a legless veteran with the observation, 'I did not send you to Afghanistan'. The resulting uproar caused some local officials to be punished for 'callous, formal, and bureaucratic treatment' of veterans.[33]

Little changed. Numerous letters to *Pravda*, it said in 1987, cited 'more and more new instances of indifference and callousness and of reluctance to even lift a finger in order to give elementary assistance or simply human attention and to get involved in the fate of men who have been through the grim school of Afghanistan...'.[34] In 1988, invalids and widows of *Afghantsi* (Afghans), as Soviet veterans came to be known, were still being treated 'poorly, even shamefully'. By April 1989 'no bureaucrat or paperpusher on the path of the *Afghantsi* [had] been punished for his callous attitude'.[35] Soviet newspapers, which had a CPSU-assigned job 'to create the impression of caring about the workers', received numerous letters telling of 'a negligent, heartless attitude toward [Afghanistan veterans] and [a] negative attitude of a section of the population toward the benefits which they can enjoy'. Some World War II veterans resented giving those who had served in Afghanistan the same special considerations they continued to receive.[36]

Unrealizable Benefits

Priorities were legally granted to Afghanistan veterans for things in perennial short supply in the straitened Soviet economy, including allocation of housing, technical and vocational training, and use of vacation centres. A 17 January

1983 benefits decree was kept virtually secret, however, and many local authorities failed to reflect it in their operating rules.[37] One decorated veteran said he 'didn't even know about [the benefits] when I returned home in the spring of 1985'.[38] As late as April 1989 a report on benefits said '*almost all* [pertinent] decrees have been declassified'.[39] The secrecy prevented public justification of benefits while censorship denied the public any understanding that the soldiers had earned them in a tough war. It also kept down demands for benefits that the Soviet economy could not satisfy—housing benefits for World War II widows had still not been fully honoured, and there were some 18 categories of people with theoretical but unfulfillable preferences for housing.[40]

The inability to fulfill the promises caused bitterness. 'The state has taken care of those it sent to Afghanistan,' one journalist wrote sarcastically. 'They have been given great privileges. But just try and make use of them.' Another writer said the Soviet state left veterans 'to the whim of uncontrollable social and national forces,...[and] betrayed [them] by paying them off with empty benefits...'.[41] As the Soviet economy declined and the USSR then collapsed, many *Afghantsi* 'were left all alone with their problems', the president of Russia, Boris N. Yeltsin, said in 1993. They 'have been abandoned', a newly independent *Izvestiya* commented.[42]

Unable to meet the needs of healthy veterans or of widows and other dependents, the USSR was even more poorly equipped to deal with medical problems. In the war, 23 258 Soviets were officially reported as wounded, another 26 798 were 'injured, maimed, or shocked', and 11 600 were later reported to have become invalids.[43] In addition, more than 400 000—that is, 65 per cent of all the Soviets who served in Afghanistan—'suffered illnesses of varying degrees of severity—mainly infectious ones' that, a military hospital director said, would mean 'tough going for about three years...[with possible] recurrences, very serious complications, and invalidism...'.[44] Hospital and rehabilitation facilities were inadequate. Particular attention focused on the failure of a country, whose people had suffered huge numbers of lost limbs in World War II, ever to have developed an adequate prosthetic industry, while the best Soviet technology was devoted to weaponry. 'The shortage of good artificial limbs is very tangible,' Gromov complained.[45]

Veterans' Drug and Psychological Problems

The veterans also suffered from drug and psychological problems. Some took drug habits home from Afghanistan, stimulating demand for drugs in the USSR and leading to an increase of trafficking from Afghanistan.[46] Psychologically, some *Afghantsi* 'can't take it and go to pieces', Gromov observed. Some soldiers 'came out of battle stronger while others went directly to the psycho wards', a Soviet writer said. '...[V]odka, drugs, and despair' hit them hard.[47] In one large city, Sverdlovsk, nine veterans had committed suicide by 1990 and 'many [others] need psychological help'.[48] In Moscow in 1990, some 44 per cent of *Afghantsi* —between 30 000 and 40 000 veterans and family members—'require psychological help to one degree or another...[but] there is no competent psychological rehabilitation—and those who need it are being drawn to alcohol, toxic substance abuse, narcotics addiction, and even suicide'.[49] In 1996, a prominent Afghan veteran said, one-fifth of all veterans had 'severe phase displacement', and every third veteran was reported to have committed a crime.[50]

Organizing 'Internationalists'

The *Afghantsi* made Soviet officials uncomfortable. As various informal blocs of veterans began to form around the

USSR, including vigilante groups trying to fight anti-social behaviour, officials feared that strong, maverick pressure groups would develop. They tried with little success to corral the veterans into tame organizations, but the government ignored or rebuffed various new organizations and pressure groups.[51]

The war in Afghanistan exacerbated regional and ethnic differences that were to split the USSR asunder. Some non-Russian peoples saw the war as an example of Russian colonialism of the kind they had suffered. Sympathy for the Afghan resistance was, therefore, strong among minority intellectuals, if not among unaroused masses. The Baltic peoples complained in numerous semi-clandestine ways, and so did some writers in the Ukraine, the Caucasus, and Soviet Central Asia.[52] Some minority peoples felt that their sons had been disproportionately singled out for service in Afghanistan and had suffered a higher percentage of casualties than others, making this a latent political issue. Statistics available after the war showed, however, that only Turkmen, Belorusians, Ukrainians, and Moldavians were killed in numbers significantly above the nationwide average, while Baltic and Caucasian combat deaths were well below the average.[53]

SOVIET CASUALTIES

By 1987, *glasnost* had made it possible publicly to voice complaints about the lack of information on casualties. But Moscow Radio said on 6 February 1987 that making Soviet losses known would aid the enemy. A military spokesman insisted that casualties were 'a state secret'.[54] In fact, according to Sergei Tarasenko of the Soviet foreign ministry, Defence Minister Dmitriy T. Yazov did not know what the casualty count was when Foreign Minister Shevardnadze— as head of a CPSU politburo commission on the war— began asking for one, about 1987.[55]

Casualty figures were finally announced shortly after the Soviet military withdrawal had begun in 1988. General Aleksey D. Lizichev, chief political commissar for the armed forces, buried in prepared remarks the statement that 'we lost in Afghanistan, by the beginning of May this year, 13 310 men killed, 35 478 wounded, and 311 missing'.[56] While this was a front-page story in the West, Soviet newspapers 'hid the bitter figures on their inside pages, in the middle of brief reports about the press conference', *Izvestiya* commented later.[57] After the withdrawal was completed, updated figures were made public.

The defence ministry newspaper *Krasnaya Zvezda* said in mid-1990, and later repeated with minor variations, that Soviet 'victims of the war in Afghanistan...were 14 454 men killed in action and dead as a result of wounds; 309 missing in action; about 50 000 wounded; [and] 11 600 maimed and invalided'.[58] Russian Defence Minister Pavel S. Grachev added in 1994 that '23 258 [Soviet] people were wounded, 26 798 people were injured, maimed, or shocked, and over 400 000 suffered illnesses of varying degrees of severity— mainly infectious ones'.[59] The ratio of 1.61 wounded for each death, when compared with the American ratio of 6.4 wounded for each death in Vietnam, shows how bad was Soviet battlefield medical care—most Americans hit in the field survived, few Soviets did.

A 1992 book from the Military Publishing House in Moscow said war dead in Afghanistan numbered 13833 from the armed forces, 572 from border guards and other KGB units, 28 interior ministry personnel who advised Afghan militia and police, and 20 from such other Soviet government units as the ministry of construction and the state committee for cinematography—a total of 14 453. In addition, 417 servicemen 'ended up as prisoners or missing in action, of which 119 men were released...'.[60] A breakdown of the armed services' 13 833 deaths by year, and by officers and conscripts, was also published.[61]

After Soviet rumours throughout the war of far more deaths—30 000 or more—there were suspicions that Moscow had not admitted the full total.[62] The first death count to be made public, Lizichev's figure of 13 310, was curiously close to an estimate published five months before by the United States Department of State of 'at least 33 000-38 000 [casualties], more than one-third of whom were killed', not including 'heavy losses to disease'.[63] Western economists had long suspected that some figures they heard from Soviet economists were calculations of the Central Intelligence Agency and other Western sources which were played back to them in a slightly disguised form by a government that lacked accurate figures of its own. Was something similar happening with the casualty figures to hide a higher, more painful truth? Soviet officials denied this. They insisted in 1989 that the completeness of their count would be shown by the publication by 1991 of 'a memorial book...list[ing] all the dead by name',[64] so that any omissions would be obvious to families and friends. The book never appeared. Nonetheless, after the Soviet Union's breakup, Afghan war death figures that became available separately and independently for various republics and some other political subdivisions were, within a margin of statistical error, consistent with the reported total of 14 453 killed.[65]

OTHER WAR COSTS

The war was costly in other ways. Soviet officials gave various figures for rouble expenses, suggesting that only estimates were available. The figure most often cited was 60 billion roubles, or $96 billion at the official exchange rate in the 1980s. Other figures ranged from 5 billion to 10 billion roubles a year, for a total of $76 billion to $152 billion.[66] Such vague figures apparently represent only the incremental costs of fighting in Afghanistan, because there was no mention of a proportionate share of total Soviet military expenses, the cost of sustaining the Afghan regime, or such related things as medical and rehabilitation costs for Soviet veterans.

A different kind of cost was in international relations. The Soviet foreign ministry said after the troop withdrawal that the war had been an

> oppressive moral and material burden... [It] was actually seen in most countries...as a bid to expand our sphere of influence by taking advantage of a regional conflict. The presence of Soviet troops in Afghanistan not only froze our relations with many countries...but [also] called in[to] question what had been accomplished in the years of *detente*.

Soviet commentators said President 'Reagan has used Afghanistan as a kind of visual aid and prime example in his constant denunciations of "Soviet expansionism"—[T]he Afghan question was political capital for our Western opponents...[and] a stumbling block for Soviet policy in practically all spheres'.[67] It may, however, have prevented another, even worse stumbling block. According to several Soviet accounts, being bogged down in Afghanistan deterred Kremlin leaders from using military power to influence Polish internal developments in 1980 and 1981.[68] The war also 'led to our country's estrangement from the Muslim world', a Soviet journal said.[69] Moscow worked hard to overcome Islamic disapproval, marshalling front organizations of Soviet Muslims to support the Kabul regime.[70] Although the Islamic Conference Organization did not sustain its initial outrage at the Soviet invasion, it rebuffed Kabul's efforts to participate and finally gave the ICO membership to a *mujahideen* group in March 1989.[71]

Moscow found Tehran's position especially troublesome. Iran's active support for the Shi'ite Afghan resistance only complicated a relationship already made complex by the Khomeini regime's suppression of pro-Soviet Iranian Marxists—many of whom found refuge with the PDPA in

Afghanistan—and by Iran's war with an old Soviet client, Iraq, after September 1980.[72] '...[D]ifferences of opinion [on Afghanistan] generally cast a shadow on Soviet-Iranian relations,' Moscow Radio said.[73] At various times the Soviets and their Afghan proteges tried to affect Iranian policy by threats or accusations, by cross-border attacks on *mujahideen* camps in Iran, as well as by soft words.[74] But Tehran remained staunchly opposed first to the Soviet troop presence and later to continued control by Najibullah.

United Nations Votes

Afghanistan was a Soviet stumbling block at the United Nations General Assembly's regular autumn meetings. From its initial vote in 1980 against the Soviet position until the troop withdrawal began in 1988, the assembly annually passed, over Moscow's objections, a resolution calling for the withdrawal of foreign troops. The 10 November 1987 passage of a resolution by a slightly larger margin than usual, 123 votes to 19, with 11 abstentions, was particularly important because it meant the failure of an unprecedented diplomatic campaign organized by Moscow on Kabul's behalf to woo support from the non-aligned world.[75] The 20 or so Soviet allies and clients who opposed the resolutions throughout the 1980s 'supported us...even when we were in the wrong', Foreign Minister Shevardnadze remarked after the withdrawal.[76]

SOVIET REASSESSMENT ON THE THIRD WORLD

Moscow's outlook on the Third World changed during the Afghan war years. Doubts about jumping into virtually any Third World political opportunity that had developed among Soviet foreign ministry and academic specialists in the 1970s, emerged cautiously as official policy once Brezhnev was dead.

Soviet aid was reduced. The CPSU programme adopted under Gorbachev in March 1986, introduced an important qualification to the aid programmes begun by Khrushchev three decades earlier, reflecting the change from a growing economy to a stagnant or even contracting one. The programme said, 'To the extent of its abilities the Soviet Union has given and will continue to give' aid.[77] A past official glossing over of unsavoury facts to create 'a distorted image of [other] countr[ies] in the [Soviet] public awareness' was recognized, and a Soviet commentator said 'many Third World recipients of Soviet aid are notorious for their authoritarian or dictatorial methods of rule, the cults of their leaders, a ruthless suppression of the opposition, and for corruption'.[78] The CPSU's theoretical journal *Kommunist* found in January 1988, 'The known discrepancy between our country's enormous foreign policy role and relative economic and scientific-technological power has recently become increasingly alarming...'. It argued for concentrating Soviet energies on more pressing domestic restructuring.[79] 'The incorporation of new thinking in international politics,' the CPSU said in a May 1988 policy statement, 'has been marked by major practical results—[including the beginning of] the withdrawal of forces from Afghanistan...'.[80] But it took a long, difficult diplomatic effort, and finally the abandonment of Soviet positions, to make possible the practical result of withdrawal.

NOTES

1. Genrikh A. Trofimenko, 'With an Inexperienced Hand...', *SSHA: Ekonomika, Politika, Ideologiya* 6 (June 1989): 70-77, in *JPRS-USA-89-013*, 24 October 1989, p. 26.
2. *Washington Post*, 14 November 1990, p. A1.
3. *Ogonek*, No. 30, 1988: 25-7; Moscow Television, 14 July 1992, in *FBIS/CE*, 17 July 1992, p. 32; *Rossiyskaya Gazeta*, 11 July 1992, p. 1.

4. *Moscow News*, No. 35, 1988: 5; *New York Times Magazine*, 14 February 1988, p. 28; *Washington Post*, 3 January 1988, p. B5; Girardet, 'Russia's War in Afghanistan', p. 107.

5. *Washington Post*, 14 February 1989, p. A1; Radio Liberty Research, RL 143/84, 6 April 1984.

6. Radio Liberty Research, RL 109/80, 1980; Roy, *Islam and Resistance*, p. 197.

7. Moscow Television, 19 August 1987, in *FBIS/SU*, 21 August 1987, p. CC10.

8. Moscow Television, 14 July 1992, in *FBIS/SU*, 17 July 1992, p. 32; *Rossiyskaya Gazeta*, 11 July 1992, p. 1.

9. *Krasnaya Zvezda*, 30 September 1981, p. 2. Media casualty reports from the author's survey of national print and broadcast media.

10. *Glasnost*, No. 11, 1991: 5; *Komsomolskaya Pravda*, 25 November 1989, p. 1, in *FBIS/SU*, 29 November 1989, p. 120.

11. Ibid.; *Pravda*, 5 August 1987, p. 3, in *FBIS/SU*, 7 August 1987, pp. R11-12; *Literaturnaya Gazeta*, 3 August 1988, p. 11, in *JPRS-UMA-88-024*, 11 October 1988, p. 29; Moscow Radio, 15 May 1987, in *FBIS/SU*, 18 May 1987, p. CC4; *Molodezh Estonii*, 25 January 1989, p. 2, in *JPRS-UMA-89-009*, 20 April 1989, p. 87.

12. Moscow Television, 3 March 1990, in *FBIS/SU*, 6 March 1990, p. 103.

13. *Ogonek*, No. 30 (July 1988): 25-7.

14. *Pravda*, 2 August 1984, p. 6, in *FBIS/SU*, 3 August 1984, pp. D13-14; *New York Times*, 16 January 1985, p. A2.

15. E.g., *Krasnaya Zvezda*, quoted by Tass, 10 January 1988, in *FBIS/SU*, 11 January 1988, p. 33; *Komsomolskaya Pravda*, 19 October 1985, p. 3.

16. *New York Times*, 21 November 1984, p. A21; *New York Review of Books*, 17 January 1985, p. 4; Sikorski, 'Coda', p. 22.

17. *Washington Post*, 24 December 1987 and 8 July 1992, pp. A9 and C1; *Christian Science Monitor*, 27 November and 24 December 1987, pp. 12 and 12.

18. Malhuret, 'Report from Afghanistan', pp. 426-35.

19. Moscow Television, 27 December 1991, in *FBIS/SU*, 31 December 1991, p. 4.

20. AFP from Moscow, 21 July 1987, in *FBIS/SU*, 22 July 1987, p. E8; Borovik, *Hidden War*, p. 72.

21. *Komsomolskaya Pravda*, 24 February 1988, p. 3, in *FBIS/SU*, 9 March 1988, p. 22.

22. *New York Times*, 16 April 1987, p. A14.

23. E.g., compare Kabul Radio, 12 May 1987, in *FBIS/SA*, 22 May 1987, pp. C1-10, with *New Times*, 1 June 1987, pp. 18-21.

24. Alexiev, 'Inside the Soviet Army', pp. 11-14; Wimbush and Alexiev, 'Ethnic Factor', pp. 10-11; *Washington Post*, 14 February 1989, p. A17.
25. *Pravda*, 18 May 1987, p. 4, in *FBIS/SU*, 9 June 1987, pp. V2-3.
26. *Krasnaya Zvezda*, 11 July 1986, cited in *Washington Post*, 12 July 1986, p. A14; Bohdan Nahaylo, 'When Ivan Comes Marching Home: The Domestic Impact of the War in Afghanistan', *American Spectator*, July 1987: 17; *Komsomolskaya Pravda*, 25 November 1989, p. 1, in *FBIS/SU*, 29 November 1989, pp. 120-21; *Stolitsa*, No. 22 (June 1991): 7-10.
27. *Pravda*, 25 November 1987, p. 6, in *FBIS/SU*, 27 November 1987, p. 60.
28. *Literaturnaya Gazeta*, 14 October 1987, p. 14, in *FBIS/SU*, 27 October 1987, p. 36.
29. *Kommunist Tadzhikistan*, 30 December 1987, p. 2, in *FBIS/SU*, 11 January 1988, pp. 58-9; *Krasnaya Zvezda*, 24 June 1988, p. 4, in *FBIS/SU*, 30 June 1988, p. 71.
30. *Washington Post*, 23 March 1986, p. F2; AFP from Moscow, 14 June 1985, in *FBIS/SU*, 18 June 1985, p. R1; State Department, 'Afghanistan: Six Years', p. 9; Taras Kuzio, 'Opposition in the USSR to the Occupation of Afghanistan', *Central Asian Survey*, Vol. 6, No. 1 (1987): 109.
31. *Sotsialisticheskaya Industriya*, 10 March 1988, pp. 3-4, in *FBIS/SU*, 22 March 1988, p. 73.
32. *Komsomolskaya Pravda*, 26 February, 13 and 30 March 1984, pp. 4, 2, and 2, in *FBIS/SU*, 2 and 26 March, 3 April 1984, pp. D1-2, V7-9, and V1.
33. *Pravda*, 4 April, 5 and 20 August 1987, pp. 3 and 2, in *FBIS/SU*, 7 and 21 August 1987, pp. R9-13 and R8-9; *Pravda Ukrainy*, 18 August 1987, p. 1, in *FBIS/SU*, 26 August 1987, p. R4.
34. *Pravda*, 5 August 1987, p. 3, in *FBIS/SU*, 7 August 1987, p. R9.
35. Moscow Television, 16 January 1988, in *FBIS/SU*, 20 January 1988, p. 74; *Sovetskaya Belorussiya*, 5 February 1989, p. 1, in *FBIS/SU*, 10 April 1989, pp. 72-4.
36. *Izvestiya*, 2 January 1992; *Argumenty i Fakty*, 24 December 1988, pp. 4-5, in *FBIS/SU*, 27 December 1988, p. 29; *Radyanska Ukraina*, 1 April 1988, p. 3, in *FBIS/SU*, 13 April 1988, p. 48.
37. *Krasnaya Zvezda*, 24 September and 12 October 1989, pp. 3 and 2, in *JPRS-UMA-89-023*, 4 October 1989, p. 7, and *JPRS-UMA-89-025*, 27 October 1989, pp. 9-10.
38. *Moskovskaya Pravda*, 27 February 1987, p. 3, in *FBIS/SU*, 16 March 1987, p. D2.
39. *Trud*, 26 April 1989, p. 4, in *JPRS-UMA-89-017*, 13 July 1989, p. 14 (emphasis added).

40. *Izvestiya*, 9 May 1988, p. 3, in *FBIS/SU*, 10 May 1988, pp. 60-61; *Komsomolskaya Pravda*, 22 December 1988, p. 1, in *JPRS-UMA-89-006*, 6 March 1989, p. 67.
41. *Sotsialisticheskaya Industriya*, 10 March 1988, pp. 3-4, in *FBIS/SU*, 22 March 1988, p. 74; *Nash Sovremennik*, No. 5 (May 1990): 85-98.
42. *Krasnaya Zvezda*, 23 February 1993, in *FBIS/CE*, 24 February 1993, p. 23; *Izvestiya*, 2 July 1992, p. 2, in *FBIS/CE*, 8 July 1992, p. 50.
43. Moscow Television, 15 February 1994; *Krasnaya Zvezda*, 28 June 1990, p. 3, in *JPRS-UMA-90-018*, 6 August 1990, p. 26.
44. Moscow Television, 21 June 1989, in *FBIS/SU*, 27 June 1989, p. 19, and 15 February 1994; *Sovetskaya Rossiya*, 8 February 1989, p. 1, in *FBIS/SU*, 10 February 1989, p. 78.
45. Moscow Television, 23 December 1990; *Pravda*, 10 March 1989, p. 2, in *FBIS/SU*, 14 March 1989, p. 89; *Sovetskaya Rossiya*, 15 November 1989, p. 4, in *FBIS/SU*, 21 November 1989, p. 104.
46. *New York Times*, 3 October 1988, p. A12; *Argumenty i Fakty*, 24 December 1988, pp. 4-5, in *FBIS/SU*, 27 December 1988, p. 31.
47. *Sovetskaya Rossiya*, 15 November 1989, p. 4, in *FBIS/SU*, 21 November 1989, p. 104; *Literaturnaya Gazeta*, 15 February 1989, pp. 13-14, in *FBIS/SU*, 17 February 1989, p. 17; *Sotsialisticheskaya Industriya*, 10 March 1988, pp. 3-4, in *FBIS/SU*, 22 March 1988, p. 74.
48. *Izvestiya*, 13 July 1990, p. 6, in *FBIS/SU*, 18 July 1990, p. 16.
49. *Soyuz*, No. 23 (June 1990): 15, in *JPRS-UPA-90-049*, 16 August 1990, p. 73.
50. Aleksandr Lebed in *Rossiyskiye Vesti*, 28 December 1996, p. 2.
51. Moscow Television, 23 December 1987, in *FBIS/SU*, 4 January 1988, p. 59; *Pravda*, 10 March 1989, p. 2, in *FBIS/SU*, 14 March 1989, pp. 88-9; *Krasnaya Zvezda*, 26 March 1988, p. 5, in *FBIS/SU*, 29 March 1988, p. 52; *Izvestiya*, 1 May 1991, p. 1, in *FBIS/SU*, 6 May 1991, p. 28.
52. Radio Liberty Research, RL 143/84 and RL 448/87, 6 April 1984 and 27 October 1987; Kuzio, 'Opposition in the USSR', pp. 99-117.
53. Galeotti, *Afghanistan*, p. 28, who fails to give his source.
54. Moscow Radio, 6 February 1987, in *FBIS/SU*, 10 February 1987, p. CC3; Moscow Radio, 15 May 1987.
55. Tarasenko remarks, Princeton, 27 February 1993.
56. Moscow Television, 25 May 1988, in *FBIS/SU*, 26 May 1988, p. 25.
57. *Izvestiya*, 1 March 1989, p. 5, in *FBIS/SU*, 2 March 1989, p. 15.
58. *Krasnaya Zvezda*, 28 June 1990, 10 October 1991, and 31 December 1992, pp. 3, 1, and 3, in *JPRS-UMA-90-018*, *JPRS-UMA -91-029*, and *JPRS-UMA-93-002*, 6 August 1990, 25 November 1991, and 12 January 1993, pp. 26, 18, and 6 (the last says 14 453).

59. Moscow Television, 15 February 1994.
60. G. F. Krivosheyev, ed., *USSR Armed Forces Losses in Wars, Combat Operations and Military Conflicts* (Moscow, 1992), cited in *Krasnaya Zvezda*, 31 December 1992, p. 3, in *JPRS-UMA-93-002*, 12 January 1993, p. 6.
61. *Pravda* said (17 August 1989, p. 6, in *FBIS/SU*, 17 August 1989, p. 14) the armed forces' general staff reported 86 killed in 1979 (including 10 officers); 1980: 1484 (199 officers); 1981: 1298 (189); 1982: 1948 (238); 1983: 1446 (210); 1984: 2343 (305); 1985: 1868 (273); 1986: 1333 (216); 1987: 1215 (212); 1988: 759 (117); 1989: 53 (10). Of this total of 13 833 dead (including 1979 officers), 11 381 (1755 officers) were said to have been combat deaths, the remaining 2452 deaths being 'through careless handling of their weapons,...from wounds, and from illnesses'. The small number of deaths by illness is difficult to reconcile with other published figures, including a statement in *Voyenno Meditsinskiy Zhurnal* (Military Medical Journal), July 1991, pp. 27-31, that more than eight times as many soldiers died in hospitals of diseases as died there of combat wounds, unless few wounded soldiers made it to hospital—as is implied by the ratio of wounded to dead, cited in the text above.
62. E.g., *Argumenty i Fakty*, 4 November 1989, p. 7, in *FBIS/SU*, 8 November 1989, p. 107.
63. State Department, 'Afghanistan: Eight Years', p. 9.
64. *Komsomolskaya Pravda*, 27 May 1989, p. 2, in *FBIS/SU*, 6 June 1989, p. 59.
65. Two kinds of breakdowns offer a possible check on the official death total. They are based on deaths as a percentage of soldiers who served in Afghanistan and as a percentage of populations from which the soldiers were drawn. In considering this evidence, Gorbachev's generalization that more than one million Soviets served in Afghanistan can be ignored and Gromov's more detailed figure of 620 000 used. The 14 453 death figure is 2.331 per cent of 620 000. Figures available for the Ukrainian, Uzbek, Belorussian, Lithuanian, and Latvian republics and for the cities of Moscow, Volgograd, and Kostroma total 264 526 who served in Afghanistan and 6386 who died. This is 2.414 per cent. It is close enough statistically and in its implied death toll of 14 968 out of 620 000 to be within a normal margin of variation from one republic or region to another. The 14 453 deaths are also 0.005275 per cent of the mid-war Soviet population of 274 million. Available figures for the Ukrainian, Uzbek, Kazakh, Belorussian, Kirghiz, and Lithuanian republics and for the city of Volgograd and the Moscow district of Lyubertsi, which had a total mid-war population of 99 293 000, show that 6866 died. This is 0.00691 per cent. The implied national death toll from this

percentage is 18 933, significantly above the official figure. But within the nine population areas, the percentage killed ranges from a high 0.01277 in Lyubertsi to a low of 0.00166 in Latvia—such wide variations that the sample leaves the overall figures valid.

66. Moscow Television, 3 July 1990, in *FBIS/SU Supplement*, 5 July 1990, p. 8; *Mezhdunarodnaya Zhizn*, No. 8, 1988: 60; *New York Times*, 24 May 1989, p. A12; ITAR-Tass, 1 October 1992, in *FBIS/ CE Supplement*, 23 October 1992, p. 1.

67. *International Affairs*, January 1990: 12; *Izvestiya*, 20 February 1988, p. 5, in *FBIS/SU*, 2 March 1988, p. 25; *New Times*, No. 30, 1988: 14.

68. PAP from Moscow, 9 February 1993; Moscow Television, 13 March 1993.

69. *Novoye Vremya*, No. 25 (June 1991): 24-25, in *JPRS-UMA-91-021*, 7 August 1991, p. 71. See also Robert O. Freedman, *Moscow and the Middle East: Soviet Policy Since the Invasion of Afghanistan* (Cambridge, 1991).

70. Tass from Moscow, 24 October 1985, in *FBIS/SU*, 28 October 1985, pp. D11-12.

71. Kabul Radio, 14 October 1986, in *FBIS/SA*, 20 October 1986, p. C5; SPA from Jeddah, 29 December 1987, in *FBIS/NE*, 31 December 1987, p. 2; SPA from Riyadh, 16 March 1989, in *FBIS/ NE*, 17 March 1989, p. 5.

72. State Department, 'Afghanistan: Seven Years', pp. 17-18, and 'Afghanistan: Eight Years', p. 21; *New York Times*, 30 November 1988, p. A14.

73. Moscow Radio, 10 December 1988, in *FBIS/SU*, 13 December 1988, p. 13.

74. E.g., threats: *Pravda*, 6 March 1985, p. 4, in *FBIS/SU*, 7 March 1985, pp. H1-3; *Izvestiya*, 13 May and 2 December 1986, pp 4 and 5, in *FBIS/SU*, 15 May and 3 December 1986, pp. D4 and H1-2; cross-border attacks: *Pravda*, 6 March 1985, p. 4, in *FBIS/SU*, 7 March 1985, pp. H1-3; Moscow Radio, 8 July 1988, in *FBIS/SU*, 11 July 1988, p. 16; soft words: Moscow Radio, 7 January 1985, in *FBIS/SU*, 15 January 1985, p. D2; *Die Welt*, 10 August 1987, p. 7.

75. *New York Times*, 11 November 1987, p. A12; Tass from Moscow, 12 November 1987, in *FBIS/SU*, 13 November 1987, pp. 12-13.

76. *Pravda*, 24 October 1989, pp. 2-4, in *FBIS/SU*, 24 October 1989, pp. 45-6.

77. *Pravda*, 7 March 1986, pp. 3-8, in *FBIS/SU Supplement*, 10 March 1986, p. O3 [*sic* —O20] (emphasis added).

78. *Literaturnaya Gazeta*, 7 October 1987, p. 14, in *FBIS/SU*, 16 October 1987, pp. 38-40; *Moscow News*, 3 December 1989, p. 6.

79. *Kommunist*, January 1988, pp. 42-50.
80. *Pravda*, 27 May 1988, pp. 1-3, in *FBIS/SU*, 27 May 1988, p. 49.

CHAPTER 9

THE WITHDRAWAL DECISION

The Soviet Union withdrew its 'limited contingent' from Afghanistan under the terms of an agreement signed in Geneva on 14 April 1988. The four-part agreement was the result of long, difficult negotiations under United Nations' auspices, but they were not what got the Soviets out. Gorbachev had decided that reasons broader than the Afghanistan problem required withdrawal. The agreement simply provided a weak excuse for Moscow to accept less than the terms it had long sought. Acceptance was not easy. The withdrawal decision met 'resistance in Soviet military-political circles..., rejection on the part of the Afghan leadership, [and]...disbelief' abroad, a Soviet foreign ministry journal said.[1]

The basic reason for withdrawal was the USSR's domestic situation, which was worsening because of factors more profound than the peripheral Afghan problem. When Gorbachev became CPSU general secretary in March 1985, he faced systemic weaknesses that Brezhnev had allowed to fester behind a cloak of censorship into crisis proportions; that Brezhnev's successor, Andropov, had begun to recognize but had not had time enough or health to address; that the next leader, Chernenko, had tried to ignore. A disgruntled public perceived living standards no longer to be rising, even to have begun declining. This was primarily a result of trying to maintain a superpower status from an inefficient economic base. The armed forces were eating up far more resources for competition with the United States than the country could rationally afford. Their demand for higher budgets grew while overall national output was stagnant or shrinking. This structural problem was compounded by the disaffection of the impoverished Soviet people with the old Stalinist social contract. The satisfaction and security they derived from cheap but poor housing and medical care, from guaranteed jobs and other returns on acceptance of dictatorial rule, were so minimal that they felt little obligation to work productively in return. Corruption undermined ideology. Social ills arising from the Afghan war only exacerbated existent disaffection.

Gorbachev and a clique of iconoclastic thinkers around him, men who saw the need and had the willingness to question Brezhnevian orthodoxies, recognized that continuing on the path he had inherited would only lead to greater problems and unrest at home as well as undermining the base on which rested the appearance of strength abroad. The long-term health of the USSR and of its Communist system required an improved economy. The leadership had to regain the confidence of a sullenly uncooperative people and give them incentives to work more productively. That required a reallocation of resources and qualitative improvements through cutting a growing military burden. It also meant raising the technological level of an antiquated civilian economy with the import of Western technology.

Afghanistan figured in the necessary reforms in three ways, none of them a primary driving reason for change. Its direct cost was only a minor factor, since military and foreign aid expenditures were overwhelmingly devoted to competition and confrontation with the West and China. The war's contribution to Soviet public malaise was real but only another element in decades of accumulated grievances. In the third way, the war was significant but not decisive. Gorbachev needed to reorder foreign policy in a quest for relaxing international relations, thus justifying to the Soviet military-industrial complex and other Communist traditionalists a reduction of the arms burden and seeking access to Western loans and technology. Arms control agreements, not armed confrontations, were needed. '...[O]ur international policy is more than ever determined by domestic policy, by our interest in concentrating on constructive endeavors to improve our country,' Gorbachev said in 1987.[2] He added in 1990, '...without a new foreign policy, we would have been in no position to transform our own country'.[3]

The situation had come full circle since 1979. Then, the Brezhnev leadership felt it had little to lose in already poor East-West relations and stalled SALT II negotiations from invading Afghanistan. Now, the need for better relations and new arms control agreements argued for removing Western and Chinese complaints about the Soviet role in Afghanistan. The 'limited contingent' came to be seen by the reformers around Gorbachev as blocking their country's greater good.[4]

OPPOSITION TO CHANGING AFGHAN POLICY

Gorbachev had to fight on three fronts to bring the troops home. One was the home front. Efforts to end the Afghanistan commitment were opposed by senior soldiers, security officials, ideologues, and other conservatives. They served as a sea anchor that kept Soviet policy pointed into the storm of continued warfare and international criticism long after Gorbachev had started exploring ways to withdraw. Brezhnev's ill health had in his later years enhanced a feudalization of Soviet power, dispersing it to such centres as the defence ministry and the KGB that pursued their own interests. Gorbachev began trying to recentralize some of this authority by, for example, giving the CPSU in its October 1985 programme a previously unspecified key role in formulating military doctrine.[5] He had a hard struggle that culminated in the KGB- and military-based attempt to overthrow him in August 1991 which, in failing, destroyed the USSR.

The second front was against Afghanistan. Najibullah, knowing his regime's weakness, resisted Gorbachev's efforts to win his endorsement of a withdrawal. Gorbachev said on 28 July 1986 that the USSR was prepared to bring troops home 'at the request of the [Afghan] government'.[6] Najibullah would not willingly ask and ultimately had to be coerced into agreeing. The third front was international. Gorbachev's negotiators tried long and hard to win an agreement with the main foreign backers of the *mujahideen* that would cut off all aid to them, so that the Kabul regime might have some chance of surviving without Soviet troops. When agreement proved unattainable, the USSR settled for a fig leaf that did not hide continued fuelling of a prolonged civil war.

To many in the West, negotiations seemed fruitless. The conventional wisdom was that the Soviets, whose record was virtually never to yield any foothold they had attained,[7] had entered Afghanistan to stay forever and the *mujahideen* would not be able to drive them out.[8] The United States seemed only to make the situation more intractable by insisting on not only a Soviet withdrawal but also the restoration of 'a neutral, nonaligned Afghan Government that would be responsive to the wishes of the Afghan people'. That meant ending the PDPA dictatorship, although American officials said Washington would not stand in the way of an honourable withdrawal.[9] Moscow interpreted this position to mean the United States did not want to settle but instead preferred to keep Afghanistan an issue to justify its arms buildup. But Western Europe and the Islamic world also called for the Afghan people freely to choose their government and return to nonalignment after a Soviet withdrawal.

EARLY PEACE EFFORTS

The Soviet leadership decided within a few months of the invasion that it needed a plan for an Afghan settlement, both as a ploy to seem responsive to vague plans offered in Western Europe and as political cover behind which to prosecute an unexpectedly tough war. In February 1980, Fidel Castro offered to try to organize negotiations between Afghanistan and Pakistan. In response, on 10 March 1980, the CPSU politburo commission said 'the outline of a political settlement could consist of a complex of bilateral agreements between Afghanistan and its neighbours, above all Pakistan, and systems of corresponding guarantees from the USSR, USA, and certain other states' acceptable to both sides. Writing to Castro, Brezhnev added, 'It seems inadvisable to us to have any degree of involvement on the part of the general secretary of the UN in these affairs'.[10]

As a result, the Afghan government announced on 14 May 1980 what was ostensibly its own proposal for a 'political solution'. It had been written in Moscow by officials on the foreign ministry's Afghanistan and United States desks, in consultation with the KGB and the defence ministry—which made sure that it left open the possibility of retaining Soviet military bases in Afghanistan.[11] Safronchuk, the Soviet diplomat who had overseen Afghan foreign policy from June 1979 until shortly before the invasion, returned to Kabul in March 1980 to supervise Afghan cooperation with the proposal.[12]

It called for Afghanistan to hold separate, direct talks with Iran and Pakistan on normalizing relations—meaning halting help for guerrillas—and on refugees' returning home under an amnesty. 'Practical measures should be taken to prove that armed interventions...are being halted,' with guarantees from the United States 'regarding the banning of subversive activities against Afghanistan'. If effective guarantees were received, then the question of a Soviet troop withdrawal could be resolved, the proposal said vaguely.[13] Implicit in the proposal was an assumption that any armed resistance to the Kabul regime had to be the result of outside intervention. Safronchuk knew this was 'a totally unrealistic assessment of the situation'.[14]

The failure to mention self-determination was significant because the proposal helped frame later United Nations' efforts to find a solution that did not require a free choice of government. Pakistani Foreign Minister Agha Shahi agreed with the omission on tactical grounds. Once Soviet withdrawal, non-interference guarantees, and refugee return conditions had been worked out, he said, Moscow would have 'to face the moment of truth that the Babrak Karmal regime would not survive when the occupying Soviet forces were pulled out'.[15] Despite implied acceptance by the United States and other key players, this omission was to become controversial in the 1988 end game.

The May 1980 proposal had no initial impact. Neither Pakistan nor Iran would talk to the anathematized regime. In the summer of 1981, the USSR rebuffed American efforts to start secret discussions on a face-saving way to get its troops out by insisting it needed solid assurance that the regime would survive a withdrawal.[16] Instead, after contacts with the United Nations to explore possible negotiating procedures, Soviet officials worked out a revised settlement proposal that was issued by the Kabul regime on 24 August 1981. The basic elements were the same, but Brezhnev's opposition to United Nations' involvement was dropped. Instead of bilateral talks with Pakistan and Iran, Afghanistan said it 'does not object' to some 'participation' by a United Nations' representative in the meetings.[17] With this modification, the CPSU's 10 March 1980 outline indicated the shape of the eventual Geneva agreement.

GENEVA TALKS

The United Nations became the medium through which an agreement was eventually reached, but its role was that of facilitator rather than conciliator. The UN under-secretary for special political affairs, Peruvian diplomat Javier Perez de Cuellar, was named in February 1981 as an intermediary for indirect talks. After he became UN secretary-general in January 1982, he named an Ecuadorean lawyer Diego Cordovez who became under-secretary for political affairs.

United Nations' efforts were slow in getting started. Afghanistan kept insisting on face-to-face talks with Pakistan and Iran, who refused. Talks finally began in Geneva on 16 June 1982, within a framework fixed by Cordovez after consultations. These 'proximity talks' were held according to a formula that eventually led to Cordovez's shuttling between rooms occupied by Afghan diplomats—with Soviet advisers lurking in the background—and Pakistanis, who kept the Americans informed. Iran refused to be represented.[18] Cordovez quickly won concurrence that the basic elements would be an agreement on the withdrawal of foreign forces from Afghanistan, mutual promises of non-interference in each other's internal affairs, some guarantees of these promises, and arrangements for the return home of refugees. Details remained to be filled in. There was no direct mention of elections or any change in the PDPA-controlled Afghan government.[19]

Great skepticism surrounded the talks. 'Each side believes that the other doesn't want a settlement', Cordovez said in 1986. He later commented that 'these negotiations have been conducted in an atmosphere of enormous distrust'.[20] But he persevered; the war went on. Cordovez conducted twelve rounds of talks in Geneva and made six tours of the region from June 1982 up to the signing in April 1988.[21] A key issue became a timetable for the departure of Soviet troops and its relationship to a guaranteed halt of 'outside interference', by which the Communists meant not only the supply of weapons but also any guerrilla opposition, including indigenous resistance. Not until the eighth session in Geneva, in May 1986, did Kabul offer a withdrawal timetable: Soviet troops to leave within four years, aid to the *mujahideen* to stop at the beginning of this period. Pakistan scorned this as intended to give the Soviets time to clean up guerrillas as they ran out of ammunition. Pakistan suggested a six-month withdrawal.[22] Kabul—that is, Moscow—slowly whittled down the time period, asking in February 1987 for an 18-month withdrawal, in September 1987 for 16 months, and in November 1987 for only 12 months, while Pakistan's counterproposals rose to eight months.[23] The question of guaranteeing non-interference— reduced to its narrowest definition of halting outside weapons deliveries—at the beginning of a withdrawal, however short, remained vexed.

Soviet-American Side Talks

After Gorbachev became the CPSU general secretary in March 1985, what developed into regular Soviet-American talks on regional problems began with a discussion of Afghanistan. At the opening round in June 1985, Moscow offered to join the United States in guaranteeing the results of the Geneva talks and to commit itself to a withdrawal timetable, whose length was still unspecified.[24] In November, during a brief discussion of Afghanistan at his first meeting with President Reagan, Gorbachev omitted linking 'outside interference' to withdrawal terms. Perceiving a hint, the State Department wrote to Cordovez on 11 December 1985 that the United States was willing 'to play an appropriate guarantor's role in the context of a comprehensive and balanced settlement...provided that the central issue of Soviet troop withdrawal and its inter-relationship to [other issues] was resolved'.[25] As settlement terms were then formulated by Cordovez, a guarantee meant an aid cutoff when a withdrawal began. Although there was some disagreement within the Reagan administration on such linkage, American policymakers foresaw no possibility that the Soviets would leave Afghanistan. The letter to Cordovez therefore seemed at the time like a way to encourage Gorbachev—or to put him on the defensive diplomatically—

without really committing the United States ever to have to stop aid to the *mujahideen*.[26]

As sporadic, desultory talks occurred in Geneva, the nature of a post-withdrawal government came to be seen by all sides as increasingly important. This became a focus of secret diplomacy in Soviet-American summit conferences and numerous lower-level meetings and in Pakistani contacts with the Soviets.[27] Cordovez suggested in July 1987 a regime that would 'not be dominated by any one party', but the Soviet and Afghan approach was to broaden the regime by drawing in other elements without sacrificing PDPA control,[28] as described in Chapter 5. Cordovez, Moscow, Kabul, and Islamabad all toyed with the idea of having former king Zahir Shah return to Kabul, but neither the PDPA nor its Islamist enemies wanted him to have a significant role.[29]

SOVIET POLITICS AND NEGOTIATIONS

At this point it is necessary to back up and fill in the changing Soviet political background to negotiations. Brezhnev died five months after the Geneva talks began in June 1982. When Andropov succeeded him as head of the CPSU and Soviet government, Soviet sources spread reports that depicted Andropov as the early 1979 opponent of involvement in Afghanistan, not the stout supporter of invasion that he became later in 1979. Andropov was represented as recognizing that the invasion had been a mistake, and he would bring the boys home, if only the West would cooperate.[30] When President Zia met him after attending Brezhnev's funeral, Andropov spoke of a Soviet preference for a political settlement, disclaimed any Soviet intention of absorbing Afghanistan, and expressed hope for better relations with Pakistan.[31]

Then, possibly because Andropov never meant it or because of discussion in the Kremlin, there was a policy decision to reassure a worried Karmal and Soviet clients elsewhere of Moscow's constancy. On 16 December 1982, five weeks after Andropov took over, *Pravda* declared that the Marxist revolution in Afghanistan 'is irreversible because it is a people's revolution, because the support and solidarity of the Soviet Union...are on the side of the Afghan people and its government...[who] will be able to defend their interests...'.[32] Kremlin archives show that Moscow already knew it was not a people's revolution that could defend itself. The new Andropov leadership was making a political statement. It was reinforced two weeks later by a CPSU-written government statement that 'the Soviet Union will do its internationalist duty to the end in defending Afghanistan against foreign armed intervention'.[33] On 10 March 1983 Andropov told the CPSU politburo that 'we cannot give up' in Afghanistan.[34] The following month he said that 'we have a rather long common border with Afghanistan. And so, in assisting friends, we at the same time think of ensuring the interests of our security'.[35]

Andropov's Attitude

Nonetheless, Andropov reportedly ordered a high-level policy review in 1983 that concluded the Afghan problem could not be resolved by military means.[36] He told Perez de Cuellar on 28 March 1983 that the USSR felt a settlement was needed. Holding up a hand and bending down his fingers one by one, Andropov gave five reasons: the war was harming Soviet relations with the West, with socialist states, with the Islamic world, and with other Third World states, and—lowering his thumb—was harming his country internally, both economically and socially.[37]

There was, however, no public discussion of the wisdom of continuing the war. As Andropov's health worsened in mid-1983, Brezhnevian old-thinkers reiterated the usual hard line on Afghanistan. Brezhnev's aide, Chernenko, was manœuvered into the general secretary's post after Andropov died in February 1984. Moscow media quoted—with curious delay—Karmal's claim to have been reassured of support by Chernenko at Andropov's funeral.[38] Chernenko pointedly refused to meet Zia, who also attended the funeral. Soviet media adopted a more militant tone in reporting the war. Showing its lack of interest in a political settlement, Moscow failed for the first time to send an adviser with the Afghan delegation for talks in Geneva.

THE GORBACHEV ERA

When Chernenko died after 13 months in office, Gorbachev became the first Soviet leader who had not participated in the CPSU politburo's 1979 invasion vote. As a provincial official and then as the party secretary for agriculture since November 1978, Gorbachev lacked foreign policy experience. On one of his few foreign trips, to Canada in 1983, he reportedly remarked privately that the invasion 'was a mistake'.[39] In a 1989 comment about how unlucky the USSR had been in efforts to revive the economy, Gorbachev cited the decline in prices for oil exports, the 1986 nuclear accident at Chernobyl, the 1988 earthquake in Armenia, 'Afghanistan, our old sins, and so on and so forth'.[40] The next day Moscow Television said continuing Soviet aid to Kabul was partly 'a desire to atone for what...Gorbachev called "our old sins"...', and the idea that Soviet involvement in Afghanistan had been sinful was repeated later.[41] But when *Pravda* published a cleaned-up official version of Gorbachev's extemporaneous remark after an unusual three-day delay, the words 'our old sins' had disappeared, and he was alleged to have said, 'There are considerable costs involved in Afghanistan'.[42]

Following precedent, Gorbachev met Karmal after Chernenko's funeral in March 1985. Karmal told the PDPA central committee that Gorbachev had 'sincerely expressed the principled stand of the CPSU central committee in connection with support for the [Afghan] revolution...',[43] a curious formulation that left in doubt Gorbachev's personal commitment. Gorbachev also met Zia. He told the general that 'aggressive actions are being launched' against Afghanistan from Pakistani territory that 'cannot but have a most unfavourable effect on the state of Soviet-Pakistani relations', Tass said.[44] A Pakistani account said the meeting was harsh, and Zia called it intense. But Zia publicly tried to put a good face on what was rumoured to have been a threatening Soviet attitude. Threats were carried out: from 294 artillery and air strikes into Pakistan in 1984, the total rose to 753 in 1985, and in 1986 it doubled to 1437, and terrorist incidents rose similarly, as indicated in Chapter 7.[45]

Putting Afghanistan First

As soon as the funeral guests had left, Gorbachev met on 16 March with two advisers, Georgiy A. Arbatov and Anatoly S. Chernyaev. Gorbachev had a list of international questions; Afghanistan was number seven or eight. Arbatov, director of the Soviet institute studying relations with the United States, said Afghanistan should top the list, apparently because it was a key to unlocking other problems. Gorbachev agreed. He later told Chernyaev, a personal aide, that Afghanistan should be the first foreign problem to solve.[46] Aleksandr N. Yakovlev, perhaps Gorbachev's most important adviser, said later that from the time Gorbachev became general secretary he felt 'that a peaceful withdrawal should be effected'.[47]

At the time, United States support for the *mujahideen* was just beginning to gain momentum. It was in the following month, April 1985, that President Reagan signed his directive for arming the *mujahideen* enough for them to try to defeat the Soviets, as described in Chapter 7. Although the greater military effectiveness of the resistance that came later undoubtedly played a role in convincing key Soviet officials that the Afghan problem could not be solved on the battlefield, the political leadership for a withdrawal was already in place before the US Congress reshaped American involvement.

For a time Gorbachev avoided public comment on Afghanistan. He ignored it in speeches surveying international issues. He seemed too wary to tackle immediately the many Soviet vested interests in Afghan policy. But the Soviet leaders' message to Kabul on the April 1985 anniversary of the Saur *coup* was noticeably cooler than earlier ones, omitting the usual promise of continued Soviet assistance in 'defending the April Revolution's gains...'.[48] Karmal desperately resorted to claiming that a Gorbachev speech promised support when in fact Gorbachev had avoided the subject.[49]

Cordovez said that in May 1985 the USSR offered 'a number of ideas on how the [Geneva] negotiations should move forward'.[50] Shortly after, Gorbachev told his politburo that it was necessary to remove Karmal and put in an Afghan leader who would discuss a Soviet troop withdrawal. Gorbachev also began trying to sway the politburo's thinking by reading to its meetings from stacks of letters from soldiers, their mothers, and even two generals serving in Afghanistan. The letters, which Chernyaev described as 'very traumatic documents', expressed uncertainty over the Soviet role, asked how it was 'internationalist duty' to destroy villages and kill Afghans, and said *Pravda* lied about the war.[51] In June the Soviet state committee for broadcasting reversed its order against realistic accounts of the war and ordered television reports on Soviet combat operations, as mentioned in Chapter 8.[52] This reflected a decision to inform the public on how nasty a war it really was, to overcome years of conditioned acceptance of it, and to prepare public understanding for a withdrawal.

Resistance to a Settlement

Gorbachev encountered resistance. Men like Gromyko, senior soldiers, and KGB officials felt that backing away from a militant policy would compromise Communist ideological principles, Soviet foreign policy tenets, and defence ministry prestige. 'There was a battle' in the leadership, Shevardnadze said later. 'It was quite painful for the military. I would not say everybody, but certain people were bound up with the war.'[53] Yakovlev said the Soviet military-industrial complex wanted the war to continue rather than see military spending cut.[54]

Gorbachev found it necessary to prove to the war's supporters that a military solution would not work. General Varennikov said unspecified conditions, apparently referring to Soviet institutional opposition, 'unfortunately forced us...[in] 1985, and especially in 1986,...to return to the resolution of issues by means of military measures'.[55] General Mikhail M. Zaitsev was put in supervisory charge of the OKSVA in mid-1985. He was given one year—at most, two years—to quell the resistance and stabilize the situation, with more troops trained to conduct ambushes in guerrilla territory but without the increase in the size of the 'limited contingent' that some generals sought.[56] The pressure of a deadline led to the 1986 high point of Soviet successes and low point of *mujahideen* morale, as related in Chapter 7, but failed to solve Moscow's problem.

The CPSU politburo decided in October 1985, Gorbachev said later, on 'a course of settling the Afghan question...[by] expedit[ing] the withdrawal of our forces and simultaneously ensur[ing] a friendly Afghanistan... through a combination of military and political measures'.[57] Karmal was warned to prepare for Soviet troops to leave.[58]

The job 'of settling the Afghan question' was given to Shevardnadze, the leader of Soviet Georgia who had become foreign minister in July 1985 after Gorbachev pushed Gromyko into the then-weak Soviet presidency.

Shevardnadze headed a new CPSU politburo commission on Afghanistan, created about the end of 1985, perhaps at the October 1985 politburo session.[59] The politburo members on it were CPSU secretary and Gorbachev adviser Yakovlev, KGB chairman Viktor M. Chebrikov, and the defence minister, first Marshal Sergei L. Sokolov and later his successor, General Dmitriy T. Yazov. Other members were the CPSU secretary for foreign affairs, Anatoliy F. Dobrynin; Chebrikov's deputy Kryuchkov, who personally supervised the KGB's large role in Kabul affairs; chief of general staff Akhromeyev; the general staff's supervisor of the war, Varennikov; and Konstantin F. Katuchev, the chairman of the USSR State Committee for Foreign Economic Relations. An interdepartmental working group prepared materials for meetings that the commission held every week or ten days.[60]

THE 'BLEEDING WOUND'

While politburo discussions and the existence of Shevardnazde's commission were kept secret, Gorbachev's first major public pronouncement on Afghanistan was buried in his omnibus report of the central committee to the CPSU's 27th congress on 25 February 1986. A general secretary's report to a congress was a collective statement of the leadership. Shevardnadze indicated that he and others had to fight unspecified opposition within the leadership to any hint of changing Afghan policy in order to get something into the speech.[61] Gorbachev told the congress that

counter-revolution and imperialism have turned Afghanistan into a running sore [*or* bleeding wound]. The Soviet Union supports this country's efforts which are directed at the defence of its own sovereignty. We would like in the near future to bring the Soviet forces—situated in Afghanistan at the request of its government—back to their homeland. The time scale for the step-by-step withdrawal has been worked out with the Afghan side, as soon as a political settlement has been achieved which will provide for a real end to and reliably guarantee a non-renewal of the outside armed interference in the internal affairs of [Afghanistan].[62]

Gorbachev's statement became a landmark in both Soviet and Western perceptions of the war because his graphic 'bleeding wound' indicated Afghanistan was having an impact on the USSR. By continuing to blame outside interference for the war, he left it unclear whether the Soviet position had changed enough to make a settlement possible. Shevardnadze said later that at the party congress, 'following large-scale, vehement debates, we reached our political conclusion' to withdraw.[63] Other evidence casts doubt on this, but, if true, it meant debates and conclusion behind the scenes, because Afghanistan was studiedly not discussed in congress speeches.

Babrak Karmal did not support Gorbachev's line in his own brief address to the congress, as mentioned in Chapter 5. Instead, he emphasized the second half of a Lenin quotation whose first half is usually all that is cited: 'Any revolution is only worth something when it knows how to defend itself, but a revolution does not learn how to defend itself all at once.'[64] Soon after snubbing Karmal by not letting him meet privately with Gorbachev or any other CPSU leader, Moscow deposed him.

THE SOVIET DECISION

The Soviet military's failure to meet the deadline for mastering the Afghan situation, compounded by the introduction of Stinger missiles in September 1986, pushed Soviet leaders further. The decisive politburo meeting was held on 13 November 1986. Noting the politburo's October 1985 decisions, Gorbachev complained that 'there is no

movement in either' the troop withdrawal or ensuring a
friendly Afghanistan. 'If the approach is not changed, we
will continue to fight for another 20 or 30 years.' Gromyko
was also despondent: 'Right now the situation is worse today
than half a year ago.' Akhromeyev told politburo members,
'on occupied territory, we cannot establish authority. We
have lost the battle for the Afghan people'.[65]

Summing up the discussion, Gorbachev elaborated on the
failure of the politburo's October 1985 thinking.

> The strengthening of the military position of the Afghan
> government has not taken place. National consolidation has
> not been ensured, mainly because Comrade Karmal continues
> to hope to sit in Kabul under our assistance. [Now we must]...in
> the course of two years effect the withdrawal of our troops
> from Afghanistan. In 1987 withdraw 50 per cent of our troops,
> and in the following [year]—another 50 per cent. Second, we
> must pursue a widening of the social base of the regime, taking
> into account the realistic arrangement of political forces. ...We
> must start talks with Pakistan. Most importantly, [we must make
> sure] that the Americans don't get into Afghanistan. But I
> think that Americans will not go into Afghanistan militarily.[66]

Gorbachev's statement reflected the findings of
Shevardnadze's commission. The politburo decision to
accept and implement them was kept secret but began to
have veiled effects. In November a senior adviser to
Gorbachev who had earlier spoken confidently of success in
Afghanistan told American diplomatic and regional
specialists, 'We know we have to get out, but we don't
know how to get out. Please help us'.[67] First Deputy Foreign
Minister Yuliy M. Vorontsov, who had become the senior
Soviet spokesman on Afghan affairs, invited Pakistani Foreign
Secretary Abdul Sattar to Moscow in early December. 'We
are leaving,' Vorontsov told him as he sought to work out a
political solution that would avert a possible bloodbath after
the departure.[68]

Deadline for Najibullah

Najibullah was summoned to Moscow for talks with Gorbachev on 12 December 1986. Publicly, Gorbachev said, 'We will not abandon our southern neighbour in a difficult situation...[but w]e have no intention to leave for long our troops in Afghanistan...'. It is up to the Americans 'to start scaling down the interference' in Afghan internal affairs, he added.[69] Najibullah went home and secretly told the PDPA central committee on 30 December that Gorbachev had privately told him Soviet troops would withdraw within 18 months to two years[70]—that is, by June or December 1988.

That PDPA central committee meeting adopted the concept of national reconciliation. Six days later, Shevardnadze and Dobrynin arrived in Kabul for talks.[71] The reason for their visit was unclear, but it probably was related to Najibullah's refusal to bait the hook of national reconciliation with enough dilution of PDPA control to catch any significant non-Communists and thus ease the way toward a compromise that would enable Soviet troops to leave gracefully. About that time, Moscow sent word to Washington that it was ready to discuss a withdrawal timetable and a government of national unity in Kabul, but the State Department considered the Soviet agenda premature.[72]

Najibullah did not want to believe Shevardnadze's statement in Kabul that a Soviet withdrawal 'is not far off'.[73] Najibullah said on 18 January that only an end to fighting and international guarantees against interference would prompt a Soviet withdrawal, obviously knowing neither condition was 'not far off'. He also denied any disagreement with the USSR on a solution.[74] Perhaps he was counting on allies in Moscow who oppposed a withdrawal under the then foreseeable circumstances, despite Gorbachev's ability to carry the CPSU politburo with his intention to quit Afghanistan. Two episodes related in Chapter 7 need to be re-examined in this context.

RESISTANCE IN MOSCOW

One episode was what the United States labelled a sham withdrawal of six regiments from Afghanistan in the autumn of 1986. One of Shevardnadze's closest advisers said the foreign minister was surprised by the American charge because the Soviet defence ministry had always kept civilian officials uninformed about its actions in Afghanistan.[75] The implication is that the ministry flouted Gorbachev's intentions, if not his direct orders. Yakovlev said that when, a year and a half later, Gorbachev called for the general withdrawal, everyone in the top leadership agreed—for the record. 'But then the most terrible things started happening. The implementation was sabotaged.'[76]

The Soviet armed forces were later accused of deliberately deceiving their civilian bosses on such other issues as the nature of a radar installation at Krasnoyarsk, responsibility for the deaths of 21 demonstrators in Tbilisi on 9 April 1989, the scrapping of bacteriological weapons production facilities, and the disposition of tanks under an arms control agreement.[77] The other main Soviet player in Afghanistan, the KGB, was also accused of deception, such as KGB boss Chebrikov's lying to other politburo members by denying that the KGB had secretly installed listening devices during the construction of a new American embassy in Moscow.[78] Insubordination apparently accounted for some of the irregularities of Afghanistan policy.

Resistance to a policy change also seemed to explain the publicity in the spring of 1987 for *mujahideen* attacks across the Soviet border. Both the defence ministry and the KGB, which was responsible for border guards, had suppressed reports of earlier raids that impugned their ability to protect the motherland. But, when Gorbachev was pressing for withdrawal, two cross-border raids were publicized to support the contention, as expressed by one prominent military spokesman, that '[a]n attack on one's country must be caught as far as possible from the border' by keeping troops in a frontline position in Afghanistan.[79]

Testimony in later years from Shevardnadze, Yakovlev, and others reinforced this evidence. Shevardnadze said the troop withdrawal encountered 'considerable resistance from the CPSU...extraordinarily tough fights within the party'.[80] Yakovlev said Kryuchkov, the godfather of PDPA rule first as head of the KGB's foreign intelligence and later as KGB boss, 'together with the military, wanted to drag on the war in Afghanistan...'.[81] Safronchuk said both the Soviet military and the KGB argued in 1987 that they needed more time to build up the Afghan army before withdrawal.[82]

Some of these arguments occurred in Shevardnadze's politburo commission. The military representatives, supported by KGB officials, hammered at the pro-withdrawal Shevardnadze and Yakovlev with questions they could not answer and put 'forward seemingly objective and reasonable arguments' that amounted to 'deliberately holding...up' a decision, Yakovlev said. Without ever asserting that the war should continue, military and KGB officials used 'contrived and devious ways of spinning it out'. They warned that, without the Soviet Army, 'everything will collapse. Afghanistan will quickly fall into the hands of the Americans, through Pakistan.... We will have the real enemy on our doorstep'. Yakovlev added that Gorbachev's determination to withdraw was the decisive factor in the commission's work.[83]

The policy struggle in secret meetings moved into the public media. Whenever Afghanistan came up in Kremlin meetings under Gorbachev, Yakovlev said, 'voices of outright advocates of the war...were not all that prominent, for some reason. They—the former foreign minister [Gromyko], for instance—they only raised their voices when challenged'.[84] But in January 1988 Gromyko publicly hinted at his opposition to withdrawal by recalling—abstractly, with no context—for praise, Stalin's determined fight and Soviet 'iron patience' in 1945 to ensure that Poland would be a friendly

Communist state 'and not an appendage of the Western bloc'.[85] A Moscow Radio commentator asked, 'Did our boys perish in the Afghan mountains and deserts so that Afghanistan could return to its medieval past?'[86] The defence ministry newspaper said 'we have never abandoned friends in trouble.... [It was a] source of pain...that the cause of the Afghan revolution has not yet been seen through to the end...because sacrifices should have some point and result'.[87] Contrary to other evidence, however, Vorontsov contended later that Soviet military officers were 'the main proponents of getting out' of Afghanistan.[88] Perhaps there was a difference between officers who did the actual fighting and senior generals.

Talking in July 1989 about civilian control over the military, Gorbachev said that, when he became CPSU general secretary in 1985, there was 'a situation which was fraught with serious dangers', and one of the central committee's first moves had been 'strengthening discipline' in the armed forces.[89] He seized an opportunity to weaken military opposition by firing several senior officers for unpreparedness after a young West German landed a light plane unchallenged beside the Kremlin on 28 May 1987. Ustinov's successor as defence minister, Sokolov, who had commanded the invasion of Afghanistan, was replaced by Yazov, a general personally known and beholden to Gorbachev.[90] Less than a month later, Gorbachev promoted allies into the CPSU politburo. These moves strengthened his position to carry out such controversial policies as bringing troops home from Afghanistan.

Apprehensions in Moscow

Apprehensions were growing in Moscow that the Kabul regime was not strong enough to survive Soviet troops' departure, that there would be 'a blood bath after we leave'.[91] With the Communist idea of a compromise, national reconciliation, generally rejected, Cordovez offered his own compromise idea in July 1987. He proposed a Geneva meeting of the seven Peshawar leaders, resistance commanders, refugee and tribal leaders, the PDPA, and 'selected personalities' among Afghan exiles, including Zahir Shah or his supporters. Their *jirgah* would set up 'broadly based transitional arrangements' under which 'no party would be assured a predominant role...'.[92] But no one was prepared to compromise. *Mujahideen* leaders rejected any PDPA role, Moscow feared the PDPA would be eclipsed, and both the Islamists and Pakistan rejected the king. In Pakistan, ISI—where General Hamid Gul succeeded Akhtar Abdur Rahman as commander in March 1987—as well as President Zia's fundamentalist Islamic supporters opposed any solution that did not put into power their favourite, Hekmatyar. Pakistani diplomats' manœuverability in seeking a settlement was thus restricted.[93]

A recalcitrant Najibullah was summoned back to Moscow. The communique on his meeting with Gorbachev on 20 July 1987 was notably lacking in cordiality or Soviet assurances of support. Apparently referring to KGB and Soviet military attitudes, Gorbachev told a shaken Najibullah, 'No matter what else you may have heard, I hope you are ready in twelve months, because we will be leaving whether you are or not'.[94] The next day Gorbachev said in an interview, 'In principle, the question of the withdrawal... already has been decided.... However, the interference in Afghanistan's internal affairs must be ended and the nonresumption of this interference guaranteed'. Soviet diplomats were told to publicize the decision, not the 'however'.[95]

PREPARING THE SOVIET AND AFGHAN PUBLICS

The Soviet public also had to be prepared. More honest media accounts of the war did not help people understand how it might be possible to walk away from an oft-repeated commitment to Kabul or see a Soviet-sponsored regime violate the Leninist principle of one-party rule. A tortured defence of Afghan national reconciliation on Moscow Television in August 1987 called it only realistic for the regime to drop its slogans of building socialism and propose a coalition government. Rather than being 'a retreat of the revolution', such steps were 'a strengthening of the revolution', a panel of experts on Afghanistan averred. One of them, Deputy Foreign Minister Anatoliy L. Adamishin, played the classic trump card in any Soviet policy argument, a claim that Lenin had set a precedent for whatever policy his successors currently favoured. Adamishin compared the 'sharp change' in Afghanistan to Russia's 3 March 1918 treaty of Brest-Litovsk with Germany.[96] To buy peace during World War I in order to preserve his fragile new regime, Lenin had narrowly overcome strong resistance in the Bolshevik leadership to the treaty's major concessions. Adamishin thus indicated that Marxist control of Afghanistan had to be sacrificed for a greater goal—which he did not spell out. Still, the Soviet public had doubts. A young officer wrote to *Krasnaya Zvezda* suggesting that offering to 'be reconciled with inveterate enemies [is]...a sign of weakness or gullibility.... Doesn't [this] smack of capitulationism?'—a dirty word in the Leninist lexicon. Denying this, the defence ministry newspaper said Lenin had 'pointed out that it is childish to reject compromise "on principle"'.[97]

Still Najibullah dragged his heels. At a belatedly scheduled round of Geneva 'proximity talks' from 7 to 11 September 1987, Afghan Foreign Minister Abdol Wakil offered a reduction in the Soviet withdrawal time from eighteen to sixteen months. *Pravda* promptly reiterated that twelve months probably would be acceptable.[98] On 16 September, Shevardnadze privately told Secretary of State Shultz that the USSR would leave Afghanistan soon, possibly by the end of the Reagan administration sixteen months later, and he wanted American help to achieve a peaceful solution.[99]

Worries about Soviet support surfaced at the PDPA's second nationwide conference, held 18-20 October 1987. Najibullah warned that opposition to national reconciliation—a policy that many members felt threatened their jobs—could no longer be tolerated. Afghanistan 'will be eternally grateful' for Soviet military support. He added pointedly, 'many questions relating to military building and strengthening of our armed forces' military might have still not been resolved. At present, by no means all military units and formations can independently and successfully oppose the enemy'.[100] Najibullah met Gorbachev again in Moscow on 3 November 1987. Unconfirmed Kabul reports said Gorbachev strongly criticized Najibullah for squandering Soviet aid, for PDPA strife, and for the regime's inability to turn the military tide, and he said there was 'increasing internal pressure' in the USSR for a troop withdrawal, on which Najibullah must help.[101] Speaking two days later to foreign Communists, Gorbachev sounded defensive in explaining his policy of cutting foreign commitments and turning inward for 'developing and renewing Soviet society'.[102]

CONCLUDING COMPLICATIONS

Vorontsov told Michael H. Armacost, the United States under-secretary of state for political affairs, on 16 November 1987 that the next round of 'proximity talks' should be held by the end of February as 'the final round'. Vorontsov significantly did not add the condition that withdrawal still depended on piecing together a national reconciliation coalition to share power in Kabul.[103] When Najibullah assumed the Afghan presidency two weeks later, he announced that, in discussions with the Soviets, 'it was decided that the withdrawal...will take place...within a time not longer than twelve months. We will present this proposal at the next round of the Geneva talks'. Although he added his usual call for interference to stop and stay stopped, Najibullah had been coerced into accepting twelve months by Gorbachev, who was considering an even shorter withdrawal period.[104] Najibullah was asked a few days later, 'What will happen in Afghanistan after the withdrawal of Soviet troops?' He replied, 'This question worries every one of us'.[105]

After Gorbachev had forced Najibullah into line in preparation for the Soviet leader's December 1987 talks with President Reagan in Washington, Reagan complicated the Geneva end game and turned settlement efforts into an American domestic political issue. A journalist asked if he would 'make a commitment not to supply the anti-government forces for a year if the Soviets committed to get out of Afghanistan within that period of time'. Reagan replied, 'I don't think we could do anything of that kind.... You can't suddenly disarm [the *mujahideen*] and leave them prey to the [Kabul regime]...'.[106] This contradicted the United States' commitment to Cordovez dated 11 December 1985 to halt aid to the *mujahideen* at the beginning of a withdrawal, as part of guaranteeing 'a comprehensive and balanced settlement'. Americans officials said later that Reagan either had not known about or had not understood the 1985 letter.[107]

This issue obstructed any progress on Afghanistan during Reagan's meetings with Gorbachev.[108] After their talks, Gorbachev said that 'the beginning of the withdrawal...must at the same time become the beginning of the termination of assistance with arms and money to the *dushmans* [bandits, i.e., *mujahideen*]. From the very first day this is declared, our troops will start withdrawing' and will only fight in self-defence. He added, 'We do not strive for a pro-Soviet regime in Afghanistan', and the United States should not seek a pro-American one.[109]

At the State Department, Armacost quickly reiterated the 1985 promise to accept the Geneva package, including cutting off aid when withdrawal began.[110] This provoked confused statements from the White House about what the aid cut off policy was. Members of Congress who had led the fight to help the *mujahideen*, accused the State Department of selling out the resistance and called on Reagan to ensure continued aid.[111] Shultz tried to split the difference by suggesting that the need for American aid would decline 'as the withdrawal proceeds...and it would cease' at an unspecified date. At the same time, he introduced a new element: Soviet military aid to Kabul should also be halted.[112] Congressional pressure and angry outside accusations of a sellout influenced the Geneva agreement's final shape.[113]

Shevardnadze's Notice

Shevardnadze flew to Kabul again on 4 January 1988. As he left, on 6 January, he told the Afghan news agency, 'We would like the new year of 1988 to be the last year of the stay of Soviet troops in your country'. Claiming that the United States had agreed to guarantee a settlement and halt aid, Shevardnadze said, 'We shall leave Afghanistan with a clear conscience and awareness that we have done our duty, when external interference ceases. Complete understanding on this point exists between ourselves and the Afghan leadership'. While the withdrawal did not depend on the creation of a transitional government acceptable to the resistance, he said, an internal political settlement required that 'no one will claim a monopoly on power'. Shevardnadze added an indirect warning to Najibullah not to put 'some ancilliary, transitory, and personal considerations and ambitions before national interests' by evading 'broad political dialogue...'.[114]

Opposition within the Soviet leadership to Shevardnadze's—and Gorbachev's—Afghan policy was shown by an unusual Soviet media blackout of the foreign minister's trip to Kabul and by a failure of the CPSU politburo to announce its routine review and endorsement of a member's talks with a foreign leader. Nor was Najibullah happy. He tried unsuccessfully to complicate the Geneva negotiations by introducing new requirements: the dismantling of *mujahideen* training camps in Pakistan before the withdrawal began, and a *mujahideen* ceasefire not only with departing Soviets but also with the Afghan army.[115]

President Zia introduced a more serious complication. He said Pakistan could not sign the Geneva accords with Najibullah, 'the man appointed by the Soviet Union who is responsible for killing so many people.... The present regime is Soviet-oriented. It cannot, therefore, be accepted...'. He would only reach a Geneva agreement with a coalition Afghan government, which might have some PDPA representatives.[116] This reversed Pakistan's position at Geneva that the nature of the future government was not a condition. It also picked up the Soviet insistence on a national reconciliation coalition that had been dropped by Vorontsov in November 1987. Agha Shahi, who had set Pakistan's position in 1981, suggested Pakistan was beginning to doubt whether the PDPA regime would collapse once the Soviets were gone and the burden of Afghan refugees would end.[117]

GORBACHEV'S DECISIVE STATEMENT

With both Reagan and Zia seeming to back away from an agreement as Moscow became more eager to get one, Gorbachev felt betrayed in his peace efforts.[118] He acted abruptly, decisively, and apparently over continuing opposition—presenting Soviet opponents of withdrawal with a *fait accompli*. Without warning, a statement was read for him on Moscow Television on 8 February 1988, and a short time later Najibullah broadcast his obviously coerced concurrence. Gorbachev said 'all aspects of a settlement have been almost fully worked out at the Geneva negotiations', including non-interference—meaning a halt in aid to the *mujahideen*—and international guarantees of it. In fact, he knew the halt was not 'almost fully worked out', but his obvious purpose was to commit the Soviet Army to coming home regardless of further complications. What remained to be done, Gorbachev said, was to establish a time frame for the withdrawal. He said Soviet troops would begin withdrawing on 15 May 1988 if the Geneva agreements were signed by 15 March, and they would be gone within ten months.[119]

Gorbachev added that the withdrawal was not 'linked with the completion of efforts to set up a new, coalition government in Afghanistan,...[with] bringing the policy of national reconciliation to fruition.... This is a purely internal Afghan issue'. If fighting continued after the withdrawal, '[t]he Geneva obligations will close the channels for outside assistance.... If necessary', Gorbachev added unrealistically, 'consideration could be given at that state to using the possibilities available to the United Nations and its Security Council'. Gorbachev concluded hopefully, 'when the Afghan knot is untied, it will have the most profound impact on other regional conflicts'.[120]

Gorbachev's position was a far cry from his CPSU congress statement two years earlier that a withdrawal would occur 'as soon as a political settlement has been achieved which will provide for a real end to and reliably guarantee a non-renewal of outside armed interference...'.[121] But eliminating the Afghanistan problem from Soviet domestic and foreign policy had become more important than attaining those conditions. 'This conflict must be concluded,' Gorbachev said in April 1988. 'It has dragged on too long. The country needs peace'[122]—referring to the USSR, not Afghanistan.

Reactions to the Decision

Dissent from the 8 February statement was immediately obvious. The next day Shevardnadze and fellow politburo member Yegor K. Ligachev praised it at a joint session of the Supreme Soviet's two foreign affairs commissions.[123] But Defence Minister Yazov's speech to the commissions was notably silent on it, and he only commented opaquely thirteen days later that the statement was 'of immense significance'.[124] President Gromyko used carefully neutral language about the withdrawal decision while awarding a Hero's gold star to a colonel who had helped 'that fraternal country'.[125] KGB boss Chebrikov avoided the subject in public remarks that were otherwise harsh on compromise with the West.[126]

To defend the decision, Gorbachev and his supporters took two kinds of offensive actions. One was to begin making the public disclosures, cited in Chapter 3, that the invasion was decided by a small, ill-informed clique around Brezhnev. The other was discrediting the Kabul regime. For example, Gorbachev's adviser Yevgeniy M. Primakov said 'history has not confirmed' that the PDPA 'government was really good, really revolutionary, and that those who had come to power could extend their influence over the whole country'.[127]

Moscow sent special envoys to important Islamic nations to seek aid in convincing the United States and Pakistan to complete the Geneva agreement with commitments on halting aid. Vorontsov went to Islamabad, but President Zia argued that a new government in Kabul was essential for getting the refugees to leave Pakistan.[128] Zia and the ISI-led military establishment were convinced that the Soviets had been defeated and Pakistan could therefore hold out for a favourable Afghan regime. However, Prime Minister Mohammed Khan Junejo mobilized domestic opinion and American pressure behind the idea that it was an acceptable risk to sign the agreement and wait for a new Afghan government to be worked out later.[129] *Mujahideen* leaders in Peshawar were naturally also dissatisfied with leaving the Kabul regime intact, as were Iran-based guerrillas.

FINISHING IN GENEVA

When talks resumed in Geneva on 2 March 1988, Pakistan's minister of state for foreign affairs, Zain Noorani, let Zia's demand for a transitional government in Kabul fade away gradually. Pakistan ended up agreeing to a vague commitment of continued United Nations involvement in the peace process.[130] This left Reagan's insistence on continuing arms aid to the *mujahideen* as the key issue. After confusion and conflict in Washington, the administration agreed in mid-January 1988 on a policy that became known as 'symmetry'. If the USSR would stop military aid to Kabul when the withdrawal began, United States aid to the *mujahideen* would also end— 'negative symmetry'. But if the Soviets continued arming Kabul, American aid would also continue—'positive symmetry'— despite any American signature in Geneva guaranteeing jointly with the USSR non-interference in Afghan internal affairs.[131] Moscow argued that its arms supply agreements with Afghanistan were long-standing, legitimate arrangements between governments that had to continue, whereas US aid was an illegitimate arrangement that violated international law.[132]

Although the United States wanted a signed agreement that should make Moscow's actions predictable, the Soviet foreign ministry eliminated any leverage this might have gained for Washington. The ministry announced on 17 March that it wanted 'the withdrawal [to] be part of the [Geneva] package', but if the impasse continued then 'the withdrawal of Soviet troops will be carried out in some other way'.[133] In Washington on 22 and 23 March, Shevardnadze pleaded with Shultz in often emotional tones that the USSR had done nearly everything the United States had asked on Afghanistan, but it needed 'this one last piece' of an American aid cut off. Shultz was adamant: no further aid from either, or else aid from both.[134] Frustrated and unhappy, Shevardnadze left saying that '[t]he Afghan question can be settled without an American guarantee' to halt outside interference.[135] This meant that all the United States, Pakistan, and the *mujahideen* had to do was wait for the withdrawal, conceding nothing.

Agreeing with Crossed Fingers

Nonetheless, the Geneva agreement that Pakistan was moving toward signing was a problem. One part said Pakistan would 'prevent within its territory the training, equipping, financing, and recruitment of mercenaries from whatever origin for the purpose of hostile activities against' Afghanistan, and it would deny them facilities.[136] Shevardnadze contended that by 'positive symmetry' the Americans were 'out to make Pakistan violate its commitments'.[137] This did not bother Islamabad. Junejo telephoned Shultz on 30 March to say Pakistan intended to sign and to urge that the United States sign as a guarantor of non-interference. But, the prime minister added, Pakistan would continue to be the base and supply channel for the *mujahideen*. To confirm this deliberate deceit, Zia phoned Reagan later the same day. Pakistan, Zia said, would 'just lie about' violating the agreement. 'We've been denying our activities there for eight years. Muslims have the right to lie in a good cause', Zia reportedly explained.[138]

American officials rationalized the contradiction between guaranteeing non-interference and continuing aid, despite warnings from legal experts and misgivings from Congress about making international agreements with the intention of breaking them. As both Washington and Moscow rushed last-minute supply buildups for their clients, just in case there was an agreed cutoff, the Soviets were so eager to wrap up the Geneva accords and begin withdrawing that they were willing to ignore the intended deception.

Bludgeoning Najibullah into Line

The remaining problem was Najibullah. He strongly opposed being left without Soviet aid, nor did he want his enemies to continue to receive aid. Needing an Afghan signature in Geneva for a face-saving way out of the war, Shevardnadze flew to Kabul on 3 April. Reflecting what he told Najibullah, Tass made it clear that the USSR would withdraw its troops even without an American guarantee, even if Pakistan refused to sign. Still, Najibullah threatened not to sign in Geneva.[139] So Shevardnadze took him to Tashkent on 6 April to meet Gorbachev, who flew in from Moscow. Before meeting, each leader had held a session of his party politburo to obtain approval for his course. Gorbachev could threaten to withhold aid if Najibullah did not cooperate, but Najibullah had reluctant PDPA authority to agree to the Geneva accords. After a tense night in Tashkent as Najibullah had an emotional telephone discussion with Kabul's recalcitrant delegation in Geneva, Afghan concurrence was assured.[140] The two Communist leaders said on 7 April that 'the last obstacles to concluding the agreements have now been removed...'.[141] Although Najibullah's arm had obviously been twisted hard, he later claimed that 'we decided to send the Soviet Union off', and a Supreme Soviet report diplomatically accepted his pretence.[142]

One other issue that arose in the Geneva conclusion was the boundary between Pakistan and Afghanistan. The 10 March 1980 CPSU politburo commission's outline of a political settlement, which foreshadowed the shape of the Geneva agreement, recognized 'that Pakistan will strive to secure Afghanistan's recognition of the Durand Line'. The commission thought it would be 'advantageous for the

Afghans to use this issue to receive from Pakistan maximal concessions...'.[143] Eight years later the issue was fought to a draw. The draft section on non-interference used the phrase 'existing internationally recognized boundaries'. Wakil objected, with more political posturing than historical accuracy, that 'no regime in Afghanistan...has accepted' the Durand Line. Although irritated by the disruptive argument, the Soviets backed him. Finally, Pakistan came up with acceptable language that it and Afghanistan were 'not to violate the boundaries of each other...'.[144]

THE GENEVA AGREEMENT

With all the issues resolved, or finessed, officials of the four principal countries gathered on 14 April 1988 at the United Nations' European headquarters—the old League of Nations' *Palais des Nations* in Geneva. It was the first time representatives of Afghanistan and of Pakistan, which refused to recognize the Kabul regime, had officially met across one table. Perez de Cuellar and Diego Cordovez presided. No one shook hands. 'There were no smiles and little celebration', a key Pakistani official observed.[145]

Wakil and Noorani each signed three of the agreement's four accords, which were to come into effect on 15 May. One 'on non-interference and non-intervention' said Afghanistan and Pakistan each would

refrain from the threat or use of force...so as not to violate the boundaries of each other..., [would] refrain from armed intervention, subversion, military occupation, or any other form of intervention and interference, overt or covert..., [would] prevent within its territory the training, equipping, financing, and recruitment of mercenaries from whatever origin for the purpose of hostile activities against the other [country]..., [would] prevent any assistance to or use of or tolerance of terrorist groups, saboteurs, or subversive against the other..., [and would] prevent within its territory the presence, harbouring, in camps and bases or otherwise, organizing, training, financing, equipping, and arming of...groups for the purpose of creating subversion, disorder, or unrest in the territory of the other....[146]

A second accord said 'Pakistan shall facilitate the voluntary, orderly, and peaceful repatriation of all Afghan refugees staying within its territory...'. Afghanistan promised that they could return freely, live where they wanted, have the right to work, be able 'to participate on an equal basis in the civic affairs of...Afghanistan', and 'enjoy the same rights and privileges' as other Afghan citizens 'without discrimination'. The third accord 'on the inter-relationships for the settlement' said that by agreement between the USSR and Afghanistan

> there will be a phased withdrawal of the foreign troops which will start on [15 May 1988]. One-half of the troops will be withdrawn by 15 August 1988 and the withdrawal of all troops will be completed within nine months.... [Representatives of Afghanistan and Pakistan would meet when needed t]o consider alleged violations and to work out prompt and mutually satisfactory solutions to questions that may arise.... A representative of the Secretary-General of the United Nations shall lend his good offices ....

Shevardnadze and Shultz signed as witnesses to this accord, thus committing the USSR to the withdrawal timetable.

A 'declaration on international guarantees' that also went into effect on 15 May was signed by Shultz and Shevardnadze. It said their countries undertook 'to invariably refrain from any form of interference and intervention in the internal affairs of...Afghanistan and...Pakistan and to respect the commitments contained in the...non-interference and non-intervention' agreement, and would urge other countries to do the same. Under an unsigned 'memorandum of understanding' promising cooperation, Perez de Cuellar established on 26 April a UN Good Offices Mission in

Afghanistan and Pakistan to 'ascertain on the ground any violation' of the accords. General Rauli Helminen of Finland and 50 officers drawn from existing UN peacekeeping operations formed the mission.[147]

An American Qualification

After the signing ceremony, Shultz made public a statement sent to Perez de Cuellar that was 'integral to [American] undertakings as guarantor'. The key paragraph said, 'The obligations undertaken by the guarantors are symmetrical. In this regard, the United States has advised the Soviet Union that the US retains the right, consistent with its obligations as guarantor, to provide military assistance to parties in Afghanistan. Should the Soviet Union exercise restraint in providing military assistance to parties in Afghanistan, the US similarly will exercise restraint'. The State Department later insisted, 'The Soviets and the other Geneva parties signed...with full knowledge of' the position expressed in the American statement, which it denied was inconsistent with Shultz's signing the guarantee declaration.[148] But a journalist at the signing commented that the American statement and a parallel Pakistani statement 'gave the whole ceremony something of an unreal quality...'.[149] When pressed at a news conference, Shevardnadze groped for some way to deny the unreality. After first claiming that 'actions to meddle in the affairs of Afghanistan [have] finally been all blocked', he added, 'frankly', that continued American arms deliveries 'will not have a decisive influence...[if Pakistan] observe[s] all the principles' of the accords[150]—an obvious contradiction, because there could be no American deliveries without Pakistan's violating its pledges.

Shevardnadze said that, when he flew home from Geneva,

> [i]t might have seemed that I should have been happy: there
> would be an end to the caskets arriving in the country. The
> account of deaths and expenditure...would be closed. But,
> despite this, I felt profoundly depressed.... It was hard for me
> to see myself as a foreign minister who had signed by no means
> a victory agreement. Such had not been a frequent occurrence
> in the history of Russia and the Soviet Union. And I was further
> troubled by the thought of people whom we ourselves had
> nursed and roused to revolution and whom we were now leaving
> one-on-one with a deadly enemy.[151]

But in Geneva Shevardnadze rejected a journalist's
question about Soviet generals' having 'lost a war'. He
insisted, 'There is no defeat here'.[152] Years later he claimed,
'By making the decision to withdraw our troops, we won
the Afghan war'.[153] In fact, the Geneva accords were neither
victory nor defeat for the Soviets—nor a settlement for the
Afghans. A Soviet commentator said later it would have
been naive to expect the accords to lead to peace. What they
did provide was 'relief, relief', another Soviet said.[154]

The reverse of Soviet relief was Kabul worry. Col. Gen.
Shahnawaz Tanai, the chief of the Afghan army general staff
who was soon to become defence minister, said 'a
considerable proportion of leftist [PDPA] members—
including [those] in the army—were dispirited, and there
was even talk that the Soviet Union had allegedly changed
its principles'.[155] Yakovlev reported that Kabul 'accused us
of leaving it in the lurch. It moaned that Afghanistan would
soon collapse, that reprisals would start and so on'.[156]

A *mujahideen* statement issued in Peshawar on the eve of
the signing said the resistance was not bound by the
agreement because it had not participated in the talks, self-
determination was not guaranteed, and Najibullah was left in
power. Guerrilla leaders called for a continued fight and urged
refugees not to go home until the Kabul regime had been
overthrown. Iran agreed, calling the accords 'legally invalid'.[157]

NOTES

1. *International Affairs*, March 1990: 89.
2. Moscow Television, 16 February 1987, in *FBIS/SU*, 17 February 1987, p. AA17.
3. *Pravda*, 11 July 1990, pp. 1-2, in *FBIS/SU Supplement*, 13 July 1990, p. 77.
4. Moscow Television, 19 August 1987, in *FBIS/SU*, 21 August 1987, p. CC2.
5. *Pravda*, 26 October 1985, in *FBIS/SU*, 28 October 1985, pp. 1-28.
6. Moscow Television, 28 July 1986, in *FBIS/SU*, 29 July 1986, p. R19.
7. The only partially, but not directly, comparable withdrawals were from Chinese Sinkiang (now Xinjiang) in 1943 and Iranian Azerbaijan in 1946.
8. E.g., Shahi, *Pakistan's Security*, p. 111; Zhores Medvedev, *Andropov* (New York, 1983), p. 172. This author assumed the Soviets would use whatever force was needed to hold onto Afghanistan, in *Afghanistan and the Soviet Union* (Durham, 1983).
9. State Department, *Bulletin*, April 1980: 12; *New York Times*, 6 August 1981, p. A1.
10. *CWIHPB*, Nos. 8-9: 167-9.
11. Sergei Tarasenko, remarks, Princeton, 27 February 1993.
12. Ibid.; Safronchuk, remarks, Austin, 20-21 October 1989.
13. Kabul Radio, 14 May 1980, in *FBIS/SA*, 15 May 1980, pp. C1-3.
14. Safronchuk, 'Afghanistan in the Taraki Period', p. 91.
15. Shahi, *Pakistan's Security*, pp. 37-8.
16. *New York Times*, 6 August 1981, p. A1.
17. Kabul Radio, 24 August 1981, in *FBIS/SA*, 25 August 1981, pp. C1-2.
18. Riaz Khan, *Untying*, pp. 49-51, 95.
19. Selig S. Harrison, 'Inside the Afghan Talks', *Foreign Policy*, Fall 1988: 38-9; Riaz Khan, *Untying*, p. 95; Diego Cordovez and Selig S. Harrison, *Out of Afghanistan: The Inside Story of the Soviet Withdrawal* (New York, 1995).
20. *Washington Post*, 5 May 1986, p. A24; *Muslim*, 24 January 1988, p. 1, in *FBIS/NE*, 4 February 1988, p. 55.
21. Details in one of the Geneva accords, Tass from Geneva, 14 April 1988, in *FBIS/SU*, 15 April 1988, p. 29.
22. *New York Times*, 29 June, 19 July, and 10 December 1986, pp. 14, 5, and A10; Karachi Radio, 24 July 1986, in *FBIS/SA*, 30 July 1986, p. F2.
23. State Department, 'Afghanistan: Eight Years', p. 11.

24. Harrison, 'Paths to Peace', p. 12; Reagan, *American Life*, pp. 618-19.
25. Ibid., p. 644; AP from Washington, 22 November 1985; *New York Times*, 14 December 1985, 11 February and 24 March 1988, pp. A3, A3, and A35.
26. *Christian Science Monitor*, 26 February 1986, p. 4.
27. *New York Times*, 23 January 1987, p. A3; Riaz Khan, *Untying*, Chapter VI.
28. *Washington Post*, 17 April 1988, p. C2; Tass from Cairo, 16 October 1987, in *FBIS/SU*, 16 October 1987, p. 33.
29. *New York Times*, 11 December 1987, p. A17; *Der Spiegel*, 30 March 1987, p. 172, in *FBIS/SA*, 31 March 1987, p. C1; Riaz Khan, *Untying*, pp. 195-201; *Muslim*, 29 April 1987, p. 1, in *FBIS/SA*, 7 May 1987, p. C1.
30. *Washington Post*, 16 April 1991, p. A12.
31. Riaz Khan, *Untying*, p. 106.
32. *Pravda*, 16 December 1982, in *FBIS/SU*, 16 December 1982, p. D1-4.
33. 'Tass Statement', 31 December 1982, in *FBIS/SU*, 3 January 1983, pp. D1-2.
34. Transcript of politburo session; *Washington Post*, 16 November 1992, p. A16.
35. Tass from Moscow, 24 April 1983, in *FBIS/SU*, 25 April 1983, pp. AA1-10.
36. Sarah E. Mendelson, 'Internal Battles and External Wars: Politics, Learning, and the Soviet Withdrawal from Afghanistan', *World Politics*, April 1993: 341, 346.
37. Cordovez, who was present, to the author.
38. Kabul Radio, 14 February 1984, in *FBIS/SU*, 15 February 1984, p. P25; *Izvestiya*, 21 February 1984, p. 4, in *FBIS/SU*, 23 February 1984, p. D1.
39. *Time*, 4 January 1988, p. 27.
40. Moscow Television, 21 January 1989, in *FBIS/SU*, 23 January 1989, p. 50.
41. Moscow Television, 22 January 1989, in *FBIS/SU*, 23 January 1989, p. 36; *SSHA: Ekonomika, Politika, Ideologiya*, June 1989: 62-68, in *JPRS-USA-89-013*, 24 October 1989, p. 19.
42. *Pravda*, 24 January 1989, pp. 1-2, in *FBIS/SU*, 24 January 1989, p. 50.
43. Kabul Radio, 27 March 1985, in *FBIS/SA*, 3 April 1985, p. C10.
44. Tass in *Krasnaya Zvezda*, 15 March 1985, p. 3, in *FBIS/SU*, 15 March 1985, p. D1.
45. Riaz Khan, *Untying*, p. 134; Karachi Radio, 15 March 1985, in *FBIS/SA*, 15 March 1985, p. F1; *Diario de Noticias*, 30 June 1985,

pp. 30-32, in *FBIS/SA*, 12 July 1985, p. F2; Arif, *Working with Zia*, p. 329.

46. Anatoly S. Chernyaev, remarks, Princeton, 27 February 1993.

47. Moscow Television, 27 December 1991, in *FBIS/SU*, 31 December 1991, p. 3.

48. Compare *Pravda*, 27 April 1983 and 26 April 1984, both p. 1, with 27 April 1985, buried on p. 2, in *FBIS/SU*, 28 April 1983, 27 April 1984, and 30 April 1985, all pp. D1.

49. Compare Kabul Radio, 25 April 1985, in *FBIS/SA*, 1 May 1985, pp. C10-13, with *Pravda*, 24 April 1985, pp. 1-2, in *FBIS/SU*, 24 April 1985, pp. R3-18.

50. Don Oberdorfer, 'A Diplomatic Solution to Stalemate: Afghanistan: The Soviet Decision to Pull Out', *Washington Post*, 17 April 1988, p. A1.

51. Chernayev, remarks, Princeton, 27 February 1993.

52. Moscow Television, 27 December 1991, in *FBIS/SU*, 31 December 1991, p. 4.

53. Moscow Television, 24 December 1991, in *FBIS/SU*, 27 December 1991, p. 5.

54. Moscow Television, 27 December 1991, in *FBIS/SU*, 31 December 1991, p. 4.

55. *Ogonek*, 18 March 1989, p. 6; Budapest Television, 28 June 1989, in *FBIS/SU*, 30 June 1989, p. 73.

56. Oberdorfer, *Turn*, p. 238; Alexiev,' 'United States and the War', p. 13; Mendelson, 'Internal Battles', p. 349f.

57. *CWIHPB*, Nos. 8-9: 180.

58. *Pravda*, 19 February 1988, pp. 1-3, in *FBIS/SU*, 19 February 1988, p. 56.

59. Moscow Television, 3 July 1990, in *FBIS/SU Supplement*, 5 July 1990, p. 8; Moscow Television, 24 December 1991, in *FBIS/SU*, 27 December 1991, p. 5.

60. Moscow Television, 27 December 1991, in *FBIS/SU*, 31 December 1991, p. 4; Sergei Tarasenko, remarks, Princeton, 27 February 1993; *Pravda*, 4 July 1990, p. 3, in *FBIS/SU Supplement*, 5 July 1990, p. 3.

61. Shevardnadze, *Future Belongs to Freedom*, p. 47; Moscow Television, 24 December 1991, in *FBIS/SU*, 27 December 1991, p. 5.

62. Moscow Television, 25 February 1986, in *FBIS/SU Supplement*, 26 February 1986, p. O31 (BBC translation as 'running sore'); Tass from Moscow in English, 25 February 1986, in *FBIS/SU Supplement*, 25 February 1986, p. O12 (Tass translation as 'bleeding wound').

63. Moscow Television, 22 January 1992, in *FBIS/CE*, 23 January 1992, p. 6.

64. *Pravda*, 1 March 1986, p. 11, in *FBIS/SU Supplement*, 19 March 1986, p. O15.

65. *CWIHPB*, Nos. 8-9: 178-80.

66. Ibid., pp. 180-81.

67. Oberdorfer, 'Diplomatic Solution'.

68. Oberdorfer, *Turn*, p. 239; *Washington Post*, 26 December 1986, p. A25.

69. *Pravda*, 14 December 1986, pp. 1-2, in *FBIS/SU*, 15 December 1986, pp. D1-9.

70. *International Affairs*, February 1990: 20; Oberdorfer, 'Diplomatic Solution'.

71. Tass from Kabul, 5 January 1987, in *FBIS/SU*, 6 January 1987, p. D1.

72. George P. Shultz, *Turmoil and Triumph: My Years as Secretary of State* (New York, 1993), p. 870.

73. Bakhtar from Kabul, 8 January 1987, in *FBIS/SA*, 9 January 1987, p. C1; *Pravda*, 8 January 1987, p. 5, in *FBIS/SU*, 8 January 1987, p. D4.

74. Kabul Radio, 18 January 1987, in *FBIS/SA*, 21 January 1987, pp. C2-6.

75. Sergei Tarasenko, interview, Princeton, 27 February 1993.

76. Moscow Television, 27 December 1991, in *FBIS/SU*, 31 December 1991, p. 3.

77. *Pravda*, 24 October 1989, pp. 2-4, in *FBIS/SU*, 24 October 1989, p. 50; Mikhail Tsypkin, 'The Soviet Military: *Glasnost*' Against Secrecy', *Problems of Communism*, May-June 1991: 58; *Komsomolskaya Pravda*, 27 May 1992, p. 2, in *FBIS/CE*, 28 May 1992, p. 33; Shevardnadze, *Future*, p. 214.

78. *Literaturnaya Gazeta*, 22 January 1992, p. 11, in *FBIS/SU*, 28 January 1992, p. 20.

79. Moscow Radio, 6 February and 15 May 1987, in *FBIS/SU*, 10 February and 18 May 1987, pp. CC4 and CC3.

80. *Neue Zeit*, 21 October 1992, p. 6; *Die Welt*, 12 October 1992, p. 9.

81. *Literaturnaya Gazeta*, 24 February 1993, p. 2, in *FBIS-R/CE*, 13 March 1993, p. 10; *Trud*, 23 February 1993, p. 1.

82. Safronchuk, remarks, Austin, Texas, 20 October 1989.

83. Moscow Television, 27 December 1991, in *FBIS/SU*, 31 December 1991, p. 4.

84. Ibid.

85. *Pravda*, 9 January 1988, p. 4, in *FBIS/SU*, 12 January 1988, p. 40.

86. Moscow Radio, 9 October 1987, in *FBIS/SU*, 15 October 1987, p. 18.

87. *Krasnaya Zvezda*, 10 December 1987, p. 4; and 22 May 1988, p. 2, in *FBIS/SU*, 24 May 1988, p. 33.
88. Oberdorfer, *Turn*, p. 241.
89. Moscow Radio, 3 July 1989, in *FBIS/SU*, 5 July 1989, p. 49; *Christian Science Monitor*, 12 July 1989, p. 1.
90. Oberdorfer, 'Diplomatic Solution'; Dale R. Herspring, 'On *Perestroyka*: Gorbachev, Yazov, and the Military', *Problems of Communism*, July-August 1987: 99-107; *Stolitsa*, June 1991: 7-10.
91. PAP from Warsaw, 2 September 1987, in *FBIS/SU*, 3 September 1987, p. 6; *Al-Musawwar*, 23 October 1987, pp. 26-9, in *FBIS/SU*, 27 October 1987, p. 31.
92. Harrison, 'Inside', p. 53; Rubin, 'Next Round', pp. 62-3.
93. Riaz Khan, *Untying*, pp. 207-208.
94. Tass from Moscow, 20 July 1987, in *FBIS/SU*, 21 July 1987, pp. E1-2; Oberdorfer, *Turn*, p. 242 (quoting Gorbachev at second- or third-hand).
95. *Pravda*, 23 July 1987, pp. 1-2, in *FBIS/SU*, 23 July 1987, p. CC7; Oberdorfer, *Turn*, p. 243.
96. Moscow Television, 19 August 1987, in *FBIS/SU*, 21 August 1987, pp. CC7-11.
97. *Krasnaya Zvezda*, 5 February 1988, p. 3, in *FBIS/SU*, 11 February 1988, pp. 11-12.
98. *New York Times*, 11 September 1987, p. A3; State Department, 'Afghanistan: Eight Years', pp. 11, 23, Riaz Khan, *Untying*, pp. 218-24.
99. Shultz, *Turmoil and Triumph*, p. 987.
100. *Pravda*, 19 October 1987, p. 5, in *FBIS/SU*, 21 October 1987, pp. 26-9; *FBIS Trends*, 5 November 1987.
101. *Sueddeutsche Zeitung*, 16 November 1987, pp. 1-2, in *FBIS/SU*, 16 November 1987, pp. 22-3.
102. Moscow Radio, 5 November 1987, in *FBIS/SU*, 6 November 1987, p. 28.
103. Oberdorfer, 'Diplomatic Solution'.
104. Kabul Radio, 30 November 1987, in *FBIS/NE*, 2 December 1987, p. 57; Oberdorfer, 'Diplomatic Solution'; *New York Times*, 2 December 1987, p. A8.
105. Bakhtar from Kabul, 2 December 1987, in *FBIS/NE*, 7 December 1987, p. 55.
106. *New York Times*, 4 December 1987, p. A16.
107. *New York Times*, 14 December 1987 and 11 February 1988, pp. A3 and A3.
108. *New York Times*, 11, 15, and 22 December 1987, pp. A22, A8, and A14.

109. *Pravda*, 12 December 1987, pp. 3-4, in *FBIS/SU*, 15 December 1987, p. 21.
110. *Washington Post*, 14 December 1987, p. A17.
111. *Washington Post*, 14 and 22 December 1987, pp. A17 and A19; *Washington Times*, 15 and 16 December 1987, pp. A11 and A1; *Christian Science Monitor*, 21 December 1987, p. 7; *New York Times*, 15 January 1988, p. A3.
112. *New York Times*, 8 January 1988, p. A1; Shultz, *Turmoil and Triumph*, p. 1087.
113. *Washington Post*, 7 February, 1 March, and 13 April 1988, pp. A22, A9, and A30; *Washington Times*, 1 March 1988, p. A10; *New York Times*, 7 April 1988, p. A12.
114. Bakhtar from Kabul, 6 January 1988, in *FBIS/NE*, 7 January 1988, pp. 44-5; Tass from Kabul (in Tass foreign service), 6 January 1988, in *FBIS/SU*, 7 January 1988, pp. 23-5.
115. *Washington Post*, 17 January 1988, p. C2.
116. *New York Times*, 13 January 1988, p. A1.
117. Shahi, *Pakistan's Security*, pp. 104-105; *Washington Post*, 22 February 1988, p. A16.
118. Shultz, *Turmoil and Triumph*, p. 1089.
119. Moscow Radio, 8 February 1988, in *FBIS/SU*, 8 February 1988, pp. 34-6; Kabul Radio, 8 February 1988, in *FBIS/NE*, 9 February 1988, pp. 53-4.
120. Moscow Radio, 8 February 1988, in *FBIS/SU*, 8 February 1988, pp. 34-6.
121. Moscow Television 25 February 1986, in *FBIS/SU Supplement*, 26 February 1986, p. O31.
122. *Pravda*, 8 April 1988, p. 1, in *FBIS/SU*, 11 April 1988, p. 62.
123. Moscow Television, 9 February 1988, in *FBIS/SU*, 9 February 1988, pp. 5 and 1.
124. *Krasnaya Zvezda*, 10 and 23 February 1988, in *FBIS/SU*, 10 and 23 February 1988, pp. 1-3 and 70.
125. *Pravda*, 13 February 1988, p. 1, in *FBIS/SU*, 19 February 1988, p. 59.
126. Radio Liberty Research, RL 252/88, 21 June 1988.
127. Moscow Radio, 10 April 1988, in *FBIS/SU*, 11 April 1988, p. 10.
128. Tass from Islamabad, 11 February 1988, in *FBIS/SU*, 11 February 1988, pp. 24-5; Islamabad Radio, 11 February 1988, in *FBIS/NE*, 12 February 1988, p. 56.
129. *New York Times*, 29 February and 1 April 1988, pp. A2 and A1; Arif, *Working with Zia*, p. 324.
130. *Washington Post*, 16 March 1988, p. A16; Riaz Khan, *Untying*, pp. 264, 267-9.

131. Oberdorfer, 'Diplomatic Solution'; *New York Times*, 25 and 31 March, 8 April 1988, pp. A1, A1, and A11.
132. Tass from Moscow, 29 March 1988.
133. *New York Times*, 18 March 1988, p. A12.
134. Shultz, *Turmoil and Triumph*, p. 1090.
135. Tass from Washington, 24 March 1988.
136. Tass from Geneva, 14 April 1988, in *FBIS/SU*, 15 April 1988, p. 26.
137. *Izvestiya*, 1 April 1988, p. 5, in *FBIS/SU*, 1 April 1988, p. 5.
138. Shultz, *Turmoil and Triumph*, p. 1091; Oberdorfer, *Turn*, p. 280.
139. Ibid., p. 281; Tass from Kabul, 3 and 4 April 1988, in *FBIS/SU*, 4 April 1988, pp. 18-19.
140. Moscow Television, 9 April 1988, in *FBIS/SU*, 11 April 1988, p. 66; Pyadyshev, 'Najibullah', p. 20.
141. *Izvestiya*, 8 April 1988, p. 1, in *FBIS/SU*, 7 April 1988, p. 35.
142. Kabul Radio, 8 April 1991, in *FBIS/NE*, 9 April 1991, p. 66; *Kabul Times*, 17 December 1990, p. 1; Moscow Television, 24 December 1989, in *FBIS/SU*, 28 December 1989, p. 73.
143. *CWIHPB*, Nos. 8-9: 168.
144. Riaz Khan, *Untying*, pp. 277-82; *New York Times*, 23 March 1988, p. A6; Kabul Radio, 17 March 1988, in *FBIS/NE*, 18 March 1988, pp. 10-11; Islamabad Radio, 17 March 1988, in *FBIS/NE*, 17 March 1988, pp. 8-9; *Izvestiya*, 1 April 1988, p. 5, in *FBIS/SU*, 1 April 1988, pp. 4-5.
145. Riaz Khan, *Untying*, pp. 284-5.
146. Texts of the four Geneva accords and the accompanying 'memorandum of understanding', cited here and below, are in a number of sources, including Riaz Khan, *Untying*, pp. 315-31, and Tass from Geneva, 14 April 1988, in *FBIS/SU*, 15 April 1988.
147. State Department, 'Afghanistan: Soviet Occupation and Withdrawal', p. 4.
148. House of Representatives, Foreign Affairs Committee, hearing, Washington, 19 May 1988, pp. 17-19, 24-5.
149. *Washington Post*, 15 April 1988, p. A27.
150. *Pravda*, 15 April 1988, p. 6, in *FBIS/SU*, 15 April 1988, pp. 34-5.
151. *Literaturnaya Gazeta*, 18 April 1990, p. 1, in *FBIS/SU*, 26 April 1990, p. 9; Shevardnadze, *Future*, pp. 68-9.
152. *Pravda*, 15 April 1988, p. 6, in *FBIS/SU*, 15 April 1988, p. 36.
153. Moscow Television, 24 December 1991, in *FBIS/SU*, 27 December 1991, p. 6.
154. Moscow Television, 17 September 1988, in *FBIS/SU*, 20 September 1988, p. 24; Moscow Radio, 17 April 1988, in *FBIS/SU*, 19 April 1988, p. 24.

155. *Krasnaya Zvezda*, 14 August 1988, p. 3, in *FBIS/SU*, 15 August 1988, p. 31.
156. Moscow Television, 27 December 1991, in *FBIS/SU*, 31 December 1991, p. 4.
157. *Afghan Jehad*, April-June 1988: 37-38; *Washington Post*, 17 April 1988, p. A29; Tehran Radio, 14 April 1988, in *FBIS/NE*, 15 April 1988, pp. 55-6.

CHAPTER 10

WITHDRAWAL

The Soviet Army's withdrawal from Afghanistan was completed as scheduled on 15 February 1989, after the last troops out of Kabul struggled across the Hindu Kush in an unusually cold winter. In the final months, Moscow sent a first deputy foreign minister, Yuliy M. Vorontsov, as ambassador to Kabul to seek a political compromise that might preserve some elements of the regime. Compromise eluded him, however, because of the PDPA leadership's refusal to yield any meaningful power and the Peshawar seven's inability to submerge their separate ambitions in cooperation. The withdrawal period ended in uncertainty and continued fighting.

A sense of doom permeated the reporting of Moscow media and the attitude of Soviet academic specialists and others in the final months before the last troops left Afghanistan. Shevardnadze's politburo commission said on 23 January 1989 that '[t]he Afghan comrades...point out that they cannot manage completely without our military assistance'.[1] Nonetheless, the Kremlin publicly pretended that prospects for the Kabul regime were not too bad.[2] Only after the regime had survived a while did Moscow media admit how pessimistic the official Soviet view had been. 'Soviet generals [were] unanimous in insisting that the Kabul regime would fall shortly after the 40th Army withdrawal', a Soviet journal said. *Izvestiya* reported that 'observers in our country and in the West unanimously predicted that the capital would fall within a matter of weeks without Soviet military cover'.[3] Najibullah said later that Afghan 'public opinion in general thought that the state would collapse, inevitably and quickly'.[4] The United States Department of State said at the end of 1988, 'Most experts agree that [the Afghan army] probably can survive no more than a matter of months after a complete Soviet withdrawal'.[5] Western journalists covering the war from Peshawar thought it would be one or two months, eight months at most, and *mujahideen* leaders were optimistic of a quick victory.[6] 'The projections of Pakistan's intelligence services and the CIA about the inability of Dr. Najibullah's government to survive after the Soviet forces had left Afghanistan proved wrong,' Zia's aide wrote later.[7]

MILITARY MOVEMENTS

A reduction of the 'limited contingent' was already underway before the withdrawal officially began on 15 May 1988. Small garrisons pulled out of thirteen provinces, leaving Soviet forces in fourteen provinces. Soviet troops in Afghanistan were announced as numbering 100 300 in 183 'military townships and facilities' as of 15 May.[8] The withdrawal was under overall control of General Varennikov from the Soviet general staff group in Kabul, and direct command of the 40th Army's Lt.-Gen. Gromov, but was plagued by other senior Soviet officers who rushed to Kabul to seek a role. Troops began leaving the eastern area around Jalalabad to the Afghan army a few days before 15 May, the Panjshir Valley was abandoned to Massoud's forces by the end of May, and Badakhshan was evacuated—including the Wakhan corridor that had often been falsely reported to have been annexed by the USSR.[9] Despite trouble in 'sizzling Qandahar', where Soviet troops had to be flown out just before 15 August, the United Nations Good Offices Mission was satisfied that half the 'limited contingent' was gone by then. All women and children of Soviet diplomats and advisers had also left.[10] The *mujahideen* made little effort to hinder the first stage of the withdrawal, but fighting intensified at the approach of 15 November, the date set by the Soviets to begin the final stage. On 4 November, Moscow announced it was suspending the withdrawal 'for the time being' because the resistance was 'whipping up the situation' and Pakistan was committing 'glaring violations' of the Geneva accords with American support, and it said Soviet troops were being given 'more advanced weaponry'.[11] The withdrawal soon resumed.

As the 15 February 1989 deadline neared, Soviet troops were deployed along two corridors. The western one from Shindand through Herat to Kushka in Turkmenistan was evacuated without major problems.[12] The more vital Salang tunnel route from Kabul to the Amu Darya bridge at Termez in Uzbekistan became the focus of Soviet worries. The final stage of withdrawal up these highways began in mid-January amid an upsurge of fighting. Afghan truck convoys with supplies coming from the USSR as well as Soviet troops going there came under *mujahideen* attack. On 21 January the Soviets began flying food into Kabul, where 'children were dying of the cold in bread lines', malnutrition became widespread, and heavy snow sometimes paralysed activity.[13] Yazov made on 27 and 28 January the first visit of a Soviet defence minister to Afghanistan since the invasion in order to reassure Najibullah of continuing military aid. The day after he left, Yuriy D. Maslyukov, the chairman of the Soviet state planning commission, arrived in Kabul to promise continued economic aid.[14] But a statement by Gromov, 'We will not leave our southern neighbour in the lurch', that appeared in the first edition of *Pravda* on 2 February was deleted from the second edition.[15]

Soviet commanders, who presumably knew of the British army that was annihilated by Afghan guerrillas while withdrawing from Kabul through mountains in the hard winter of 1842, considered the crossing of the Hindu Kush via the Salang tunnel their most critical problem. Road conditions had been deteriorating for months as avalanches and rockfalls added to ambush casualties. In the worst winter for a decade or more, snow depths at the northern end of the 11 100-foot-high tunnel reached ten feet.[16] After Afghan soldiers abandoned their posts of guarding the road by October, the Soviets tried to get Massoud to leave it alone in return for a promise that the Kabul regime would supply him 'with everything necessary'. He rejected the bribe. Massoud said later, however, that he had told the Soviets his forces 'would not put forth any obstacles' to the withdrawal'.[17]

Whatever was said, the 40th Army unleashed one final campaign of terror in an effort to prevent attacks on its last troops on the road, with Gorbachev's personal authorization.[18] Heavy bombing and artillery attacks devastated dozens of villages close to the road that were feared to harbour *mujahideen*. At least 377 and perhaps 700 villagers, few if any of them guerrillas, were killed. In one case, women, children, and old men who were fleeing to the road from artillery attacks on their village near it, were gunned down by a Soviet colonel.[19] 'It was dreadful,' Massoud said.[20] Either because or in spite of this policy—Massoud said the villagers were killed after Soviet generals had told his local commander 'they would not fire upon *mujahideen*'—some withdrawing Soviet convoys were attacked. Gromov said that, 'although we expected it to be difficult in Salang, we did not expect it to be that difficult'.[21]

Kremlin Arguments

As the time approached for the last Soviet troops to leave Kabul, the Kremlin argument over withdrawal was rekindled, pitting reformers against the military and KGB. 'There was indeed some tough talking, disagreement' at a politburo meeting in early February, Yakovlev said. 'Each side tried...to force the other to accept responsibility' for abandoning Najibullah's regime to its expected collapse and 'a bloodbath'. But Gorbachev decided the troops must leave.[22] After Najibullah made a speech vowing to fight on, and PDPA members were armed to defend themselves, the last 40th Army convoy rolled out of Kabul on 6 February.[23] In the Hindu Kush, guerrillas stood by the road mocking them, but neither side fired. On 15 February, Gromov walked across the Amu Darya bridge behind an armoured column, with 'a sense of bitterness...[and] tears in my eyes'. To the waiting television cameras, he declared, dry-eyed and incorrectly, 'There is not a single Soviet soldier or officer left behind me. Our nine-year stay ends with this'.[24] At CIA headquarters outside Washington, those who had funnelled weapons to the *mujahideen* had a party, while State Department officials who had worked on the Afghan problem partied in nearby Georgetown.[25]

About 200 persons remained in the fortified Soviet embassy compound in Kabul, including some thirty military advisers.[26] Many embassies in Kabul had evacuated dependents and cut staffs in the summer of 1988 as the *mujahideen* intensified rocket attacks on the capital. Najibullah said that between 15 May and 5 November, when the attacks virtually ended, more than 750 civilians had been killed in Kabul city and province by rocket attacks, car bombs, and other guerrilla actions.[27] In mid-January 1989, West Germany and Britain ordered their diplomats to leave because of food shortages as well as mounting violence. The American embassy was ordered closed on 25 January, although the *charge d'affaires*, Jon D. Glassman, disagreed with the conventional wisdom that the regime would fall quickly, chaotically. Several other countries, including Italy and France, also pulled their personnel out.[28]

As the withdrawal went on, Moscow media began preparing the Soviet public for the regime's collapse. Soviet reports from Kabul described 'alarming factors' in the Afghan defence picture, such as 'poor conscription into the army and the growing number of deserters'.[29] The editor of Afghanistan's defence newspaper was quoted as saying 'attitudes of dependence were developing in the army, a desire to sit it out under [Soviet] protection'.[30] A Soviet commentator said many Afghan officers, long accustomed to taking orders from and generally depending upon the Soviets, 'started learning to fight too late'.[31]

The Afghan army redeployed its limited manpower to defend important towns and communications lines that had been protected by the Soviet Army. The resistance cause was significantly damaged by the way some *mujahideen* groups took advantage of the changing situation. For example, after Soviet troops left a provincial capital, Konduz, on 9 August 1988, some 1200 *mujahideen* from several groups, including Massoud's, overwhelmed the surprised Afghan army garrison and looted, raped, and burned. One commander reportedly ordered the summary execution of 650 officials in Konduz, apparently blaming them for hospitality to the Soviet occupiers; and Afghan militia were mutilated and girls kidnapped.[32] At the Afghan garrison at Torkham, where the Peshawar-Kabul road descends from the Khyber Pass to enter Afghanistan, 141 soldiers surrendered in November 1988 to Pakistani border authorities. The Pakistanis turned them over to *mujahideen* under Khales, who executed 74 of them, packed their bodies into tea crates, and dumped them inside Afghanistan.[33] Such brutality sent an electrifying message to Afghan soldiers and civilians who might have been reluctant to stick with the regime but seemed to be left with no alternative, thus ensuring a longer, harder war ahead.

More Soviet Weapons

To such psychological stimuli to keep fighting, the Soviets added 'extra consignments of more powerful weapons' for the Afghan armed forces.[34] Moscow said the rocketing of Kabul necessitated its beginning to supply Scud-Bs, surface-to-surface missiles with a range of about 175 miles that were being retired from Soviet arsenals. More than 2000 Scuds were reported to have been launched by Soviet crews up to the end of 1991. Not very accurate, however, they had almost no effect on the war.[35] Nor was the Soviet supply of 30 MiG-27 fighter-bombers, an improvement over warplanes previously provided to the Afghan air force, very effective.[36] Both types of weapons were significant mainly as a political statement of Soviet support.

POLITICS IN KABUL

The Soviet withdrawal and PDPA policies associated with it exacerbated old strains within the PDPA. The CPSU politburo commission observed on 23 January 1989 that 'there is still no real unity within the PDPA...'.[37] Khalqis, led by Interior Minister Gulabzoy, and dissident Parchami supporters of the exiled Karmal, opposed the weakening of party control implied—but not implemented—by national reconciliation. They also accused Najibullah of selling out the revolutionary cause by agreeing to the Soviet withdrawal without achieving the original Geneva goal of halting aid to the resistance.[38] The removal of Keshtmand from the prime minister's job in late May 1988 and the replacement of Rafi with Tanai as defence minister, related in Chapter 5, added to PDPA turmoil. In June the party expelled Abdul Qadir, who had become disillusioned after helping put the PDPA in power.[39] A Soviet report said 'clashes [between PDPA factions], sometimes more embittered than the clashes with the common enemy,...[are] undermin[ing] the country's defence capabilities...'.[40]

On 19 October, Najibullah confirmed to the PDPA central committee rumours that there had been a *coup* attempt, reportedly on 8 October. He said actions of 'factionalists—in particular, those opposing the national reconciliation policy—...have been transformed into open anti-state activities and provocations with the armed

forces...to seize power...'.[41] At least seventeen PDPA and
regime officials had been arrested—according to some
reports the number of persons apprehended was 165 or
even 300 persons. They included Karmal's half-brother,
Mahmud Barialay, and Karmal's old friend, Anahita
Ratebzad.[42] The committee removed two men from the
politburo and secretariat. One was the adaptable Khalqi,
Saleh Mohammed Ziray. The only person to serve in the
politburo continuously since the PDPA came to power, Ziray
had become outspokenly critical of Najibullah's policies.
Western diplomats heard that the committee meeting 'broke
up in chaos as some members rejected concessions to the
mujahideen'.[43]

Other changes followed. Gulabzoy, the Khalqi leader and
interior minister, reportedly had made one or several trips to
Moscow in the late summer or early autumn of 1988 to try
to talk Soviet leaders into deposing Najibullah, who he
argued could not prevent a collapse at the end of the Soviet
withdrawal, and putting himself in power.[44] But Moscow
stuck with Najibullah. A few weeks after the alleged *coup*
attempt, Gulabzoy was banished to Moscow as the Afghan
ambassador.[45] This decapitated the most difficult regime
element trying to obstruct a political compromise with the
mujahideen during the Soviet departure. Soviet and PDPA
sources said Gulabzoy's move was arranged by Vorontsov,
who had been abruptly posted as Soviet ambassador to Kabul
in October. This senior diplomat was charged with seeking
some political compromise that could stabilize the military
withdrawal period.[46] Watanjar succeeded Gulabzoy as interior
minister, taking the job for the third time. Watanjar was
generally considered a Khalqi but was not militantly factional
because his primary loyalty ran directly to Moscow. After
Taraki, Amin, Sarwari, and Gulabzoy, the Khalqi faction was
left without clear leadership, and a less dominant factional
authority passed to the new defence minister, Tanai.[47]
Despite the changes, tensions continued in Kabul.

The regime was unable to broaden its political base during the withdrawal. 'The people have no more confidence in the People's Democratic Party of Afghanistan than they have in the opposition,' Sharq, the ostensibly non-Communist prime minister, said in October.[48] A deputy premier conceded in November that the 'proportion of Afghans [who] have retained their faith in the PDPA...[p]erhaps...do not constitute the majority of the population, arithmetically speaking'.[49] Sharq's government never lived up to its billing as a broad coalition. 'Feeble, to say the least, are the actions of...Sharq and many ministers in his cabinet,' the CPSU politburo commission observed.[50] The fault was primarily Najibullah's. He made it clear that Sharq and his cabinet had no real power. 'The power of the presidency is the axis of our government system,' he declared, with parties needed to rally popular support.[51] As soon as the last Soviet troops were gone, Najibullah abandoned the symbolism of broader, more conciliatory government. He ousted Sharq.

MUJAHIDEEN ANARCHY

The trouble in Kabul was matched by the anarchic condition of the *mujahideen*. The expectation of victory after Gorbachev's 8 February 1988 statement seemed to sharpen differences among the seven Peshawar groups. Mojaddedi charged that Hekmatyar tried to have him assassinated on several occasions, and they reportedly drew pistols in one meeting of the seven.[52] As mentioned in Chapter 6, Sayed B. Majrooh was gunned down on 11 February. A Western scholar found 'a reign of terror against "insufficiently Islamic" intellectuals in Peshawar' by Hekmatyar and his fellow Islamist Yunis Khales.[53] Hekmatyar's followers inside Afghanistan were accused of attacking other resistance bands and stealing their supplies. In December 1988 his men looted a United Nations truck convoy taking relief supplies to Massoud. Rather than denying such attacks, Hekmatyar alleged that many of the commanders attacked had been financed by the CIA or the KGB.[54] His hatred for both intelligence services—while trying to obscure his dependence on weapons from the CIA pipeline—seemed matched only by his jealousy of Massoud.

President Zia worried in early 1988 that a continued PDPA regime would mean refugees stayed in Pakistan, so Islamabad exerted pressure on the *mujahideen* alliance to come up with an alternative government. After weeks of argument, the alliance announced, on 23 February 1988, plans for a government headed by a council of the seven party leaders that, it unrealistically suggested, should replace the Kabul regime in time to sign the Geneva accords itself. It was supposed to hand over power to a government elected within six months after the Soviets had left.[55] Aside from the fact that the seven leaders never yielded any of their small authority to this shadow government, it was not widely accepted and had faded away before the Soviet withdrawal was over.

Despite the Shi'ite rejection of the Pushtun- and Sunni-oriented Peshawar political process, Rabbani as the head of the alliance in late 1988 was able to patch up relations with Iranian interests.[56] Iran's policy had changed by then. In regional relations, Islamic ideology had been replaced by power politics. The end of Iran's war with Iraq, the failure to export the ayatollahs' revolution, and competition with the Saudis who were backing Islamabad and Peshawar, as well as Iran's internal power shifts, caused Tehran to broaden Afghan policy beyond the Shi'ite minority in the Hazarajat. Rather than being left out, it dropped in the autumn of 1988 its severe criticism of the Geneva accords and began supporting Pakistan's role in negotiations. Under government pressure, the eight resistance groups fostered by Iran united in December 1988 into an Islamic Coalition Council of Afghanistan, the better to voice Shi'ite views against Sunnis in Peshawar.[57]

SETTLEMENT EFFORTS

In his continuing United Nations role after the Geneva signing, Diego Cordovez offered a plan to resolve the Afghanistan conflict before the Soviet withdrawal ended. He had suggested in 1987 'broadly based transitional arrangements' that would bring together the PDPA, the Peshawar seven, and 'selected personalities' from among Afghan exiles, but the *mujahideen* continued to refuse to have anything to do with the PDPA.[58] Cordovez kept working on variations of this, including having a transitional government of members who would be barred from serving in a permanent government that they would establish within six months by some agreed method, which Cordovez suggested be a *loya jirgah*.[59] Although the plan died because Pakistan, the *mujahideen*, and the United States all thought they could do better than the implied compromise with the PDPA, a version of it was used in 1992 to ease the PDPA out of power.

Najibullah made fruitless proposals for talks 'with the opposition' or an international conference on Afghanistan.[60] Gorbachev proposed to the United Nations General Assembly on 7 December 1988 a ceasefire and 'a halt to arms deliveries to all belligerent parties' beginning 1 January, the dispatch of United Nations' peace-keeping forces to Afghanistan, and speedy implementation of Najibullah's call for an international conference on Afghan neutrality and demilitarization.[61] The halt of arms deliveries meant Soviet acceptance of 'negative symmetry' after rejecting United States' efforts to obtain it before the Geneva signing. Moscow had now become more desperate to find a last-minute solution. But the United States was no longer interested, and Shevardnadze commented a week later that Soviet diplomacy did not adequately follow through on Gorbachev's proposal. Anyway, Rabbani flatly rejected the proposal on behalf of the Peshawar alliance.[62]

VORONTSOV'S DIPLOMACY

Vorontsov was unexpectedly named Soviet ambassador to Afghanistan on 13 October 1988. A foreign ministry spokesman, recalling Gorbachev's 'bleeding wound' statement two and a half years earlier, explained that 'a highly skilled healer' was needed.[63] The description fit Vorontsov, the Kremlin's chief diplomatic troubleshooter and a member of the CPSU central committee. The unusual urgency of the assignment, as well as its intended limited duration, was emphasized by Vorontsov's retaining his first deputy foreign minister status while in Kabul. His job was to ease the last Soviet troops out with the least possible political trauma, to broker some sort of deal intended to avoid a bloody and embarrassing collapse of the client regime.

The USSR had refused to deal directly with Peshawar leaders, who insisted that bilateral talks were the only way to reach a settlement. Moscow feared such talks would imply the resistance's legitimacy, thus damaging the standing of the Kabul regime. But, as Moscow grew more desperate, Soviet diplomats quietly began in September 1988 trying to negotiate with the *mujahideen*. After initial rebuffs, Soviet diplomats in Islamabad met at the Pakistani foreign ministry on 27 November with representatives of Rabbani, the current head of the Peshawar alliance, and Hekmatyar. The only subject discussed was Soviet soldiers held by the *mujahideen*. Rabbani's and Hekmatyar's groups held the largest numbers.[64] Prisoner exchanges had already occurred locally, and representatives of Hekmatyar had been holding unpublicized talks on prisoners with the Soviets in Europe for at least three years, but the Islamabad talks were unproductive. The Soviets said the *mujahideen* wanted to hold general political talks rather than just deal with prisoner questions.[65]

Soviet-*Mujahideen* Meetings

More significantly, Vorontsov met resistance leaders. As well as legitimizing those whom Moscow had long labelled as bandits, this began an effort to reposition Soviet diplomacy from supporting a combined Moscow-Kabul attitude toward the war to a neutral stance of 'honest mediation'.[66] With no other option, Najibullah accepted this weakening of Soviet support with a public show of good grace, describing Vorontsov as a mediator and claiming that his search for a compromise had been suggested by Afghanistan and was part of a joint plan.[67] Vorontsov's unprecedented meeting was held in Taif, Saudi Arabia, from 3 to 5 December, with a delegation from Peshawar headed by Rabbani, the alliance chairman. The Soviet purpose, a spokesman said, was to 'organiz[e] inter-Afghan dialogue' that might achieve an internal settlement 'as soon as possible'. While both sides talked about the need for a 'broad-based government', Vorontsov insisted that the PDPA should have a place in it, but Rabbani rejected this. Massoud rebuffed Vorontsov's efforts to meet him separately.[68]

Before Vorontsov's second meeting with *mujahideen* leaders, in Islamabad on 6 January 1989, Soviet diplomacy searched frantically for a break in the political deadlock. The efforts included Gorbachev's United Nations proposals two days after the Taif talks and Vorontsov's talks with the American ambassador in Moscow, Zahir Shah in Rome, Foreign Minister Ali Akbar Velayati and representatives of the Iranian-backed guerrillas in Tehran, and Pakistani officials in Islamabad. The Iranian-based *mujahideen*, who had not been represented in Taif, joined the Islamabad talks. Mojaddedi, now taking a turn heading the alliance, said Vorontsov insisted on the Kabul regime's participation in a transitional government, so 'there was no reason for the negotiations to continue...'.[69]

Shevardnadze's Role

As the end of Soviet protection for Kabul drew closer, Shevardnadze reinforced Vorontsov. Visiting Kabul on 14 and 15 January, the foreign minister emphasized that he had come 'to provid[e] the services of a mediator' who sought to get Afghans 'to conduct direct dialogue at the negotiating table', but he also promised continued Soviet military supplies if the war went on.[70] On 5 and 6 February, Shevardnadze became the first Soviet foreign minister ever to visit Pakistan. Talking to Pakistani officials, without meeting *mujahideen* representatives, he insisted that the USSR could not let down the Kabul regime by allowing the withdrawal to 'be the doorway to civil war'. But the visit failed to find a face-saving way for Moscow to end the fighting and preserve some role for the PDPA.[71]

ZIA'S DEATH

Shevardnadze met in Islamabad with the successors to President Ziaul Haq. Zia and 29 others were killed when a Pakistani air force C-130 transport plane crashed on 17 August 1988, probably because of 'a criminal act or sabotage', according to an official report.[72] The others included Gen. Akhtar Abdul Rahman, who as head of the Interservices Intelligence Directorate had directed the build up of aid to the *mujahideen*. The deaths of Zia and Akhtar stimulated reports that the Soviet KGB or its Afghan protégé WAD had carried out a revenge plot, and some suspicion also fell on India and on Zia's domestic enemies, but responsibility for the crash was never fixed.[73]

Pakistan's policy did not change. Shortly before his death, Zia had told an interviewer that Pakistan 'will help the Afghan resistance in every way we can', and, after 'a big fight', the *mujahideen* will capture Kabul within a matter of weeks, or 'at the most a few months', of the Soviet departure. Then Pakistan would install its favourites in power. Zia reportedly added, 'We have earned the right to have a very friendly regime there. We took risks as a front-line state, and we won't permit it to be like it was before, with Indian and Soviet influence there and claims on our territory. It will be a real Islamic state, part of a pan-Islamic revival that will one day win over the Muslims in the Soviet Union'.[74]

After Zia's death this goal continued to be pursued by the Pakistani army and ISI, which dominated Afghan policy, with encouragement and support from Hussain Ahmad's Jamaat party. It became a key element in three more years of Afghan civil war.

NOTES

1. *CWIHPB*, Nos. 8-9: 181.
2. *FBIS Trends*, 3 August and 16 November 1988, pp. 6-10 and 7-8.
3. *New Times*, 27 November 1990, pp. 28-31; *Izvestiya*, 16 September 1991, p. 5, in *FBIS/SU*, 17 September 1991, p. 13.
4. Kabul Radio, 27 June 1990, in *FBIS/NE*, 3 July 1990, p. 47.
5. State Department: 'Afghanistan: Soviet Occupation and Withdrawal', p. 7. For agreement by such specialists as Olivier Roy, Thomas E. Gouttierre, and Zalmay Khalilzad, see *Washington Post*, 3 March 1988, p. A32, and *New York Times*, 19 June 1988, p. 4. This author said in lectures that he expected the Kabul regime to collapse very quickly; *e. g.*, at Air University, Montgomery, Ala., 12 January 1989.
6. *New York Times*, 24 January 1989, p. A8; *Christian Science Monitor*, 4 April 1988, p. 11.
7. Arif, *Working with Zia*, p. 328.
8. *Pravda*, 15 May 1988, p. 1, in *FBIS/SU*, 17 May 1988, p. 32; Tass from Moscow, 26 May 1988, in *FBIS/SU*, 26 May 1988, p. 27. Throughout the PDPA period, the number of provinces fluctuated with political reorganizations.
9. AFP from Islamabad, 12 and 30 May 1988, in *FBIS/NE*, 12 and 31 May 1988, pp. 32 and 44; Tass from Kabul, 22 May 1988, in *FBIS/SU*, 23 May 1988, p. 41.
10. State Department press statement, 17 August 1988; Moscow Television, 14 August 1988, in *FBIS/SU*, 15 August 1988, p. 31.

11. Tass from Moscow, 4 November 1988, in *FBIS/SU*, 4 November 1988, pp. 17-18.
12. Tass from Termez, 15 February 1989, in *FBIS/SU*, 16 February 1989, pp. 24-5.
13. *Izvestiya*, 24 January and 7 February 1989, pp. 4 and 1, in *FBIS/SU*, 27 January and 7 February 1989, pp. 29-30 and 38; AP from Kabul, 25 January 1989.
14. Tass from Kabul, 28 and 29 January 1989, in *FBIS/SU*, 30 January 1989, p. 34.
15. *Pravda*, 2 February 1989, p. 5, in *FBIS/SU*, 2 February 1989, p. 34.
16. Moscow Television, 5 November 1988, and *Krasnaya Zvezda*, 14 January 1989, p. 5, in *FBIS/SU*, 7 November 1988 and 19 January 1989, pp. 27 and 28.
17. Moscow Television, 9 October 1988, in *FBIS/SU*, 12 October 1988, p. 22; Tass from Kabul, 11 October 1988, in *FBIS/SU*, 12 October 1988, p. 20; Richard Mackenzie, 'Amid Bombs and Rockets, the Gestation of a Government', *Insight*, 20 February 1989, p. 28; Moscow Television, 5 October 1997.
18. Moscow Television, 28 January 1992, in *FBIS/CE*, 5 February 1992, p. 16.
19. *New York Times*, 21 January and 6 May 1989, pp. 3 and 1; *Washington Post*, 31 January and 1 February 1989, pp. A23 and A1; 'Mike Winchester' [Anthony Davis], 'Guerrilla Gauntlet', *Soldier of Fortune*, March 1990, p. 56; *Trud*, 22 January 1992, p. 1, in *FBIS-R/CE*, 5 March 1992, p. 104; Borovik, *Hidden War*, p. 258.
20. Moscow Television, 5 October 1997.
21. *Trud*, 22 January 1992, p. 1, in *FBIS-R/CE*, 5 March 1992, p. 104; *Washington Post*, 10 February 1989, p. A35; *Pravda*, 6 February 1989, p. 1, in *FBIS/SU*, 6 February 1989, p. 38.
22. Moscow Television, 27 December 1991, in *FBIS/SU*, 31 December 1991, p. 5.
23. AP from Kabul, 6 February 1989; *New York Times*, 8 February 1989, p. A6.
24. *New York Times*, 16 February 1989, p. A1; Moscow Television, 3 March 1989, in *FBIS/SU*, 6 March 1989, p. 105. Some KGB border guards left later on 15 February than Gromov; *Komsomolskaya Pravda*, 11 October 1990, p. 3, in *FBIS/SU*, 18 October 1990, p. 60.
25. *Washington Times*, 2 May 1989, p. A3; *New York Times*, 1 March 1989, p. A22.
26. Moscow Television, 19 February 1989, in *FBIS/SU*, 22 February 1989, p. 26.

27. Kabul Radio, 26 November 1988, in *FBIS/NE*, 29 November 1988, p. 53; AFP from Kabul, 13 May 1988, in *FBIS/NE*, 13 May 1988, p. 31.
28. *New York Times*, 22 and 27 January 1989, pp. 3 and A1; Moscow Radio, 27 January and 11 February 1989, in *FBIS/SU*, 30 January and 13 February 1989, pp. 34 and 29.
29. Moscow Radio, 30 November 1988, in *FBIS/SU*, 6 December 1988, p. 28.
30. *Sotsialisticheskaya Industriya*, 23 June 1988, p. 3, in *FBIS/SU*, 28 June 1988, p. 31.
31. Moscow Radio, 11 September 1988, in *FBIS/SU*, 12 September 1988, p. 12.
32. AFP from Termez, 12 August 1988, in *FBIS/SU*, 12 August 1988, p. 24; *Economist*, 20 August 1988, p. 28.
33. Asia Watch, 'Afghanistan: The Forgotten War', February 1991, p. 34.
34. Tass from Moscow, 4 November 1988, in *FBIS/SU*, 4 November 1988, pp. 17-18; *CWIHPB*, Nos. 8-9: 184.
35. Tass from Kabul, 1 November 1988, in *FBIS/SU*, 2 November 1988, p. 24; AFP from Kabul, 20 November 1991, in *FBIS/NE*, 21 November 1991, p. 44; *Jane's Intelligence Review*, February 1992: 51-58.
36. State Department, 'Afghanistan: Soviet Occupation', p. 6; *Jane's Defence Weekly*, 27 May 88, p. 999.
37. *CWIHPB*, Nos. 8-9: 182.
38. State Department, 'Afghanistan: Soviet Occupation', p. 9.
39. Kabul Radio, 22 June 1988, in *FBIS/NE*, 23 June 1988, pp. 31-2. Qadir was named ambassador to Poland, but he defected to seek refuge in Bulgaria; *Central Asia and Caucasus Chronicle*, March 1989: 13.
40. *Sotsialisticheskaya Industriya*, 23 June 1988, p. 3, in *FBIS/SU*, 28 June 1988, p. 31.
41. Kabul Radio, 23 October 1988, in *FBIS/NE*, 24 October 1988, p. 55.
42. Bakhtar from Kabul, 5 November 1988, in *FBIS/NE*, 7 November 1988, p. 49; AFP from Islamabad, 25 October 1988, in *FBIS/NE*, 26 October 1988, p. 39.
43. AFP from Islamabad, 25 October 1988, in *FBIS/NE*, 26 October 1988, p. 39; transcript, news conference by Jon D. Glassman, New Delhi, 1 February 1989.
44. *New York Times*, 19 October 1988, p. A3; Mackenzie, 'Brutal Force', p. 16.
45. Ibid.; *Izvestiya*, 13 November 1988, p. 4, in *FBIS/SU*, 14 November 1988, p. 35.
46. *Christian Science Monitor*, 6 December 1988, p. 1.

47. *Danas*, 20 December 1988, pp. 55-7, in *FBIS/NE*, 4 January 1989, pp. 41-2.

48. AFP from Kabul, 12 October 1988, in *FBIS/NE*, 13 October 1988, p. 53.

49. Muhammad Sarwar Mangal, *Izvestiya*, 11 November 1988, p. 5, in *FBIS/SU*, 16 November 1988, p. 26.

50. *CWIHPB*, Nos. 8-9: 182.

51. Kabul Radio, 1 September 1988, in *FBIS/NE*, 6 September 1988, p. 51.

52. Richard Mackenzie, 'When Policy Tolls in Fool's Paradise', *Insight*, 11 September 1989, p. 10.

53. Barnett R. Rubin, testimony, US House of Representatives, Foreign Affairs Committee, 7 March 1990, p. 33.

54. *New York Times*, 12 January and 1 December 1988, pp. A1 and A1.

55. *Afghan Jehad*, January-March 1988 and April-June 1988, pp. 26-7 and 22-7.

56. Tehran Radio, 28 December 1988, in *FBIS/NE*, 29 December 1988, p. 50.

57. IRNA from Tehran, 23 December 1988, in *FBIS/NE*, 29 December 1988, p. 50; Lorentz, 'Anatomy', p. 52; IISS, 'Strategic Survey 1988-1989' (London, 1989): 146.

58. Harrison, 'Paths', pp. 14-15.

59. Islamabad Radio, 9 July 1988, in *FBIS/NE*, 11 July 1988, p. 59.

60. Kabul Radio, 22 and 29 October 1988, in *FBIS/NE*, 24 and 31 October 1988, pp. 57 and 58.

61. *Pravda*, 8 December 1988, pp. 1-2, in *FBIS/SU*, 8 December 1988, pp. 15-16.

62. *Vestnik Ministerstva Inostrannykh del SSSR*, 15 December 1988, pp. Annex ii-viii; *'Ukaz*, 10 December 1988, p. 5, in *FBIS/NE*, 15 December 1988, p. 46.

63. Tass from Moscow, 13 October 1988, in *FBIS/SU*, 13 October 1988, pp. 16. Nikolay G. Yegorychev had been the Soviet ambassador in Kabul for seven months; Kabul Radio, 14 October 1988, in *FBIS/NE*, 17 October 1988, p. 40.

64. *Christian Science Monitor*, 29 November 1988, p. 7; *Izvestiya*, 8 December 1988, p. 5, in *FBIS/SU*, 9 December 1988, pp. 24-5.

65. State Department, 'Afghanistan: Soviet Occupation', p. 11; *Christian Science Monitor*, 29 November 1988, p. 7; *La Stampa*, 9 February 1988, pp. 1-2; *Izvestiya*, 8 December 1988, p. 5, in *FBIS/SU*, 9 December 1988, pp. 24-5.

66. Moscow Radio, 20 January 1989, in *FBIS/SU*, 25 January 1989, pp. 10.

67. Bakhtar from Kabul, 8 December 1988, in *FBIS/NE*, 12 December 1988, p. 54; Kabul Radio, 3 December 1988 and 25 February 1989,

in *FBIS/NE*, 5 December 1988 and 27 December 1989, pp. 52 and 37.

68. Moscow Radio, 5 December 1988, in *FBIS/SU*, 6 December 1988, p. 26; *FBIS Trends*, 7 December 1988, p. 7; *Washington Post*, 19 December 1988, p. A21; *Al-Siyasah*, 28 December 1988, p. 17, in *FBIS/NE*, 4 January 1989, p. 46; *Trud*, 22 January 1992, p. 1, in *FBIS-R/CE*, 5 March 1992, p. 105.

69. AFP from Islamabad, 9 and 19 January 1989, in *FBIS/NE*, 9 and 23 January 1989, pp. 71 and 56-7; *'Ukaz*, 14 January 1989, p. 5, in *FBIS/NE*, 25 January 1989, p. 54; *Washington Post*, 10 January 1989, p. A18; Moscow Radio, 10 January 1989, in *FBIS/SU*, 11 January 1989, p. 16.

70. Kabul Radio, 14 and 16 January 1989, in *FBIS/NE*, 17 and 18 January 1989, pp. 54-6.

71. *Pravda*, 7 February 1989, p. 4, in *FBIS/SU*, 7 February 1989, p. 27; *New York Times*, 7 February 1989, p. A11; *Muslim*, 7 February 1989, p. 1.

72. *New York Times*, 19 October 1988, p. A11.

73. *Washington Post*, 28 August 1988, p. B1; *Wall Street Journal*, 4 November 1988, p. A14.

74. *Washington Post*, 29 January 1989, p. D1.

CHAPTER 11

LAST YEARS OF AFGHAN COMMUNISM

For three years after the Soviet Army's departure, Afghan Communism clung to a dwindling space in a situation that had been transformed by the Soviet presence. What was in December 1979 an ill-focused struggle between the Kabul regime and disparate opponents had by February 1989 become more viciously chaotic. The theme of Communism versus Islam had weakened; the theme of strong central government versus local autonomy had strengthened. From February 1989 until the regime collapsed in April 1992, regional and ethnic differences became more important. Parochial authority grew more assertive, national leadership more conspicuously absent. Hatred of outside interference shifted its focus from brutal Soviet intervention to devious Pakistani manipulation of *mujahideen* politics.

As the PDPA regime professed to transform itself into a non-Communist, pragmatic government, its opponents' *jihad* turned into a power struggle over an anticipated succession to Kabul officials who stubbornly refused to relinquish their dictatorial rule. A united resistance with a clear message might have made short work of the regime, but there was neither unity nor clarity. The fight for political control of Afghanistan was prolonged by questions of the future kind of government and the form of the state, the role of religion in government, the place of intensified ethnic awareness, and the influence of external forces.

Those external forces fuelled a high level of continuing struggle. Although public attention to Afghanistan faded in the USSR,[1] Gorbachev's government—particularly elements of the KGB and military—remained concerned enough about not abandoning a client to provide sufficient military and economic aid to sustain Kabul. Not until KGB and military leaders failed in an attempt to overthrow Gorbachev in August 1991 and consequently lost their power, did Soviet policy adapt to the fact that aid in the needed amounts was neither affordable nor rewarding. Pakistan, Iran, and Saudi Arabia remained involved, but the United States started to lose interest as the failing USSR began to abandon their broader confrontation.

INTERIM *MUJAHIDEEN* GOVERNMENT

In the last days of the Soviet withdrawal, efforts intensified to replace the February 1988 governmental arrangement of Peshawar groups with some more viable interim government that could take over from the expected PDPA collapse and hold elections within six months. However, the efforts began in prejudice, were carried through in secrecy and corruption, produced divisive bitterness, and ended in worse than futility by making a peace settlement more difficult. Pakistani and Saudi sponsors of the efforts ensured that the result was not representative of the resistance's diversity or the Afghan nation's complexity. Instead, the result further divorced *mujahideen* politics from Afghan realities, detracting from a solution to the country's tensions.

After torturous preliminary negotiations, a *shura* (council) convened in Rawalpindi, adjacent to Islamabad, on 10 February 1989—four days after the last Soviet troops had left Kabul. Following several breakdowns, much anger, and considerable backstage manipulation, the *shura*'s outcome on 24 February was widely believed by Afghans to have been dictated by Pakistan, with Saudi help in bribing delegates. Spoils of the anticipated victory were to be shared among the same old Peshawar seven in a way that emphasized Pushtun nationalism, Ghilzay Pushtun dominance, and Islamist determination, to the virtual exclusion of ethnic minorities, Shi'ites, royalists, and commanders actually fighting the war. A contrived election named as president of the interim government Sibghatullah Mojaddedi, a moderate leader whose perceived honesty and unthreatening weakness made him acceptable to others. Other leaders were assigned fictional jobs according to the number of votes that ISI engineered for them, rather than the importance of their groups.[2] Shi'ite alliance leaders rejected the small role left to them, neither refugees nor expatriates were represented, and commanders inside Afghanistan expressed displeasure with the results.[3] Lacking control of any significant Afghan town, claimant government leaders continued to live in Peshawar. Their ministries existed only on paper to justify foreign-subsidized jobs for their followers.

Sparse Diplomatic Acceptance

The Islamic Conference Organization awarded the interim government Afghanistan's membership, which had been kept vacant since the Soviet invasion. Bahrain, Malaysia, Saudi Arabia, and Sudan extended diplomatic recognition.[4] Pakistan did not, apparently to avoid the precedent of recognizing an ostensibly foreign government operating from its own soil and to keep its foreign ministry from having in effect to negotiate with its intelligence service, ISI, the guiding hand behind the pretender regime. Most nations took the position enunciated by the United States: diplomatic relations could be opened only when the new government had shown that it met such criteria as 'control over territory, a functioning civil administration, broad popular support, and ability to honour international obligations'.[5]

The interim government, which never acquired these attributes, had a turbulent but inconsequential life. Repeatedly announced dates by which it intended to hold elections in Afghanistan passed without any action. Various leaders angrily left the government—for a time, Hekmatyar's Hezb set itself up as a rival to it—and quietly returned. After Pakistan virtually ordered the *mujahideen* to cooperate, the feckless cabinet was replaced on 3 December 1991 with a leadership council that included Iranian-backed *mujahideen*.[6] Tehran controlled, or at least heavily influenced, the Shi'ite alliance of what grew to nine groups and was collectively called the *Wahdat-e Islami-ye Afghanistan* (Afghanistan Islamic Unity Party), or Wahdat.[7] After lengthy and difficult negotiations, agreement on cooperation between *mujahideen* based in Peshawar and Wahdat—operating from Bamyan—was reached in Islamabad on 29 July 1991, with the participation of Pakistani and Iranian officials. The new umbrella raised later by the leadership council was not broad enough, however, to cover Zahir Shah, despite his quiet efforts to help find a way to unite all Afghan factions.[8]

Mujahideen Infighting

As the expected fall of Kabul failed to materialize, Peshawar politics became more violent and bitter, and hostility toward outsiders sharpened. Hekmatyar in particular was accused of ruthless determination to use on fellow *mujahideen* whatever savagery he chose toward his goal of dominating a future Afghanistan, while his ISI sponsors looked the other way if not being actually complicitous. In a long, bloody record of clashes, torture, and assassinations, one incident stood out. It was the killing of 36 of Massoud's best commanders and officers by Hekmatyar's Hezb forces in Takhar province. Five were killed in ambush on 9 July 1989 and the rest captured and executed the next day, reportedly on Hekmatyar's radioed orders or agreement.[9]

Other clashes inside Afghanistan had diverse causes. After 70 or 80 guerrillas were killed in August 1989, fighting for a Helmand province bridge vital to the opium trade, one of the commanders involved was killed while visiting Peshawar in March 1990, with Hekmatyar widely believed to have had an opium trade rival eliminated.[10] In June 1990 while visiting Peshawar, one of Hekmatyar's top commanders became the fifth important Afghan killed in the city within two weeks.[11] In August 1989 one of the most important commanders around Qandahar, Abdul Latif, a supporter of Zahir Shah and critic of the interim government, was poisoned and his two accused killers executed with suspicious haste.[12] After Soviet and regime forces withdrew from the Konar valley in 1988, Arab money and several hundred Arab volunteers won control for former Hekmatyar commander Jamil-ur-Rahman at the head of a puritanical Wahhabi regime. It applied an allegedly Islamic concept of conquest that considered any Kabul-aligned areas to be heretic, permitting pillaging of property, execution of men, and enslavement of women and children—Wahhabi practices in other parts of Afghanistan, too. The resulting hatreds erupted in fighting in August 1991 in which Hekmatyar's Hezb drove Rahman's Salfi group from the provincial capital, Asadabad. After Rahman took refuge in Pakistan and was assassinated by an Egyptian Arab, Saudi Arabia used its financial influence over both factions to mediate a truce, but fighting continued in the Konar valley.[13] Such internecine savagery occurred in other areas, too, as a harbinger of the civil war that followed the PDPA's collapse.

Mujahideen Atrocities

The United States Department of State, after years of chronicling only Kabul regime atrocities in its annual reports to Congress on human rights in Afghanistan, began noting in 1990 that various *mujahideen* groups, 'most frequently' Hekmatyar's, were alleged to have committed 'politically motivated murders and kidnappings of Afghan refugee intellectuals, killing of prisoners', and other crimes.[14] A year later it said 'there have been credible reports that some resistance groups have attacked, tortured, killed, or imprisoned persons opposed to their programmes', with Hekmatyar again singled out. Several thousand political prisoners were reported held in *mujahideen* prisons in Afghanistan and in refugee camps in Pakistan, with some 'routinely subject[ed]...to torture'. Islamist groups of Hekmatyar, Khales, and Sayyaf were 'most frequently linked to these prisons and cited for poor prisoner treatment', the State Department said.[15] The New York-based human rights organization, Asia Watch, added that 'Pakistani authorities, especially the ISI, have participated in abuses, including the detention of Afghan refugees suspected of opposing some of the parties favoured by Pakistan, or handing over suspects to the parties for interrogation and torture'.[16] Mojaddedi accused Hekmatyar of having had hundreds of innocent people killed, with the cooperation or connivance of Pakistani military authorities.[17]

Violence was used not only among *mujahideen* groups and against supporters of Zahir Shah or other opponents of the Islamists. It was also employed with growing frequency into the early 1990s against foreigners and Afghan employees of international relief organizations that were providing medical, educational, nutritional, and other care to refugees. Many were warned to leave Peshawar for allegedly corrupting Islam with irreligious ideas. Death lists were published, and a number of people were murdered.[18] Mobs believed to have been organized by Hekmatyar attacked some Western relief centres, destroying supplies and workshops for helping refugees. Projects helping Afghan women were particularly targeted.[19] Despite appeals from relief organizations to the Afghan interim government, the seven groups, and the

Pakistani government, many organizations had to curtail or even close operations by early 1991. Pakistani authorities did little to investigate and nothing to prosecute such persecution.[20]

This lawlessness was accompanied by accusations from Hekmatyar, the leader who had benefited the most from ISI's distribution of American-supplied armaments and money, that the United States was trying to subvert the resistance cause. Supported by such Islamists as Sayyaf, Hekmatyar took the lead in charging, 'The US and Soviet Union are allies in an anti-Islamic campaign', and he accused the CIA of plotting his assassination.[21] The United States sought in late 1989 to restrict the amount of its aid that Pakistan gave Hekmatyar, but supplies were fungible, and those financed by Saudi Arabia and other outside sources could still be used by ISI to favour him.[22]

THE COMMANDERS' *SHURA*

The virtual exclusion of *mujahideen* commanders fighting inside Afghanistan from the February 1989 Rawalpindi *shura*, and the unrepresentative, incompetent nature of the interim government that it established, led to an attempt to establish an alternative guerrilla voice. Most field commanders had earned local legitimacy; their authority did not depend upon groups based in Peshawar or Tehran. The Peshawar seven's interests were increasingly seen as inimical to those doing the fighting, although many fighters were tied to Peshawar by ISI's initial policy of distributing weapons only through the seven. Those commanders who were able to cooperate with each other—rather than pursuing internecine warfare, as Hekmatyar's men did— began to broaden their contacts.

The leading commander in the west, Mohammad Ismail Khan, who was loosely affiliated with Rabbani's Jamiat party, convened the first important commanders' conference before the interim government was set up. A claimed total of 1200 commanders, mostly from central, western, and southern Afghanistan, met from 11 to 23 July 1987 in the Saghar area of Ghowr province. In obvious criticism of Peshawar, Tehran, and foreign supporters, they proclaimed that only 'the heirs of the martyrs and...the Muslims of the trenches who are struggling in hot fronts and are ready to be martyred' had the right to determine Afghanistan's future. They called for a broader conference in six months.[23]

Not until three years later, when the biases and incompetence of the interim government had disgusted fighters, did another significant meeting of field commanders occur. This time the initiative came from the east. Meeting in Paktia province from 7 to 9 May 1990, some 40 or 50 commanders 'categorically rejected any attempts or formulas' for a political settlement 'without direct participation of the commanders'.[24] This led to another Paktia meeting from 22 to 25 June of some 300 commanders, said to represent all 29 provinces. They reiterated the demand for a voice in political developments but insisted they were not looking for a confrontation with the interim government.[25] Massoud did not attend the Paktia meetings but hosted the next one, held from 9 to 12 October in Badakhshan. With Hekmatyar not represented, the commanders rejected an ISI plan for a Hekmatyar-led attack on Kabul, as discussed below. They called instead for a single military strategy with 'coordinated and organized operations' simultaneously throughout the country. They said Afghanistan should be divided into nine zones, with religious leaders, commanders, and elders appointing 'a responsible person' for each zone.[26]

The commanders' *shura* failed to fulfil its promise of fresh leadership, free from the mess in Peshawar and the influence of ISI and other outside elements. The idea of setting up a political committee was rejected because too many commanders were unwilling to challenge their nominal bosses in Peshawar. Plans to name individuals responsible for combat zones were never accepted, and nationally coordinated military operations were never implemented. By mid-1991, many commanders, beset with rivalries and other troubles within their home territories which made it difficult for them to focus on the larger picture, had lost interest in their *shura*.[27]

After the Badakhshan meeting, Massoud made his first visit to Pakistan since the war began. Senior ISI officers, who disliked his independence of the control they sought over the resistance, had visited him inside Afghanistan in 1988 to offer armaments, although he received little directly from them.[28] Now they had him meet in mid-October 1990 with Pakistani President Ghulam Ishaq Khan, the army chief, General Mirza Aslam Beg, and the director general of ISI, Maj. Gen. Mohammad Assad Durrani. Massoud also met Hekmatyar, and they supposedly patched up their differences. This did not prove lasting, however, nor did Massoud receive the arms and ammunition that he thought Pakistan had promised him.[29]

ENLARGED ARMS PIPELINE

With the Soviet withdrawal, the supply of armaments from Pakistan to the *mujahideen* became less a smuggling operation involving evasion of military interdiction and more of a virtually open trucking business.[30] ISI tried to tighten its control by what became known as 'subcontracting'— delivering supplies directly to commanders who followed its operational orders, rather than channelling them through the Peshawar seven.[31] In mid-1988, the United States temporarily stopped providing Stingers, for fear that the withdrawal would free the missiles for use by terrorists elsewhere; and supplies were generally slowed in the expectation that needs would decrease when all Soviets were gone. But as the USSR continued to pour in massive military aid to the regime, American and Saudi money kept the Pakistani pipeline filled.[32]

Value of Aid to the Resistance

After more than $700 million worth of American and Saudi funded aid had been pumped through the pipeline in 1988, the plan was raised to $715 million in just the three months of December 1989 through February 1990, because Soviet aid to Kabul had increased.[33] But in Washington questions were increasingly raised about aid, and they fuelled an internal conflict. By early 1990, the once solid congressional support for arming the *mujahideen* had begun to crumble as fast as the perception of a threatening Soviet Union waned. The share of aid going to Islamists such as Hekmatyar came under more skeptical scrutiny. Congress cut the 1991 programme $50 million below the 1990 level of $300 million.[34] Also hanging over the programme were American worries about Pakistan's efforts to develop nuclear weapons. Under a law that banned aid to countries trying to make their first nuclear weapons—a law whose possible applications to Pakistan had been ignored while driving the Soviets out of Afghanistan was the highest policy consideration—the United States suspended a planned $237 million in aid for the 12-month period beginning 1 October 1990.[35] Although angered, Pakistan continued cooperating with the CIA's Afghan programme because of its national interests in what happened in Afghanistan.

Aid to the *mujahideen* was complicated by Iraq's seizure of Kuwait in August 1990. The action split the Peshawar leadership. As head of the almost dormant interim government, Mojaddedi dispatched 308 guerrilla fighters to Saudi Arabia as a token of support for the Kuwaiti and Saudi governments that had provided so much aid to the resistance. This was denounced by Hekmatyar and Sayyaf—persistent critics of the United States, which now led the anti-Iraqi coalition—and by Rabbani, an irresolute occasional critic of Washington. Their attitude probably was affected by hopes of recovering from Iraq money that the leaders had in looted Kuwaiti banks, and by the pro-Iraqi views of some senior Pakistani military officers. The three leaders found themselves curiously aligned with Kabul, which rewarded Iraq's support of previous years by backing Baghdad. After the Persian Gulf war in January and February 1991, in which the *mujahideen* did not see action, the three opportunists gladly shared with other leaders the captured Iraqi tanks and other equipment turned over by the Americans and Saudis.[36]

Afghanistan angrily denounced the continued aid to the *mujahideen*. In the 626 days between the Geneva signing and the end of 1989, it sent 1018 notes to the United Nations Good Offices Mission charging 8002 violations of the accords. The mission, little more than a transparent fig leaf, never made a finding that a violation had occurred.[37] In April 1989, Afghanistan took its complaints to the UN Security Council, which had never debated Afghan developments. Foreign Minister Abdol Wakil contended that Pakistani interference met the United Nations' definition of aggression, but the council was unable to agree on any resolution or statement, much less any action.[38] This made the predictable mockery of Gorbachev's 8 February 1988 withdrawal statement that the United Nations was the proper resort if interference continued. While Kabul waxed indignant, Moscow blamed Islamabad for the continued aid but played down criticism of Washington, whose goodwill it saw as essential to implementing Soviet domestic changes.[39]

SOVIET AID TO KABUL

Moscow unhappily accepted that each side would continue supplying its client—positive symmetry—because negative symmetry of cutting all aid was not an option if the Kabul regime were to survive, as powerful Soviet interests wanted. Soviet aid was essential and massive. With the Salang highway no longer safe after the Soviets quit guarding it—Najibullah said guerrillas destroyed 275 vehicles on it from 21 March to 21 June 1989, compared with 150 in the last full year of the Soviet presence[40]—Moscow sustained Kabul with the largest airlift in Soviet military history at a cost of more than $490 million a year. In its initial period, Western diplomats estimated 3800 cargo flights were made in 196 days from the end of the withdrawal through September 1989.[41]

Soviet soldiers in Afghanistan supervised the delivery and use of arms aid. Western estimates ran as high as 700 soldiers in mid-1991, but Moscow insisted in 1989 that only 25 or 30 logistical specialists remained, 'depending on the type of armaments supplied to the Afghan army at the moment'. This ignored the later-admitted presence of Soviet crews to fire Scud missiles.[42] There were many unconfirmed reports of other Soviet personnel's involvement both inside Afghanistan and in aerial support from across the border.[43] Apparently confirming a continuing Soviet combat role, an Afghan general paid tribute in April 1991 to 'such [Soviet] military specialists as the sappers, tankmen, airmen, and artillerymen...[who are] bold and fearless people who have risked their lives repeatedly'.[44]

Various Soviet reports on military aid to Afghanistan valued it at some 2.5 billion roubles ($4 billion) in 1989, and 4 billion roubles ($6.4 billion) in 1990.[45] Western estimates of the value of post-withdrawal Soviet aid ranged from $2 billion to $3.5 billion for arms aid in 1990 and $3 billion in 1991, plus $700 million worth of civilian supplies in 1990 and $500 million in 1991.[46] Of its 4000 million rouble worldwide economic aid grants budgeted for 1991, the USSR allocated to Afghanistan 280 million roubles or $448 million at the decreasingly realistic official rate—not all of which seems to have been delivered—plus about 150 million roubles of credits that were not expected to be repaid.[47] As the USSR's ability to supply its own people with civilian goods declined, Soviet criticism of aid secretly allocated to Afghanistan increased. Shevardnadze argued, however, that denying further aid 'would devalue all the sacrifices made by our people'.[48]

After initial testiness over Soviet criticism of the aid, Kabul began to talk unrealistically of its long-term trade possibilities with the USSR. But Najibullah described in June 1991 the immediate fact of an 'ugly economic crisis.... The gross national product, national output, and per capita income declined noticeably', while inflation was 'horrifying'.[49] Kabul suffered food shortages every winter, and other parts of the country experienced them occasionally. Although private trade continued to flourish between regime-held towns and *mujahideen*-controlled countryside, as well as across borders with Pakistan and Iran, the regime remained dependent upon the USSR for food and other essential supplies.

CHANGING THE REGIME'S IMAGE

After the Soviet withdrawal, the regime accelerated efforts begun with national reconciliation more than two years earlier to improve its public image. The widely publicized manipulation by Pakistan of the *mujahideen* interim government it had created enabled Najibullah to take a nationalistic stance. '...[T]his is not a war of Afghans, but a war between Afghanistan and Pakistan,' he said.[50] He conceded that 'it might still have been applicable somehow' to call his government 'Moscow's puppet' before the withdrawal ended. '...[T]he opposition was [then] able to present itself as a patriotic force that for many years had opposed the foreign military presence,' and it would have benefited by agreeing to an election, Najibullah said, as if an election might have been conducted honestly. But now, he said in 1991, 'they themselves are in fact puppets in the hands of the Pakistani military'.[51] While there was much truth in this description of the Peshawar pretenders, although inapplicable to many *mujahideen* commanders inside

Afghanistan, it was also true that Najibullah's regime was a kept artifact of Soviet hardliners.

Two other factors helped the regime: a general war weariness and apprehension or even fear of what would happen, particularly in Kabul, if the resistance won. Beyond the danger of revenge on regime stalwarts, the worst worries were over Hekmatyar's trying to realize his vision of an Islamic state with one dictatorial ruler and a place for women only in the home. A growing number of Afghans seemed to accept Najibullah's moderating changes, despite continuing bitterness that the PDPA 'ruined the country, and now they want us to rally behind them', as one Kabul resident said.[52]

The most important symbolic change was the PDPA's name to the Watan (Homeland) Party. The PDPA had not held a congress to approve policies and renew its leaders' mandate since its founding in 1965, although its charter specified a congress every four years. Corrupted by power and fearful of losing it, many members resisted a fresh look at the party.[53] Najibullah complained of members' dogmatism. '...[O]ne of the reasons for *the party's defeat* was the unrealistic efforts of the party leadership to impose aspirations on the hard, uncompromising realities.... [I]t is clear that Marxism is not acceptable in Afghanistan,' he said shortly before the party congress was held in Kabul on 27 and 28 June 1990.[54]

The Second Party Congress

It met after the Berlin Wall had fallen, and the long-subservient East European members of the Soviet bloc were rejecting Communism. The 868 congress delegates represented a claimed membership of 173 614, although a Soviet specialist on Afghanistan had asserted the year before that only 30 000 PDPA members were active or committed.[55] In Najibullah's lengthy, defensive report, the claim of a small minority to decide policy for all Afghans was renounced. It had been 'a historic mistake' to have come under 'a specific ideology...[that] set up great obstacles for the creation of a broad national base for the party...'.[56] The congress approved a new charter that dropped the PDPA's claim to be a ruling party, pledged to uphold democracy, promised special attention for peaceful reconstruction, and changed the name. The cosmetic nature of such changes was shown by the unanimous election of virtually all 144 members and 59 candidate members of the old central committee to the newly renamed central council, and ten out of eleven politburo members to the renamed executive committee. Najibullah was unanimously elected Watan's president.[57]

Some things were swept under the congress rug. Najibullah had called beforehand for investigations of party members' participation in 'plundering, misuse of funds, bribery, embezzlement, and mismanagement in the [governmental] departments...'.[58] His fast-rising deputy, Farid Ahmad Mazdaq, an ethnic Tajik born in 1958, who reportedly had been charged with preparing the congress in a way that would make the party more democratic, said just before its commencement that 'PDPA leaders include thieves and bribe takers, and there are plenty of abuses'.[59] The congress did nothing about reforms.

The worsening economic situation cut into the party organization. The PDPA claimed to have given up secret— and probably illegal—government subsidies in late 1988, but it continued to receive money secretly from the CPSU to help support its sizeable bureaucracy. This stipend ended as the CPSU fell apart in late 1991. Watan was forced to begin dismissing full-time, paid party workers in the government and armed forces.[60]

As part of its new look, the party relinquished its special place in the government—in theory, only not in practice. In 1989, an election law was broadcast on 14 May, an election for *loya jirgah* members supposedly held on 17 May, and the *loya jirgah* convened in Kabul on 20 and 21 May.[61]

When this membership met again a year later, on 28 and 29 May 1990, with some provincials virtually kidnapped to fill out the delegate count, they amended the national constitution to eliminate any mention of the PDPA as having any special role, to insert political pluralism as a basic principle, and to declare the Islamic character of the state.[62] In August 1991, Najibullah approved a decree dropping 'the words "the Saur revolution, People's Democratic Party of Afghanistan, and primary party organizations" from all legislative documents in force in the country'.[63] In Kabul schools, pre-1978 textbooks were brought back, and the teaching of Russian was replaced with English or French.[64] But with Najibullah as the all-powerful national president as well as Watan leader, the official changes in the party's status had little practical effect. No real challenge to the old ruling clique was permitted. The discredited old National Front was replaced in July 1990 with a Peace Front as an umbrella for all political organizations; it never achieved any greater respectability or significance.[65]

GOVERNMENT CHANGES

Shortly after the Soviet Army had left, Najibullah fired Sharq, whose prime ministerial authority had been circumvented through PDPA channels, and brought back Solton Ali Keshtmand as prime minister in all but name.[66] Keshtmand was known as excessively corrupt, even by Kabul's low standards, and he helped establish a wealthy merchant class of his fellow Hazara Shi'ites. A high percentage of Soviet aid reportedly ended up in such pockets.[67] Although corruption did not disqualify him, Keshtmand was kicked upstairs on 6 May 1990 to a newly created, meaningless post of first vice president.[68]

Returning to appearances of non-partisanship, Najibullah named on 7 May, a non-party official, Fazl Haq Khaliqyar, to become prime minister. A career civil servant born in

Herat in 1934, who had risen to first deputy minister of finance, Khaliqyar was then serving as governor general of Herat.[69] He had been seriously wounded on 6 April by bullets intended for Najibullah while standing in for the president at a provincial ceremony for the surrender of 1000 guerrillas, some of whom turned the occasion into an ambush that killed several generals and up to 125 others.[70] After proposing a pragmatic programme to parliament while lying on a stretcher, Khaliqyar was sworn in on 27 May. Key posts in his cabinet went to party members.[71]

This cabinet was part of an effort to overcome factionalism. Najibullah had already reached out to old Khalqi rivals as well as supporters of Karmal in Parcham. Dr Shah Wali, Amin's deputy who had been released from eight years' imprisonment in April 1988, was appointed in April 1989 as a minister-counsellor. Abdul Karim Misaq, a PDPA founder and a politburo member under Amin, was rehabilitated in 1989 and named mayor of Kabul in 1990. Mahmud Barialay, Karmal's half-brother who had been imprisoned for opposing national reconciliation, was appointed first deputy prime minister in June 1989 and elected to Watan's executive committee.[72] Other selected political prisoners, mostly Khalqis, were released in early 1990, although some 3000 more stayed in prison.[73]

COUP ATTEMPTS

Factionalism remained. There were several *coup* attempts in 1989. A major attempt to overthrow the government in March 1990 led to fighting in Kabul more severe than during either the 1973 or 1978 *coups*. After Gulabzoy was banished to Moscow in November 1988, some Khalqis looked for leadership to the defence minister, Col. Gen. Shahnawaz Tanai. Born in 1950 in the Tanai tribal area of Pushtuns around Khost in Paktia province, the diminutive Soviet-trained career soldier had taken part in the 1978 *coup* and then risen through a succession of commands that earned him a reputation as a butcher. Tanai opposed Najibullah's softening of the PDPA's Communist principles intended to broaden support.[74]

The arrests of Tanai's army colleagues for 1989 *coup* attempts in which apparently he was involved led to a trial beginning on 5 March 1990. The regime said later that Tanai, apparently fearing that the testimony would implicate him, ordered a *coup* the next day.[75] His supporters seized the defence ministry headquarters at Darulaman and Bagram air base. Artillery shells hit downtown Kabul, and planes from Bagram bombed key buildings including the presidential palace where they narrowly missed Najibullah. Tanks of interior ministry forces, then headed by Watanjar, and WAD troops under Yaqubi, turned back rebellious army tank columns downtown and, after severe fighting, recaptured a wrecked defence ministry headquarters on 7 March. A loyal army division recaptured Bagram the next day. At least 300 were killed and downtown Kabul was extensively damaged. While the fighting was going on, Najibullah replaced Tanai as defence minister with Watanjar, who was ostensibly a Khalqi but primarily a Moscow loyalist. Raz Muhammad Paktin, also a Khalqi, took over the interior ministry. Tanai, his wife and three children, five generals, and 15 pilots fled to Pakistan on 7 March.[76] Kabul Radio said 623 persons were arrested. Various unconfirmed reports said 54 or 'more than 800 officers and soldiers were executed...'.[77]

With his usual opportunism, Hekmatyar claimed credit for helping Tanai fight Najibullah and appealed for other *mujahideen* to join in. But the interim government angrily refused to have anything to do with Tanai.[78] Although it was unclear whether Tanai and Hekmatyar had somehow worked together in the 1989 *coup* attempts or in advance of the March 1990 *coup*, Hekmatyar's claim was enough for Kabul to begin referring to what had happened as a 'failed Shahnawaz-Gulbuddin [Hekmatyar] *coup d'état*' that had been planned by ISI. Cynical Afghan exiles concluded that not only was Hekmatyar willing to make any unprincipled deal to attain power but also ISI would do anything to put its protege in power.[79]

On 18 March, the PDPA central committee expelled 24 persons from the party. In addition to Tanai and his rebel generals, they included three men who had been major PDPA and government figures: Ziray and Panjshiri, who were temporarily imprisoned, and Gulabzoy, who was replaced as ambassador in Moscow. Sarwari was accused of having worked with ISI to set up the *coup* attempt.[80] Sarwari had left his minor post as Afghanistan's ambassador to South Yemen in January and gone to India, where the Afghan embassy seized his passport on 2 February as he tried to fly to Kabul. After the regime denounced him as a *coup* organizer and reportedly asked India to take him out of circulation, he was jailed in New Delhi on 11 June. The official reason was he lacked a valid passport and visa, a crime punishable by up to five years in prison. Sarwari, who had personally tortured prisoners as head of Kabul's lawless political police in 1978 and 1979, was still languishing in an Indian jail when the Afghan regime fell almost two years later.[81]

The post-*coup* purge was followed by government and party changes, related above. Najibullah continued to tighten his control by replacing old party stalwarts with protégés such as Mazdaq. Keshtmand was removed from his vice presidential post on 8 April 1991. In July he quit the party, which he accused of being authoritarian and of not believing in its new professions of political pluralism.[82] By that time, the only survivors in Kabul's leadership who had played a significant role in bringing the PDPA to power thirteen years earlier were Moscow's man Watanjar, along with his less important comrade Rafi. Taraki, Amin, and others were dead; Abdul Qadir, Sarwari, Gulabzoy, Karmal, and others were in exile; others who remained in Kabul, such as

Ratebzad, were forced to be inactive; and some were in prison.

The Return of Karmal

On 20 June 1991, Karmal returned to Kabul from Moscow. He had been living there since 4 May 1987 in enforced exile, trying unsuccessfully to go home, visited only by minor CPSU officials who 'tell me what I can do and what I cannot'.[83] The lack of a satisfactory explanation to Watan members for the return caused speculation that Moscow wanted to stir up the Kabul political scene in a way that might weaken Najibullah's refusal to compromise on a peace settlement, thus leading to a reduction in the Soviet burden of continuing to finance the regime.[84] As numerous followers called at Karmal's small Kabul apartment, a Watan leader said his 'sudden return has drawn dormant hostilities out into the open in our party...'.[85]

CONTINUING WAR

Looming over and shaping politics was the continuing war. A Soviet report said the 'disarray in party ranks has considerably diminished the combat ability of the armed forces'.[86] The regime became heavily dependent on militia units, which roughly doubled its military strength. Two units came to play a critical role in preserving the regime by acting as mobile firefighting forces with greater daring, brutality, and effectiveness than the Afghan army showed. Dostam's 53rd militia division—the Jowzjani unit of Uzbeks and Turkmen—and to a lesser extent Jaffar Naderi's 80th militia division of Ismaeli Tajiks were flown to trouble spots to beat back *mujahideen* threats.[87] By 1991 they were doing most of the regime's fighting in return for payment in dollars—no afghanis or roubles accepted. Described by one observer as 'mercenaries, corrupt and degenerate', these militiamen were as much a danger to civilians whom they robbed and raped as to the *mujahideen*.[88]

The Battle of Jalalabad

Shortly after the Soviet withdrawal, a four-month-long battle in which the *mujahideen* failed to capture Jalalabad clarified the military and political patterns of three more years of civil war. It showed that the *mujahideen* were unable or unwilling to submerge their personal, political, ethnic, and regional differences in the common cause of destroying the regime; the interim government in Peshawar lacked any real authority; ISI was determined to win the war at great guerrilla cost in order to install its favourites in Kabul; the *mujahideen* were unready to make or incapable of making the change from irregular to conventional warfare that the ISI determination required; and the regime was capable of fighting desperately and well as long as Moscow continued to provide supplies. Jalalabad was a psychological defeat for the *mujahideen*, who had expected an unassisted Afghan army to crumple.

In the bloodiest battle in more than a decade, Jalalabad was heavily damaged, and 500 or more civilians died out of a pre-war population of perhaps 170 000. Some 1000 or more soldiers were killed, and the *mujahideen* suffered some 4000 deaths. Many guerrilla groups lost as many men in that one battle as in all previous fighting. They came to realize that it was a mistake for men equipped and experienced only for guerrilla warfare to try to capture a well-defended city in frontal assault.[89] Some *mujahideen* groups refused to accept ISI assignments to take turns blocking regime reinforcements on the road from Kabul to Jalalabad or to launch major diversionary attacks elsewhere in Afghanistan.[90] Their refusal arose from a perception that Jalalabad was an ISI effort to defeat Najibullah so it could install its favourite, the Ghilzai Pushtun, Hekmatyar, in Kabul. Few Ghilzais outside his party, and still fewer Durrani Pushtuns, Tajiks, or other Afghans wanted to die for that.[91] The failure was ISI's, with the agreement of Peshawar leaders who were eager to have an Afghan capital for their interim government. Jalalabad was a proxy battle by ISI— maybe not even proxy, because there were reports of Pakistani Army units' being involved.[92] The decision to launch the attack was taken in Islamabad on 5 March at a meeting of Pakistani officials attended by United States Ambassador Robert B. Oakley but not by any *mujahideen* officials. When scapegoats were being sought after the failure, Prime Minister Benazir Bhutto and ISI's director general, Lt.-Gen. Hamid Gul, each blamed the other.[93] By over-reaching itself politically as well as militarily, Pakistan damaged prospects for ending the war and ridding itself of Afghan refugees.

As fighting subsided around Jalalabad, the war went on sporadically elsewhere. *De facto* truces developed in more areas, partly from general weariness, partly from guerrilla reluctance to follow ISI suggestions for such things as blowing up dams to discomfort the regime, that would harm ordinary Afghans.[94] On his October 1990 visit to Pakistan, Massoud tried with little apparent success to get ISI officials to understand *mujahideen* political considerations as well as the military ramifications of the situation.[95]

The next military action of political significance was the capture of Khost on 31 March 1991. Under seiges of varying seriousness since 1979, the town had withstood several rounds of intensified attacks after the Soviet withdrawal. It finally fell to a 16-day offensive, led by Hezb-Khales commander Jalaluddin Haqqani, that involved other *mujahideen* groups and strong Pakistani army logistical and advisory support.[96] ISI rushed Hekmatyar to Khost in time for the victory. He claimed it as his own, although other groups had done all the fighting, thus reaffirming that

Pakistan was determined to try to manœuver him into power.[97]

After Khost, ISI pointed its *mujahideen* forces at capturing Gardez, 60 miles south of Kabul, but they failed. The regime destroyed in April 1991 a conventional military force that ISI had armed and trained for Hekmatyar astride the road south of Kabul, in the hope of taking the capital. Frustrated, ISI switched their attention back to Jalalabad, but an attack there later in 1991 brought no progress despite the presence of Pakistani officers who were commanding tanks.[98] During this period, Massoud steadily consolidated his control of the northeast, which included taking control of the Wakhan corridor.[99]

The victories of Massoud and other northern commanders increased *mujahideen* pressure on the Soviet border. Vocal support by Massoud and Rabbani for separatist tendencies in Soviet Tajikistan, as well as statements by Hekmatyar, and old remarks by President Zia about bringing Soviet Central Asia into a new unified Islamic region, fanned Soviet fears.[100] KGB border guards were unable to prevent the planting of mines within the USSR by *mujahideen*, the smuggling of anti-Soviet literature, narcotics smuggling— some by Soviet diplomats and generals—and simple age-old banditry.[101] Soviet officials blamed ISI, the CIA, and other 'special services' for inciting and sometimes organizing border trouble. They claimed several men captured along the border had been trained by Pakistanis or Americans for sabotage or anti-Soviet agitation.[102]

REFUGEES AND LAND MINES

The Afghan civil war after the Soviet withdrawal discouraged the return home of refugees that had been envisaged by the Geneva accords. Most refugees wanted to wait for peace before tackling the daunting problems of rebuilding war-ravaged villages, reclaiming fields weedy and hardened by disuse, replanting orchards, cleaning out or rebuilding irrigation systems, replacing draft animals and tools, and obtaining seed and fertilizer.

These problems were compounded by land mines. Afghanistan was strewn with them. The danger lurked silently everywhere—limbs being blown off, eyes blinded— or death. The Soviet and Afghan armies had planted minefields to defend their installations, booby-trapped villages after offensive sweeps, and sown mines indiscriminately by artillery fire or aircraft in an effort to close the guerrillas' supply routes, hamper their movements, and terrorize those civilians who were beyond the reach of the regime. The *mujahideen* mined roads and areas of enemy operations. The Soviets said mines were 'the cause of considerable losses',[103] but the number of casualties they inflicted on both sides was unknown. One estimate for resistance and civilian personnel handicapped and disabled by mines was 30 000 by late 1988, when mines were causing more casualties than any other type of weapon. The International Committee of the Red Cross reported that some 1400 mine victims reached three medical centres in 1992, and 8000 mine wounds or deaths a year were reported by 1993—with half the victims dying for lack of treatment.[104]

No one knew how many mines poisoned the land, or where they were. Neither side had kept count, and few maps were made, as they deployed mines for immediate purposes without consideration of long-term dangers.[105] Estimates of the number of still lethal mines in place after the Soviet departure started at three million and ran up to sixty million. More than 25 000 were cleared from just two villages in the Panjshir valley.[106] The United States Department of State said 'Afghanistan is perhaps the most heavily mined country in the world'.[107] Under a United Nations programme announced in 1988, specialists from Australia, Britain, Canada, Egypt, France, Italy, New Zealand, Norway, Pakistan, Thailand, Turkey, and the United States began teaching refugees how to recognize the danger of mines. They also instructed the Afghans on how to demine their country and taught them some medical skills.[108] In 1994, they estimated that it would take another five or six years to finish clearing mines just from 'high priority areas'.

HUMANITARIAN EFFORTS

The demining programme was part of a broader United Nations effort to provide humanitarian aid to all sides in the Afghan tragedy. But member countries were slow to provide funding for a new Office of the Coordinator for Humanitarian Assistance Relations to Afghanistan, known as UNOCA, headed by a former UN High Commissioner for Refugees, Prince Sadruddin Aga Khan. Some donors were already making humanitarian efforts amid difficulties from Pakistan, *mujahideen* corruption and hostility, regime obtuseness, and inadequate logistics. A number of planned projects had to be cut back or cancelled.[109] Before resigning in December 1990, Sadruddin complained of a vicious circle: donors would honour pledges only when refugees started returning, but refugees would not go back until 'basic requirements for a secure and sustainable existence' had been met.[110]

The United States had by April 1992 put $50 million into the UN programme, but that was only a minor part of its humanitarian contribution. Up to 1985 it gave more than $430 million for refugees in Pakistan under a programme run jointly by the World Food programme and the UN High Commissioner for Refugees, which was also supported by Japan, Saudi Arabia, and West European and other countries.[111] As the United States Congress began increasing military aid for the *mujahideen* in 1985, it decided to supplement aid to refugees by sending humanitarian assistance to non-Communist parts of Afghanistan. An unfulfilled goal of this assistance was unifying the resistance.[112] After a slow start because of disagreements with Pakistan, the American programme based there was by 1987 employing Afghans and giving money to private voluntary organizations to deliver medical supplies, clothing, educational materials, fruit tree plants, advisory services, and other items to *mujahideen* areas of Afghanistan. Almost $400 million worth of funding and grain had been disbursed by April 1992.[113]

How much of the humanitarian aid funnelled through Peshawar resistance groups reached the intended recipients is uncertain. Corruption was rampant. Some sources estimated that only 15 to 30 per cent of the aid was delivered. American officials temporarily suspended the $30-million food aid part of the programme on several occasions in 1989, because *mujahideen* leaders refused to allow monitoring of deliveries. After 2400 tons of wheat were diverted by ISI officers, apparently for private gain, another temporary halt was ordered in January 1990 to work out new monitoring procedures.[114] The private voluntary aid organizations from many countries operating from Peshawar regularly had to bribe Pakistani police and military as well as some *mujahideen* groups, in order to carry out humanitarian work in border areas.[115]

THE DIPLOMATIC SEARCH FOR PEACE

Peace efforts after the Soviet withdrawal were frustrated by the diversity of elements involved. Competition in Kabul sapped Najibullah's ability to make deals, while rivalries, hatreds, and ideological, ethnic, and religious differences divided regime opponents. Despite lip service to the idea, few resistance factions were prepared to accept majority rule—if a valid way could have been found to determine a majority—in composing one unified side to face the regime. The main outsiders were equally divided. United Nations officials, Soviets, and Americans had different viewpoints on how to achieve peace, or even what it would mean, while in Pakistan the dominant voice belonged to those who wanted to ensure that a future Afghanistan would be a loyal ally or even an obedient satellite state.

After the UN General Assembly asked Perez de Cuellar in 1988 to promote the creation of a coalition government that would take power before the last Soviet soldier left, the Secretary-General assigned the working role to Benon V. Sevan, an American-educated career United Nations official of Armenian extraction from Cyprus. Sevan found strong disagreement on who should speak for the resistance—exiled Afghans, Zahir Shah, others—or whether they should talk to Kabul at all.[116] After numerous rebuffs from those who still wanted the war to come out their way, and extensive consultations by Sevan with 'all concerned parties', Perez de Cuellar made public on 21 May 1991, five 'elements [that] would serve as a good basis for a political settlement... acceptable to the vast majority of the Afghan people'. This plan called for 'an intra-Afghan dialogue' to work out details of a transitional period under a ceasefire that would lead 'to the establishment of a broad-based government'. Transitional arrangements would include 'a credible and impartial transition mechanism with appropriate powers and authority (yet to be specified) that...[would assure] free and fair elections...for the establishment of a broad-based government...[and] an agreement...to end arms supplies to all Afghan sides...'.[117] On paper, at least, Perez de Cuellar had agreement of all the parties except Hekmatyar, Sayyaf, and Khales.[118]

Perez de Cuellar said later, referring to Najibullah, he had been assured 'that some of the controversial personalities concerned would not insist on' participating in settlement talks 'or in the transition mechanism'. He called for action on 'organizing an Afghan gathering with a wider participation, as well as defin[ing] the structure and powers of the transition mechanism...[by] which all powers and all executive authority could be transferred in an orderly manner'. The Secretary-General added that he believed 'other questions can be resolved in that context...'.[119]

Kabul's Peace Plans

Not waiting for the results of the United Nations proposal, the Kabul regime offered its own peace plans, wooed diplomatic support, and conducted secret talks with aides to Zahir Shah and with various *mujahideen* leaders. Talks were held with Hekmatyar's representatives in 1988 and 1989, each side later saying the other had taken the initiative. Najibullah claimed in November 1990 that talks had been held 'with almost all of' the Peshawar leaders.[120] In April 1991, the head of WAD, Yaqubi, met secretly in Geneva with the director general of ISI, Durrani. Durrani reportedly proposed a deal to get Hekmatyar and Sayyaf into a coalition government with Najibullah, but it was rejected.[121] The only thing this intrigue produced was proof that, while peace was desired, opportunism outweighed principle for many players.

Najibullah made various proposals that won India's support and encouraged Switzerland in a short-lived peace effort, but Pakistan rejected anything that gave the regime a voice in future arrangements.[122] After more secret talks and contradictory statements about what role he intended to play in a new arrangement, if any,[123] Najibullah proposed a transitional national unity government on 25 September 1991, with the king coming home to placate the Afghans. That plan too was stillborn.[124]

Soviet Efforts

Moscow's post-withdrawal policy was 'not...supporting a particular regime' in Afghanistan, but supporting the state. Gorbachev reportedly asked Najibullah, when the latter secretly visited Moscow in late 1989, to promise in writing that he would quit once a settlement outline was agreed.[125] Obviously concerned about his future, Najibullah contended in 1990 that 'the Soviet Union has a certain moral duty to ensure that those forces dedicated to the ideals of Afghan-Soviet friendship are assigned a fitting place in the future structure of Afghan society'.[126] Despite new Russian Foreign Minister Andrey V. Kozyrev's description of Najibullah as Afghanistan's Beria—Stalin's notorious police boss—some Soviets still argued that Najibullah's resignation would cause the regime to fall, the governmental infrastructure to collapse, and 'general chaos' to result.[127]

In this complex situation, the Soviet foreign ministry suggested peace plans and worked with United Nations efforts, while the Soviet armed forces and the KGB continued to sustain Kabul[128]—a situation similar to the division between Pakistan's foreign ministry and ISI. A sign of dwindling Soviet interest, however, was Vorontsov's becoming just a part-time resident ambassador after the withdrawal was completed. He was finally replaced in Kabul on 4 October 1989 with Boris N. Pastukhov, a throwback to earlier ambassadors whose CPSU careers had peaked and who were shunted off to diplomatic work.[129] Soviet patience with funding a continuing war was running out.

Periodic Soviet-American discussions of a political solution for Afghanistan were usually secondary in talks on arms control and other East-West issues. Although there was dissension in the State Department,[130] United States policy was for a time based on the assumption that the *mujahideen* would win after the Soviet withdrawal. By early 1990, however, the Bush administration had given up on a *mujahideen* victory and become interested in a negotiated settlement.[131] This led to discussions with Moscow on transitional arrangements and elections, as well as both sides' endorsement of Perez de Cuellar's five-point plan.[132] At mention of Najibullah in one meeting, Shevardnadze reportedly blurted out, 'Sometimes I wish all these people would just kill each other and end the whole thing'.[133] By

June 1991, an American commentator was writing about Soviet-American 'failed efforts to end the war in Afghanistan...'.[134] Soviet talks with Pakistan and Iran about Afghanistan were also unproductive.

MISSING SOVIET SERVICEMEN

Moscow's most active contacts with Pakistan were on the subject of 311 Soviet servicemen reported missing in Afghanistan. They were not mentioned in the Geneva negotiations or accords, but the subject grew in domestic Soviet political importance after the troop withdrawal began. For Moscow, efforts to recover the servicemen came to overshadow diplomatic attempts to find peace in Afghanistan. Finally, when Russia and other Soviet successor states had become too absorbed in their own internal problems to care much any more about Afghanistan's troubles, the quest for the missing men remained their main interest in the Afghan situation.

Neither side took prisoners in the first days of Soviet involvement in Afghanistan's savage war. Captured fighters were killed, often with extreme brutality.[135] Then in May 1982, after Moscow had refused to exchange 50 imprisoned Afghans for a captured Soviet geologist and he was killed, the USSR agreed to an International Committee of the Red Cross (ICRC) arrangement with 14 resistance groups for Soviet prisoners to be interned for up to two years in Switzerland at Moscow's expense. Only eleven prisoners had been transferred by 1984, when distrustful *mujahideen* quit turning over any more to the ICRC, and after the two years three of the prisoners opted to stay in the West while the rest went home.[136] Several downed Soviet pilots, who came into Pakistani hands from 1981 onward were repatriated, the last of them being Col. Aleksandr V. Rutskoy on 20 August 1988.[137] Some captured Soviet and regime soldiers were held in prisons in refugee camps in Pakistan, probably with ISI's knowledge. On 26 April 1985, a group of them in Jamiat's Zangali camp south of Peshawar, overcame their guards, seized weapons, and demanded that they be released. In the ensuing fight, the camp's ammunition dump blew up, killing between nine and twelve Soviets. Moscow angrily protested to Islamabad.[138] But Pakistan's civilian officials were not prepared to interfere with ISI arrangements except when it was convenient. As a result, Soviet prisoners became political pawns. When Pakistani diplomats wanted to improve the atmosphere for a February 1987 meeting in Moscow, they prevailed on ISI to provide one of the *mujahideen*'s Soviet prisoners for repatriation as a goodwill gesture.[139]

Prisoner Exchanges

When the son of a senior CPSU official in Kiev was captured, the official apparently got Moscow to put pressure on Kabul for the first exchange of Soviets for *mujahideen* held by the regime. Two Soviets were traded for six guerrillas in August 1985.[140] This opened the way for further exchanges. Soviet generals Varennikov and Gromov said informers were paid for information on prisoners who were then ransomed for money and for 'various kinds of property, including military hardware'.[141]

Many missing Soviets had not been captured, but had deserted because of brutal army conditions or disgust with having to kill unarmed Afghans. Some of them later became homesick and decided to return home. But others—mostly Soviet Central Asians with religious and ethnic affinity with the resistance—began new lives in Afghanistan. And some joined the guerrillas. A Soviet parliamentarian said eight or ten men 'went over to the enemy', and an American study found 'at least two dozen documented cases' of Soviets fighting alongside the *mujahideen*.[142]

Soviet media discussion of missing soldiers built up public pressure to get them back. This gave the *mujahideen* a bargaining chip for seeking an end to Soviet aid for Kabul. It also raised unrealistic hopes that most of the 311 missing men would eventually come home.[143] Gradually the numbers of those said to be still alive was scaled down.[144] A resistance spokesman said in 1989 that only 50 to 75 Soviet soldiers were prisoners.[145] By late 1991 Soviet experts on the subject were said to believe that 200 to 250 of the missing were dead, 30 to 40 of them had been assimilated into Afghan life and established families, some were fighting alongside the *mujahideen*, and only 30 or 40 'can be properly regarded as war prisoners'.[146]

A major public relations campaign was launched in the USSR on behalf of the prisoners—help was even sought from such long-scorned organizations as Amnesty International[147]—but there was an undercurrent of controversy. Some people still believed Stalin's World War II attitude: anyone who was captured, rather than fighting to the death, was a traitor who on return should be imprisoned or even shot, and his family should suffer.[148] A 4 July 1988 amnesty for former prisoners who had chosen the West but then returned home was publicly criticized. There was opposition to a Supreme Soviet amnesty effective 15 December 1989 for servicemen who committed crimes in Afghanistan, including murder, or were taken prisoner or reported missing there. One man who went home through Pakistani intervention in 1994 was charged with treason, desertion, and arms theft.[149]

Taking advantage of Soviet desperation, the *mujahideen* raised the prisoner trade ratio from 1985's two-for-six. Massoud made a one-for-seven exchange in 1988, and by 1990 the ratio was one or two Soviets for 25 or even 33 guerrillas.[150] How much pressure Moscow had to exert on Kabul to make imprisoned *mujahideen* available for these trades is unclear, but Afghan dependence on Soviet aid probably was the key. Najibullah said in December 1991 that nine Soviets had been released through his regime's efforts, apparently meaning since the withdrawal—the total was soon raised to ten—and 'we will not spare our humanitarian efforts' in the future.[151]

The effort to bring home these prisoners continued after the USSR disappeared and Najibullah fell. When two returned in May 1996, a spokesman in Moscow for the Committee for the Affairs of Soldiers-Internationalists said 'some 300 Russian boys' were still being held in Afghanistan and Pakistan, while a Ukrainian official had said a few months earlier that 80 Ukrainian citizens were still being held.[152] These imprecise figures apparently included some who had been killed but their bodies not recovered.

NOTES

1. *Komsomolskaya Pravda*, 14 June 1990, p. 3, in *FBIS/SU*, 19 June 1990, p. 14.
2. Barnett R. Rubin, 'The Fragmentation of Afghanistan', *Foreign Affairs*, Winter 1989/90: 155; Roy, 'Afghanistan: back to tribalism'; *Washington Post*, 11 February and 7 August 1989, pp. A14 and A11; Islamabad Radio, 24 February 1989, in *FBIS/NE*, 24 February 1989, p. 50; *Afghan Jehad*, October 1988-December 1989, pp. 10 and 19-21.
3. INRA from Tehran, 9 March 1989, in *FBIS/NE*, 10 March 1989, p. 43; *New Times*, No. 6, 1991: 36-8; *Soldier of Fortune*, November 1989, p. 38.
4. SPA from Riyadh, 16 March 1989, in *FBIS/NE*, 20 March 1989, pp. 8-9; *Washington Post*, 10 May 1989, p. A33.
5. *Washington Post*, 25 February 1989, p. A18.
6. Reuter from Islamabad, 5 December 1991; *Afghan Jehad*, October-December 1991, p. 21; *Frontier Post*, 27 January 1991, p. 1; IISS, 'Strategic Survey 1989-1990' (London, 1990): 162-3.
7. IRNA from Tehran, 16 June 1990, in *FBIS/NE*, 20 June 1990, p. 33; *Nouvelles d'Afghanistan*, Nos. 74-5: 29-31.
8. *Washington Post*, 10 September 1989, p. C1; *Keyhan*, 24 May 1990, p. 3, in *FBIS/NE*, 31 May 1990, pp. 35-6; *New York Times*, 3 June 1990, p. 14.

9. Richard Mackenzie, 'A Murderous Jolt for U. S. Policy' and '"Essential Justice" After a Massacre', *Insight*, 14 August 1989 and 22 January 1990, pp. 38-40 and 28-30; *New York Times*, 18 July and 6 August 1989, pp. A6 and 8.

10. *Washington Post*, 29 August 1989, p. A15; Asia Watch Report, 'Afghanistan: The Forgotten War': Human Rights Abuses and Violations of the Laws of War Since the Soviet Withdrawal' (New York, February 1991), p. 70.

11. AFP from Peshawar, 13 June 1990, in *FBIS/NE*, 14 June 1990, p. 59.

12. AFP from Quetta, 8 August 1989, in *FBIS/NE*, 9 August 1989, pp. 49-50; *Washington Post*, 12 August 1989, p. A16; Asia Watch Report, 'Afghanistan: Forgotten War', p. 70.

13. Rubin, 'Fragmentation', p. 155; *New York Times*, 31 January 1989, p. A1; *Christian Science Monitor*, 20 June 1990, p. 1; AFP from Peshawar, 27 August and 3 September 1991, in *FBIS/NE*, 28 August and 6 September 1991, pp. 21 and 19.

14. State Department, 'Country Reports on Human Rights Practices for 1989', (Washington, February 1990), pp. 1322-3.

15. State Department, 'Country Reports on Human Rights Practices for 1990', (Washington, February 1991), pp. 1361-3; State Department, 'Country Reports...for 1991,' (Washington, February 1992), p. 1327.

16. Asia Watch, 'Afghanistan: Forgotten War', p. 99.

17. *Washington Times*, 8 August 1989, p. A7.

18. State Department, 'Country Reports...for 1991', p. 1327; 'News from Asia Watch', 3 November 1989, pp. 1-4; Asia Watch, 'Afghanistan: Forgotten War', pp. 99-123.

19. AFP from Peshawar, 29 April 1990, in *FBIS/NE*, 1 May 1990, pp. 40-41; *Economist*, 12 May 1990, pp. 35-8.

20. Statement by Agency Coordinating Body for Afghan Relief (ACBAR), Peshawar, 15 May 1990; *AFGHANews*, 1 February 1991; Mackenzie, 'Split Force', p. 35.

21. AFP from Peshawar, 28 July 1991, in *FBIS/NE*, 29 July 1991, p. 51; press release, (Hekmatyar's) Afghan News Agency, 27 May 1990.

22. *New York Times*, 2 February and 19 November 1989, pp. A3 and 16; *Los Angeles Times*, 19 November 1989, p. 1.

23. *Afghan Jehad*, June-August 1987: 35-6.

24. AFP from Islamabad, 13 May 1990, in *FBIS/NE*, 14 May 1990, p. 29.

25. AFP from Peshawar, 28 June 1990, in *FBIS/NE*, 29 June 1990, p. 41; *Afghan Jehad*, April-June 1990 and July-September 1990: 30-31 and 23-6.

26. *Afghan Jehad*, October-December 1990: 34-5; *New York Times*, 17 October 1990, p. A7; Richard Mackenzie, 'Rebels Calling Their Own Shots', *Insight*, 26 November 1990, p. 20.

27. *Wall Street Journal*, 17 May 1990, p. A14; Weinbaum, 'Pakistan and Afghanistan', p. 504.

28. Richard Mackenzie, 'After Victory Comes the Hard Part', *Insight*, 31 October 1988, p. 35; *Washington Times*, 8 May 1990, p. A3.

29. *Far Eastern Economic Review*, 25 October 1990, p. 14; *International Defence Review*, No. 7, 1991: 705; AFP from Peshawar, 28 October 1990, in *FBIS/NE*, 29 October 1990, p. 55; *Le Monde*, 6 July 1991, p. 5.

30. *Pravda*, 17 June 1988 and 5 April 1989, p. 5, in *FBIS/SU*, 22 June 1988 and 10 April 1989, pp. 18 and 19; *New York Times Magazine*, 29 December 1991, p. 16.

31. *Washington Post*, 31 August 1988 and 3 September 1989, pp. A19 and A1; IISS, 'Strategic Survey 1989-1990', p. 163.

32. *Los Angeles Times*, 19 November 1989, p. 1; *Washington Post*, 16 August 1988, 16 July, 2 September, and 15 October 1989, pp. A1 and B7; *New York Times*, 17 July 1988 and 17 July 1989, pp. 8 and A5.

33. *New York Times*, 26 February 1989 and 24 October 1990, pp. 15 and A7; *Los Angeles Times*, 19 November 1989, p. 1; *Wall Street Journal*, 9 November 1989, p. A18.

34. *New York Times*, 22 May 1989 and 24 October 1990, pp. A17 and A7; *Wall Street Journal*, 9 November 1989, 16 July and 25 September 1990, pp. A18, A14, and A4.

35. *Bulletin of the Atomic Scientists*, June 1989: 20-26; *New York Times*, 30 March 1987 and 19 May 1989, pp. A18 and A7.

36. *Dawn*, 11 and 19 February 1991, pp. 16 and 6, in *FBIS/NE*, 13 and 21 February 1991, pp. 36 and 55; *Nation*, 28 January 1991, p. 1; *Frontier Post*, 2 March 1991, p. 5; remarks, Tom Gouttierre, Washington, 23 April 1991; *Christian Science Monitor*, 17 July 1991, p. 6; *AFGHANews*, 1 February 1991, p. 1; *Washington Post*, 1 October 1991, p. A12.

37. Kabul Radio, 21 September 1988 and 1 January 1990, in *FBIS/ NE*, 22 September 1988 and 5 January 1990, pp. 33 and 35; State Department, 'Soviet Occupation and Withdrawal', p. 4.

38. *New York Times*, 25 April 1989, p. A10; Tass from New York, 25 and 27 April 1989, in *FBIS/SU*, 25 and 28 April 1989, pp. 29-30 and 8-9.

39. E.g., *Izvestiya*, 16 August 1988, p. 1, and *Pravda*, 23 September 1988 and 7 May 1989, pp. 1 and 5, in *FBIS/SU*, 16 August and 23 September 1988, 8 May 1989, pp. 20-21, 28, and 23-5.

40. Kabul Radio, 21 July 1989, in *FBIS/NE*, 26 July 1989, p. 47.

41. *New York Times*, 24 May 1989, p. A12; *Washington Times*, 4 October 1989, p. A7.
42. *International Defence Review*, No. 7, 1991: 704; David C. Isby, 'Soviet Advisers in Afghanistan—the Involvement Continues', *Jane's Intelligence Review*, June 1991: 244-8; *Moscow News*, No. 34, 1989: 1; *Krasnaya Zvezda*, 17 December 1989, p. 3, in *FBIS/SU*, 27 December 1989, p. 11.
43. *New York Times Magazine*, 29 December 1991, p. 17; David C. Isby, 'Airstrikes on Afghanistan 1989-91', *Jane's Intelligence Review*, November 1991: 506-507.
44. *Krasnaya Zvezda*, 24 April 1991, p. 5, in *FBIS/SU*, 25 April 1991, p. 8.
45. *Izvestiya*, 25 May 1992, p. 5; Radio Odin, Moscow, 8 July 1992.
46. David C. Isby, 'Soviet Arms Deliveries and Aid to Afghanistan, 1989-91', *Jane's Intelligence Review*, August 1991; *International Defence Review*, No. 7, 1991: 704.
47. Tass from Moscow, 11 January 1991, in *FBIS/SU*, 14 January 1991, p. 20; *Komsomolskaya Pravda*, 29 June 1991, p. 4, in *FBIS/SU*, 12 July 1991, p. 16; Bakhtar from Kabul, 28 January 1990, in *FBIS/NE*, 1 February 1990, pp. 51-2.
48. *Pravda*, 24 October 1989, pp. 2-4, in *FBIS/SU*, 24 October 1989, p. 46. See also Moscow Radio, 4 January 1990, and Moscow Television, 24 December 1991, in *FBIS/SU*, 8 January 1990 and 27 December 1991, pp. 14 and 5-6.
49. Kabul Radio, 11 June 1991, in *FBIS/NE*, 14 June 1991, p. 31.
50. Kabul Radio, 13 April 1989, in *FBIS/NE*, 14 April 1989, p. 41.
51. *Pravda*, 4 November 1991, p. 4, in *FBIS/SU*, 6 November 1991, p. 10.
52. *New York Times*, 22 and 31 March 1989, pp. A14 and A3.
53. Kabul Radio, 23 and 27 June 1990, in *FBIS/NE*, 26 June and 3 July 1990, pp. 42 and 52.
54. *Aziya i Afrika Segodnya*, No. 8, 1990: 22-4; Kabul Radio, 22 April and 23 June 1990, in *FBIS/NE*, 23 April and 26 June 1990, pp. 23 and 43 (emphasis added); BBC Television, 10 July 1990.
55. Kabul Radio, 29 June 1990, in *FBIS/NE*, 5 July 1990, p. 30; *Far Eastern Economic Review*, 13 April 1989, p. 21.
56. Kabul Radio, 27 June 1990, in *FBIS/NE*, 3 July 1990, pp. 55-6.
57. Kabul Radio, 27, 28, and 29 June 1990, in *FBIS/NE*, 2, 3, and 5 July 1990, pp. 35, 53, and 30.
58. Kabul Radio, 18 March 1990, in *FBIS/NE*, 20 March 1990, p. 34.
59. *Komsomolskaya Pravda*, 13 June 1990, p. 3, in *FBIS/SU*, 19 June 1990, pp. 18-19; *New York Times*, 5 May 1990, p. 6; Kabul Radio, 26 October 1989, in *FBIS/NE*, 26 October 1989, p. 59.

LAST YEARS OF AFGHAN COMMUNISM 361

60. *Pravda*, 29 December 1990, p. 5, in *FBIS/SU*, 9 January 1991, p. 14; AFP from Kabul, 20 October 1991, in *JPRS-NEA-91-080*, 26 November 1991, p. 50.

61. Kabul Radio, 14, 19, and 21 May 1989, in *FBIS/NE*, 17 and 24 May 1989, pp. 56-9 and 46-9; Bakhtar from Kabul, 19 and 22 May 1989, in *FBIS/NE*, 24 May 1989, pp. 46-9; *Daily Telegraph*, 18 May 1989, p. 12.

62. *Komsomolskaya Pravda*, 12 June 1990, p. 3, and *Pravda*, 25 June 1990, p. 1, in *FBIS/SU*, 19 June and 3 July 1990, pp. 18 and 19; Bakhtar from Kabul, 4 June 1990, in *FBIS/NE*, 6 June 1990, p. 38.

63. Kabul Radio, 17 August 1991, in *FBIS/NE*, 20 August 1991, p. 40.

64. *Afghan Jehad*, April-June 1991: 15; *Nation*, 1 October 1991, p. 1, in *JPRS-NEA-91-080*, 26 November 1991, pp. 51-2; *Far Eastern Econonic Review*, 19 December 1991, pp. 55-7.

65. Kabul Radio, 25 April and 16 July 1990, in *FBIS/NE*, 26 April and 17 July 1990, pp. 36 and 46.

66. *Guardian*, 28 February 1989, p. 5; AFP from Kabul, 8 May 1990, in *FBIS/NE*, 2 February 1989, p. 51; Kabul Radio, 21 February 1989, in *FBIS/NE*, 22 February 1989, p. 51.

67. Notes from a Soviet specialist on Afghanistan, provided to the author by Anthony Arnold, 21 April 1991.

68. Kabul Radio, 6 May 1990, in *FBIS/NE*, 7 May 1990, p. 43; *Izvestiya*, 4 May 1990, p. 1, in *FBIS/SU*, 11 May 1990, p. 14.

69. Kabul Radio, 7 and 10 May 1990, in *FBIS/NE*, 8 and 11 May 1990, pp. 34 and 27; *Le Figaro*, 18 December 1991, p. 4.

70. *New York Times*, 7 April 1990, p. 5; *Keyhan*, 19 April 1990, p. 1, in *FBIS/NE*, 7 May 1990, p. 45; AFP from Kabul, 7 May 1990, in *FBIS/NE*, 8 May 1990, p. 34.

71. Kabul Radio, 27 May 1990, in *FBIS/NE*, 29 May 1990, pp. 46-7.

72. Kabul Radio, 4 April and 24 June 1989, 28 June 1990, in *FBIS/NE*, 5 April and 26 June 1989, 2 July 1990, pp. 41, 22, and 35; *Muslim*, 31 January 1989, p. 1; *Muslim*, 20 April 1990, p. 1, in *FBIS/NE*, 25 April 1990, p. 41.

73. State Department, 'Country Reports...on Human Rights' February 1991, p. 1361.

74. *Za Rubezhom*, No. 3, 1986: 12-13; *Danas*, 20 December 1988, pp. 55-7, in *FBIS/NE*, 4 January 1989, p. 42; BBC, 7 March 1990, in *FBIS/NE*, 7 March 1990, p. 37.

75. AFP from Kabul, 5 March 1990, in *FBIS/NE*, 5 March 1990, p. 40.

76. Tass from Kabul, 6, 7, and 8 March 1990, in *FBIS/SU*, 6, 7, 8, and 9 March 1990, pp. 19-20, 21-2, 34-5, and 6-7; Kabul Radio, 6, 8, 10, and 11 March 1990, in *FBIS/NE*, 6, 9, 12, and 13 March

1990, pp. 35, 38-40, 38, and 46; AFP from Kabul, 6 and 10 March 1990, in *FBIS/NE*, 6 and 12 March 1990, pp. 33 and 32; *New York Times*, 29 April and 10 May 1990, pp. 12 and A4.

77. Kabul Radio, 2 April 1990, in *FBIS/NE*, 3 April 1990, p. 47; *Nation*, 30 June 1990, p. 10, in *FBIS/NE*, 2 July 1990, p. 38; *Afghan Jehad*, January-March 1990: 17.

78. AFP from Islamabad, 7 March 1990, in *FBIS/NE*, 7 and 8 March 1990, pp. 36 and 39; *Pakistan Times*, 7 March 1990, p. 1, in *FBIS/NE*, 7 March 1990, p. 31; BBC, 8 and 17 March 1990, in *FBIS/NE*, 8 and 19 March 1990, pp. 39-40 and 44-5; *Washington Post*, 17 March 1990, p. A19; *New York Times*, 21 March 1990, p. A7.

79. Kabul Radio, 9, 15 March, and 6 May 1990, in *FBIS/NE*, 12, 16 March, and 14 May 1990, pp. 34, 41, and 33; *Al-Sharq Al-Awsat*, 22 March 1990, p. 7, in *FBIS/NE*, 30 March 1990, p. 30; *Washington Post*, 17 March 1990, p. A25.

80. Kabul Radio, 7 and 18 March 1990, in *FBIS/NE*, 7 and 19 March 1990, pp. 33 and 39; AFP from Islamabad, 17 April 1990, in *FBIS/NE*, 18 April 1990, p. 32.

81. *Al-Ittihad*, 12 March 1990, p. 1, in *FBIS/NE*, 14 March 1990, pp. 26-7; Kabul Radio, 7 March 1990, in *FBIS/NE*, 7 March 1990, p. 33; AFP from New Delhi, 12 July 1990 and 10 April 1991, in *FBIS/NE*, 13 July 1990 and 10 April 1991, pp. 35 and 44-5.

82. Kabul Radio, 8 April 1991, in *FBIS/NE*, 9 April 1991, p. 70; AFP from Kabul, 14 November 1991, in *FBIS/NE*, 15 November 1991, p. 40.

83. AFP from Kabul, 20 June and 21 July 1991, in *FBIS/NE*, 20 June and 24 July 1991, pp. 34 and 44; *Trud*, 24 October 1991, p. 4, in *JPRS-UIA-91-027*, 27 November 1991, p. 56.

84. Ibid.; *Economist*, 27 July•1991, p. 34.

85. AFP from Kabul, 30 June, 10 and 21 July 1991, in *FBIS/NE*, 1, 12, and 24 July 1991, pp. 35, 46, and 45.

86. *New Times*, No. 12, 1990: 9.

87. Reuter from Kabul, 10 March 1992; AFP from Mazar-e-Sharif, 8 April 1992.

88. *New York Times Magazine*, 29 December 1991, p. 27; *New Times*, No. 48, 1990: 28; Reuter from Kabul, 10 March 1992.

89. *Izvestiya*, 13 March 1989, p. 4, in *FBIS/SU*, 14 March 1989, p. 14; *New York Times*, 12 August and 13 September 1989, pp. 3 and A12; *New York Times Magazine*, 4 February 1990, p. 27; AFP from Peshawar, 17 April 1989, in *FBIS/NE*, 18 April 1989, p. 45.

90. *Wall Street Journal*, 27 March 1989, p. A1; interview of Brig. Gen. Rahmatullah Safi by Afghan Information and Documentation Centre, Peshawar, May 1989; Tarzi, 'Politics', p. 491; Rubin, 'Soviet Involvement', p. 42.

91. *Washington Post*, 7 August 1989, p. A11.
92. The CPSU politburo commission believed the reports; *CWIHPB*, Nos. 8-9: 184.
93. *New York Times*, 23 April 1989, p. 1; *Christian Science Monitor*, 24 May 1989, p. 3.
94. AFP from Islamabad, 29 October 1991, in *FBIS/NE*, 29 October 1991, p. 49; Kabul Radio, 28 October 1991, in *FBIS/NE*, 31 October 1991, p. 51.
95. Mackenzie, 'Split Force', p. 35; Mackenzie, 'Rebels Calling', p. 20.
96. *Izvestiya*, 8 August 1989, p. 5, in *FBIS/SU*, 9 August 1989, p. 16; *New York Times*, 2 and 16 April 1991, pp. A7 and A10; *Washington Post*, 2 April and 1 June 1991, pp. A9 and A19; Bruce Richardson, 'Khost Busters', *Soldier of Fortune*, November 1991, pp. 61-5.
97. AFP from Peshawar, 5 April 1991, and AFP from Miran Shah, 10 April 1991, in *FBIS/NE*, 5 and 11 April 1991, pp. 42 and 52; *New York Times*, 7 April 1991, p. 10; *Al-Sharq Al-Awsat*, 11 April 1991, p. 14, and *Muslim*, 16 April 1991, p. 2, in *FBIS/NE*, 17 April 1991, p. 30.
98. *New York Times Magazine*, 29 December 1991, p. 27; *Foreign Report*, 14 November 1991, pp. 7-8.
99. *Le Monde*, 6 July 1991; AFP from Islamabad, 13 August 1991, in *FBIS/NE*, 14 August 1991, p. 33.
100. AFP from Peshawar, 28 January and 15 February 1989, 14 February 1990, in *FBIS/NE*, 29 January and 16 February 1989, 14 February 1990, pp. 37, 41-2, and 42; *Al-Ittihad*, 20 February 1989, p. 1, in *FBIS/NE*, 22 February 1989, p. 58.
101. *Trud*, 14 June 1991, p. 3, in *JPRS-UMA-91-021*, 7 August 1991, p. 47; Tajikta-Tass from Dushanbe, 1 August and 5 September 1991, in *FBIS/SU*, 1 August and 6 September 1991, pp. 73 and 12; *Turkmenskaya Iskra*, 11 July 1989, p. 3, in *FBIS/SU*, 28 August 1989, p. 18; *Krasnaya Zvezda*, 27 March 1990 and 6 September 1991, p. 3, in *FBIS/SU*, 29 March 1990 and 13 September 1991, pp. 17 and 22; David C. Isby, 'The Soviet Military and Afghanistan: The Trans-Border War, 1989-91', *Jane's Intelligence Review*, March 1992: 113-18.
102. *Kommunist Tadzhikistana*, 30 December 1987, p. 2, in *FBIS/SU*, 11 January 1988, p. 58; Tass from Dushanbe, 1 December 1989, 12 July 1990, and 11 April 1991, in *FBIS/SU*, 5 December 1989, 13 July 1990, and 12 April 1991, pp. 91, 17-18, and 74-5.
103. *Danas*, 10 January 1988 [*sic*—1989], pp. 54-5, in *FBIS/NE*, 18 January 1989, p. 32.
104. Asia Watch, 'Afghanistan: Forgotten War', pp. 55-60; David C. Isby, 'Postwar Peril: Soviet Minefields', *Soldier of Fortune*, April 1989, p. 35; State Department, 'Hidden Killers: The Global

Problem With Uncleared Landmines: A Report on International Demining' (Washington, July 1993), pp. 9, 30; State Department, 'Hidden Killers: The Global Landmine Crisis' (Washington, January 1995), p. 45.

105. *New York Times*, 17 August 1988 and 3 December 1989, pp. A8 and 23; State Department, 'Country Reports...for 1990', p. 1363; *Washington Post*, 16 May 1988, p. A22.

106. FCO, 'Afghanistan: Continuing Conflict', May 1989, p. 5; *New York Times*, 14 August 1988, p. 9; *Washington Post*, 8 January and 5 July 1989, pp. C2 and A2; AFP from Islamabad, 27 November 1991, in *FBIS/NE*, 29 November 1991, p. 42.

107. State Department, 'Hidden Killers' (1993), p. 43.

108. *New York Times*, 8 September and 8 October 1988, pp. A17 and 5; AFP from Risalpur, 22 March 1989, and from Islamabad, 31 August 1989, in *FBIS/NE*, 22 March and 31 August 1989, pp. 49-50 and 45; *Washington Post*, 21 March and 12 April 1990, pp. A15 and A25.

109. *Afghan Jehad*, July-September 1988: 50-52; Weinbaum, 'Politics of Afghan Resettlement', pp. 287-98; *New York Times*, 18 and 23 June 1988, pp. 5 and A3; *New York Times*, 3 February and 21 November 1989, pp. A6 and A5.

110. *Afghan Jehad*, October-December 1991: 55-8; *Washington Post*, 12 April 1990, p. A25.

111. Transcript, State Department briefing, 22 April 1992; State Department, 'Afghanistan: Six Years', p. 15.

112. *Washington Post*, 14 October 1986, p. A32.

113. *Washington Post*, 10 June 1986 and 18 February 1989, pp. A22 and A33; transcript, State Department briefing, 22 April 1992; U. S. House, Committee on Appropriations, 'Foreign Operations, Export Financing, and Related Programmes Appropriations', Washington, annual series through 1992.

114. *Christian Science Monitor*, 9 September 1987, p. 3; Weinbaum, 'Politics of Afghan Resettlement', p. 298; BBC World Service, 12 January 1988; *Washington Times*, 6 February 1990, p. A7; *Washington Post*, 15 February 1990, p. A46; *New York Times*, 16 February 1990, p. A5.

115. *Christian Science Monitor*, 7 September 1988, p. 1.

116. *New York Times*, 2 November 1989 and 14 January 1990, pp. A13 and 15; *Christian Science Monitor*, 15 October 1991, p. 18.

117. *Afghan Jehad*, April-June 1991: 30-32.

118. Ibid., pp. 13-15; *Izvestiya*, 27 May 1991, p. 4, in *FBIS/SU*, 28 May 1991, pp. 17-18; *Pakistan Times*, 24 May 1991, p. 10, in *FBIS/NE*, 29 May 1991, p. 26.

119. *Afghan Jehad*, October-December 1991: 63-4.

120. *Al-Siyasah*, 18 March 1990, p. 27, in *FBIS/NE*, 22 March 1990, pp. 36-7; *Nation*, 24 December 1990, p. 8, in *FBIS/NE*, 7 January 1991, p. 44; *Al-Sharq Al-Awsat*, 21 April 1990, p. 9, in *FBIS/NE*, 25 April 1990, p. 24; Kabul Radio, 21 October and 29 November 1990, in *FBIS/NE*, 23 October and 3 December 1990, pp. 56 and 52-3.

121. *Washington Post*, 9 May 1991, p. A37.

122. Delhi Radio, 29 August 1990, in *FBIS/NE*, 29 August 1990, p. 50; Weinbaum, 'Pakistan and Afghanistan', p. 505; *Neue Zuercher Zeitung*, 23 November 1990, p. 2; AFP from Kabul, 2 July 1991, in *FBIS/NE*, 3 July 1991, p. 49.

123. Bakhtar from Kabul, 25 January 1990, and Kabul Radio, 28 August 1990 and 31 May 1991, in *FBIS/NE*, 2 February and 29 August 1990, 6 June 1991, pp. 32, 47, and 35.

124. Kabul Radio, 25 September 1991, in *FBIS/NE*, 25 September 1991, pp. 18-26; *New York Times*, 1 October 1991, p. A3.

125. *Pravda*, 27 April 1990, p. 1, in *FBIS/SU*, 30 April 1990, p. 30; *New York Times*, 17 December 1989, p. 26.

126. *International Affairs*, November 1990: 81.

127. *Komsomolskaya Pravda*, 28 August 1991, p. 3, in *FBIS/SU*, 29 August 1991, p. 98; Moscow Radio, 29 May 1991, in *FBIS/SU*, 29 May 1991, p. 23.

128. *Izvestiya*, 15 February 1990, p. 5, in *FBIS/SU*, 15 February 1990, pp. 28-31.

129. Tass from Moscow, 6 June and 4 October 1989, in *FBIS/SU*, 8 June and 5 October 1989, pp. 12 and 18-19. Pastukhov ran the Soviet Komsomol from 1977 to 1982.

130. *Washington Post*, 10 August 1989, p. A27; *New York Times*, 15 December 1989, p. A9.

131. *Washington Times*, 11 January 1990, p. A1; *Washington Post*, 31 January 1990, p. A16; *New York Times*, 14 and 20 January, 24 February 1990, pp. 1, 8, and 8.

132. *New York Times*, 5 and 9 February, 3 May, 5 June, 15 July, and 2 August 1990, pp. A1, A9, A1, A18, 8, and A3; AFP from Islamabad, 12 April 1990, in *FBIS/NE*, 12 April 1990, p. 28; Moscow Radio, 2 August 1990, in *FBIS/SU*, 3 August 1990, pp. 11-12; *FBIS Trends*, 8 August 1990, pp. 6-8; Interfax from Moscow, 23 May 1991, in *FBIS/SU*, 24 May 1991, p. 3.

133. Michael R. Beschloss and Strobe Talbott, *At the Highest Levels: The Inside Story of the End of the Cold War* (Boston, 1993), p. 180.

134. *Washington Post*, 1 June 1991, p. A18.

135. Girardet, *Afghanistan*, pp. 225-32; Bonner, *Among the Afghans*, Chapter 8; Roy, *Islam and Resistance*, pp. 202-03; *New York Times*, 1 November 1985, p. A1.

136. Girardet, *Afghanistan*, pp. 226-30; State Department, 'Afghanistan: Three Years', p. 5, and '... Six Years', p. 8; *Pravda*, 31 March 1989, p. 7, in *FBIS/SU*, 5 April 1989, p. 22. On Soviet prisoners who went West, and some who later returned home, see *Izvestiya*, 10 July 1988, p. 3, in *FBIS/SU*, 14 July 1988, p. 21; *New York Times*, 2 December 1984, 17 October and 23 November 1986, pp. 13, A20, and 22; Tass from Moscow, 19 July 1988, in *FBIS/SU*, 20 July 1988, pp. 25-6; Borovik, *Hidden War*, pp. 127, 201; *Argumenty i Fakty*, No. 31, 1988: 4, in *FBIS/SU*, 3 August 1988, p. 27.

137. *Pravda*, 18 August 1988, p. 6, and *Izvestiya*, 17 July 1989, p. 3, in *FBIS/SU*, 18 August 1988, and 19 July 1989, pp. 18-19 and 31. Gromov said 'several million dollars' were paid to ransom Rutskoy; *Argumenty i Fakty*, No. 8, 1994: 1.

138. Bakhtar from Kabul, 7 May 1985, in *FBIS/SA*, 8 May 1985, pp. C1-2; *Krasnaya Zvezda*, 15 May 1985, p. 3, and *Izvestiya*, 2 June 1985, pp. 4-5, in *FBIS/SU*, 15 May and 5 June 1985, pp. D1-2 and D1-4.

139. Riaz Khan, *Untying*, pp. 363-4.

140. Radio Liberty Research, RL-356-85, 25 October 1985; Kyodo from Islamabad, 19 October 1985, in *FBIS/SU*, 21 October 1985, p. D1.

141. *Moscow News*, No. 38, 1989: 6; Moscow Radio, 1 July 1989, in *FBIS/SU*, 3 July 1989, p. 27.

142. Ludmilla Thorne, testimony, US Congress, Commission on Security and Cooperation in Europe, 'Soviet Army Defectors and Prisoners of War from Afghanistan', 23 March 1988, pp. 8-9; *Wall Street Journal*, 27 June 1988, p. 12; Alexiev, 'Inside', pp. 38 and 61-2; *Komsomolskaya Pravda*, 21 December 1989, p. 2, in *JPRS-UMA-90-006*, 20 March 1990, pp. 24-5; Moscow Television, 2 October 1989, in *FBIS/SU*, 4 October 1989, p. 53; *New York Times*, 17 October 1986, p. A20.

143. Kabul Radio, 14 October 1991, in *FBIS/NE*, 17 October 1991, p. 48; *Pravda*, 21 November 1988, p. 6, in *FBIS/SU*, 25 November 1988, p. 17.

144. E.g., Tass from Moscow, 13 June 1988, and Moscow Radio, 1 July 1989, in *FBIS/SU*, 15 June 1988 and 3 July 1989, pp. 24 and 27; *Komsomolskaya Pravda*, 17 October 1989, p. 4, in *FBIS/SU*, 20 October 1989, p. 61.

145. *Izvestiya*, 29 June 1989, p. 4, in *FBIS/SU*, 30 June 1989, p. 16.

146. Tass from Moscow, 22 November 1991, Interfax from Moscow, 29 November 1991, and Moscow Television, 8 January 1992, in *FBIS/SU*, 25 November and 3 December 1991, 15 January 1992, pp. 24, 23, and 23. On assimilation, see also Kabul Radio, 14 October 1991, in *FBIS/NE*, 17 October 1991, p. 48; *Soldier of*

Fortune, October 1989, pp. 46-7; *Komsomolskaya Pravda*, 29 June 1991, p. 4, and *Trud*, 20 August 1991, p. 3, in *FBIS/SU*, 12 July and 29 August 1991, pp. 17 and 16.

147. E.g., Moscow Radio, 21 June 1988, *Literaturnaya Gazeta*, 29 June 1988, p. 14, Tass from Moscow, 18 October 1988, and *Komsomolskaya Pravda*, 25 November 1988, p. 3, in *FBIS/SU*, 23 and 30 June, 18 October, and 1 December 1988, pp. 13-14, 21, 27, and 16; *Argumenty i Fakty*, No. 8, 1989: 5, in *JPRS-UMA-89-010*, 4 May 1989, p. 84.

148. Ibid.; Moscow Radio, 17 June 1988, *Trud*, 10 January 1989, p. 3, and *Krasnaya Zvezda*, 11 May 1989, p. 1, in *FBIS/SU*, 21 June 1988, 11 January and 16 May 1989, pp. 7, 20-22, and 92; *Moscow News*, No. 29, 1988, p. 4, and No. 30, 1989, p. 9.

149. Tass from Moscow, 4 July 1988, in *FBIS/SU*, 5 July 1988, p. 24; ITAR-Tass from Samara, 20 June 1994; Moscow Television, 2 October 1989, and Tass from Moscow, 28 and 29 November 1989, in *FBIS/SU*, 4 October, 29 and 30 November 1989, pp. 53, 72, 77, and 51; *New York Times*, 29 November 1989, p. A10.

150. Koydo from Islamabad, 20 June 1988, and *Al-Siyasah*, 28 December 1988, p. 17, in *FBIS/NE*, 21 June 1988 and 4 January 1989, pp. 39 and 46; Moscow Radio, 28 November 1989, Tass from Moscow, 15 January 1990, and Moscow Television, 13 August 1991, in *FBIS/SU*, 29 November 1989, 18 January 1990, and 14 August 1991, pp. 26, 20, and 24.

151. *Argumenty i Fakty*, No. 52, 1989: 4-5, in *FBIS/SU*, 9 January 1990, p. 122; Tass from Moscow, 22 November 1991, and Tass from Kabul, 16 and 23 December 1991, in *FBIS/SU*, 25 November, 17 and 24 December 1991, pp. 25, 13, and 55; Kabul Radio, 9 December 1991, in *FBIS/NE*, 16 December 1991, p. 71.

152. ITAR-Tass from Moscow, 23 May 1996; Intelnews from Kiev, 4 November 1995.

CHAPTER 12

MUJAHIDEEN VICTORY

Fourteen years and a day after the 1978 *coup* that brought the PDPA to power, the Kabul regime gave up its few remaining bits of that shattered power. A cutoff of Soviet aid led to the downfall of a leadership decimated by internecine strife, deserted by key domestic supporters, demoralized, and overwhelmed by enemies. But the *mujahideen* interim council that assumed the tattered trappings of an Afghan state on 28 April 1992 was disunited. While the victory ended the Communist effort to shape Afghanistan, it only began another bloody stage in the struggle over power and policy that had wracked the country for decades. Authority was dispersed into regional fiefdoms as a fight for the national symbolism of Kabul devastated the capital.

The USSR's ability and willingness to sustain its old client state had been dwindling for several years. They were dealt a fatal blow by the unsuccessful attempt of hard-liners from the CPSU, KGB, and interior ministry, plus some military leaders though not the Soviet armed forces as a whole, to oust Gorbachev in August 1991. Many of these were the same people who had resisted Gorbachev's efforts to withdraw the Soviet Army and who then insisted on continuing aid to Kabul. The key ones were General Varennikov and KGB chief Kryuchkov. The failed *coup* attempt meant that those 'who had insisted on keeping Najibullah at any price have been removed from power', a senior Soviet diplomat said.[1] Kryuchkov in particular was accused of having kept the war going and of sabotaging efforts to obtain the *mujahideen*'s release of Soviet war prisoners in return for a halt of Soviet arms to Kabul.[2]

Under civilian officials who were newly enfranchised by the removal of *coup* leaders, the USSR was able to begin 'freeing itself step by step from its commitments to remain on the side of the Najibullah regime to the last', *Izvestiya* commented.[3] Officials around the fast-fading Gorbachev were acutely aware of their country's deteriorating economy. They saw aid for Afghanistan not only as an unsupportable drain but also as an obstacle to negotiating badly needed Western aid.

NEGATIVE SYMMETRY

Less than a month after the *coup*'s failure, the USSR and the United States agreed on negative symmetry, the halt of arms supplies to both sides in Afghanistan that had been discussed fruitlessly since the closing rounds of the Geneva negotiations three and a half years earlier. An agreement signed in Moscow on 13 September 1991 by the post-*coup* foreign minister, Boris D. Pankin, and Secretary of State James A. Baker III, said their governments would stop arms deliveries by 1 January 1992, with no increase in the scale of deliveries up to then. It also called for 'a ceasefire and a cutoff of weapons deliveries from all other sources...'. Adding what diplomats called 'negative symmetry plus', it said the two countries would 'work toward withdrawal of major weapons systems from Afghanistan'. This referred in particular to Scud missiles and possibly MIG-27 fighter-bombers on the Soviet side, and possibly Stinger missiles from the United States.[4]

The United States closed the arms pipeline to Pakistan in September. Gorbachev ordered in November the withdrawal of military advisers from Afghanistan, including Scud launching crews. Soviet military deliveries ended on 15 December,[5] and the USSR was dissolved eleven days later.

None of its successor republics had the resources or will to send significant amounts of armaments to help the Kabul regime. A general on the Afghan general staff said his troops had battle reserves for only five or six months.[6]

Pakistan welcomed the Moscow agreement but refused to commit itself to stop deliveries, which Afghan military intelligence said continued to be trucked across the Durand Line after 1 January 1992.[7] Islamabad, whose influence over the *mujahideen* had always depended upon its control of the arms pipeline, apparently worried that giving up that tool would enable such outsiders as Iran and Libya to influence the future of the sensitive border area and Afghanistan as a whole. Saudi Arabia also made no public commitment to halt arms aid. *Mujahideen* leaders unanimously rejected a ceasefire suggestion from Najibullah but differed in reactions to the arms cutoff. The more anti-American leaders, who only admitted their long dependence on the CIA pipeline by complaining during dry periods, reacted predictably. Khales called the agreement a 'typical US betrayal', while Sayyaf termed it 'unjust, self-motivated, and one-sided'.[8]

End of Economic Aid

Just as ominous for Najibullah as a halt to arms aid was the looming end to economic support. After the Moscow *coup* attempt, Soviet officials told Kabul they would honour the 1991 economic aid commitment. But they refused to comment on prospects for 1992 or beyond, despite pleas from Prime Minister Khaliqyar on an early October trip to Moscow.[9] Soviet media reflected a debate within the government, and with an increasingly dominant Russian republic government, over the possible effects of cutting off Kabul.[10]

Moscow tried to drive what Afghan officials thought a hard bargain for expanded commercial ties with Russia, Central Asian republics, and other Soviet successor states.[11]

But Najibullah's withered area of control lacked a productive economic base from which to make trade agreements. Not even the gas fields around Sheberghan could help, though they had long proved Afghanistan's main export earner as they paid for Soviet loans. Pipelines to the USSR, which had been closed before the Soviet army's withdrawal, had not reopened by the end of 1991. Besides, gas-surplus Central Asian republics did not need Afghan gas. Afghan officials talked grandly but unrealistically of piping gas to central Europe. Expensive new pipelines would have been needed, however, and the caloric value of Afghan gas was so low that its ability to cover pipeline costs to distant markets was doubtful. While casting around desperately for economic help from such countries as India, Turkey, and even China, the Kabul regime had to turn increasingly to Afghan private traders to import grain, fuel, and other essentials. They staved off disaster for a time.

MUJAHIDEEN IN MOSCOW

In mid-November 1991, Moscow received the first official visit of a *mujahideen* delegation. It was headed by the Peshawar interim government's foreign minister, Burhanuddin Rabbani—over opposition from Hekmatyar, Sayyaf, and Khales that Pakistan and Saudi Arabia had to quell—and included the president of the Tehran-based coalition of Shi'ite guerrillas, Rakhmatullah Mortazavi. The delegation negotiated with Soviet Foreign Minister Pankin, Russia's new Vice President Aleksandr V. Rutskoy—a Hero of the Soviet Union for flying 428 missions, bombing, rocketing, and strafing the *mujahideen*, and for being shot down twice—and Russian Foreign Minister Andrey V. Kozyrev, as well as representatives of some other republics.[12] The Russian role signified the USSR's dying authority as well as dissension over Afghanistan policy. Russia under President Boris N. Yeltsin was more eager than Soviet officials to be rid of the Afghan problem at any cost except giving up the chance to recover prisoners. It was also more ready to scuttle Najibullah.[13] Russian participation in the negotiations therefore put pressure on Pankin to accede to *mujahideen* demands.

As one of the last major diplomatic actions of the crumbling Soviet state, Pankin issued with Rabbani on 15 November a joint statement that condemned the Soviet invasion and wartime role in Afghanistan. This remarkable—indeed, only a short time before, unthinkable—position of a Soviet foreign minister completed the transition from Brezhnevian bluster in 1979 through Andropov's incomplete reassessment to Gorbachev's discrediting of the invasion decision.

The joint statement 'confirmed the necessity for complete transfer of state power to an interim Islamic government', said this interim government would decide 'the validity of all agreements signed after 1978 between the Soviet Union' and the Kabul regime, and said further that both 'sides agreed to do everything possible to release all' prisoners. Rabbani's delegation declared in the statement that 'general elections will be held in Afghanistan within a two-year period from the moment a transfer of power from the Kabul regime to an interim government takes place', with help from the United Nations and the Islamic Conference Organization. 'The Soviet side agrees prior to January 1992 to stop all supplies to the Kabul regime of arms, military goods, *and fuel for military purposes*,' and to recall all military personnel from Afghanistan. 'The Soviet Union without fail will take part in the common effort to reconstruct the ravages of war,' it promised, and also that a joint body would be established within a month to implement the decisions and carry out further negotiations.[14] Instead, the USSR collapsed.

The halt of military fuel was an important addition to the Soviet-American negative symmetry agreement that meant the regime's armed forces would soon quit running. The statement included almost everything Rabbani sought except removing Najibullah, a subject that had been argued among Soviet officials. Pankin said he told Rabbani that the USSR had burned its fingers once changing Afghan leaders, and 'we do not want to interfere again from the other side'.[15] Despite this, *Pravda* reported 'harsh questions' in Kabul on why 'Moscow reacted with such uncommon thoughtlessness to the *mujahideen*'s demands for power...'.[16] Najibullah tried to put the best possible face on the situation, ignoring the psychological damage to his cause from both the dying USSR and its main successor, Russia, opting out of the Afghanistan problem.[17] Hekmatyar, Sayyaf, and Khales, the Peshawar leaders closest to ISI's hard-liners who wanted to fight on to absolute victory rather than cut any deal, denounced Rabbani's success and became obstructive.[18]

Prisoner Problems

Rabbani promised the *mujahideen* 'will take measures to release the first batch of [Soviet prisoners] before 1 January 1992'. One soldier was released two days after the Moscow statement. Then Islamists, who held most of the prisoners, refused to cooperate.[19] Rutskoy visited Pakistan at the end of 1991 for talks with its government and the *mujahideen*. His hopes of taking home a sizeable number of prisoners were disappointed. The main reason was that Hekmatyar was uncooperative, insulting, and contemptuous of Pakistani attempts to work something out, possibly reflecting ISI's attitude toward foreign ministry peace efforts. Rutskoy reported later that all he got was a list of 56 prisoners, fourteen of whom were definitely still alive. In the following 15 months, the *mujahideen* released six Soviet prisoners.[20] A few more went home later, but most remaining prisoners were caught in Moscow politics, disputes among resistance groups, and *mujahideen* hopes of trading them for missing Afghans who might be held in former Soviet states— although, other than about 25 Afghan criminals, authorities in Russia denied holding any.[21] The issue gradually faded into obscurity, and misery for the prisoners' families.

PAKISTAN'S CHANGED POSITION

With both the United States and Saudi Arabia firmly behind a political solution in Afghanistan, Pakistan began to resolve the split in its position between the foreign ministry and ISI. The politically powerful chief of Pakistan's army staff, Gen. Asif Nawaz Janjua, reportedly was embarrassed by the failure of *mujahideen* leaders—particularly Hekmatyar—to be more forthcoming with Rutskoy. He also apparently felt that negative symmetry made a military solution no longer feasible.[22] On 25 January 1992, Pakistani officials who made policy on Afghanistan held their first meeting in almost nine months. Prime Minister Mohammad Nawaz Sharif presided, Asif Nawaz and ISI chief Durrani attended, and so did senior foreign ministry officials. Pakistani sources said three factors shaped their discussion: the *mujahideen* failure at Gardez that indicated military victory was beyond reach, especially after negative symmetry took effect; loss of patience with obstructionist Islamists, particularly Hekmatyar, as a result of the Rutskoy visit debacle and of the Islamists' inability to offer any alternative path toward peace; and Pakistan's hopes of opening trade routes across a pacified Afghanistan in order to benefit economically from becoming the outlet to the sea for newly independent republics of the former Soviet Central Asia. Later reports suggested that another factor was a desire to improve relations with the United States, which had cut off aid and major military sales to Pakistan because it was believed to be pursuing a nuclear weapons programme.[23]

The group of officials decided, and the foreign ministry announced two days later, that Pakistan would 'support the UN Secretary-General's efforts for convening of an Afghan assembly to decide an interim government acceptable to the Afghans'. All *mujahideen* 'and patriotic Afghan elements' were urged to cooperate.[24] This was immediately seen by the Islamists as Pakistan's abandoning its determination to put them in power in Kabul. Such leaders as Sayyaf attacked the decision. So did the Islamists' Pakistani supporters; Jamaat leader Hussain Ahmad in particular tried to use the new policy as a domestic political tool to force Nawaz Sharif's government into a more fundamentalist policy.[25] Kabul reacted by halting its virulent anti-Pakistani propaganda. The new United Nations Secretary-General, Boutros Boutros-Ghali, said he was sending Sevan back to the region because '[t]he time is ripe…to take concrete steps to promote a comprehensive political settlement'.[26]

REVIVED UN EFFORTS

Sevan canvassed a plan not unlike the one Cordovez had offered in July 1987. Some 150 leading Afghans selected from lists prepared by and acceptable to all factions—the regime, *mujahideen* in Peshawar and Tehran, the former king and his backers, other exiles, and some independent Afghans—would, by late April, select 30 or 35 members of a working group. It would organize a decision-making *loya jirgah* and name an interim government, from which working group members would be excluded. The interim government and *jirgah* would be responsible for holding elections for a permanent government, whose form the *jirgah* would decide.[27]

Najibullah announced on 18 March that he would 'not insist on my personal participation in the proposed Afghan gathering…'. He said the regime would transfer power to 'the interim government as of the first day of the transition period', but three weeks later Najibullah said he would give up the presidency when the working group was organized, without waiting for it to set up an interim government.[28] With Sevan proclaiming that 'peace is at hand', Boutros-Ghali announced on 10 April agreement in principle for a

15-man pre-transitional council to be announced soon and take power in Kabul.[29] But Islamist hard-liners Hekmatyar, Sayyaf, and Khales denounced the plan. They insisted that only *mujahideen* could take part in any new arrangement, barring regime survivors, neutral Afghans, exiles, supporters of Zahir Shah, and others.[30] None the less, *mujahideen* chiefs, in danger of being marginalized by the United Nations process, were 'engulfed by despair', Rabbani said later.[31] Briefly, it seemed that the collapse of the USSR, the weariness of other outsiders with the struggle, and United Nations' diplomacy might finally be bringing together a settlement.

REVOLT IN THE NORTH

In late 1991 Najibullah began to doubt the loyalty of Dostam, the Uzbek commander of the Jowzjan militia that had, since the Soviet withdrawal, been the regime's most effective fighting force. Massoud had long been wooing Dostam and, by some reports, Dostam had made a private peace with him while continuing to let Kabul deploy the Jowzjanis in other parts of the country.[32] Fearing trouble, Najibullah banished Dostam and his troops from Kabul. In late January 1992, the regime tried to replace a Tajik general, who sat on the Watan ruling council, with a Pushtun general as commander of the Afghan army garrison at Heiraton, the big base stocked with Soviet military supplies near the Afghan end of the Amu Darya bridge from Termez. The Tajik, Maj.-Gen. Abdul Momen, refused to relinquish command. He was supported by Dostam and by Sayyed Jaffar Naderi, the Tajik militia commander who controlled most of the road from Heiraton to the Salang pass.[33]

The end of Soviet subsidies for Kabul apparently was a key factor in this defiance. With the regime no longer able to pay their mercenaries, Dostam and Naderi calculated that it was time to begin repositioning themselves with their old enemies, the *mujahideen*. It was also time to seize control of the large Soviet military stocks built up at Heiraton just before the aid cutoff, rather than have them pass on to Kabul. In addition, there was an ethnic factor: Tajiks and Uzbeks who had long been dominated by Pushtuns united to defy the predominately Pushtun regime and insist on a larger national voice. Although the rebellion seemed pure opportunism, Dostam later asserted with questionable honesty that, ever since Najibullah came to power in 1986, he had been gaining his confidence in order to acquire weapons to overthrow him.[34]

The mercenaries, joined by some regime generals in the north, got in touch with Massoud and agreed to work under the orders of one leader for a united Islamic state, putting aside 'all secessionist inclinations', and to 'show remorse for their past', Massoud said.[35] Massoud's Supervisory Council of the North, which already dominated northeastern Afghanistan, was paralleled in the northwest by Dostam and Naderi with a new National Islamic Movement formed in Mazar-e-Sharif. By March, virtually all of the country north of the Hindu Kush was united in defiance of Kabul and determination to end the war. This meant the fading away of the Islam versus Communism motivation that had contributed to years of war, although the opportunism of a Dostam or a Hekmatyar had always flourished in non-ideological ways. The new alignment showed that the old Afghan contest over power, central authority, and ethnic balance still existed, but with new players, more and better weapons, and different rules.

The Kabul Cabal

On 9 March Najibullah angrily accused Dostam, Naderi, and several Kabul political leaders, including Karmal and Barialay, of threatening national unity.[36] His statement seemed to reach out for a broader consensus, but instead it caused many regime officials to begin to adjust to his not being around much longer. The Afghan army lost heart for continuing to fight the *mujahideen*, particularly without Dostam's and Naderi's troops to deal with the toughest challenges. So Najibullah's 18 March acceptance of Sevan's plan and promise to step down came as he was already losing control. On 21 March the commander of the Kabul garrison, Deputy Defence Minister Mohammad Nabi Azimi, flew to Mazar-e-Sharif, ostensibly to try to put down the rebellion. Instead, he showed understanding of it.[37] Some reports suggested that Azimi was part of a Kabul cabal that had encouraged the northern revolt as one element in a plot against Najibullah that involved Karmal and his personal following of dissident Parchamis.[38]

As the regime began to crumble, Russian President Yeltsin learned on 7 April—reportedly to his surprise—that some 200 specialists from the former Soviet Army and KGB were still advising Kabul. Such defiance of Gorbachev's November order to withdraw all advisers showed continued opposition in Moscow to abandoning Afghanistan. Yeltsin had the specialists flown out between 9 and 15 April.[39] This further eroded regime stability.

NAJIBULLAH'S DOWNFALL

Smelling victory, *mujahideen* leaders rushed to seize Kabul, the symbol of national control. By 15 April Kabul lay virtually defenceless before Massoud's forces, but after taking Bagram he held his men north of the capital. On 17 or 18 April, Massoud met in Jabal Saraj with Dostam, Naderi, and Momen to reach a formal agreement on cooperation.[40] In reaction to Massoud's moves and Kabul's weakening, Hekmatyar—who left Peshawar on 18 April to take field command of his forces—started moving his ISI-aided forces up from south of Kabul. Elsewhere, Afghan army commanders began making deals that enabled resistance forces and local notables to take control of Herat, Qandahar, Jalalabad, and other key towns. The war had ended almost everywhere except Kabul by about 20 April.[41]

The regime shattered under the growing military and political pressure. Some officials hoped for a consensus transition; others were divided between those who preferred that Massoud or Hekmatyar seize the capital. Hekmatyar's supporters included many of the same hard-line Pushtun Khalqis who had sympathized with if not backed Tanai's *coup* attempt two years earlier, particularly in the interior ministry and parts of WAD, and the army.[42] They were, however, outmanœuvered by those who for ethnic or other reasons preferred to see the northern coalition take over. Najibullah summoned WAD and army leaders to a reportedly stormy meeting on 15 April. His Pushtun supporters, led by the head of military intelligence, General Mohammad Omar, and by WAD boss Yaqubi, accused four officials of treason for negotiating with Dostam and allowing Massoud to advance. The four were Azimi, Vice President Mohammed Rafi, army chief of staff Mohammed Asif Delawar, and the third-rank WAD official, Yor Muhammad.[43] But, seemingly confirming the accusation that Azimi and others had already made a deal with the northerners, Azimi sent some fifteen planes to Mazar-e-Sharif on the day of Najibullah's meeting. They brought back about 600 of Dostam's troops who seized Kabul airport and fanned out south of the city to block Hekmatyar's advance.[44]

Najibullah went home from the meeting, found that his security detail had been disarmed by men answering to Azimi, and panicked.[45] Sevan, who had been in Pakistan negotiating with *mujahideen* groups on the transition plan, flew into Kabul around midnight in his chartered United Nations' plane. At about 2 a.m. on 16 April, Najibullah with his brother Hamadzai and an aide tried to go to the airport to fly in the UN plane to India, which had offered him asylum and where his family already was.[46] But troops— Dostam said later they were the regime's Republican Guard forces—turned Najibullah back from the airport, saying they had no instructions to let him leave. He then found refuge in a UN compound in Kabul with Sevan, who took on a moral obligation for Najibullah because of his cooperation in trying to work out a peaceful transition. The failure of Sevan's peace efforts left his position untenable with the *mujahideen*, and he was recalled by UN headquarters on 19 June.[47] Yaqubi was reported to have committed suicide— with 'four bullets in the head', by one account. Defence Minister Watanjar ended up in hospital seriously wounded for unexplained reasons, while Omar and others were arrested by Azimi's supporters.[48]

Najibullah's foreign minister, Abdul Wakil, followed tradition by turning on him in a manner reminiscent of Amin's 1979 criticism of the fallen Taraki and Najibullah's own 1986 criticism of Karmal. Wakil said on 16 April that Najibullah had, contrary to expectations of government and Watan party leaders, 'resorted to fleeing the country irresponsibly...because of the fear of peace and because of the fear...that he might be held accountable for a number of his actions before the people of Afghanistan.... [He was] a major obstacle for the restoration of peace'. Watan's executive committee denounced Najibullah as having 'wanted to create a so-called power vacuum and to bring about chaos in the country'. The government said he had 'illegally resigned contrary to the provisions of the constitution and ha[d] steathily fled...'. Power was now held, Wakil said, by the Watan executive committee and the government's four vice presidents—whom Najibullah had ordered dismissed on 26 March, apparently to clear the way for the United Nations' transition plan. Vice President Abdul Rahim Hatef became acting president, but Azimi seemed temporarily to hold the most power while Wakil was publicly most active. Hatef publicly invited the *mujahideen* to 'come along and run the state apparatus'.[49]

The change in Kabul was symbolized by the secret removal on the night of 18-19 April of tank No. 815 from a pedestal in front of the Arg, the old royal and now presidential palace. The tank in which Watanjar had led the attack that brought the PDPA to power fourteen years earlier was replaced with red and pink geraniums. The regime began releasing both ordinary criminals and political prisoners from Pul-i-Charki prison. The latter included Panjshiri and other former PDPA leaders involved in Tanai's *coup* attempt.[50]

STRUGGLE OVER KABUL

Wakil flew north to talk with Massoud, who was too wary to rush into the vacuum. 'If I enter the city, it is likely to whip up disagreements between Pushtun and non-Pushtun,' he explained. 'It is therefore preferable to persuade everybody of the need for a peaceful solution.'[51] Typically, Hekmatyar was not so moderate. While criticizing Massoud for having talked to Wakil, he demanded that the regime surrender unconditionally by 26 April to a council named by him alone to form a provisional government, or, he said, he would capture Kabul.[52] But with *mujahideen* leaders in Peshawar working on an agreed, shared takeover, Hekmatyar decided he could not wait until 26 April. Before dawn on 24 April, the Friday holy day, some 450 of his Hezb fighters were smuggled into the downtown Kabul compound of the interior ministry. The minister, Paktin, was a hard-line Pushtun Khalqi with whom Hekmatyar was prepared to cooperate, as he had done with Tanai in 1990. Again, personal ambition and Pushtun solidarity were more important to Hekmatyar than anti-Communism or *mujahideen* solidarity. Other Hezb troops infiltrated around Dostam's men. Massoud charged that this was a conspiracy with Paktin, a *coup* attempt to snatch power from a *mujahideen* coalition that was agreed on in Peshawar on 25 April.[53] On that day Hekmatyar claimed control of Kabul, said there was no need for coalition leaders to come to the capital, and warned he would shoot their plane down if they tried.[54]

In response, Massoud finally sent his men into Kabul to join with Dostam's forces in seizing many important points before Hezb could get to them and in driving Hezb out of such already seized places as the Arg. Following a decision by Peshawar leaders, Massoud announced the formation of a six-man commission headed by himself to administer the capital. Azimi ordered all Afghan armed forces to obey Massoud's orders, but the military split along ethnic and political lines. For several days, battle-torn Kabul was chaotically divided among loosely cooperating fighters of Massoud and Dostam with some army support, Hekmatyar's Hezb cooperating with some interior troops and regular army men, Shi'ite guerrillas, and miscellaneous other armed men. By 28 April, with Dostam's men in the fighting vanguard, Hezb had been cleared from central Kabul but remained in positions from which they could fire artillery and rockets into it.[55]

Manœuvering in Peshawar

The coalition decision in Peshawar followed an intensification of squabbling for position. Pakistan had tried immediately after Boutros-Ghali's 10 April statement, to get the *mujahideen* leaders to agree on a transitional council representing all Afghan elements. But, with victory in sight, leaders who had been built up—if not simply created—by Pakistan's decisions on distributing American, Saudi, and other aid, were not very susceptible to high-level Pakistani efforts to exert influence.[56] Hekmatyar's arrogance forced the other leaders to reach late on 24 April a partial agreement in the presence of Nawaz Sharif, other Pakistani officials, and Hussain Ahmad. United Nations' representatives were also present, but the world body had been discredited in *mujahideen* eyes by Sevan's commitment to help Najibullah leave Kabul.[57]

The Peshawar agreement called for a council headed by Mojaddedi and composed of ten nominees of the main Peshawar groups, ten *ulema* (Islamic scholars), and 30 *mujahideen* field commanders. After two months, the council was to be converted into or superceded by a government with Rabbani as president, Hekmatyar or his nominee as prime minister, Massoud as defence minister, and other ministerial posts distributed among other Peshawar groups according to an agreed list. The division of power between the president and prime minister was left vague. This government was supposed to organize within a further four months a *loya jirgah*—its composition was unclear—that would choose a broader-based government, which would conduct elections for a permanent government within a year.[58] The timetable was similar to the United Nations' broadly representative plan, but this was a narrowly *mujahideen* arrangement. Representatives of Hekmatyar and of the Iran-based Shi'ite coalition, the *Wahdat-e-Islami-ye* (Islamic Unity Party), known as Wahdat, walked out of the final meeting with Nawaz Sharif because they felt they had not been given large enough roles.[59]

A NEW REGIME

Had it not been for Hekmatyar's threat to shoot down the coalition's plane, *mujahideen* leaders headed by Mojaddedi might have flown to Kabul on 27 April and assumed charge on the fourteenth anniversary of the Saur *coup*. But the threat caused Mojaddedi's group to drive over the Khyber Pass to Kabul. It arrived at 11 a.m. on 28 April as *mujahideen* fired jubilantly into the air and chanted '*Allah o Akbar*'.[60] In a ceremony that afternoon at the foreign ministry, described as the first meeting of the Islamic Jihad Council of Afghanistan, Mojaddedi assumed the country's interim presidency. Although he said he was 'receiving power from the Kabul regime', there was in the confusion no clear turnover, no formal surrender or transfer of power. Instead, former top officials simply congratulated Mojaddedi and his colleagues on claiming the authority that they had lost.[61] However, with the symbolism of a Kabul ceremony went virtually no real authority. Anarchy reigned. Shortly after the ceremony, fighting broke out nearby between the council's supporters and Hekmatyar's men, with each group eagerly enlisting former PDPA stalwarts on its side. This fight went on for years with shifting lineups of combatants.

Thus ended, with the proverbial whimper, a disastrous PDPA rule in Kabul that had begun with naively Marxist ideas, become dominated by Soviet imperialism, and ended up outlasting Communist rule in Moscow and the Soviet Union itself.

NOTES

1. Tass from Moscow, 14 November 1991, in *FBIS/SU*, 19 November 1991, p. 19; *Komsomolskaya Pravda*, 15 October 1991, p. 5, in *JPRS-UIA-91-025*, 5 November 1991, pp. 28-9.
2. Moscow Television, 20 and 29 September 1991, in *FBIS/SU*, 23 and 30 September 1991, pp. 55 and 69.
3. *Izvestiya*, 9 October 1991, p. 6, in *FBIS/SU*, 11 October 1991, p. 70.
4. Tass from Moscow, 13 September 1991, in *FBIS/SU*, 13 September 1991, pp. 3-4; *New York Times* and *Washington Post*, 14 September 1991, both p. A1.
5. Reuter from Kabul, 30 December 1991; *Izvestiya*, 20 November 1991, p. 1, in *FBIS/SU*, 20 November 1991, p. 13.
6. *Krasnaya Zvezda*, 31 January 1992, p. 3, in *FBIS-R/CE*, 20 February 1992, p. 104.
7. Ibid.; Reuter from Islamabad, 16 September and 31 December 1991.
8. AFP from Islamabad, 13 and 14 September 1991, in *FBIS/NE*, 16 and 17 September 1991, pp. 45-6 and 49-50; *Pakistan Times*, 16 September 1991, p. 10.
9. Kabul Radio, 14 October 1991, and Bakhtar from Kabul, 30 October and 3 November 1991, in *FBIS/NE*, 17 and 31 October,

5 November 1991, pp. 47, 51-2, and 62; Interfax and Tass from Moscow, 4 October 1991, in *FBIS/SU*, 7 October 1991, pp. 22 and 65-6.

10. *Izvestiya*, 16 September 1991, p. 5, and *Pravda*, 18 November 1991, p. 4, in *FBIS/SU*, 17 September and 20 November 1991, pp. 12-14 and 15-16; *Rabochaya Tribuna*, 19 October 1991, p. 1.

11. AFP from Kabul, 8 November 1991, in *FBIS/NE*, 8 November 1991, pp. 42-3.

12. Moscow Radio, 14 November 1991, and Interfax from Moscow, 18 November 1991, in *FBIS/SU*, 15 and 19 November 1991, pp. 73-4 and 16; *Afghan Jehad*, October-December 1991: 22-3.

13. Tass from Moscow, 3 October 1991, in *FBIS/SU*, 4 October 1991, pp. 62-3; *Komsomolskaya Pravda*, 15 October 1991, p. 5, in *JPRS-UIA-91-025*, 5 November 1991, p. 29.

14. Text, *Afghan Jehad*, October-December 1991: 22-3 (emphasis added).

15. *Komsomolskaya Pravda*, 15 October 1991, p. 5, and *Delovoy Mir*, 20 November 1991, p. 2, in *JPRS-UIA-91-025* and *JPRS-UIA-92-001*, 5 November 1991 and 17 January 1992, pp. 28 and 70; Reuter from Moscow, 12 November 1991.

16. *Pravda*, 22 November 1991, p. 4, in *FBIS/SU*, 26 November 1991, p. 15.

17. Kabul Radio, 18 November 1991, in *FBIS/NE*, 19 November 1991, pp. 43-4; *Kabul Times*, 7 December 1991, p. 1.

18. AFP from Islamabad, 17 November 1991, in *FBIS/NE*, 18 November 1991, pp. 49-50.

19. Ibid.; AFP from Peshawar, 26 November 1991, in *FBIS/NE*, 26 November 1991, p. 49.

20. Reuter from Islamabad, 27 January 1992; *News*, 28 January 1992, p. 1; Moscow Television, 26 December 1991, in *FBIS/SU*, 27 December 1991, p. 44; *Nezavisimaya Gazeta*, 31 March 1993, p. 4, in *FBIS-R/CE*, 23 April 1993, p. 71.

21. Moscow Television, 12 July 1993, in *FBIS/CE*, 13 July 1993, p. 53; Interfax from Moscow, 24 June 1992 and 9 March 1993, in *FBIS/CE*, 26 June 1992 and 10 March 1993, pp. 31-2 and 17; *Izvestiya*, 6 October 1992, p. 8.

22. *Muslim*, 5 January 1992, p. 1, in *FBIS/NE*, 6 January 1992, pp. 69-70; *News*, 28 January 1992, p. 1.

23. *News*, 28 January 1992, p. 1; Reuter from Islamabad, 27 January 1992; Islamabad Radio, 30 January 1992, in *FBIS/NE*, 31 January 1992, p. 72; *New York Times*, 19 February 1992, p. A10.

24. Text of foreign ministry statement, 27 January 1992, obtained privately.

25. *News*, 1 February 1992, p. 12; *Muslim*, 29 January and 8 April 1992, pp. 1 and 5.

26. Reuter from United Nations, 27 January 1992.

27. AFP from Peshawar, 6 February 1992, in *FBIS/NE*, 7 February 1992, p. 16.

28. *New York Times*, 13 March 1992, p. A1; Kabul Radio, 18 March 1992, in *FBIS/NE*, 19 March 1992, p. 29; AFP from Kabul, 9 April 1992.

29. AP from Islamabad, 2 April 1992; Reuter from Geneva, 10 April 1992.

30. AFP from Islamabad, 9 April 1992, and *News*, 10 April 1992, p. 12, in *FBIS/NE*, 10 and 13 April 1992, pp. 31 and 41; Reuter from Islamabad, 10 April 1992.

31. Kabul Radio, 6 May 1992, in *FBIS/NE*, 7 May 1992, p. 33.

32. *Financial Times*, 27 April 1992, p. 14; *Washington Times*, 18 May 1992, p. A8.

33. *News* and *Nation*, 28 January 1992, p. 1, in *FBIS/NE*, 30 January 1992, pp. 38-9; AFP from Kabul, 8 February 1992; AFP from Mazar-e-Sharif, 8 April 1992.

34. Winchester, 'Blood Feud', p. 32; *Al-Wasat*, 29 June 1992, pp. 22-3, in *JPRS-NEA-92-087*, 14 July 1992, p. 54.

35. Ibid.; *Al-Hayah*, 7 May 1992, p. 4, in *FBIS/NE*, 13 May 1992, pp. 45-6.

36. Reuter from Kabul, 10 March 1992.

37. AFP from Kabul, 19 March 1992, in *FBIS/NE*, 20 March 1992, pp. 39-41; Reuter from Kabul, 19 April 1992; *New York Times*, 20 April 1992, p. A8.

38. AFP from Kabul, 13 May 1992, in *FBIS/NE*, 14 May 1992, p. 37; *News*, 17 May 1992, p. 12, in *FBIS/NE*, 19 May 1992, p. 57.

39. Tass from Moscow, 16 April 1992, and *Kuranty*, 23 April 1992, 1, in *FBIS/CE*, 17 and 24 April 1992, pp. 14 and 19-20; AFP from Kabul, 13 April 1992.

40. Davis, 'Afghan Army', p. 136.

41. AFP from Islamabad, 14 April, AFP from Kabul, 16 April, and AFP from Quetta, 20 April 1992, in *FBIS/NE*, 15, 16, and 21 April 1992, pp. 61, 50, and 48; Islamabad Radio, 20 April 1992, in *FBIS/NE*, 21 April 1992, p. 49.

42. Davis, 'Afghan Army', p. 134; Winchester, 'Blood Feud', p. 34.

43. *Nation*, 23 April 1992, p. 1, in *FBIS/NE*, 24 April 1992, p. 28; *Le Monde*, 25 April 1992, p. 4, in *FBIS/NE*, 29 April 1992, p. 38.

44. AFP from Kabul, 15 and 16 April 1992, in *FBIS/NE*, 16 April 1992, pp. 48-50; Reuter from Kabul, 30 April 1992.

45. *Nation*, 23 April 1992, p. 1, in *FBIS/NE*, 24 April 1992, p. 28; *Le Monde*, 25 April 1992, p. 4, in *FBIS/NE*, 29 April 1992, p. 38.

46. Kabul Radio, 31 March and 16 April 1992, in *FBIS/NE*, 7 and 17 April 1992, pp. 20 and 29-30; Delhi Radio, 19 April 1992, in *FBIS/NE*, 20 April 1992, pp. 32-3.

47. AFP from New Delhi, 18 April 1992, in *FBIS/NE*, 20 April 1992, pp. 33-4; Reuter from Kabul, 22 and 30 April, 20 June 1992, 10 August 1993.

48. Kabul Radio, 16 April 1992, in *FBIS/NE*, 17 April 1992, p. 31; *Frontier Post*, 18 April 1992, p. 8, *Nation*, 23 April 1992, p. 1, and *Le Monde*, 25 April 1992, p. 4, in *FBIS/NE*, 20, 24, and 29 April 1992, pp. 30, 28, and 38; Reuter from Kabul, 13 May 1992.

49. Reuter from Kabul, 16 April 1992; Kabul Radio, 16, 19 and 22 April 1992, in *FBIS/NE*, 17, 20, and 24 April 1992, pp. 26, 29-30, 32; 26, and 25-7.

50. Reuter from Kabul, 19 April 1992; AFP from Kabul, 19 April 1992.

51. Tehran Radio, 19 April 1992, in *FBIS/NE*, 20 April 1992, p. 30; *Le Monde*, 21 April 1992, p. 4, in *FBIS/NE*, 21 April 1992, p. 46.

52. AFP from Islamabad, 20 and 21 April 1992, in *FBIS/NE*, 21 April 1992, p. 47; Radio Message of Freedom [Hekmaktyar's station], 22, 25, and 27 April 1992, in *FBIS/NE*, 23 and 27 April 1992, pp. 34-5 and 39-41.

53. *New York Times*, 25 April 1992, p. 1; *Muslim*, 26 April 1992, p. 1.

54. Radio Message of Freedom, 27 April 1992, in *FBIS/NE*, 27 April 1992, p. 40.

55. Winchester, 'Blood Feud'; Davis, 'Afghan Army', pp. 135-37; Reuter from Kabul, 25 April 1992; *New York Times*, 26 April 1992, p. 1.

56. *News*, 13 and 17 April 1992, p. 1, in *FBIS/NE*, 13 and 20 April 1992, pp. 50 and 43-4; Reuter from Islamabad, 16 April 1992; Islamabad Radio, 18, 19, and 22 April 1992, in *FBIS/NE*, 20 and 23 April 1992, pp. 43-4; *New York Times*, 22 April 1992, p. A12.

57. *New York Times*, 25 April 1992, p. 4; AFP from Islamabad, 21 April 1992, and from Peshawar, 24 April 1992, in *FBIS/NE*, 21 and 24 April 1992, pp. 46 and 29.

58. *Nation*, 25 April 1992, pp. I, IV, in *FBIS/NE*, 27 April 1992, pp. 34-5; *New York Times*, 25 April and 1 May 1992, pp. 4 and A10.

59. Ibid.; AFP from Peshawar, 28 April 1992, in *FBIS/NE*, 28 April 1992, p. 38.

60. *New York Times*, 30 April 1992, p. A10; AP from Kabul, 28 April 1992.

61. *New York Times*, 29 April 1992, p. A1; Kabul Radio, 28 April 1992, in *FBIS/NE*, 29 April 1992, pp. 32-4.

CHAPTER 13

LEGACIES

The Communist period in Afghanistan and the Soviet Union's involvement in it left different legacies south and north of the Amu Darya. In Afghanistan the effects would long be felt socially, economically, militarily, and politically. In destroying the *status quo*, the PDPA created uncertainty about whether the multi-ethnic land would remain a single cohesive political entity. The civil war that followed the collapse of Najibullah's regime magnified problems created by the PDPA period. To the north, a rush of events that culminated in the collapse of the USSR muted or buried most of the war's effects in states that had been ruled from Moscow. In addition, the region surrounding Afghanistan was affected by overlapping problems, particularly in an increasingly violent and drug-sickened Pakistan and in a conflict-racked Tajikistan. And the broader Islamic world was affected by the military skills taken home from Afghanistan to challenge governments and social practices.

FADING FOCUS IN THE FORMER SOVIET UNION

The breakup of Moscow's empire into many separate republics was not a result of the Afghan war, much as such people as Mojaddedi wanted pridefully to believe that the war had destroyed the Soviet Union.[1] Memories of this particular war were overwhelmed by other events so important, even traumatic, that Afghanistan quickly came to echo only faintly in Soviet dialogue, unlike the way the

Vietnam involvement reverberated for years in the United States. Afghanistan was eclipsed as an example of the Soviet empire's contracting world reach by the beginnings of far more important change in Eastern Europe in the autumn of 1989 and independence drives of the Baltic states in 1990. And the Kabul regime's long refusal to fall spared Gorbachev responsibility for having destroyed a client state. No angry debate on 'who lost Afghanistan?' developed because, by the time Najibullah fell, the Soviet Union itself had been lost. Gorbachev won the Nobel Peace Prize in 1990 for his contributions to ending the Cold War and promoting international peace, with the withdrawal from Afghanistan cited as one component. But a Soviet public with new crises on its mind gave him little credit for having cauterized the 'bleeding wound' of Afghanistan.

Political issues of the war faded; warriors did not. By May 1991 Afghanistan veterans commanded eight Soviet armies and twenty-three divisions.[2] After the Soviet Union was dissolved in December 1991, Rutskoy became the most prominent veteran as Russia's vice president, but armed defiance of Yeltsin in 1993 resulted in his ouster. The invasion commander, Marshal Sokolov, served as Soviet defence minister. Pavel S. Grachev, a Hero of the Soviet Union for commanding an airborne division in Afghanistan, became Russia's defence minister in May 1992, and his successor was Col. Gen. Igor N. Rodionov, commander of the 40th Army during 1985 and 1986. The army's last commander, Gromov, was for a time a deputy defence minister before being sidelined, and talk of his being a future Russian leader faded—to be succeeded by speculation about another *Afghantsi* general, Aleksandr Lebed, who ran for president in 1996 and then briefly held high positions under Yeltsin. Yeltsin's bodyguard and powerful confidant until his abrupt dismissal in 1996, Aleksandr Korzhakov, had served for a time as Najibullah's KGB bodyguard. Akhromeyev, the chief of staff of the Soviet operations group in Kabul during the first two years of the war, hanged himself after taking part in the August 1991 *coup* attempt. Varennikov, who directed the last four years of Soviet military action in Afghanistan and later commanded Soviet ground forces, and his boss, Defence Minister Yazov, were temporarily imprisoned as 'active organizers of the *coup*' against Gorbachev, whom Varennikov later accused in court of betraying the army in Afghanistan.[3] Yuliy Vorontsov became Russia's ambassador to the United States, while his successor as ambassador in Kabul, Boris Pastukhov, rose to become first deputy foreign minister of Russia. Many *Afghantsi* went into politics; others used their military skills in the flourishing realm of Russian organized crime.

Russian writers said the Soviet Army made little effort 'to extract lessons from [Afghanistan, which had]...proved our lack of preparedness for effective and low-expenditure participation in low intensity conflicts'. The experience of the USSR's only war in almost half a century—and its last war—'was not fully studied or summarized, and by [1993] has been largely lost'. Archives of military units withdrawn from Afghanistan reportedly were destroyed. The army sank first into peacetime sloth, then splintered into post-union republic units, and finally fell into such neglect that few Russian military units were battle-ready by 1993.[4] For a time there was no stomach for further battles. Moscow commentators talked of an 'Afghanistan syndrome', although Russians argued whether their Afghanistan experience paralleled the American experience in Vietnam.[5] The USSR's syndrome showed in a refusal to become directly involved in the 1991 Persian Gulf war resulting from Iraq's seizure of Kuwait. 'Afghanistan was enough for us,' Prime Minister Nikolay Ryzhkov declared.[6] Later, Grachev opposed committing forces to peace efforts in Bosnia, saying 'Russia does not need a second Afghanistan'.[7] But, despite widespread warnings that Chechnya could become 'another Afghanistan', Russia conducted a military campaign against the successionist Muslim enclave in the Caucasian mountains in 1994-5. The army's ineptness there proved the failure to learn from the Afghanistan experience and the general decline in military standards.

Although, as it faded the Soviet Union had abandoned the Marxist version of 'the white man's burden' to improve the world by making it socialist, post-Communist Russia showed another interest that revived memories of the Afghanistan experience. Tajikistan lies 800 miles across two other newly independent republics from the nearest Russian territory, but it was important to Moscow because of some 200 000 Russian residents whom Russia could ill afford to absorb, economic ties, and Tajikistan's perceived forward position to protect Russia from Islamic fundamentalism and narcotics trafficking.[8] Under a 1992 collective security agreement by most of the former Soviet republics, former KGB border troops now in a separate Russian Federal Border Service remained on the Tajik border facing Afghanistan, supplemented by a division of the Russian army. Declaring that Russia's national security was involved on the Tajik-Afghan border, President Boris N. Yeltsin said in 1993, 'everyone must understand [that this] is effectively Russia's, not Tajikistan's, border'.[9] Russians periodically died in armed clashes with Afghanistan-based insurgents opposed to the Tajik government and with smugglers of drugs and other contraband toward Russian and West European markets.

The exacerbation of Tajikistan's internal fight for post-Soviet power resulting from the proximity of Afghanistan was just one regional aftermath. Pakistan suffered from an increased flow of narcotics from Afghanistan as a result of the war, as well as from having far more weapons in an already volatile society. The slide of its main financial, industrial, and port city, Karachi, toward anarchy in the mid-1990s was partly an Afghan war effect. So, partly, were campaigns by Afghan-trained guerrillas in countries spanning the Eastern Hemisphere, from the Philippines to Algeria. Fighters trained in Afghanistan participated in the Chechnya and Bosnia wars, and other men—freedom fighters to some, terrorists to others—continued to shelter, train, and sally forth from Afghanistan years after Najibullah's fall.

CONTINUING AFGHAN PROBLEMS

The battle for control of Kabul and its symbolism of national power that erupted as the PDPA regime collapsed continued spasmodically for years. Internal alliances treacherously changed. External influences varied as foreign countries shifted their roles.

This struggle for dominance in Afghanistan is a sad story that cannot properly be told until peace returns. But some bitter ironies in the aftermath of the PDPA period can be noted. Dostam, who had helped Massoud seize Kabul in 1992, turned against the Tajik leader in 1994, but had become his ally again before Dostam temporarily lost control of the predominately Uzbek and Turkmen ethnic area of northwestern Afghanistan to a former deputy in 1997. After 1992, Hekmatyar's Hezb wrecked Kabul with indiscriminate artillery and rocket attacks on Massoud's forces. Some of this ammunition had been paid for by the United States and Saudi Arabia, supplied by ISI, and hoarded by Hezb while it had let other *mujahideen* now in Kabul do most of the fighting to oust the Soviets and the Communist regime, but some of it reportedly was supplied later by elements in Pakistan or purchased with money from various Arab fundamentalists.[10]

ISI gave up, however, on Hekmatyar's prospects of ever reaching its goal of having him rule a pro-Pakistani country. Islamabad switched its support to—some reports said created—a new force of Pushtun 'seekers of knowledge', or *taliban*. The fanatically fundamentalist *taliban* appeared in mid-1994 in the Qandahar area, claiming to be reformers trying to end the lawlessness and anarchy of the post-Communist period. Islamabad saw them as a way to pacify routes across Afghanistan so that Pakistan could benefit from

Central Asian markets. The *taliban* quickly pulled together a mixture of former *mujahideen*, Communist regime soldiers, Islamic students, and others to become more of a religious and political force than a fighting army.[11] It seized Herat from Ismail Khan on 4 September 1995 and, after setbacks, occupied Kabul on 27 September 1996, as Massoud retreated to the Panjshir valley. This left Afghanistan roughly divided along the Hindu Kush between a predominately Pushtun southern three-quarters of the country and a northern alliance of Tajiks, Uzbeks, Turkmen, and Hazaras.

According to Massoud, Najibullah rejected Massoud's offer to leave the United Nations' building where he had been sheltered since April 1992 and quit Kabul with Massoud's forces, to be free then to go anywhere he wanted. Immediately upon entering the capital, *taliban* troops pulled Najibullah out of the UN building, castrated him, killed him by bludgeoning or by dragging him behind a truck, and hung his body on display outside the Arg.[12] A few months later, on 3 December 1996, Babrak Karmal died of liver cancer in a Moscow hospital.[13] Of the four PDPA leaders who were responsible for and presided over a violent period—Taraki, Amin, Karmal, and Najibullah—Karmal alone did not die by violence.

The changing internal alliances were matched by changes in the involvement of foreign countries. Russia, the heart of the Soviet Union that had fought Massoud, became his supporter and arms supplier. Moscow's motive was to block first Hekmatyar's and then the *taliban's* versions of Muslim fundamentalism from the old Soviet borders that Russia still helped to guard. Iran, which had been on the opposite side from Moscow, joined in helping the northerners. So did India, a friend of the PDPA regime to its end, which reflexively supported those fighting whoever was backed by Pakistan. Massoud and other northern commanders charged that Pakistani army soldiers were fighting with the *taliban*, in the way that ISI officials had, after the fact, admitted direct involvement during the war against the Soviet army;

but Islamabad denied this. The United States was widely assumed to be backing the *taliban* despite its denials of doing anything more than supporting ineffective United Nations' efforts to arrange a peace agreement.[14]

Communists and Refugees

While the victors fought, Afghan Communists went in many directions. Some, such as Mazdaq, Abdul Wakil, and Gulabzoy, sought temporary refuge in Moscow, while Ziray and Watanjar ended up in London. Besides the mysteriously dead Yaqubi, some other Communist leaders failed to get away. The regime's last chief justice, Abdol Karim Shadan, who had earlier sentenced *mujahideen* in an interior ministry court, was abducted, tortured, and killed by unknown persons in early May 1992. Car bombs killed former senior security officials in Kabul on 1 August and 3 November 1992, and others were assassinated in apparent revenge for their regime roles. Yet the notable fact was not these isolated killings; it was the lack of a widespread, organized settling of scores between the *mujahideen* and regime supporters in a society noted for long-lasting blood feuds. One reason was that many apparent supporters had reinsured with the resistance through family ties and covert cooperation. But the main reason apparently was the way both victors and vanquished divided. In the realignment that accompanied the fall of Najibullah, there was no single, overall regime element left to blame or victimize. Virtually every military force that continued to ravage the country combined elements of PDPA supporters and opponents.

By 1994, some 30 000 Afghans were stuck as unwanted refugees in Russia, and illegal migration of Afghans across Russia toward the West had become a problem for other European nations. The post-Communist fighting deterred the return of refugees from Pakistan and Iran while putting new people to flight, particularly residents of Kabul, who fled to refugee camps at Jalalabad or on to Pakistan. By 1996 some 1.5 million refugees remained in Pakistan, and more joined them rather than accept restrictions on women and other limitations to modern life imposed by the *taliban*. Iran forced many refugees to leave. Foreign aid programmes in Afghanistan were limited partly by the chaos, and because United Nations officials believed that some aid workers were killed by those who wanted to restrict foreign influence; and partly by *taliban* refusal to let women work with men.[15] Aid was also scarce because of competition from new refugee crises in Africa as well as 'donor fatigue'. None the less, masses of Afghanistan's people remained malnourished, sick, uneducated, ill-housed, and desperate.

AFGHANISTAN'S PROSPECTS

Post-Communist Afghanistan was burdened by four basic kinds of difficulties. One was the broad problem arising from its internal ethnic balance, its borders, and its relations with neighbours. The 1978-92 war ended centuries of Pushtun dominance while shifting leadership among Pushtuns from the Durranis to the rival Ghilzais. The *taliban* sought to reimpose Pushtun control with power moving back to the Durranis, creating unrest among Ghilzai Pushtun recruits to the *taliban* cause. Across the northern border, the independence of Tajik, Uzbek, and Turkmen peoples, after the Soviet Union dissolved in 1991 created possible alternatives to Kabul as attractions for Afghan minorities that had been separated from their ethnic brethren and placed in a Pushtun-dominated state by the border drawing of 19th-century British and Russian colonialism. Across the Iranian border, where the division of waters flowing from Afghanistan in the Helmand River remained a latent issue, Tehran exerted influence on Afghan Shi'ites, particularly Hazaras, a group disaffected within the Afghan polity as a result of being consigned second-class status for generations.

But the most obvious continuing issue was the border with Pakistan. Decades of efforts by ISI to create an Afghan leadership that would not question the Durand Line had failed to resolve the problem of Pushtuns' being divided by another colonially drawn border. Both Karmal and Najibullah had kept the issue of Pushtunistan alive during the 1980s.[16] The contending factions that succeeded them in Kabul had no immediate time for such subjects. But the *taliban*'s recruitment of Pushtun youths from Islamic schools in Pakistan's Northwest Frontier and Balochistan to fight Tajiks, Uzbeks, and other minorities blurred the border distinction even more than Pakistan's official involvement in Afghan warfare.

Related to ethnic questions was the second problem of redefining the nature of the Afghan state. The drastically changed circumstances required a new consensus on the powers of government, the mode of popular participation in it, and relations among ethnic groups and geographic regions. These matters had begun to emerge from traditional Asian autocracy and come into modern political focus starting in the late 1940s and accelerating with Daoud's changes in the 1950s. They became critical issues with the PDPA's acquisition of power and were exacerbated by civil war, Soviet intervention, and more post-PDPA civil war. Religious questions that affected social organization were also part of the political problem. Islamists sought a government in which religious law was predominant, but this created the issue of how and by whom the large body of Quranic injunctions and Muslim traditions was to be interpreted. Some Islamists sought to use religion to ensure that traditionalists did not return the country to secular government. Many Afghans suspected that this was a power struggle veiled in piety. There was only limited evidence of popular support for Islamist determination of policies. Indeed, there was some evidence to the contrary, because many of the strict Islamist policies challenged the old relaxed blend of Islam and pre-Islamic traditions by which the masses lived. But no tested method of determining the popular will existed. Neither the elections of the 1960s constitutional period nor the PDPA's supposed elections provided models for democracy with broad, informed public participation. The *taliban* introduced an even more rigid interpetation of religion as a guide to life without recourse to public opinion. Organizing meaningful elections in Afghanistan remained a daunting task, and few power groups showed any desire for them.

Reaching agreement on a new structure for the state depended upon resolving the third problem, re-establishing cultural and social conventions that had been upset by the PDPA and reactions to its use of power, and moving beyond these conventions to new political forms. PDPA decrees and the civil war accelerated cultural and social changes already underway under pressures of modernization. What had been a consensual society grew confrontational. The role of religion became controversial. In particular, establishing the role of women in a post-Communist society was a test case for preserving the steps toward a modern economy that Daoud had begun more than three decades earlier by making it possible for them to work outside their homes. The *taliban* banished them back to an unseen role.

The limits of governmental authority had become uncertain and needed to be redefined. Beyond the positions established by local leaders who offered protection within their limited areas, neither the PDPA regime nor resistance leaders had had much claim to any legitimacy other than the gun, although some claimed exclusive rights to interpret Islam as giving them legitimacy. The old social system had been overturned as valiant warriors rose quickly to positions once awarded primarily on seniority, but no new hierarchy was defined with the clarity needed for domestic tranquillity. Even the traditional way of settling local disputes by mediation of respected elders was upset by Islamists and then by the *taliban* in even more absolutist form. In rejecting white-bearded authority in favour of their own often revolutionary reading of Muslim rules, they added to Islam as religion the disruptive role of Islam as political ideology. The old ways had been destroyed, but competition for the advantage of individuals or small groups or self-proclaimed religious authorities took precedence over finding new ways to work for agreement on the national good.

While some new leaders voiced beliefs in electoral democracy, sincerely or otherwise, the political habits for such a system were lacking. Afghanistan had never had a working tradition of political parties that formed alliances or coalitions, agreed on programmes and sought broader support on the basis of them, or submerged individual interests in any sense of public welfare. It had been a land of hierarchial, top-down control, with a consensus often formed as people fell into line behind what the strongest or shrewdest man thought could be attained without provoking too much opposition. The war had enfranchised many new political elements that were not accustomed to submerging their interests for a common benefit, that were unwilling to yield the authority won in the heat of conflict, that did not know how to negotiate or compromise or that claimed divine authority for not needing to negotiate or compromise. This made it difficult to combine different interests into the sort of cooperation implied by talk of electoral politics and government, along Western parliamentary lines.

It was both Afghanistan's nature and its misfortune not to have produced from the war any single leader who could be widely accepted as rising above the traditional divisions of the country by tribe, ethnic group, variety of Islamic interpretation, and other factors. Indeed, the war only hardened the divisiveness of such factors. This compounded the lack of a parliamentary tradition to point toward an inability to construct a working government. There were, in short, tremendous problems of holding meaningful elections in which people made informed choices and the results were generally accepted in a spirit of majority rule. The very concept of elections was in doubt.

Rebuilding

Complicating these three problems was the fourth one of loss of material and human capital in a land with one of the world's lowest life expectancies, an estimated 42 years, and highest infant mortality rates, some 3 per cent. The illiteracy rate was estimated at 75 per cent and more than half the population was believed by 1997 to be suffering from malnutrition.[17] Innumerable homes had to be rebuilt, entire villages reconstructed, refugees resettled. Millions of land mines had to be removed or at least located and cordoned off. Weed-infested fields needed to be returned to productivity, silted-up irrigation systems restored, orchards and vineyards replanted. The infrastructure for economic modernization—roads, bridges, airports, telecommunications, pipelines, governmental buildings—needed to be rehabilitated, rebuilt, and extended. Schools and health clinics had to be reconstructed and restocked, teachers and medical personnel trained. And tens of thousands of persons needed artificial limbs.

Prospects for returning Afghanistan to self-sufficiency, much less prosperity, were daunting. Destruction and neglect had blighted old economic ways. The export of rugs, fruit, and other products of a primitive economy that had gone on throughout the war could not pay for new needs, and low-calory gas or other capital-intensive extractive industries were not practical hopes for the foreseeable future. A large proportion of the human talent accumulated over several decades of educational efforts had been lost. Few of the educated and technically trained Afghans who fled the PDPA regime to start new lives abroad were willing to return to the post-war chaos and *taliban* restrictions on women, which inhibited the beginning of the long, slow effort to educate the people needed for recovery. For many villagers who returned to ruined farms, the quickest way to earn a little money to buy new supplies was by growing opium poppies.

Poppy cultivation increased annually, making Afghanistan by 1996 second only to Burma as an opium producer.[18]

While foreign aid was tiny compared with the need, Afghan hopes of getting compensation from the USSR or later from its successor republics for the damage done to their country were in vain. When Russian Foreign Minister Kozyrev flew to Kabul 13 May 1992 to deliver food and medical aid, Afghans 'raised the question of reparations'. They suggested $100 billion, a totally unrealistic figure for Russia, which was then seeking foreign aid for itself. Kozyrev contended Russia was 'not responsible for the actions of the Soviet communist regime', and Russia and Afghanistan had both been 'victims of Communist totalitarianism'.[19]

Obscurity had long been Afghanistan's lot. It attracted little attention or help from a world that had many other things to distract it. For a time, that changed. Cold War aid competition beginning in the 1950s brought a little notice. Then the world paid some attention to the start of PDPA rule and much more to the Soviet involvement. But after that involvement ended, leaving its effects on the USSR as well as Afghanistan, the world began to forget. And yet the convulsion of this tragic episode in Afghanistan's tumultuous history was not played out. The changes begun in its Communist period will affect Afghanistan for years to come.

NOTES

1. Kabul Radio, 1 May 1992, in *FBIS/NE*, 4 May 1992, p. 41.
2. *Krasnaya Zvezda*, 24 May 1991, p. 2, in *JPRS-UMA-91-015*, 21 June 1991, p. 17.
3. Moscow Radio, 25 August 1991, in *FBIS/SU*, 26 August 1991, p. 29; Tass from Moscow, 16 September 1991, in *FBIS/SU*, 17 September 1991, p. 30; Reuter from Moscow, 8 July 1994.
4. *Komsomolskaya Pravda*, 15 June 1988, p. 2, in *FBIS/SU*, 21 June 1988, p. 40; *Izvestiya*, 19 September 1991, p. 2, and 16 April 1991, p. 1; *SSHA: Ekonomika, Politika, Ideologiya*, No. 3, 1993: 33-41; *Krasnaya Zvezda*, 16 April and 28 October 1989, 25 May 1991,

pp. 1, 2, and 3, in *JPRS-UMA-89-017*, *JPRS-UMA-089-028*, and *JPRS-UMA-091-020*, 13 July and 27 November 1989, 25 July 1991, pp. 13, 16, and 5-8; *Sotsialisticheskaya Industriya*, 4 June 1989, p. 1, in *FBIS/SU*, 5 June 1989, p. 57; *Voyennaya Mysl*, No. 11, 1993: 13-21; *Wall Street Journal*, 2 July 1993, p. A4.

5. E.g., *Komsomolskaya Pravda*, 4 May 1990, p. 1; *New Times*, No. 37, 1990: 12-13; NHK Television, 14 February 1991, in *FBIS/East Asia*, 15 February 1991, p. 3.

6. Moscow Television, 6 October 1990; Radio Liberty Research, RFE/RL Daily Report 230, 5 December 1990; Radio Liberty Research, 5 October 1990.

7. ITAR-Tass from St. Petersburg, 1 April 1993.

8. *Komsomolskaya Pravda*, 12 August 1993, p. 7, in *FBIS/CE*, 13 August 1993, pp. 2-3; Moscow Television, 24 February 1993.

9. AFP from Moscow, 16 July 1993, in *FBIS/CE*, 16 July 1993, p. 48; ITAR-Tass from Moscow and Reuter from Moscow, 26 July 1993.

10. Anthony Davis, 'Peace Eludes Afghanistan', *Jane's Intelligence Review Yearbook*, 1994/95, pp. 111-14.

11. Anthony Davis, 'Afghanistan's Taliban', *Jane's Intelligence Review*, Vol. 7, No. 7: 315-21; Anthony Davis, 'Showdown in Kabul', *Asiaweek*, 28 April 1995, pp. 37-41; *New York Times*, 16 February 1995, p. A3; *Muslim*, 17 February 1995, p. 1; *Le Monde*, 20 February 1995, p. 2. While Hekmatyar had been supported by ISI and Pakistan's *Jamaat-i Islami* headed by Hussain Ahmad, the *Taliban* were initially backed by the Pakistani Interior Ministry headed by retired Maj.-Gen. Nasirullah Babar Khan and Pakistan's *Jamiyat-Ulema-Islami*, a clerical party at odds with *Jamaat-i Islami*.

12. *Sobesednik*, July 1997: 3; Anthony Davis, 'A Radical New Order', *Asiaweek*, 11 October 1996, pp. 18-24; *New York Times*, 24 November 1996, p. 4:9.

13. Kabul Radio, 3 December 1996; Reuter from Moscow, 5 December 1996.

14. *New York Times*, 18 February 1996, p. 4:5; *Far Eastern Economic Review*, 1 February 1996, pp. 20-21.

15. *New York Times*, 27 July 1993 and 27 July 1997, pp. A6 and 1.

16. Kabul Radio, 23 April and 14 September 1985, 9 April 1986, in *FBIS/SA*, 1 May and 19 September 1985, 11 April 1986, pp. C7, C9, and C1-2; Bakhtar from Kabul, 30 August 1988, in *FBIS/NE*, 31 August 1988, p. 42; *L'Humanite*, 6 December 1988, p. 16, in *FBIS/NE*, 15 December 1988, p. 45; *Pravda*, 26 April 1989, p. 4, in *FBIS/SU*, 26 April 1989, p. 43.

17. Shah M. Tarzi, 'Afghanistan in 1992: A Hobbesian State of Nature', *Asian Survey*, February 1993: 174; Reuter from Mazar-e-Sharif, 3 August 1997.

18. Reuter from Washington, 24 November 1992; UN Drug Control Programme, 1995; State Department, human rights report, 29 January 1997.
19. Tass from Kabul and Moscow Radio, 13 May 1992, in *FBIS/CE*, 13 and 14 May 1992, pp. 18-20 and 16-17; *Izvestiya*, 15 and 16 May 1992, pp. 1 and 6, in *FBIS/CE*, 18 May 1992, pp. 9-10.

SELECTED BIBLIOGRAPHY

Documents

Alexiev, Alexander. 'Inside the Soviet Army in Afghanistan'. RAND R-3627-A. Santa Monica, May 1988.

_____. 'The United States and the War in Afghanistan'. RAND P-7395. Santa Monica, January 1988.

American Universities Field Staff Reports, South Asia series, New York, serial.

Amnesty International. 'Afghanistan: Unlawful Killings and Torture'. London, May 1988.

Asia Watch. 'Afghanistan: The Forgotten War: Human Rights Abuses and Violations of the Laws of War Since the Soviet Withdrawal'. New York, February 1991.

Cold War International History Project Bulletin. Washington, serial.

Congressional Research Service. 'Afghanistan: Soviet Invasion and U. S. Response'. Washington, 1980.

Cronin, Richard P. 'Afghanistan After the Soviet Withdrawal: Contenders for Power'. Congressional Research Service, Washington, 2 March 1989.

_____. 'Afghanistan: United Nations-Sponsored Negotiations, An Annotated Chronology and Analysis'. Congressional Research Service, Washington, 22 November 1985 and 23 July 1986.

Defense Department. 'Soviet Military Power'. Washington, serial.

Ermacora, Felix. 'Report on the situation of human rights in Afghanistan'. United Nations documents E/CN.4/ 1985/21, 19 February 1985, and serial.

Foreign and Commonwealth Office. 'Afghanistan Report' London, serial.

———. 'Afghanistan: Continuing Conflict'. London, 1989.

———. 'Afghanistan: Opposition Groups'. London, 1980.

———. 'Afghanistan: Soviet Occupation'. London, 1980.

———. 'The Sovietisation of Afghanistan'. London, 1981.

House of Commons. 'Afghanistan: The Soviet Invasion and Its Consequences for British Policy'. London, 1980.

International Institute for Strategic Studies. *Strategic Survey*. London, serial.

———. *The Military Balance*. London, serial.

Lorentz, John H. 'Anatomy of an Entanglement: Afghanistan and Iran'. Ms., October 1989.

National Committee for Human Rights in Afghanistan. *Russia's Barbarism in Afghanistan*. n.p. [Peshawar?], October 1984.

Radio Liberty Research. Munich, serial.

Rasheed (Rashid), Abdul. 'Final Report: The War in Afghanistan, Past and Present'. Ms., November 1986.

RFE/RL [Radio Free Europe/Radio Liberty] Daily Report. Munich, serial.

State Department. 'Afghanistan Resistance and Soviet Occupation: A 5-Year Summary'. Washington, 1984.

———. 'Afghanistan: (number) Years of Soviet Occupation'. Washington, serial.

———. 'Afghanistan: Soviet Occupation and Withdrawal'. Washington, December 1988.

———. 'Chemical Warfare in Southeast Asia and Afghanistan'. Washington, March 1982.

———. 'Chemical Warfare in Southeast Asia and Afghanistan: An Update'. Washington, November 1982.

———. 'Country Reports on Human Rights Practices'. Washington, serial.

———. 'Hidden Killers: The Global Problem With Uncleared Landmines: A Report on International Demining'. Washington, July 1993.

_____. 'Soviet Influence on Afghan Youth'. Washington, 1986.

_____. *Foreign Relations of the United States.* Washington, serial.

United States Congress. House subcommittee on Europe and the Middle East. 'An Assessment of the Afghanistan Sanctions: Implications for Trade and Diplomacy in the 1980s'. Washington, April 1981.

Weekly Compilation of Presidential Documents. Washington, serial.

Periodicals, Newspapers, News Agencies, and Broadcast Sources

Afghan Jehad. Islamabad.

Afghan News Agency. Peshawar.

Afghan Realities. Paris.

AFGHANews. Peshawar.

Afghanistan Council, The Asia Society. *Newsletter.* New York.

Afghanistan Information Centre Monthly Bulletin. Peshawar.

Agence France Presse.

Argumenty i Fakty. Moscow.

Armiya. Moscow.

Asian Affairs: An American Review. St James, NY.

Asian Survey. Berkeley, Calif.

Asiaweek. Hong Kong.

Associated Press, The.

Bakhtar New Agency, Kabul

British Broadcasting Corporation. London.

Central Asian Survey. London.

Christian Science Monitor. Boston.

Cold War International History Project Bulletin. Washington.

Danas. Belgrade.

Defis Afghans. Paris.

Die Zeit. Hamburg.

The Economist. London.

Far Eastern Economic Review. Hong Kong.

The Financial Times. London.

Foreign Broadcast Information Service. *Daily Report, Central Eurasia* (from 6 Jan 1992). Washington, serial.

_____. *Daily Report, China* . Washington, serial.

_____. *Daily Report, Latin America*. Washington, serial.

_____. *Daily Report, Middle East and North Africa* (through 31 Mar 1980). Washington, serial.

_____. *Daily Report, Near East and South Asia* (from 1 Jun 1987). Washington, serial.

_____. *Daily Report, South Asia* (from 1 Apr 1980 through 31 May 1987). Washington, serial.

_____. *Daily Report, Soviet Union* (through 3 Jan 1992). Washington, serial.

_____. *Daily Report, West Europe*. Washington, serial.

_____. *Report, Central Eurasia*. Washington, serial.

_____. *Trends in Communist Media*. Washington, serial.

Frontier Post. Peshawar.

Guardian. London.

Insight. Washington.

International Affairs. London.

International Affairs. Moscow.

International Journal of Middle East Studies. New York.

ITAR-Tass (International Telegraph Agency, Russia—Telegraph Agency Soviet Soyuz). Moscow

Izvestiya. Moscow.

Jane's Defence Weekly. London.

Jane's Intelligence Review. London.

Jane's Soviet Intelligence Review. London.

Joint Publications Research Service. *Near East-South Asia Report*. Washington, serial.

_____. *Soviet Union, Economic Affairs*. Washington, serial.

_____. *Soviet Union, International Affairs*. Washington, serial.

_____. *Soviet Union, Military Affairs*. Washington, serial.

_____. *Soviet Union, Military History Journal.* Washington, serial.
_____. *Soviet Union, Political Affairs.* Washington, serial.
Journal of South Asian and Middle Eastern Studies. Villanova.
Kabul New Times.
Kabul Radio.
Kabul Television.
Kabul Times.
Kommunist Vooruzhennykh Sil. Moscow.
Kommunist. Moscow.
Komsomolskaya Pravda. Moscow.
Krasnaya Zvezda. Moscow.
Le Monde. Paris.
Les Nouvelles d'Afghanistan. Paris.
Literaturnaya Gazeta. Moscow.
Moscow News.
Moscow Radio.
Moscow Television.
The Muslim. Islamabad.
New Times. Moscow.
New York Times.
Newsweek. New York.
Nezavisimaya Gazeta. Moscow.
Novoye Vremya. Moscow.
Ogonek. Moscow.
Orbis. Philadelphia.
Pravda. Moscow.
Problems of Communism. Washington.
Reuter News Agency.
Soldier of Fortune. Boulder, Colo.
Sotsialisticheskaya Industriya. Moscow.
Sovetskaya Rossiya. Moscow.
Sovetskiy Voin. Moscow.
State Department. *Bulletin.* Washington.
Tass (Telegraph Agency Soviet Soyuz). Moscow.
Time. New York.
The Times. London.

Trud. Moscow.
US News & World Report. Washington.
Vechernaya Moskva. Moscow
Voyenno-Istoricheskiy Zhurnal. Moscow.
Wall Street Journal. New York.
Washington Post.
Washington Star.
Washington Times.
World Economics and International Relations. Moscow.
World Marxist Review. Moscow.

Books

Adamec, Ludwig W. *A Biographical Dictionary of Contemporary Afghanistan.* Graz, 1987.
Akhramovich, Roman T. *Outline History of Afghanistan After the Second World War.* Moscow, 1966.
Amstutz, J. Bruce. *Afghanistan: The First Five Years of Soviet Occupation.* Washington, 1986.
Anwar, Raja. *The Tragedy of Afghanistan: A First-hand Account.* London, 1988.
Arbatov, Georgi A. *The System: An Insider's Life in Soviet Politics.* New York, 1992.
Arif, Gen. Khalid Mahmud. *Working With Zia: Pakistan's Power Politics 1977-1988.* Karachi, 1995.
Arnold, Anthony. *Afghanistan's Two-Party Communism: Parcham and Khalq.* Stanford, 1983.
―――. *Afghanistan: The Soviet Invasion in Perspective.* Stanford, 1981.
―――. *The Fateful Pebble: Afghanistan's Role in the Fall of the Soviet Empire.* Novato, Cal., 1993.
Banuazizi, Ali, and Myron Weiner, eds. *The State, Religion, and Ethnic Politics: Afghanistan, Iran, and Pakistan.* Syracuse, 1986.
Baryalai, A. M. ed. *Democratic Republic of Afghanistan Annual, 1979.* Kabul, 1979.

Bocharov, Gennady N. *Russian Roulette: Afghanistan Through Russian Eyes.* New York, 1990.

Bonner, Arthur. *Among the Afghans.* Durham, N. C., 1987.

Borovik, Artyom. *The Hidden War: A Russian Journalist's Account of the Soviet War in Afghanistan.* New York, 1990.

Bradsher, Henry S. *Afghanistan and the Soviet Union.* Durham, N. C., 1983, 1985.

Brzezinski, Zbigniew. *Power and Principle: Memoirs of the National Security Adviser 1977-1981.* New York, 1983.

Carter, Jimmy. *Keeping Faith: Memoirs of a President.* New York, 1982.

Cordovez, Diego, and Selig S. Harrison. *Out of Afghanistan: The Inside Story of the Soviet Withdrawal.* New York, 1995.

Dobrynin, Anatoly F. *In Confidence: Moscow's Ambassador to America's Six Cold War Presidents (1962-1986).* New York, 1995.

Dupree, Louis B. *Afghanistan.* Princeton, 1973.

Dupree, Louis, and Linette Albert, eds. *Afghanistan in the 1970s.* New York, 1974.

Ekedahl, Carolyn McGiffert, and Melvin A. Goodman. *The Wars of Eduard Shevardnadze.* University Park, Pa., 1997.

Emadi, Hafizullah. *State, Revolution, and Superpowers in Afghanistan.* New York, 1990.

Farr, Grant M., and John G. Merriam, eds. *Afghan Resistance: the Politics of Survival.* Boulder, 1987.

Fraser-Tytler, W. Kerr. *Afghanistan: A Study of Political Developments in Central and Southern Asia,* 2nd ed. London, 1953.

Fullerton, John. *The Soviet Occupation of Afghanistan.* Hong Kong, 1983.

Gai, David, and Vladimir Snegirev. *Vtorzheniye: Neizvestnye Stranitsy Neobiavlennoi Voiny (Invasion: Unknown Pages of an Undeclared War).* Moscow, 1991.

Galeotti, Mark. *Afghanistan: The Soviet Union's Last War.* London, 1995.

Galiullin, Rustem. *The CIA in Asia: Covert Operations against India and Afghanistan.* Moscow, 1988.

Gankovsky, Yuri V. *A History of Afghanistan.* Moscow, 1982.

Gates, Robert M. *From the Shadows: The Ultimate Insider's Story of Five Presidents and How They Won the Cold War.* New York, 1996.

Ghaus, Abdul Samad. *The Fall of Afghanistan: An Insider's Account.* Washington, 1988.

Girardet, Edward R. *Afghanistan: The Soviet War.* New York, 1985.

Gorbachev, Mikhail. *Perestroika: New Thinking for Our Country and the World.* New York, 1987.

Grassmuck, George, and Ludwig W. Adamec. *Afghanistan: Some New Approaches.* Ann Arbor, 1969.

Hauner, Milan, and Robert L. Canfield. *Afghanistan and the Soviet Union: Collision and Transformation.* Boulder, 1989.

Huldt, Bo, and Erland Jansson, eds. *The Tragedy of Afghanistan: The Social, Cultural and Political Impact of the Soviet Invasion.* London, 1988.

Hyman, Anthony. *Afghanistan Under Soviet Domination, 1964-1983.* New York, 1984.

Isby, David C. *Russia's War in Afghanistan.* London, 1986.

———. *War in a Distant Country, Afghanistan: Invasion and Resistance.* London, 1989.

Kakar, M. Hassan. *Afghanistan: The Soviet Invasion and the Afghan Response, 1979-1982.* Berkeley, 1995.

Khan, Riaz M. *Untying the Afghan Knot: Negotiating Soviet Withdrawal.* Durham, N. C., 1991.

Khrushchev, Nikita S. *Khrushchev Remembers.* Boston, 1971.

———. *Khrushchev Remembers: The Last Testament.* Boston, 1974.

Kissinger, Henry A. *Years of Upheaval.* Boston, 1982.

Klass, Rosanne, ed. *Afghanistan: The Great Game Revisited.* New York, 1987.

Kuzichkin, Vladimir. *Inside the KGB: Myth and Reality.* London, 1990.

Laber, Jeri, and Barnett R. Rubin. *'A Nation is Dying': Afghanistan Under the Soviets 1979-87.* Evanston, 1988.

Majrooh, Sayd B., and S. M. Y. Elmi, eds. *The Sovietization of Afghanistan.* Peshawar, 1986.

Malik, Hafeez, ed. *Soviet-American Relations with Pakistan, Iran and Afghanistan.* London, 1987.

McMichael, Scott R. *Stumbling Bear: Soviet Military Performance in Afghanistan.* London, 1991.

Moslem Students Followers Imam. *Spynest Revelations: Vols. 29 and 30, Afghanistan.* Tehran, 1981.

Novosti Press Agency. *The Truth About Afghanistan: Documents, Facts, Eyewitness Reports.* Moscow, 1980.

Nyrop, Richard F., and Donald M. Seekins, eds. *Afghanistan: A Country Study.* Washington, 1986.

Oberdorfer, Don. *The Turn: From the Cold War to a New Era: the United States and the Soviet Union 1983-1990.* New York, 1991.

Reagan, Ronald. *An American Life.* New York, 1990.

Roy, Olivier. *Islam and Resistance in Afghanistan.* Cambridge, England, 1986, 1990.

Rubin, Barnett R. *The Fragmentation of Afghanistan: State Formation and Collapse in the International System.* New Haven, 1995.

Saikal, Amin, and William Maley, eds. *Regime Change in Afghanistan: Foreign Intervention and the Politics of Legitimacy.* Boulder, Colo., 1991.

_____. *The Soviet Withdrawal from Afghanistan.* Cambridge, 1989.

Shahi, Agha. *Pakistan's Security and Foreign Policy.* Lahore, 1988.

Shahrani, M. Nazif, and Robert L. Canfield, eds. *Revolutions & Rebellions in Afghanistan: Anthropological Perspectives.* Berkeley, 1984.

Shevardnadze, Eduard. *The Future Belongs to Freedom.* New York, 1991.

Shultz, George P. *Turmoil and Triumph: My Years as Secretary of State.* New York, 1993.

Sikorski, Radek. *Dust of the Saints: A Journey to Herat in Time of War.* London, 1989.

Slinkin, M. F. *A History of the Armed Forces of Afghanistan, 1747-1977.* Moscow, 1985.

Urban, Mark. *War in Afghanistan.* London, 1988, 1990.

Vance, Cyrus. *Hard Choices: Critical Years in America's Foreign Policy.* New York, 1983.

Yousaf, Mohammad. *Silent Soldier: The Man Behind the Afghan Jehad.* Lahore, 1991.

Yousaf, Mohammad, and Mark Adkin. *The Bear Trap: Afghanistan's Untold Story.* London, 1992.

Articles

Afroz, Sultana. 'Afghanistan in US-Pakistani Relations, 1947-1960'. *Central Asian Survey,* Vol. 8, No. 2.

Amin, Tahir. 'Afghan Resistance: Past, Present, and Future'. *Asian Survey,* April 1984.

Barnes, Fred. 'Victory in Afghanistan: The Inside Story'. *Reader's Digest,* December 1988.

Bernstein, Carl. 'Arms for Afghanistan'. *New Republic,* 18 July 1981.

Canfield, Robert L. 'Islamic Sources of Resistance'. *Orbis,* Vol. 29, No. 1.

Central Intelligence Agency. 'Biographic Report: Mohammad Daud'. In Moslem Students Followers Imam. *Spynest Revelations,* Vol. 29: 38-46.

Cogan, Charles G. 'Partners in Time: The CIA and Afghanistan since 1979'. *World Policy Journal,* Summer 1993.

Collins, Joseph J. 'The Soviet Military Experience in Afghanistan'. *Military Review,* May 1985.

Davis, Anthony. 'The Afghan Army'. *Jane's Intelligence Review,* March 1993.

_____. 'Afghanistan's Taliban'. *Jane's Intelligence Review*, Vol. 7, No. 7: 315-21.

Dorronsoro, Gilles, and Chantal Lobato. 'The Militia in Afghanistan'. *Central Asian Survey*, Vol. 8, No. 4.

Dupree, Louis B. 'Afghanistan Under the Khalq'. *Problems of Communism*, July-August 1979.

_____. 'Afghanistan's Big Gamble: Part II, the Economic and Strategic Aspects of Soviet Aid'. *American Universities Field Staff Reports* [hereafter *AUFS*], South Asia, Vol. 4, No. 4 (1960).

_____. 'Asia Society Occasional Paper'. New York, Spring 1976.

_____. 'The Decade of Daoud Ends: Implications of Afghanistan's Change of Government'. *AUFS*, South Asia, Vol. 7, No. 7 (1963).

_____. 'The Democratic Republic of Afghanistan, 1979'. *AUFS*, Asia, No. 3, 1979.

_____. 'Red Flag Over Hindu Kush, Part 1: Leftist Movements in Afghanistan'. *AUFS*, Asia, No. 44, 1979.

_____. 'Red Flag Over Hindu Kush, Part 2: The Accidental Coup, or Taraki in Blunderland'. *AUFS*, Asia, No. 45, 1979.

_____. 'Red Flag Over Hindu Kush, Part III: Rhetoric and Reforms, or Promises! Promises!'. *AUFS*, Asia, No. 23, 1980.

_____. 'Red Flag Over Hindu Kush, Part V: Repressions, or Security Through Terror Purges, I-IV'. *AUFS*, Asia, No. 28, 1980.

Dupree, Nancy Hatch. 'The Conscription of Afghan Writers: An Aborted Experiment in Socialist Realism'. *Central Asian Survey*, Vol. 4, No. 4.

Farr, Grant M. 'The New Afghan Middle Class as Refugees and Insurgents'. In Farr and Merriam, *Afghan Resistance*.

Halliday, Fred. 'Revolution in Afghanistan'. *New Left Review*, No. 112, 1978.

Harrison, Selig S. 'Cut a Regional Deal'. *Foreign Policy*, Spring 1986.

————. 'Dateline Afghanistan: Exit through Finland?' *Foreign Policy*, Winter 1980-81.

————. 'Inside the Afghan Talks'. *Foreign Policy*, Fall 1988.

————. 'The Afghan Arms Alliance'. *South*, March 1985.

Hart, Douglas M. 'Low-intensity Conflict in Afghanistan: The Soviet view'. *Survival*, March/April 1982.

Isby, David C. 'Airstrikes on Afghanistan 1989-91'. *Jane's Intelligence Review*, November 1991.

————. 'Fought with weapons and lost by men: Counter-insurgency and the lessons of Afghanistan' in Leebaert, Derek, and Timothy Dickinson, eds. *Soviet Strategy and New Military Thinking*. New York, 1992.

————. 'Postwar Peril: Soviet Minefields'. *Soldier of Fortune*, April 1989.

————. 'Soviet Advisers in Afghanistan—the Involvement Continues'. *Jane's Intelligence Review*, June 1991.

————. 'Soviet Arms Deliveries and Aid to Afghanistan, 1989-91'. *Jane's Intelligence Review*, August 1991.

————. 'The Soviet Military and Afghanistan: The Trans-Border War, 1989-91'. *Jane's Intelligence Review*, March 1992.

Kakar. Hasan. 'The Fall of the Afghan Monarchy in 1973'. *International Journal of Middle East Studies* 9, 1978.

Khalidi, Noor Ahmad. 'Afghanistan: Demographic Consequences of War, 1978-1987'. *Central Asian Survey*, Vol. 10, No. 3.

Korgun, V. G. 'Afghanistan in Contemporary Times'. In Gankovsky. *A History of Afghanistan*.

Kushkaki, Sabahuddin. 'Changes in Afghan Society Due to War'. *Afghan Jehad*, October-December 1991.

Kuzio, Taras. 'Opposition in the USSR to the Occupation of Afghanistan'. *Central Asian Survey*, Vol. 6, No. 1.

Lifschultz, Lawrence. 'Afghanistan: The Not-So-New Rebellion'. *Far Eastern Economic Review*, 30 January 1981.

Lobato, Chantal. 'Islam in Kabul: The Religious Politics of Babrak Karmal'. *Central Asian Survey*, Vol. 4, No. 4.

Lyakhovskiy, A. A. and V. M. Zabrodin. 'Secrets of the Afghan War'. *Armiya*, Nos. 3-4, 1992.

Mackenzie, Richard. 'Essential Justice' After a Massacre'. *Insight*. 22 January 1990.

_____. 'A Brutal Force Batters a Country'. *Insight*, 5 December 1988.

_____. 'A Murderous Jolt for U. S. Policy'. *Insight*, 14 August 1989.

_____. 'A Split Force, an Immovable Najib'. *Insight*, 15 October 1990.

_____ 'Afghan Front Rests on Capitol Hill'. *Insight*, 11 June 1990.

_____. 'Afghan Rebels Never Say Die'. *Insight*, 25 January 1988.

_____. 'After Victory Comes the Hard Part'. *Insight*, 31 October 1988.

_____. 'Amid Bombs and Rockets, the Gestation of a Government'. *Insight*, 20 February 1989.

_____. 'Pitfalls in Policy on the Path to Kabul'. *Insight*, 9 April 1990.

_____. 'Rebels Calling Their Own Shots'. *Insight*, 26 November 1990.

_____. 'When Policy Tolls in Fool's Paradise'. *Insight*, 11 September 1989.

Malhuret, Claude. 'Report from Afghanistan'. *Foreign Affairs*, Winter 1983-84.

Mehta, Jagat S. 'A Neutral Solution'. *Foreign Policy*, Summer 1982.

Mendelson, Sarah E. 'Internal Battles and External Wars: Politics, Learning, and the Soviet Withdrawal from Afghanistan'. *World Politics*, April 1993.

Morozov, Aleksandr. 'Our Man in Kabul'. *New Times*, Nos. 38-41, 1991.

Morozov, Aleksandr. 'The KGB and the Afghan leaders'. *New Times*, No. 24, 1992.

Mukerjee, Dilip. 'Afghanistan under Daud: Relations with Neighboring States'. *Asian Survey*, April 1975.

Naby, Eden. 'Islam within the Afghan Resistance'. *Third World Quarterly*, April 1988.

———. 'The Changing Role of Islam as a Unifying Force in Afghanistan'. In Banuazizi and Weiner. *The State, Religion, and Ethnic Politics.*

———. 'The Ethnic Factor in Soviet-Afghan Relations'. *Asian Survey*, March 1980.

Nahaylo, Bohdan. 'When Ivan Comes Marching Home: The Domestic Impact of the War in Afghanistan'. *American Spectator*, July 1987.

Nations, Richard. 'The Muslims' Divided Alliance'. *Far Eastern Economic Review*, 29 February 1980.

Negaran, Hannah (pseudonym). 'The Afghanistan Coup of April 1978: Revolution and International Security'. *Orbis*, Spring 1979.

Oberdorfer, Don. 'A Diplomatic Solution to Stalemate: Afghanistan: The Soviet Decision to Pull Out'. *Washington Post*, 17 April 1988.

Oliynik, Lt.-Col. A. 'The Sending of Troops to Afghanistan: Participants in the Events Tell and Documents Attest to How the Decision was Made'. *Krasnaya Zvezda*, 18 November 1989.

Pyadyshev, Boris. 'Najibullah'. *International Affairs* (Moscow), February 1990.

Roy, Olivier. 'The Origins of the Afghan Communist Party'. *Central Asian Survey*, Vol. 7, Nos. 2/3,

———. 'The Origins of the Islamist Movement in Afghanistan'. *Central Asian Survey*, Vol. 3, No. 2.

Rubin, Barnett R. 'The Fragmentation of Afghanistan'. *Foreign Affairs*, Winter 1989/90.

———. 'The Old Regime in Afghanistan: Recruitment and Training of a State Elite'. *Central Asian Survey*, Vol. 10, No. 3.

Rupert, James. 'Afghanistan's Slide Toward Civil War'. *World Policy Journal*, Fall 1989.

Safronchuk, Vasili. 'Afghanistan in the Amin Period'. *International Affairs* (Moscow), February 1991.

_____. 'Afghanistan in the Taraki Period'. *International Affairs* (Moscow), January 1991.

Safronov, Col. V. G. 'Afghanistan: Results and Conclusions; As It Was (A Historian's Commentary)'. *Voyenno-Istoricheskiy Zhurnal*, May 1990.

Schwartzstein, Stuart J. D. 'Chemical Warfare in Afghanistan: An Independent Assessment'. *World Affairs*, Winter 1982-83.

Sikorski, Radek. 'Coda to the Russo-Afghan War: A Correspondent Reports'. *Encounter*, June 1988.

Sliwinski, Marek K. 'On the Routes of '*Hijrat* '. *Central Asian Survey*, Vol. 8, No. 4.

_____. 'The Decimation of a People'. *Orbis*, Winter 1989.

Trofimenko, Genrikh A. 'With an Inexperienced Hand....'. *SSHA: Ekonomika, Politika, Ideologiya*, June 1989.

Ulyanovskiy, Rostislav A. 'The Afghan Revolution at the Current Stage'. *Problems of History of the Soviet Communist Party*, No. 4, 1982.

Weinbaum, Marvin G. 'The Politics of Afghan Resettlement and Rehabilitation' *Asian Survey*, March 1989.

_____. 'War and Peace in Afghanistan: The Pakistani Role'. *Middle East Journal*, Winter 1991.

Westad, Odd Arne. 'Prelude to Invasion: The Soviet Union and the Afghan Communists, 1978-1979'. *International History Review*, February 1994.

'Winchester, Mike' (Anthony Davis). 'Muj Invade USSR'. *Soldier of Fortune*, June 1990.

_____. 'Terrorist "U"'. *Soldier of Fortune*, April 1991.

Wirsing, Robert G. 'Pakistan and the War in Afghanistan'. *Asian Affairs*, Summer 1987.

Yevstafyev, Dmitriy G. 'Low Intensity Conflicts and Russia's Defense Policy'. *SSHA: Ekonomika, Politika, Ideologiya*, No. 3, 1993.

INDEX

A

'A group' (KGB), 98
Adamishin, Anatoliy L., 284
Advisers, Soviet: xiv, 40, 46, 47,
58, 64, 70, 115, 122-5, 127,
131, 133, 135, 141, 146, 171,
268, 272, 307; civilian, 42, 60;
CPSU, 34, 52, 83; military, 19,
38, 42, 49, 50, 51-2, 53, 58,
64, 83, 118, 310, 336, 369,
372, 378; police (KGB), 41, 58,
129, 139, 144; in Africa, 395
Afghan air force, 2, 205, 226, 312.
See also Aircraft losses
Afghan armed forces, 56, 95, 196,
198, 204-206, 209-210,
311-13, 344, 370, 382, 393;
PDPA in, 20-21; size, 64, 205;
Soviet control of, 199, 206;
Republican Guard, 379. *See also*
Afghan air force; Afghan army;
Defense Ministry, Afghan; War
Afghan Armies' Revolutionary
Organization, 10, 16, 21, 29,
30
Afghan army, xv, 2, 50, 53, 78, 89-
90, 118, 171, 204-207, 211-12,
281, 307, 309-31, 336, 344-5,
348, 376, 378-9, 382; atrocities,
51-2, 141, 178, 288, 329;
conscription, 205, 310;
desertions, xiv, 48, 51, 64, 118,
204-206, 208, 216, 310; morale
and discipline, 50, 64, 206;
mutinies, 51, 208, 377-8;

purges, 35, 64, 66; 4th Armored
Brigade, 30, 97; 17th Division,
48; 25th Division, 129-30. *See
also* Purges
'Afghan cell' in Pakistan, 17, 374
Afghan Defence Ministry, 342
Afghan Foreign Minister, 383
Afghan Interior Ministry, 342, 379,
381-2, 394; troops of, xv, 205
Afghan media, 123, 213, 226. *See
also* Kabul Radio, *Kabul New
Times, Kabul Times*
Afghan Peace Front, 340
Afghan provinces, 307, 320
Afghan Social Democratic Party, 14
Afghan-Soviet economic commis-
sion, 46
Afghan-Soviet economic ties: 1, 46-
7, 169-70, localized, 170. *See
also* Advisers, Soviet, Aid,
economic; Aid, military
'Afghanistan syndrome,' 390
Afghantsi, see Veterans, Soviet
Aga Khan, Prince Sadruddin, 349
Against National Oppression, *see
Setem-i-Melli.*
Agriculture, 44, 167-8, 170, 213,
347-8, 399
AGSA, *see* Organization for the
Protection of the Security of
Afghanistan
Ahmad, Hussain, 185, 320, 375,
382, 401
Ahmedzai, Maj.-Gen. Shapur, 35
Aid to Afghanistan, economic: xii,
18-19, 47, 371, 395, 400;